Planning programs
in recreation

Planning programs in recreation

RUTH V. RUSSELL

Lecturer in Recreation,
Indiana University, Bloomington, Indiana;
Visiting Lecturer,
West Virginia University, Morgantown, West Virginia

with 61 *illustrations*

The C. V. Mosby Company

ST. LOUIS • TORONTO • LONDON   1982

A TRADITION OF PUBLISHING EXCELLENCE

Editor: Charles K. Hirsch
Assistant editor: Michelle Turenne
Manuscript editor: Carlotta Seely
Design: Susan Trail
Production: Margaret B. Bridenbaugh

The C.V. Mosby Company
11830 Westline Industrial Drive, St. Louis, Missouri 63141

Library of Congress Cataloging in Publication Data

Russell, Ruth V., 1948-
 Planning programs in recreation.

 Bibliography: p.
 Includes index.
 1. Recreation—Planning. I. Title.
GV181.43.R87   790'.06'9   81-14098
ISBN 0-8016-4231-0   AACR2

AC/D/D 20 19 18 17 16 15 14 13 12 11   02/A/237

For
Stephen Williams

Foreword

When recreation began to be formalized as a service of local government (centers, playgrounds, small parks) at the turn of the century, the conduct of recreation activity was paramount, as evidenced in the growth and services of the National Recreation Association, cooperative extension services, and other agencies. Leadership techniques and tools were the focus of workshops and conferences, and activity books were abundant. As the recreation profession developed, especially in the 1960s and early 1970s, it became more oriented to park and recreation systems and emphasized the administration of such systems and the planning of recreation areas and facilities. Professional curriculums in the colleges and universities, as well as conferences and workshops, reduced the emphasis on the conduct of activities and leadership techniques in favor of courses in planning, administration, and management. However, these courses and the books and materials developed seldom approached programming systematically or in depth. As we move into the 1980s, the importance of the recreation experience and the role of good-quality programming has been recognized. Thus this book comes at a most appropriate time in the development of the endeavor to make the recreation experience more meaningful through organized programs. This book not only sets forth a systematic approach to program planning but also provides a valuable resource base.

While there are some traditional recreation program elements in this book, the author has tried to approach the planning process through the integration of many different aspects, which should enable the recreation programmer to apply the program planning system to many types of agencies, populations, and setting. While some of these aspects may be unfamiliar to the typical recreation programmer, programmers should welcome these new insights and use them to enrich the quality of programming and hence the quality of the recreation experience. This book is much more than a program "planning" book. It also describes program administration and evaluation and provides a philosophical foundation for programming. The author has brought to bear her experiences in a variety of recreation settings to make the book practical and has provided unusual documentation to encourage the use of additional resource materials. It should be a rich resource for both experienced and inexperienced programmers and recreation and park administrators, as well as a fine text for use in colleges and universities.

Leadership of recreation activity and administration of a recreation and park system are important, but this book adds to these the art and science of programming—an element essential for the enhancement of meaningful experiences in the total recreation services system.

Betty van der Smissen

Director, School of Health, Physical Education and Recreation
Bowling Green State University (Ohio)

Preface

The program is what recreation services are all about. All else—personnel, supplies, areas and facilities, budgets, public relations—exists primarily to see that the program occurs and that people enjoy participating. Planning is the tool that makes programs happen. Programs are those magic moments of joyous participation that occur when the available and necessary resources have been stirred together just right by planning. But programs do not just "happen," because planning does not just "happen." Planning is organized forethought. This book describes what kind of forethought is required, how to organize it, and how to execute it.

Specifically, this text concentrates on instructing the student planner in a system of recreation program planning that has been labeled the rational planning process. This label is intended to denote the intellectual stages a planner goes through to travel the territory between a problem and a solution or between a need and a fulfillment. In essence, it is as simple and as logical as effective problem solving; that is, the planner moves step by step through the stages of identification of the needs of those served by the program services, analysis of these needs, specification of the alternatives for implementation, implementation, and evaluation.

Above all, this book is intended to lead the reader into action. It is a self-help book on how to get started and a reference book on how to keep going. It assumes that the student of recreation and park services is capable of applying relevant principles from a variety of disciplines: business, sociology, psychology, research, and so on. It also assumes that recreation program planning is a serious professional endeavor and should be approached with intelligence and sophistication.

The book is divided into three major parts. Part One serves to set the stage. Chapter 1, the introduction, sets forth the basic definitions usually required at the beginning of a teaching assignment. This chapter also provides an introductory overview of the rational planning process. Each of the key steps involved in the process is described as it is employed in subsequent chapters. Finally, the chapter is concerned with the actual flow of the planning process, that is, how the specific steps covered in the later chapters fit together into a series of interlocking spirals and circles rather than separate formal steps.

Chapter 2 considers the options from which the planner might choose in organizing or administering the planning procedure. This material is designed to help the planner determine the organizational structure of the planning project—who will do what, where, and when. Citizens, outside consultants, fellow staff members, and planning committees are all considered for potential involvement in the planning task. The value of sharing the planning responsibility is discussed.

The bulk of the text's instructional material falls in Part Two, the rational planning process. A schematic outline of the chapters in Parts One and Two may be observed in the following flowchart.

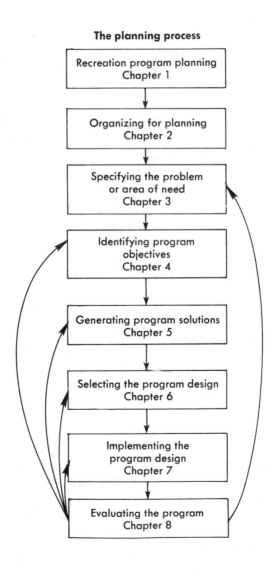

The planning process

Recreation program planning
Chapter 1

Organizing for planning
Chapter 2

Specifying the problem
or area of need
Chapter 3

Identifying program
objectives
Chapter 4

Generating program solutions
Chapter 5

Selecting the program design
Chapter 6

Implementing the
program design
Chapter 7

Evaluating the program
Chapter 8

Chapter 3 discusses the first phase in the rational planning process. The planner's most serious decision and major contribution are the formulation or definition of the planning task. To help the planner better arrive at this formulation, Chapter 3 explores indications of the demand for programmed recreation. These include demographic factors such as residential living patterns, socioeconomic status, age and occupation, as well as attitudes, preferences, behavior, and available resources. Instruction is offered in using surveys, inventories, questionnaires, and so on to gather information on these demand indicators.

Chapter 4 discusses materials pertinent to the second phase of rationally planned recreation programs. Following the determination of the planning task, the planner must consider the final outcome or result desired to properly direct the remainder of the planning process. Programs do not stand alone; they are not trophies to be lined up on a shelf; they are not worthy just because they exist. They have a far greater purpose, and determining this purpose is the subject of Chapter 4. The chapter also considers planning as a value decision made by the planner in advance. The planner's responsibility to maintain high-value choices is discussed.

Chapter 5 discusses creativity as part of the next phase of the planning process. The planner is encouraged to consider all conceivable possibilities in accomplishing the perceived program needs and interests and in meeting the established goals and objectives.

Chapter 6 brings the planner to the phase of actual program selection. Appropriateness, available leadership, budget, cost, and effectiveness evaluations assist the planner in determining which program or activity of those initially considered is the best possible solution for the particular situation.

Chapter 7 is designed to aid the planner in bridging the gap between plans on paper and action. Various marketing, motivational, scheduling, and public relations systems are suggested.

Chapter 8 considers the final phase: evaluating how well the chosen and implemented program satisfies the planning task and the program goals. This chapter also makes the plea that the planner use evaluation research not only to determine the effectiveness and worth of a past program but also as the first phase of a subsequent planning project. Thus the rational planning process comes full circle.

Part Three summarizes the preceding chapters, offers a conclusion, and proposes some open-ended questions for further thought.

The appendix is a comprehensive bibliography of current books on recreation program planning.

To accompany the text, an instructional packet is available for the teacher. This packet serves as both a workbook and a resource to enable the teacher to supplement the text with a series of class participation learning exercises. I developed this tool in conjunction with my own classroom sessions and found it the most useful and effective way of teaching this material. Student understanding of and ability in the rational planning process are virtually secured because the classroom exercises provided in the teacher packet encourage the actual practice of the material presented in the text.

I would like to express my appreciation to the publisher's reviewers for their helpful suggestions in the development of this book: James L. Bristor, Re.D., at Michigan State University; James R. Champlin, Re.D., at the University of Georgia; Effie L. Fairchild, D.Ed., at the University of Oregon; David B. Harding at the University of Florida; Bernard F. Mead, Jr., Ph.D., at the University of Wyoming; Robert M. Neely at Southwest Missouri State University; and William H. Ridinger, Ed.D., at Southern Connecticut State College.

Finally, I feel some responsibility in instructing the student planner in how to use this text. Learning is an activity. Planning is an activity. The reader is thus advised to pursue the instructional material provided here with thoughtfulness, questions, and practice.

Ruth V. Russell

Contents

Part One

Introduction

The planning process

Recreation program planning:
pressures, needs,
problems, or interests

Chapter 1

Recreation program planning

Throughout history the vast majority of mankind has been desperately poor. In the 20th century, millions of people have been escaping from poverty into affluence. With prosperity attained, what new goals will they seek to achieve? (Cleveland, 1977)

Leisure has gradually become a dominant force in modern society, and most projections indicate that its influence will increase. During the past century free time has been expanded because of technology; we now enjoy a shortened workweek, greater physical mobility, and a longer and healthier life span. As a result, our access to and demand for leisure experiences have also expanded. Today people are clamoring for more and better leisure services in which to enjoy the social, cultural, and material bounty afforded by modern technology.

Organizations and individuals concerned with the delivery of leisure services have affected and also have been affected by these changes. As a result, the function and structure of many leisure delivery systems have evolved to accommodate this society's movement from a work orientation to a leisure orientation. Leisure services must recognize changing trends and grow with them. The development of efficient and effective programs, facilities, and management practices consistent with emerging social demands is vital to the very well-being of leisure services.

For example, the entire decade of the 1980s will most likely demand that the recreation and park movement exhibit a particular tenacity if it is to not only remain viable but even survive. Certainly such factors as excessive inflation, the availability and cost of energy resources, the environmental and social costs of greater energy self-sufficiency, and increasing domestic and international tensions will exact a heavy cumulative toll on recreation program services. Simultaneously, the need for quality recreation programs will increase as the daily and cumulative effects of economic, energy, national, and personal stress reach most segments of the American people.

What are these developments likely to mean to the recreation program planner? The only certainty is that there will be no simple answer. Our collective answer to this decade of challenge must include the seeking of professional and organizational excellence; it must be an answer of commitment. We must be sure that our program services are rooted in the desires and aspirations of the public, while satisfying the requirements of the society.

Recreation: object of planning

Boredom is America's most prevalent disease (Ramey, 1974). It causes both mischief and destruction. Aside from the medical costs of boredom, the social price is evident in many ways. George Sanders, worldly star of the screen, left his last words in a suicide note in a hotel in Spain when he was 65. Sanders wrote: "I commit suicide because I am bored and because I have already lived enough" (Allen, 1974, p. 10).

Although this example is extreme, boredom is a problem of serious and pervasive consequences. Schoolteachers have known for a long time that children who are bored in class are a menace to others. The boredom of existentialists, all-night doughnut makers, housewives, truck drivers, soldiers, students, airline pilots, voters who stay home on election day, drug abusers, and animals in the zoo is all too real in many cases. A total of 85% of Americans are bored on the job (Haskell, 1980, p. 75). And unfortunately, boredom is on the increase in our society.

Erich Fromm identifies boredom as the insidious cause of catastrophes ranging from drug addiction to violence (Ramey, 1974). Bertrand Russell (1968, p. 38) claims that "boredom is a vital problem for the moralist since at least half the sins of mankind are caused by fear of it."

Boredom is essentially a thwarted desire for events, not necessarily pleasant ones, but just occurrences that will enable the victim of boredom to know one day from another. "The opposite of boredom, in a word, is not pleasure but excitement" (Russell, 1968, p. 36).

A challenge for the professional in leisure services becomes one of asking whether there is a relationship between the fascination Americans have with boredom and the requirement of effective recreation program planning. Perhaps the clue lies in Werner Graf's definition of boredom. Boredom, says Graf, is "an incomplete striving for meaning. It is the desire for meaning coupled with the inability to get it" (Allen, 1974, p. 10).

Boredom, therefore, is not apathy; it is the constant striving for meaning. It is the meaninglessness, not the monotony that we usually blame, that is perhaps the key. Knitting is monotonous. Jogging is monotonous. Yet people do them by choice. Thus it appears that meaning is the key that may link the recreation professional's collection of programs with America's most prevalent disease.

When an analysis of recreation program services is made, it becomes clear that it is not the activities or programs themselves that are central. The important thing is what happens to people as a result of experiencing these programs, the meaning that they derive from them. Recreation is the experience or the result of an activity. These results can be physical, social, psychological, or spiritual.

In this book, emphasis will be given to the program planning process, and consequently readers may find themselves absorbed in particularizing. The introductory illustration of boredom was used to show the paramount importance of planning for *meaning* in recreational programs. Program planners in recreation and parks should be providing meaningful experiences, not activities for their own sake. The real importance in program planning is not necessarily how many or what kind of activities the planner provides, but what meaning the participants experience as a result of involvement. The recreation program experience is motivated by a need for meaningful stimulation or optimal arousal. The more novel, challenging, complex, and dissonant the activity, the more arousing and fulfilling it becomes.

Recreation has been viewed by some in the field as a behavior response and by others as a stimulus to behavior; however, the foundation of meaningful recreation rests on the principle that participation needs no reward other than the participation itself. This does not forfeit any occurrence or desirability of secondary values such as physical fitness, tension release, and a well-rounded personality. In order for the program planner to meet the recreationist's need for meaningful experiences, serious attention must be given to that person's reason for participating. What does this person want or need the recreation experience to offer his or her psychological, social, or physical health? In studying the following chapters, the reader should constantly remember this question.

Definition of recreation

The term *recreation* has become increasingly familiar to all in our society. For most of us, it means what we do for fun—our hobbies, amusements, pastimes—the experiences that provide pleasure, relaxation, and amusement in our free time. Here recreation is defined as "the natural expression of certain human interests and needs seeking satisfaction during free time. It is an individual or a group experience motivated primarily by the enjoyment and satisfaction derived therefrom" (Sessoms, 1972). The program planner is therefore interested in providing opportunities for individual and group experience relative to the participants' interests and needs during free time. The program planner's main goal is participant enjoyment and satisfaction.

Thus the term *recreation* is used in this book to describe an experience rather than a specific activity. Recreation is thought of here as a feeling—a product of human behavior through which the participant becomes refreshed, renewed, contented, excited, happy, proud, rested, joyous, or recreated. Recreation is what happens to a person as the result of an activity, rather than the activity itself. This means that no activity is inherently recreational and that any experience has potential for recreation.

Although recreation has traditionally been defined as an activity characterized by certain behaviors, the real value of the activity is derived from its ability to satisfy certain underlying needs that exist within the individual. The recreation experience is thus recognized as a means to an end. This end goal usually transcends the search for diversion alone. When a person engages in recreational pursuits, he or she frequently does so for more than personal enjoyment or satisfaction; some additional reasons include the need to make friends, to keep fit, to obtain physical release, to compete, to feel successful, or to gain prestige. The recreation experience is a personal response. Therefore the selection of specific recreation activities is most likely prompted by the desire to satisfy certain personal needs.

Most definitions of recreation view it primarily as a personal phenomenon; however, because it has been institutionalized and organized, it must also be understood as an important element in our societal life, as a key aspect of our modern economy, and as a profession. This means that recreation's definition ultimately ranges from informal, free, and self-directed activity in the home to the establishment of multibillion-dollar business enterprises. Recreation may mean a single child playing a game of pick-up-sticks or millions of families swarming the highways each summer in search of the "perfect" vacation.

Therefore the definition of recreation employed in this book requires rethinking of recreation program service not only in terms of the types of activities and events typically offered, but also in terms of the human experience. Recreation should help each individual extend his or her intellectual, physical, and emotional reach—as well as that of society—through program opportunities that "improve awareness, deepen understanding, stimulate appreciation, develop one's powers, and enlarge the sources of enjoyment" (Murphy and Howard, 1977, p. 32).

Because recreation is a personal response that grows out of personal experience, recreation program agencies must develop planning goals, planning techniques, and planning skills that make available to the participant the necessary attitudes, skills, and knowledge for making relevant recreation choices.

Societal rewards of programmed recreation

The play of infants and children seems the purest form of an activity entire of itself. Yet theorists have been reluctant to leave play alone, to treat it as an autistic, self-contained activity. Recreation must, in our society, be assigned a utilitarian function and not be left in the hands of the players. Psychologists, sociologists, philosophers, psychiatrists, anthropologists, doctors, social workers, and even the clergy have devoted considerable verbal and written discussion to the positive relationship between recreation behavior and societal and individual values. The value of the recreation experience has been well defined for today's program planner. We have long held recreation to be important and have attributed to the play experience many desirable by-products. In fact, "recreation and park programs often have been promoted on the very basis of their contribution to the life of the community, the health of the individual, and the growth and security of the society" (Sessoms and others, 1975, p. 67). But the reverse is also true: recreation structures and organizations also reflect the basic values of society and the individual.

First, let us briefly explore the societal and cultural rewards of programmed play. Throughout recorded time many philosophers and pedagogues have stated that we as a society survive and flourish as a consequence of our leisure behavior. These and other professional people have pointed out that whenever one traces the origin of a practice or skill that has played a crucial role in the biological, philosophical, sociological, and psychological evolution of the human race, one usually discovers the origin to be some form of leisure behavior.

Perhaps a review of John Huizinga's classic study of the play element in culture (1955) will provide an adequate background of the relationship between recreation and society. "In culture," Huizinga writes, "we find play as a given magnitude existing before culture itself existed, accompanying it and pervading it from the earliest beginnings right up to the phase of civilization we are now living in" (p. 4). Huizinga views the activities of play and the activities of human society to be completely interrelated. He illustrates this notion in three areas: language, myth, and ritual. Language, for instance, is a societal instrument that allows us to communicate. Behind every sentence, phrase, and word is an intellectual abstract expression. This expression is no more than "a play on words" or a playful juggling of thoughts into spoken or written symbols. According to Huizinga, a similar role of play is ascribed to myth and ritual; play shapes the forms of our beliefs and daily rituals.

The value of organized recreation for society is also readily recognized via aesthetics. Inside a playground, for example, an absolute and distinct order prevails. Into an imperfect world and the confusion of life, organized play brings an aesthetic element. Rhythm and harmony are present, because to watch a player in play is to see tension, poise, balance, creativity, contrast, variation, solution, success, and failure. Organized play has rules that create for society the beauty of social order.

There are numerous other values of programmed play that can be cited. For example, such play is an economic stimulant, it defines forms of social acceptance (good sport vs. bad sport), and it equalizes population segments (sports ignore racial distinctions). James F. Murphy in *Recreation and Leisure Service* (1975) discusses the contribution of organized recreation services in what he terms the "collective search for identity." He describes this collective groping for meaning and identity as being the result of modern society's pervasive feeling of emptiness and lack of stability. Our society is in a transitional state that has left the central values of work, competition, progress, and meaning on shaky ground. Murphy claims that because of the current rootlessness of our society the emotional forms of gratification and opportunities for collective celebration and sharing are all but lost. He looks to recreation service agencies to help people realize their own potentialities, continue their self-development, be creative.

Agreement with Murphy's views, at least in part, is not difficult. Recreation programs that build cooperation among people and encourage respect for a sensitivity to people will undoubtedly help in developing a better community. One thing at least is true: as individual members of this society, we must live together.

Individual rewards of programmed recreation

Volumes have been written on the contribution of planned recreation to the growth and development of the individual. It is widely believed that recreation activities and the unique enjoyment derived from them contribute to the wholesomeness and well-being of the human personality.

Although it would be glamorous to philosophize and discuss recreation as an end in itself, as an activity that needs no justification beyond participant satisfaction, in reality, additional justification is needed for those agencies that provide such services. Therefore a brief review of the specific values of recreation to the individual that have appeared in the literature follows.

1. *Physical health.* Recreation can provide the opportunity to achieve better coordination, motor development, muscular strength, increased circulatory and respiratory capacity, and improved body tone. Recreation's contribution to physical fitness may be involved, in other words, not only with healthful living but with living at all.

2. *Mental health.* Psychological well-being is contingent upon a balance between inner desires and outer pressures. Through experiences such as art, music, social activities, and sports, people may find an outlet for self-expression otherwise denied. Many theorists also believe that recreation can offer relief from frustrations and serve as a catharsis for harmful emotions.

3. *Intellectual development.* In recreation, opportunities for broadening knowledge and skills are unlimited. Learning by doing, for example, affords the development of skills and knowledge that can result in the unparalleled education of the participant.

4. *Character development.* Recreation provides the chance for people to develop good habits. Qualities such as honesty, reliability, unselfishness, courtesy, friendliness, and courage should be encouraged and taught as a part of all recreation programs. These are the particular goals of many high-adventure wilderness programs. Organizations such as Outward Bound and The National Outdoor Leadership School offer courses lasting from 7 days to 3½ months and including wilderness expeditions, mountaineering, snow and ice climbing, ski touring, and kayaking. In typical events, all members of a group must negotiate a 12-foot wall with only the help of others in the group, or 10 people spend 12 hours in a tree. Interest in risk-taking activities has increased tremendously during the past decade.

5. *Social adjustment.* Because recreation often involves a group setting, it can be one of the most rewarding situations for the development of social relations. People must adjust to one another, at least to some degree, to enjoy the activity even when conflict and competition are a part of the activity. The Children's Experimental Workshop in Glen Echo Park, Maryland, was begun in 1974 as an instructional workshop in clay and dramatics for visually handicapped children. Among its goals was the providing of an opportunity for increased social contact.

6. *Creativeness*. Recreation, with freedom as its essential ingredient, many times makes it possible to develop creative talents; talents not only in the arts and crafts but also in motor expression and communication. Studies by Abraham Maslow have attempted to describe and rank human needs. His findings, as well as those of many other psychologists, indicate that at the apex is the need for self-realization and creative self-expression.

7. *Happiness and satisfaction*. If the recreation experience has any sole justification, it is the pleasure, the enjoyment, the gleeful expression of satisfaction that recreation can help achieve. It is the kind of feeling derived when the experience has been enriching. It is feelings such as security, recognition, accomplishment, and belonging that well-planned recreation programs can offer the participant.

There are perhaps no better or more readily available examples of these values of recreation to the individual as in the field of therapeutic recreation. The research literature is resplendent with illustrations of the actual use of programmed recreation as therapeutic treatment. For example, a study conducted in 1978 tested the use of sports programming as an alternative rehabilitation modality for emotionally disturbed adolescents (Dozier and others, 1978). The following case study from this project illustrates the findings:

> Valerie, 15, had a history of episodes of severe withdrawal and mental confusion, during which she became mute, stared into space, and was unresponsive to external stimulation. Following a brief psychiatric hospitalization, Valerie was referred to the sports group because she was a chronic underachiever, had poor interpersonal relations and was uncommunicative in psychotherapy. Initially, Valerie was silent in the group, and had little or no eye contact. One of the therapeutic tasks in working with her was to confront the withdrawal and isolation to help her become part of the group. To encourage her, Valerie was put in direct interaction with her peers and the group leaders. When she did begin to express herself, Valerie related to the leaders in an angry, defiant manner. She was allowed to express her anger fully, even when irrational, while the group leaders continued to engage her in the sports activity. Valerie became assertive and learned appropriate verbal channels for her aggression within the group. As her sports skills improved, she became able to express affection and trust in the leaders, and demonstrated the internalization of her own controls by playing the leader role with peers. She also did better at school, and at the end of the group, she enrolled in her first extracurricular activity. (p. 485)

In another 1978 study Heywood explored tension relief as a primary function of the recreative experience. The subjects in this study were students at the University of Wisconsin. They were exposed to two separate phases of treatment. The first phase was designed to induce psychophysiological stress (via mental arithmetic problem solving that was deliberately constructed to be frustrating); the second phase was designed to abate the tension generated by the first phase. The tension-reducing experiences were the following: listening to rock music, listening to classical music, reading poetry, reading a professional psychology journal, viewing a television talk show, and viewing a televised ice hockey game. The results revealed a decrease in all physiological indicators measured between phase one and phase two; subject heart rates decreased, upper back tension eased, number of respiration cycles decreased and their depth lessened, and skin resistance dropped. In other words, the findings supported the hypothesis that there is a significant physiological difference in the response to positively perceived recreative experience and induced stress.

The use of recreation programs is constantly being validated in the literature of correctional agencies as well. Professional program planners working in prisons utilize and verify recreational experiences as a means of reducing disturbances, teaching specific skills applicable on the outside, interesting the offender in constructive activity, entertaining, and building self-esteem.

The positive values of recreation for the individual have also been appreciated in nontherapeutic areas. A relative newcomer to such an appreciation is the field of business. Managers of business conventions, for instance, are learning that attendance at meetings improves when alternative activities (preferably outdoor) are made available. They are realizing that executives work better together when they have an opportunity to develop nonwork relationships. Resort companies have come to understand this too, and many have developed a variety of convention sports programs.

Although the literature on the consequences of recreation behavior has traditionally been concerned with the positive and beneficial aspects to the individual and society, a strong case is beginning to be made for the study of the negative or dysfunctional consequences. Some believe this development is precipitated by a concern for the deleterious effects of viewing violence on television and in the sports arena, the effects of too much competition (such as Little League) on childhood emotional development, and the effects of some forms of leisure pursuits on the environment. Such concern points more than ever in the direction of responsible, efficient intervention: recreation program planning.

Although the rewards of programmed play to the individual and to society, as discussed earlier, are indeed wonderful and desirable, they are not automatic. When is programmed play no longer true to the essence of the play experience? Is there such a notion as too much organized, structured, programmed play? In other words, can you have a game without playing? One simple line of demarcation lies in the following criterion: for an activity to be play, the *control*—or decision-making process—must be in the hands of the player. For example, any situation in which the recreation leader makes all the decisions with regard to game choice, paint colors, which trail to hike, what to roast over the open fire, and other variables cannot truly be called play. This control of decision making must, however, be put into proper perspective. To what extent is a player capable of making decisions about his or her play? Think about sending a young child into a candy store with a dollar. There are so many choices, and the child is not yet capable of determining what to buy. Therefore the buying experience becomes ineffective. In the beginning it would be better to present the child with only a few pieces of candy from which to choose. Likewise, in play situations it may be desirable to start with a narrow area of control and progress to wider and eventually complete control situations.

In addition to control, to be true recreation, programmed play situations must respect the concept of *intrinsic motivation*. According to Werner (1979) this means that motivation to play must come from within. It is more meaningful if play is engaged in as a result of self-motivation rather than pressure from leaders, parents, teachers, or peers.

Programmed play situations also must embrace a third determinant of true play: *internal reality*. Again according to Werner, this concept maintains that during play the concerns for survival and the realities of living are suspended and are replaced by fantasy, role playing, make-believe, escape, and pretending.

Therefore, in answer to the question of when programmed play is no longer true to the essence of play, it is when programmed play does not allow for:

1. Participant control of the play situation
2. Intrinsic motivation for participation
3. Freedom of internal reality

If the programmed play experience is not a true play experience, the rewards to society and the individual cannot be expected.

History of programmed recreation

Relaxation and enjoyment—however fleeting or momentary—have been known to all humans throughout history. Yet recreation events, experiences, and places have differed from people to people and culture to culture. The degree of advanced planning has varied according to participant needs and the number of people involved.

In ancient civilization, where mere survival consumed most attention and energy, evidence of painting, music, literature, dance, drama, and games and sports is detectable. The Egyptians were interested in music and enjoyed participation in large orchestras and choruses. Entertainment and spectator activities in Egyptian daily life were generally known only to the affluent; the lower classes reveled in their drinking houses. On holidays public festivals abounded for both classes. The therapeutic recreation field traces its origins to ancient civilization when, as a treatment for mental depression, afflicted Egyptians were sent to resorts (Sessoms and others, 1975).

The recognition of recreation experiences as a separate, identifiable part of life did not emerge until classical Greece and Rome. The arts and sports flourished during the height of Grecian civilization. The Olympic Games, for example, were first established in 732 BC in honor of the god Zeus. They continued until the fifth century AD, when commercialism, speculation, corruption, and gambling so interfered with the original ideal of the games that they were discontinued. However, by this time the Olympics had become widespread, and Rome began to exert the major influence on their purpose and form.

Rome was drawn to entertainment and spectator sports. Physical activity was seen by the ancient Romans as both an end in itself and a way of staying physically fit. Rome exploited leisure; the prevalent forms of activity were oriented to sensuous, gaudy forms of entertainment.

The recreation elements of a culture cannot be separated from its economic and political characteristics. The Middle Ages, for example, which followed the fall of the Roman Empire, were largely agricultural. The rules of a powerful church, combined with the daily toil of working the soil, left little opportunity for the lower classes to enjoy much leisure. Recreation became the telling of stories, the singing of songs, and the impromptu playing of folk games and dramas. Literature, dancing, and sports were reserved for the upper classes. Contests and tournaments in such sports as archery and fencing were popular among the knights and nobility. The shooting of wildlife was not only enjoyed, but controlled and managed during this reign of feudalism. Dancing, drama, and festivals during the Middle Ages frequently reflected religious influence, although secular recreation expressions, such as street pantomime, became more prevalent in the later period.

Up to this point in history recreational experiences were known only as a part of everyday life and work. What people did in their free time depended largely on their work, economic, and religious life-styles. As human societies became more complex and life functions became more clearly specialized, recreation became a more distinct component.

Both the attitudes toward and the opportunities for recreation took a different tack in the modern era. The Renaissance made a colossal impact in refining recreation activities. Sports and games became less brutal. New interest and new forms developed in painting and sculpture. Following the work-worshiping era of the Reformation, modern history was truly made different from the world of the ancients by the arrival of the Industrial Revolution.

The period following 1750 witnessed the rapid rise of machinery to replace human labor. The resultant growth of cities, large populations of factory workers, and long work hours during the Industrial Revolution led to a democratization of leisure and the promise that more people would be allowed to enjoy the benefits of free time and share in the values of planned recreation experiences. Thus the Industrial Revolution was a mixed blessing for the providers of social services such as recreation. On the one hand, it created new problems of city crowding, poverty, and the wear and tear of industrial labor; on the other hand, a greater wealth and productivity could be maintained and potentially shared by all. A much greater leisure could be provided by the productivity of the machine. The contradictions between the promise of comfort and leisure and the reality of discomfort, poverty, and tiresome labor became clear to the poor. They realized that a better world should be brought into being and that it is a right and duty to work for such a better world and to share in its pleasures. Much of the instability and disturbance of these centuries was the result of efforts by the workers to seize a larger share of all those things that meant a good life.

Thus the initial realization that some responsibility exists for the planning of recreation program services appeared at this time. The emergence of recreation services as a separate, distinguishable institution, particularly in America, led the way to the provision of opportunities for recreation for the public as a major social development in the twentieth century. The fact that the public was willing to support a group of professional planners for the primary purpose of fostering recreation experiences was revolutionary. But there was no alternative. Recreation agencies emerged at this time to meet the tremendous social, psychological, and general welfare needs of an urbanizing industrial nation. From the end of the eighteenth century to the middle of the twentieth century, the United States moved from being a pioneer, agricultural land to a highly industrialized, urbanized nation. However, the history of programmed recreation has its soundest origins in the opening years of this century.

The beginnings of community recreation programming included the opening of the South Park Playgrounds in Chicago in 1903; the establishment of the first playground commission by Los Angeles in 1904; the organization by Ernst T. Seton in 1902 of the Woodcraft Indians, which introduced outdoor recreation activities and formed the basis of many boys' and girls' club programs; and Luther Gulick's public school athletic leagues in New York in 1903. The years 1910 and 1912 witnessed the organization of three major youth-serving agencies: the Boy Scouts of America in 1910 and the Campfire Girls and the Girl Scouts in 1912.

These early years of the twentieth century also were marked by the rapid expansion of camping program services. Increasing in numbers, the youth camps, both public and private, focused programming on physical development and learning to live in harmony with nature. In addition, college and high school athletics advanced when the intramural program gained a foothold about 1914.

This determined trend toward organized recreation programs, as well as facilities and leaders, was centered on neighborhood and community interests. World War I served to strengthen this movement. The period from 1914 to 1918 has been referred to as the "neighborhood organization" stage of recreation in the United States. These years were defined by the emergence of self-supported, self-governed, decentralized play activities in neighborhoods (Sessoms and others, 1975). The need for recreation opportunities was recognized on a more rational and less sentimental basis.

The conditions created by World War I provoked an even greater demand for recreation services. This demand was met when the War Camp Community Service organized recreation programs in over 600 communities adjacent to military posts. On the posts themselves, in addition to the small programs operated by the U.S. Army and Navy, extensive programs were conducted by the Young Men's Christian Association.

The decade of expansion following World War I saw extensive broadening of program services in all types of recreation activities. At the same time the community began to accept responsibility for the provision of program services for all ages. There was a marked movement away from the simpler forms of recreation to activities that required increased financial resources for both participation and facilities. For many people, purchasing power increased to make automobiles, radios, sports events, motion pictures, and travel within reach. Another development was an awareness of the value of recreation to the well-being of the individual and society. "Recreation was established as a force for molding character, developing physical and mental health, and giving people a finer environment in which to dwell" (Sessoms and others, 1975, p. 36).

The period of the Great Depression (1930-1941) actually fostered the expansion of recreation services. The establishment of New Deal agencies and their "make work" projects brought forth the most extensive public recreation programs ever before attempted. Along with the construction of new areas and facilities, many recreation programs were established. It is estimated that in 1930, 22,000 volunteers and professionals were engaged in recreation services; of that figure only 2,500 were employed full time. Three years later approximately 45,000 full-time workers were added by the Work Projects Administration (Sessoms and others, 1975, pp. 38-39).

For 4 years, beginning in 1941, the United States was struggling with World War II. Organized recreation again arose to meet an increased demand for services. The Army, the Navy, the U.S.O. (United Service Organization), and the American Red Cross served close to battlefronts, in convalescent and rest centers, on troop trains and ships, in training camps, in communities adjacent to encampments, and in industrial centers.

Following World War II many towns and cities built "living" memorials to their war heroes in the form of recreation facilities; this focused greater attention on establishing recreation programs. In this same period recreation programs were developed for use in hospitals. By the 1950s services for the ill and handicapped became popular as the medical and psychiatric professions became interested in recreation's potential for treatment and rehabilitation.

Recreation exploded into a tremendous fiscal expansion in the 1960s. This was particularly evident in commercial and outdoor recreation services, as well as in federal government involvement. The federal impact was felt immediately. With funds available to local and state agencies for planning, new programs were developed in all directions. As a result of the prosperity and social upheaval of the 1960s, by the 1980s recreation planners were being challenged to plan for a very uncertain future. Responding to this challenge, they have begun to use new managerial approaches to solving administrative, resource, and policy problems. Programming also has been forced to respond in unique and efficient ways to program form and direction.

The dilemma facing recreation planners of the 1980s is whether planned, organized services as we know them today continue to provide benefits to society that exceed their cost in resources. In today's mass culture, recreation is not conceived as a noble exercise of physical and mental fulfillment as it was for the ancient Greeks and Romans. Instead it is often viewed as an opportunity for increased consumption. If organized recreation services are going to survive to the end of this century, program planners for the future may need to develop recreation experience forms that are not a part of the consuming pattern.

Planning: the recreation program tool

Planning is essentially a means of improving decisions and is therefore a prerequisite to action. For recreation and park programs, planning seeks to answer two vital questions:

- What is the purpose of an agency or program?
- What are the best means of achieving that purpose?

Planning is nothing more than a certain manner of arriving at decisions and actions to promote some good for the constituency.

Is planned recreation desirable? If so, in all or only certain instances? Why should recreation program service agencies plan? Is there such a thing as too much planned, organized recreation? When are the benefits of planning greater than its costs, and when not?

For most recreation program planners the question "why plan?" is answered readily: because planning is good. *Good* in the mind of the planner is most often synonymous with *necessary;* if planning does not occur, things will not get done. In general, the value of planning derives from its presumed ability to increase constituency welfare. But when does planning encroach on what traditionally has been highly sacred in this society: individual rights? Some argue that planning inhibits personal welfare and thus reduces the welfare of society as a whole.

Much attention has been given to this argument; even in the supposedly "safe" professions of medicine and engineering. Von Hayek (1944) and Popper (1945 and 1966) probably initiated the debate when they declared that individual freedom is a fundamental value to which comprehensive planning is hostile. Wootton (1945) responded by arguing that planning does not reduce personal freedom but, in fact, enhances it.

Big Brother worries such as these indicate a confusion about what planning does and does not provide. These critics equate a framework for future programs and development with constraints; they see planning as simply an imposition of demands from the top down. It is important that planning not fall into this description. Skeptics of planning must be shown that a plan is a tool to enhance sensible development, not an instrument to limit it. As communities become more complex and as population and social demands increase, the need for planned recreation program development must be recognized if individuals are to have any say in how their future will be shaped.

Definition of planning

For the purpose of recreation programming, planning can be defined as follows: "Planning is the process of preparing a set of decisions for action in the future, directed at achieving goals by optimal means" (Dror, 1963, p. 50). This definition can be broken down into seven different parts. A brief discussion of each part will clarify the meaning and implications of the definition.

1. *Planning is the process.* Planning is a continuous activity requiring an input of resources in order to be sustained. Because it is an ongoing process, it must be distinguished from a plan. A plan is a stable set of decisions for future action that can be arrived at with or without the help of planning. This book instructs in the process of planning, not in plan making.

2. *Of preparing.* Planning requires effort. There is a specific set of decisions or planning functions that must be approved and carried out. These are distinct though interdependent steps that can be viewed separately.

3. *A set.* It is important to determine the difference between planning and general decision making. Although planning is actually a type of decision making, its significant characteristic is that it includes a whole set of separate but related decisions.

4. *Of decisions for action.* Rather than being directed at knowledge, planning's main goal is action. An action is mobilized as a result of planning.

5. *In the future.* This is perhaps the most important element of planning. It includes prediction, uncertainty, and a certain amount of guesswork.

6. *Directed at achieving goals.* The planning process cannot function unless it has goals. This does not mean that the planning process begins to operate with clearly defined goals, but that the first phases of the process includes the formulation of planning objectives.

7. *By optimal means.* Planning is a rational process. It seeks to shape the future rationally according to desires. To be rational, the process must include collecting information, using knowledge, and processing information in a systematic and harmonious way.

It is on these elements of the definition of planning that the remaining chapters in this book are based.

Occasions for planning

All social service professionals and organizations, including the recreation profession, share in their reliance on planning. However, the different social service professions are eager for effective planning for varying reasons. There are five distinct occasions for planning.

The first occasion occurs when a particular social problem is in focus: How can we deal with increasing crime? What can the increasing numbers of working mothers do for child care while they work? What should be done about vandalism in the park?

The planning here must be directed toward the solution of a particular problem; when the problem is solved, the planning has been successful. This rationale for planning often has a role in recreation program planning.

A second reason for planning is a need to respond to gaps, fragmentation, and other inadequacies in an existing program. This approach is a relatively unimaginative and restricted rationale for planning; yet a considerable portion of planning does originate in an attempt to reform existing programs. This happens when the gap between the idealized program (derived from an earlier planning process) and reality becomes so large that renewed planning attention is needed. For example, a men's softball league, even though a success for several years, has recently been deteriorating because of a decrease in attendance, a lack of diversity in whom it serves, or another problem. Planning to improve such an existing program would be healthy and necessary.

A third reason for planning is what Alfred Kahn (1969, p. 1) defines as the translation of broad social goals into specific programs. This rationale is relatively new in this nation's social service history and is a direct result of the thinking of the 1960s. As Kahn (pp. 1-2) relates:

> At the conclusion of the work of the Joint Commission on Mental Illness and Health, the leadership of the National Institute of Mental Health was called upon to suggest strategic legislation to President John F. Kennedy. Such legislation was to advance the objective of improving treatment of the severely mentally ill by creating a service system which maximized community-based treatment and sped up the return to the community of those who must be hospitalized. Shortly thereafter authorities in each state had access to considerable planning funds, general federal guidelines, and the task of carrying through a planning process which would tie specifically to the national objectives.*

In this case the goal of planning is the formulation of general social goals and then movement toward highly specific programs.

A fourth reason for using the planning process might be to allocate scarce resources effectively. There is little dispute, particularly now in the 1980s, that much planning is initiated by the need to make do with available and limited funds. Given the likelihood of new social goals and competing demands from various interest sectors, careful planning decisions will have to be made constantly. Deciding which recreation program services represent the wisest and most beneficial use of public and private dollars will be necessary, or those dollars will be reallocated.

A fifth motive for planning is the integration of new technology and skills. There is no better example of this than the computer. Even in recreation programming, new planning has been required to accommodate computer simulation games, computer scoring, computer reservation systems, and even computer pinball. Skate-

---

*From Theory and Practice of Social Planning by Alfred J. Kahn (c) 1969 Russell Sage Foundation. Reprinted by permission of the publisher, Russell Sage Foundation.

board clinics, white-water kayaking, hang gliding, and the renaissance of hot-air ballooning are also evidence of the need to plan for the integration of new technology and skills.

Thus from this discussion we can see that planning begins with a problem, a widely felt need, a major dissatisfaction, or a crisis. At a more basic level, much of the planning literature maintains that the quality of services offered to consumers—indeed, the sheer survival of the agency itself—is dependent on planning.

History of planning

Much of what recreation programmers know and use of planning theory is derived from the experience and literature of other fields; from social work, which sees planning as a means for problem solving; from corporate or business fields, which see planning as a way of managing change; and from the efforts of the British in municipal planning.

Planning has a rather short printed history. Before the 1960s only a few books and a small assortment of articles on planning were available. In the following years there was an increased interest in comprehensive planning, beginning in the business sector and rapidly spreading into social service agencies, nonprofit organizations, and government at the national, state, and local levels.

A systematic history of planning in the social sciences has not yet been written. The story of early social planning in the United States is essentially one of partial and unintegrated efforts, of diverse conceptions and styles, and of only limited sanction. The city planning movement was founded by social welfare personnel, muckrakers, and representatives from the design and construction industries. It may be considered as beginning in 1893 with the Columbian Exposition in Chicago (Kahn, 1969, p. 23). Planning by charity organizations appeared shortly before World War I in an effort that continues today toward programming services for the less fortunate. Planning on a state level was faced seriously only after World War II, partly out of pressure to comply with and take advantage of the numerous federal offerings that increasingly made planning a prerequisite. Also since World War II there have been considerable developments in planning at the federal level as Congress continues to expand its social and welfare commitments.

For a time, planning became rather pedestaled. The master plan was the planner's "silver bullet" whose magical powers achieved great respect in the dynamic society of the 1960s. People were unhappy about injustices and gaps in society, and planners rushed to the rescue with comprehensive plans. More recently the interest in planning has been stimulated by a scarcity in resources, both natural and financial, and by the belief that there can be greater accountability by using the planning process as a mechanism for managing and controlling. At a time when resources are scarce throughout the human services network, planning has become a strategy of last resort.

Despite this interest, few social service delivery systems, recreation and park agencies included, have developed truly effective planning operations. Reasons often given for this deficiency are the following:

1. A generalized fear that planning is a business concept that is unadaptable to nonbusiness settings
2. The abstract level of planning, which scares some people
3. The pressure on administrators to solve day-to-day crises, leaving little time for planning
4. The lack of available trained planning staff
5. The fact that action is well ahead of theory in the planning field (Norman, 1979)

Yet at a time when resources for human services are scarce, these reasons must be overcome. Professionals of the future must not falter in using the comprehensive planning process effectively.

Rational approach to recreation program planning

It is estimated that by the year 2000 nearly 180 million citizens in the United States (the size of the entire population in 1960) will be living in four major urban areas: the northern half of the Atlantic coast, the area south of the Great Lakes, Florida, and the southern California coast. Along with an increase in urban population comes a surge in interest and participation in outdoor recreation, typically a 10% increase annually. By the year 2000 participation will have increased fourfold (U.S. Department of the Interior, 1974, p. 50).

Unfortunately, the nation's outdoor recreation opportunities, both resources and programs, are not now (and will not be in the future) where the people are. *The Recreation Imperative,* the draft of a nationwide outdoor recreation plan prepared by the Department of the Interior for the U.S. Senate and released in 1974, indicates that although there are 491 million acres in the public recreation estate, less than 3% of these lands are within an hour's drive of major urban areas (p. 5).

The Recreation Imperative offers a solution:

> In urban areas where the cost of land is highest, there is a particular need to identify and realize all potentials for expanding existing recreation opportunities. Imagination and willingness to step outside traditional constraints are required if these potentials are to be realized. . . . Where critical deficiencies in recreation acreage exist, cities must imaginatively assemble and use fragments of open space (p. 307).

Edward R. Walsh (1975) has proposed that one interpretation of the above solution is to use the estimated 2 million acres in this country traditionally reserved for the dead. He claims that cemetery land represents an invaluable resource in the race to recapture dwindling space for outdoor recreation. Walsh also believes that "if professionals could program this acreage for compatible leisure activities, millions of deprived city dwellers would witness the dawning of a new . . . age" (p. 29). What if you were the program planner under Mr Walsh's employ? How would you comply with this mandate?

Definition

In this book rational planning is defined as a process for determining appropriate future action through a sequence of choices. The word *determining* is used in two senses: "finding out" and "assuring." Because *appropriate* implies a criterion for making judgments regarding desired states, it suggests that planning includes attention to goals. *Action* embodies specifics and suggests the task of relating general ends and particular means. In addition, action, which is the eventual outcome of planning efforts, requires a responsible attention to problems of implementation.

The numerous choices that make up the rational planning process can be summarized into the following basic levels:

1. The selection of desired ends and criteria
2. The identification of a set of alternatives consistent with these ends, and the selection of a desired alternative
3. The guidance of action toward the determined ends

Each of these broad levels requires the planner to exercise judgment. Judgment makes planning happen. In other words, rational planning is a conscious, cerebral process directed at governing sequences of future activity.

At this point I wish to clarify two aspects of the rational planning process: the planner's unique obligation to desirable goals and the continuous nature of planning. Rational planning has been described by Joseph Bunzel (1961) as a "process where, because of faith in the ability to influence the future, one uses foresight to achieve predetermined goals." The planner takes responsibility for looking to the future and giving meaning and worth to present choices. This notion that rational planning focuses on policy determination is a central one, particularly since recreation planners are really social planners with responsibility to the best interests of their constituency. Yet the predetermined goals to which Bunzel refers are not static and rigid; rather they are dynamic and a developmental phenomenon in planning. They are the product of the complex series of interactions that is the rational planning process.

Rational planning is also a learning process. Planned behavior moves experimentally, trying various options until a "fit" is found. The planner does not merely project facts or trends in planning. Instead the planner tries to project consequences of different choices. Planning is concerned with monitoring and feedback because it is a continuous process, not a single act. Programs may be improved as the plan moves from the drawing board or planning folder to the actual operation.

Values in rational planning

Rational planning has been justified as the discipline that helps guard the public interest. Planners are assumed to possess values so useful to society that they should be charged with the responsibility of societal design, or to have some special ability that allows them to interpret the multitude of individual preferences. With these expectations comes a responsibility. There is need for mature, serious concern on the question of how planning can enhance respect for the individual, taking care not to mold him or her into a preconceived plan or to destroy privacy; in other words, how planning can avoid becoming a value-blind type of social engineering.

This means that professional integrity is of vital importance. The personal philosophy of the recreation professional and his or her interpretation of the values of the constituency play an important role in the type of recreation programs offered and the policies governing them. Because this is a diverse and complex society, not all recreation professionals think alike or interpret circumstances in the same way. Because there are a variety of planning issues with value overtones, the planner should act with a keen sense of value responsibility. As an agent of a constituency, the recreation program planner cannot impose his or her own ideas of what is right or wrong. If an ultimate objective of rational program planning is to widen choice, the planner has the obligation not to limit choice arbitrarily. If an ultimate objective of planning is efficiency, the planner cannot afford to prematurely reject alternatives based on his or her own agenda. This is crucial. I maintain that neither technical competence, educated philosophy, nor professional wisdom entitles the planner to ascribe or dictate values to those being served. This view is in keeping with the democratic precepts that govern the profession.

In conjunction with this caution, the following discussion outlines the specific personal qualities and abilities essential to the recreation program planner. They are grouped according to the behaviors that characterize planning as defined earlier in this chapter. (See Table 1 for further illustration.)

Achievement of ends This book's definition of rational planning includes the concept of a purposeful process directed toward desired, ordered results: the program. Such desired ends may be permanent program changes, slightly altered programs, or new programs. In order to perform this planning behavior well, the recreation program planner must be able to do the following:

1. Maintain a basic belief that all human beings have dignity and worth and therefore be determined to contribute toward the improvement of their lives
2. Understand and believe in the importance of recreation in modern life and its contribution both as a personal experience and as a form of social service

Exercise of choice Planning is a behavior that involves formulating values, establishing means, and selecting alternatives. This book's definition of planning stresses the exercise of choice as a characteristic of the intellectual act. In order to make good choices, the recreation program planner must be able to do the following:

1. Think clearly and logically, understand and analyze problem situations, and develop rational conclusions
2. Rely on a sound knowledge of human nature, both in an abstract sense (understanding theoretical literature on group and individual psychology) and in a practical sense (understanding everyday human responses)
3. Possess good judgment, a strong sense of personal responsibility, and high moral standards

Orientation to the future　Planning, as an end-directed process, is future oriented. It implies a need in the present for information about the future. To perform this planning behavior, the recreation program planner must be able to do the following:

1. Be flexible in the sense of being ready to grow and change over a period of time, rather than clinging to outmoded views or irrelevant professional attitudes
2. Be both visionary and practical, having high ideals of what may be possible or desired in the future while keeping a realistic sense of day-to-day matters
3. Have integrity, honesty, and loyalty to the agency with which the planner is affiliated and to its goals and philosophy

Action　Planning is employed to bring about results. Action is a step in the ends-means chain leading directly to what is desired. It is the implementation of all

Table 1　*The rational planning act and professional abilities*

Planning requirements	Abilities needed
Achievement of ends	Maintaining a basic belief that all human beings have dignity and worth Understanding and believing in the importance of recreation in modern life
Exercise of choice	Thinking clearly and logically and developing rational conclusions Relying on a sound knowledge of human nature Possessing good judgment and a strong sense of responsibility
Orientation to the future	Being flexible Being both visionary and practical Having integrity and loyalty to the agency
Action	Working effectively with others Communicating skillfully and effectively Developing specific knowledge of and enthusiasm in the recreation experience Making difficult decisions
Comprehensiveness	Being aware of the community Maintaining emotional and psychological maturity Learning from mistakes and failures

the previous planning behaviors. The planner must put the chosen alternative into operation. The recreation program planner must therefore be able to do the following:

1. Work effectively with others by bringing forth their best abilities rather than being an authoritarian director
2. Communicate skillfully and effectively, using both written and verbal forms
3. Develop specific knowledge of and enthusiasm in the forms of recreation experiences, including a personal interest and participation, and have leadership skills in some areas of activity
4. Make difficult decisions and then stand by them

Comprehensiveness The planner must be able to understand and integrate the various ramifications of planning and planned programs; the planner must be able to maintain a sense of the whole picture. Evaluation of the planned programs is a continuous process within the rational planning process itself. Accordingly, the recreation program planner must be able to do the following:

1. Be aware of the community and its diverse components, as well as the interplay of its different agencies, organizations, and social groups
2. Maintain emotional and psychological maturity by being able to understand self and others, by being as free from prejudices as possible, and by being able to manage criticism and disagreement constructively
3. Learn from mistakes and failures, not rationalizing them but facing them and turning them into positive assets

Inventory of the elements

Recreation program planning begins with a problem, a widely felt need, a major dissatisfaction, or a crisis. It may come with a transfer of power and the decision of the new leadership to change. Sometimes planning begins with the urgent need to allocate scarce resources or personnel. At other times it starts with a demand from the source of funds or power that planning be done to qualify for continued subsidy. It often begins with the acquisition of new resources or personnel. Finally, planning is undertaken because it is expected. But once the decision to plan is made, then what happens?

The following section of this chapter explains in overview fashion the critical elements within each of the steps in the rational planning process and sets the stage for more detailed study in subsequent chapters. See Fig. 1-1 for an expanded version of the planning process chart introduced in the preface.

As the chart in Fig. 1-1 indicates, planning is a developmental process in which the various steps are in constant interaction. Although a logical sequence may be listed, it is not necessarily an eternal one. To ensure a planned result that accurately reflects all the relevant planning elements, a planner must be ready to refine and revise the outcomes of earlier steps while moving toward later ones. An understand-

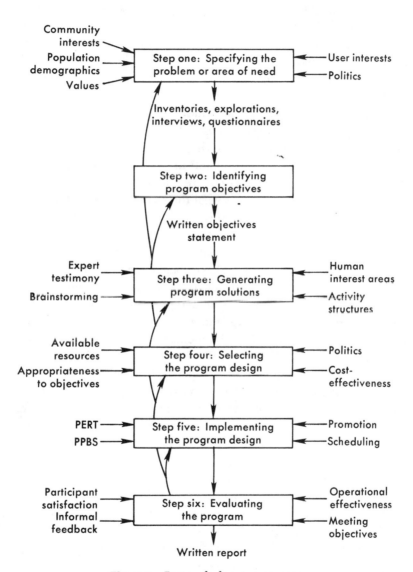

Fig. 1-1 *Rational planning process.*

ing of this need to adapt is necessary at the outset if the student planner is to master the rational planning skill. The planning must be seen as a series of interlocking circles; a change in one circle affects the overall pattern.

Step 1: Specifying the problem or area of need   Problem exploration is the cornerstone phase for the rational planning process. Its purpose is to identify, study objectively, and document problem and need priorities. Documentation of the problem and the desired solution evolves into the basis for all future steps in the planning process. Problems and needs are identified by conducting surveys of samples of the potential program users about their needs or problems. Various methods can be used to obtain information on both the quantitative and qualitative dimensions of the problem: questionnaires, interviews, statistical references, and public hearings. The purpose of all these inquiries is to define the need, to determine what is wrong with the way things are at present. This is done through a constant playing back between an assessment of the relevant aspects of the problem situation and the preferences of the constituency. This, in turn, defines what the planning task is. All else in program planning follows from the outcome of this integration.

An emphasis on the importance of defining the need as a first step in the planning process underscores the conscious and deliberate nature of the entire process. Research supporting the importance of beginning planning efforts by identifying problem/need priorities is found in all fields. Numerous studies have found that a clear and thorough understanding of needs and problems was necessary in advance of planning. In programs where the exploration of user needs was inaccurate or incomplete, comparatively more difficulties were encountered during later phases of planning (Science Policy Research Unit, 1972).

The two specific actions undertaken at this stage are investigation of the relevant realities (for example, using census data) and assessment of preferences (for example, conducting personal interviews). Although quantitative data on the user group are rather straightforward, needs and preference assessments carry with them an inherent commitment. Asking people what their problems are implies that their problems will be solved. But an investigation of what is and what ought to be is critical nonetheless and must be conducted thoroughly before going on.

Step 2: Identifying program objectives   At this juncture the planner is concerned with policy development, and so the intertwining of planning with political and special interest groups must be stressed. As the planner determines what the programming should accomplish, he or she must heed the cautions of professional responsibility to avoid uncalled-for social engineering.

Schematically (see Fig. 1-1), it is simple to understand goal development as though it were a direct linear descendant of the previous step, specifying the problem. In reality, the planners, their advisory and policy committees, and the several publics involved consider the basic possibilities in light of the facts, values, and interests explored in step 1. They formulate and reformulate policy possibilities until there is a goal outcome that represents a reasonably good "fit" in light of these factors.

Depending on the specific program planning situation, this process can be elaborate or relatively simple. Sometimes the policy choices being considered cannot be delineated without considerable background exploration. In fact, consideration of goal options may need to highlight constituency preference issues.

Goal or policy formulation is ultimately an intellectual undertaking and should be a creative one. As the recreation program planner attempts to mold a strategy for achieving what is sought, realities are weighed and values are considered.

This is a critical step in the rational planning process because in order to plan realistically and to recognize whether a relevant program solution has been reached, the planner must have some pre-established measure for evaluation. The establishment of goals and objectives at this point should give a clear sense of what programming should do. Then, after implementation, the planner will know whether or not the intended goals have been accomplished. There should be little guesswork in what the goals are meant to be.

Although schematically (see Fig. 1-1) definition of objectives follows problem exploration, the two steps are actually connected and interrelated. In many program planning situations they take place simultaneously. Many times the user value and preference data are not adequately probed before the definition of goals; therefore they must have major attention in the context of policy development. In fact, some planners divide the two major actions of step 1 (quantitative and qualitative information) between step 1 and step 2. In other words, the exploration of relevant realities, such as the quantitative census data, is performed as part of step 1, and the determination of values, preferences, and perceived needs is undertaken as part of step 2. The spiral or intersecting nature of the planning process is thus reiterated.

Step 3: Generating program solutions   At this step, the goals and objectives must be translated from general principles into program specifics. Programs are the precise actions required to achieve the stated objectives; they are the means to the clearly defined ends. A program is that combination of activities that meets the desired objectives. It is the task of this phase in the planning process to identify alternative ways or program solutions for dealing with the need priorities established in step 2.

Creative thinking is of paramount importance at the stage of generating program solutions. Each of the previously defined policy decisions must be translated into operational terms. One creative means of doing this is through a management technique known as brainstorming. In brainstorming, one or many minds are centered on the desired goals and asked to generate program ideas—new, different, practical, impractical, traditional, and far-out ones—in order to set off a spontaneous chain reaction of free association. No overt judgment is permitted in brainstorming. People hitchhike onto each other's ideas and generate new ideas that can be useful later as potential program solutions. Research has shown that applying the brainstorming technique not only results in good ideas, but also produces a greater quantity and quality of ideas than through other means.

Another way of conducting this step is for the planner to draw on the ideas of experts in the field or those of professionals with similar program problems. A survey of these expert suggestions, in the literature or in personal interviews, is made to identify alternative program solutions. After the survey, the planner summarizes and analyzes the responses by grouping compatible solution components. In this way, the full repertoire of recreation activities available to the planner, as well as the various forms of activity structures, is floated across the planner's consciousness. The result is a broad and useful list of potential activity types and forms.

Step 4: Selecting the program design A critical role for the planner in drafting the program proposal is to remain sensitive to the issues identified in prior phases. Neglect of the need priorities established during problem exploration or of the policy developed during goal definition reduces the validity of the program plan.

Having identified the problem or the need priorities (step 1), designated the program goals and objectives (step 2), and inventoried alternative ways to deal with the established goals (step 3), the program design planners integrate this information to write a specific program proposal. Whereas the purpose of the previous step was to generate a diversity of program options, the thrust of this step is to integrate these ideas into a unified, clearly specified set of action steps.

However, the distance to travel between step 3 and step 4 is tremendous. While drafting the program proposal, the planner must concentrate on the suitability, feasibility, and practicality of the various program components. A great deal of consideration also must be given to the relevant economic, political, and technical factors. At this stage those ideas generated by the free-lance atmosphere of the previous step are judged and weighed to determine which ideas are the most valuable. Then follows a judicious evaluation of the alternative program solutions according to these criteria: appropriateness; available leadership, facilities, budget; political atmosphere of the agency and the agency's sphere of operation; cost-effectiveness; and goal-effectiveness.

Skillful decision making at this step means choosing the best alternative based on all the information at hand. Yet no program solution is likely to be absolutely the best. Any final program plan more likely will be a compromise between what the planners ideally want to achieve and the realities of budgets, staff abilities, and politics. The alternative finally selected never permits a complete or perfect achievement of objectives; instead it represents the best program solution available at the time, under the circumstances. The completed program design proposal is usually submitted for review and approval for funding and implementation.

Step 5: Implementing the program design Planning is ultimately worthwhile only if the resulting product, the plan, is implemented. The implementation step is

not automatic; it too requires thought and planning. An aspect of implementation, therefore, that actually precedes the action itself is the planning of the strategy or tactic to be employed as the implementation mechanism. Whether the program plan is complex or simple, advance planning and study of the strategy or tactic to be used as the implementation mechanism are crucial.

The recreation program planner can borrow several implementation strategies from the business and management professions. These systems can aid the planner in the administrative realization, including budgeting and staging, of established program plans. The two most commonly used are the Flow Chart Method (FCM) and the Critical Path Method (CPM). These strategies offer the planner precise methodology in the actual follow-through of the program plans. As discussed more thoroughly in Chapter 7, the unique value of the FCM and CPM systems is in ensuring that all aspects of implementation (such as gathering supplies, decorating, and renting extra equipment) are accomplished in the time available. The ultimate value of these implementation strategies, therefore, is in safeguarding the intent of the original goals and objectives that could be lost while dealing with such basics as scheduling or publicity.

In many recreation agencies the program planners often become the program administrators and actually do the face-to-face leadership during implementation. This means that the planner may be the one actually teaching the games at the after-school playground program, or refereeing the basketball game in the community center gym, or even appearing on a radio talk show to promote the new family fitness program in the park. I know of few other professions in which the program professional not only must conduct a rational and relevant planning performance, but frequently must also serve as the program organizer, leader, host, coach, teacher, advertiser, clerk, first aider, authority, safety officer, and promoter. The principles of good recreation leadership need to be applied at this step even if the planner is only supervising other staff in the program implementation.

Step 6: Evaluating the program   Unlike steps 1 through 5, which primarily follow a temporal sequence, the evaluation step is really a parallel phase that begins with definition of the need and is performed throughout the planning process. However, the major task of evaluating the implemented program(s) occurs as step 6 in the rational planning process. Evaluation is intended to be an applied problem-solving tool. It attempts to make the planner's goals, criteria, and concerns explicit and to use these value judgments as a basis for assessing the worth of a planned program of action.

In this final, although never-ending, phase the evaluator analyzes the data and presents verbal and written reports that can be used to correct any inadequacies that may exist in the previous planning steps. For example, the evaluator may discover that the definition of the need was inaccurate and may wish to return to that phase and repeat the planning steps to implement a more effective program. If programs are to be and remain relevant, the cyclical nature of the process must be maintained. Evaluative research is what keeps the planning cycle going.

In the rational planning process evaluative research is used to both examine and modify a program in the formative stages and to look at the terminal effects of the implemented program. Evaluation is useful primarily as quality control; its major purpose is providing information to assist the programming decision maker. More specifically, evaluation is concerned with two functions: the measurement of congruence between performance and objectives of the program, and the professional judgment of the merits of the program.

Although the complete operation of the evaluation step is vast and detailed, covering such diverse topics as research design, statistics, and computer technology, the recreation program planner would be remiss not to make adequate provision for this step. Regardless of the level or complexity of the program planning efforts, at least some degree of evaluation must be provided. Why bother planning a program in the first place if you will never know its effectiveness?

Evaluation provides the primary method of quality control in recreation program services. By pointing out discrepancies that need correcting, it can result in better program services to the constituency. As a definite planning tool, evaluation increases the likelihood of making accurate decisions on continuation, alteration, expansion, or cancellation of programs.

CONCLUSION

The rational planning process is applicable to any agency that provides recreation program services. Regardless of which agency is sponsoring the recreation program or how large or small the program requirements, the process is the same and the same procedural steps are employed. So let us return to the programming mandate presented by Edward Walsh at the beginning of the chapter as an illustration. As a program planner, what could you do to meet the need for outdoor recreation services close to population centers? Your rational planning process might evolve in the following simplified way:

Step 1: Specifying the problem or area of need: outdoor recreation services close to the large population centers of the city.

Step 2: Identifying program objectives: to use existing urban open spaces to increase outdoor recreation program services.

Step 3: Generating program solutions.
   a. Use open space under freeways?
   b. Condemn urban private property and convert to public domain?
   c. Use community cemeteries?

Step 4: Selecting the program design. Use the natural open spaces available in community cemeteries and offer programs in wildlife feeding, berry picking, fishing, photography, walking, stone rubbing, and biking.

Step 5: Implementing the program design.
   a. Put up wildlife feeding stations throughout the grounds and schedule wildlife interpretive tours on Saturdays and Sundays.

  b. Plant blackberry and black raspberry bushes throughout.
  c. Dredge areas to form small ponds and stock with fish; schedule special events such as fishing rodeos for disabled children and fly-tying demonstrations for adults.
  d. Offer photography field trips on Sundays with instruction in picture composition.
  e. Offer after-school workshops on stone rubbing.

Step 6: Evaluating the program. Evaluate the effectiveness; is it worth the effort?

Many municipal agencies have taken planning routes similar to this one and have developed unique solutions to the problem posed in the example above. In Kalamazoo, Michigan, officials converted an old Indian burial ground into a park for family picnics. Ascension Cemetery in Libertyville, Illinois, has become a wildlife and bird sanctuary. Evergreen-Washelli Memorial Park in Seattle, Washington, lent five acres to the Northwest Pony League, which built and maintains a baseball field, bleachers, and concession stand. A Flat Rock, Michigan, cemetery provides athletic scholarships for outstanding high school seniors and the cemetery's mausoleums house a sports hall of fame. Sherwood Memorial Park in Salem, Virginia, presents religious drama in its outdoor theater. Some of New York City's cemeteries offer jogging, bicycling, ball playing, and even a nursery playground, and Woodlawn Cemetery in the Bronx provides opera recitals (Walsh, 1975).

Through proper planning and attention to the needs of the constituency, recreation programs can be effective and meaningful contributions to the quality of life. The rational planning process offers a means of accomplishing this. It does not matter whether the planner is a summer playground program supervisor, a state park naturalist, a federal prison recreation services director, or a program organizer for five preschoolers in a tiny tots program—he or she must apply rational, adaptive thought to generate program solutions relevant to the needs of the constituency. How the planner travels the territory between steps and how he or she derives results from each step is the subject of the remaining chapters of this book.

References

Allen, H. The fascination of boredom. *The Washington Post: Potomac*, August 18, 1974, p. 10.

Bunzel, J. Planning for aging. *Journal of the American Geriatrics Society*, 1961, *9:1*, 32-38.

Cleveland, H. After affluence, what? *The Futurist*, 1977, *11:5*, 279-283.

Dozier, J.E., Lewis, S., Kersey, A.C., & Charping, J.W. Sports group: An alternative treatment modality for emotionally disturbed adolescents. *Adolescence*, 1978, *13:51*, 483-488.

Dror, Y. The planning process: A facet design, *International Review of Administrative Sciences*, 1963, *29:1*, 46-58.

Haskell, H.G. Ailment: Boredom. *Parks & Recreation*, 1980, *15:1*, 75-76.

Heywood, L.A. Perceived recreative experience and the relief of tension. *Journal of Leisure Research*, 1978, *10:2*, 86-97.

Huizinga, J. *Homo ludens: A study of the play element in culture*. Boston: Beacon Press, 1955.

Kahn, A.J. *Theory and practice of social planning*. New York: Russell Sage Foundation, 1969.

Murphy, J.F. *Recreation and leisure service: A humanistic perspective*. Dubuque, Iowa: William C. Brown, 1975.

Murphy, J.F., & Howard, D.R. *Delivery of community leisure services: An holistic approach*. Philadelphia: Lea & Febiger, 1977.

Norman, A.J. Issues in promoting planning in the human service delivery system: The case of area agencies on aging. *Administration in Social Work*, 1979, *3:1*, 79-89.

Popper, K.R. *The open society and its enemies.* London: Routledge & Kegan Paul, 1945.

Popper, K.R. *The open society and its enemies* (5th ed.). Princeton, N.J.: University Press, 1966.

Ramey, E.R. Boredom: The most prevalent American disease. *Harper's,* 1974, *249:1494,* 12-14.

Russell, B. *The conquest of happiness.* New York: Bantam Books, 1968.

Science Policy Research Unit (Sappho). *Success and failure in industrial innovation.* Sussex, England: University of Sussex, Center for Study of Industrial Innovation, 1972.

Sessoms, H.D. *Glossary of recreation and park terms.* Arlington, Va.: National Recreation and Park Association, 1972.

Sessoms, H.D., Meyer, H.D., & Brightbill, C.K.

Leisure services: The organized recreation and park system. (5th ed.). Englewood Cliffs, N.J.: Prentice-Hall, 1975.

U.S. Department of the Interior. *The recreation imperative.* Washington, D.C.: U.S. Government Printing Office, 1974.

Von Hayek, F.A. *The road to serfdom.* London: George Routledge and Sons, 1944.

Walsh, E.R. Cemeteries: Recreation's new space frontier. *Parks & Recreation,* 1975, *10:6,* 28-29+.

Werner, P.J. *A movement approach to games for children.* St. Louis: C.V. Mosby, 1979.

Wootton, B. *Freedom under planning.* Chapel Hill, N.C.: University of North Carolina Press, 1945.

The planning process

```
┌─────────────────────────────────┐
│  Recreation program planning:   │
│         pressures, needs,       │
│       problems, or interests    │
└─────────────────────────────────┘
                 │
                 ▼
┌─────────────────────────────────┐
│      Organizing for planning    │
└─────────────────────────────────┘
                 │
                 ▼
```

Chapter 2

Organizing for planning

At the outset of the program planning task, a determination must be made as to who will actually carry out the planning function. Will the initiating planner perform each planning step alone? Or is it preferable that all or some of the planning be referred to a specially appointed planning committee? Will a member of the professional staff need to be appointed as the agency's official program planner? Is it desirable to bring the constituents themselves into any aspects of the planning of their own programs? Where can the planner get more help?

In many instances the planner, as the person hired for the job, will have few options in determining who does the planning; most likely the planner will do it. However, for many other planners an initial decision is required. Who are the best persons or groups of persons to carry out the planning function? Are there additional sources of planning assistance?

There are basically five options that the program planner may consider. First, as the professional best qualified, the planner may wish to perform all stages of the planning process alone. Second, the planner may choose to incorporate the particular expertise of others from the recreation agency staff in certain planning functions. Third, at certain stages it may be desirable to encourage the advice, assistance, or actual planning involvement of all or some of the program consumers. Fourth, the designation of a planning committee may be more feasible. Fifth, under some conditions it may be a good idea to bring in outside professional planning consultants for counseling, analysis, and assistance. These options are operational either separately or in combination. For example, it may prove beneficial to have constituency input in steps 1 and 2, and then let the staff assume responsibility for the latter steps in the planning process. Or a planning committee may be formed to conduct the entire planning function, with both citizens and professional staff serving as committee members. Whichever option or options are chosen, the point is that initial thoughtful consideration as to who will do the program planning is important to the ultimate success of the planning endeavor.

How recreation agencies organize for program planning

Even though the program planner may wish or be required to assume most of the responsibility for conducting the recreation program planning process, he or she will never be able to work in a vacuum or completely alone. Life has become complex. Because it is often cheaper, and more efficient, to get somebody else to carry out a task, recreation organizations have established intricate hierarchical positions to produce recreation services. This hierarchy usually goes from the policy-makers on boards and commissions, to administrators, to office support staff, to specific activity instructors, to volunteers, to interested and powerful constituents. Although the complexity of the hierarchy will vary according to the size of the organization and the breadth of its task, the persons responsible for recreation programming will need to work within their organizational and community limitations. It will be the program planner who ultimately coordinates the efforts and interprets the wishes of those both inside and outside the organization.

In fact, the positive involvement and coordination of recreation professionals, citizens, other agencies, community officials, and others is of such vital importance that it cannot be overemphasized. The program administrator, or professional responsible for planning program services, really requires the expertise and judgment of many, even of professionals from outside the field. This philosophy is supported by what Joseph Bannon has labeled the "ecological responsibility for planning" (1976, p. 18). The overall objective of any recreation plan, according to Bannon, is to add to the overall welfare of a community and not to operate in a social vacuum. Even though the focus of the plan will be recreation services, planners need to remain aware of the broader environment of the constituents. Bannon maintains that "the physical, social, and economic aspects of community life must be viewed as a total organism inseparable from any one aspect of community development" (p. 18). To be truly effective, recreation program planning must deal with people in all aspects of their lives, not just in traditional leisure concerns.

Of course it is one thing to say what is necessary for planning and quite another to achieve and sustain it. Therefore it is important to pause and review the basics of the structure and organization of most public, private, and commercial recreation and park agencies and how the program planner relates to the whole.

Types of recreation organizations

There are several distinct approaches to establishing the framework of recreation and park agencies. Usually two or more agency forms may be found operating programs in a community at the same time. In varied forms, recreation program services up through the 1970s became a major aspect of modern life. For example, between 1946 and 1966 the total number of combined recreation and park departments in U.S. cities and counties increased from 1,743 to 3,142. Recreation services offered by other governmental agencies in the United States also expanded rapidly during this period. Even commercial forms of recreation program services have blossomed. Leading economic analysts have estimated that between $150 and $200 billion per year is now spent on recreation in the United States, making commercial recreation agencies one of America's largest and most successful businesses (data reported by

Kraus and Bates, 1975, pp. 7-8). The organized provision for recreation program services may take any of the following forms, regardless of public, private, or commercial sponsorship:

1. Recreation program services can be organized as a separate, independent departmental function. Examples are the recreation department of a city, the social secretary's division of a luxurious apartment complex, and the therapeutic recreation services section in a hospital. This type of agency has a single function: to provide recreation services. When recreation services are provided as a single function, the emphasis is usually on programs and leadership rather than on the acquisition and maintenance of areas and facilities (Sessoms and others, 1975). In such cases the independent recreation department needs to rely on the resources of other departments such as parks and schools.

2. Recreation program services can be a separate park department; for example, the park department of a city or a county. This type of agency has as its single function the provision of park services. When the park system is operated by a separate park department, the focus is generally on area and facility acquisition, development, and maintenance rather than on program services.

3. Recreation program services can be part of a merged recreation and park department that includes the functions of both within a single structure. Examples are the city recreation and park department and the state recreation and park division. Although excellent examples of independent recreation commissions do exist, the current trend is toward combining the two into a single administrative unit. Even though the natural relationship between programs and facilities seems obvious, strong coordination efforts among the professional staff are necessary so that neither element, programs or facilities, is relegated to secondary consideration. Unfortunately, it is usually the program component that gets secondary attention; particularly in times of economic stress the problems of land acquisition, development, and maintenance are more visible and seemingly more pressing. On the other hand, inability to maintain the facility adequately will interfere severely with program quality.

To date there has been general agreement in the field that this agency type of organization is the most desirable. Yet in many locally combined departments full integration of the recreation and park services has not yet been achieved. In some cases the past loyalties of divisional directors have prohibited an effective working relationship. Sometimes when recreation has been absorbed into a preexisting park department, program professionals have been treated as subservient to custodial personnel, or they have not been given managing control of the programming of major facilities such as athletic fields or golf courses. One effective solution is to combine the use of both functions in all key supervisory and administrative positions and to give clear-cut responsibilities to line personnel who carry out the programs or maintain the facilities.

4. Recreation program services can be an adjunctive service provided by the local school board. Those who support this type of agency argue that schools possess

the facilities, leadership, and contact with the community needed to operate recreation programs efficiently. However, over the past few decades, the scope of recreation services has become so broad, in terms of who is being served and the variety of programs offered, that few school systems are able to meet the current challenge.

5. Recreation program services are sometimes the assigned responsibility of other governmental agencies, such as the police department, the housing authority, or the area agency on aging. Particularly in large urban areas it is sometimes useful for other municipal departments to provide recreation programs for special segments of the population. For example, some cities have youth divisions that attempt to meet the various needs (including recreation) of adolescents in a comprehensive way. Another common arrangement is special departments that serve older persons in a community with multiservice programs that include recreation, nutrition, legal counseling, and health.

6. Recreation program services can be provided by private (nongovernmental) agencies such as Girl Scouts, Boy Scouts, commercial recreation enterprises, private camps, or art galleries. These agencies operate as separate concerns from both government and schools as well as from a larger agency such as a hospital. Their sole purpose is to provide recreation services for their own membership or customers.

7. Recreation program services also can be a joint operation of two or more of the above types of agencies. For example, several governmental organizations that overlap geographically, such as a city, county, and school district, may develop contractual relationships for jointly sponsored recreation programs. Or a joint operation by a governmental department and a private agency may prove advantageous. These joint arrangements can range from merely using each other's facilities for programming to a complete sharing of budgets, staff, and facilities. For example, the Lane County Coordinating Council of Community Educatation and Recreation Agencies in Eugene, Oregon, has given every area recreation programmer (from the school districts, community college, major university, extension service, and park and recreation departments) a forum in which to explore and share trends, new ideas, and alternatives. As a result of this council, programmers are aware of other agencies' program philosophies, goals, and limitations. The council has afforded opportunities for cosponsorship and thus reduced duplication of services. Another result has been a maximal use of facility space and staff time.

These are the seven forms recreation services have most frequently employed for the organization of programs. Today various representations of all seven forms can be found in most communities across the country. Collectively they comprise what has been labeled the *community recreation system*. Although all recreation agencies are involved in providing organized recreation programs, each is different with respect to program philosophy, objectives, and service provisions. Thus recreation programs may be additionally classified according to sponsorship: public, private, or commercial. (See Table 2 for such distinction.)

Table 2 *Programming comparisons of public, private, and commercial recreation agencies*

Type of agency	Philosophy	Objectives	Program
Public (e.g., city recreation and park departments, school-sponsored recreation, other government agencies)	To enrich the life of the total community by providing opportunities for worthy use of leisure; nonprofit in nature	To provide leisure opportunities that contribute to the social, physical, educational, cultural, and general well-being of the community and its people	Designed to provide a wide variety of activities, year-round, for all groups, regardless of age, sex, race, creed, social or economic status
Private (e.g., youth agencies, church agencies, social and fraternal organizations	To enrich the life of participating members by offering opportunities for the worthy use of leisure, frequently with emphasis on the group and the individual; nonprofit in nature	Similar to public, but limited by membership, race, religion, age, and the like; to provide opportunities for close group association with emphasis on citizenship, behavior, and life philosophy values; to provide activities that appeal to members	Designed to provide programs of a specialized nature for groups and in keeping with the aims and objectives of the agency
Commercial (e.g., amusement parks, theaters, country clubs)	To attempt to satisfy public demands in an effort to produce profit; dollars from, as well as for, recreation	To provide activities or programs that will appeal to customers; to meet competition; to net profit; to serve the public	Designed to tap spending power in compliance with state and local laws

From Murphy, J.F., & Howard, D.R. Delivery of community leisure services: An holistic approach. Philadelphia: Lea & Febiger, 1977.

Recently it has become clear that the general fiscal crunch of the 1980s is putting disproportionate pressures on certain agency forms. For example, city and county recreation, park, and combined departments seem to be experiencing a declining priority status in the competition for tax dollars (Crompton and Van Doren, 1978). Two generalizations have emerged regarding which agency forms will be most viable in the 1980s:

1. As local or municipal funding of recreation programs gradually declines, people will become more dependent on higher level government agencies for the provision of these services. Probably this will mean federal assistance and in some instances state assistance.

2. These trends will also stimulate the growth of program provision by commercial agencies.

Boards and commissions

An agency that provides recreation or park services, or both, like any organization, is initially and constantly confronted with the problem of determining its own internal structure, or where the ultimate responsibility for provision of services lies within the agency. A common administrative structure is placement of this responsibility with a policymaking lay board or commission. These boards or commissions are small groups of people who are responsible for overseeing and directing the work of the professional administrator of the department. Boards and commissions may be either elected or appointed. Usually, therefore, board members are persons who possess a major influence in the community. Recreation and park boards and commissions function to translate the work of the department to the constituency and encourage support for the department (financial and attitudinal) by important constituency groups. Also, it is usually their responsibility to develop department service policies and to initiate plans for meeting the recreation needs of the community being served.

Boards and commissions are applicable within each of the seven agency types presented previously. In each case the board's overall function is the same: to determine policy for meeting recreation and park needs. Some recreation boards or commissions are quite active and assume an alert stance for the development of recreation services; others are more relaxed in their approach. Never should these groups interfere with the specific administration of the agency on a day-to-day basis. Once a board or commission has delineated the department goals, established operational policies, and hired the professional administrator, its role becomes that of delegator of the day-to-day authority to the professional staff.

The relationship among the board, the administrator, and the staff is a delicate and fickle one. For program planning to take place in the rational manner suggested in this book, the program planner must understand the contributions and limitations of the policymaking board or commission by knowing when and how much direct involvement to seek from it in the planning process. Normally the program planner must communicate with the board or commission through the agency's chief administrator. Usually the administrator interprets board programming policies and goals and objectives to the program staff and in turn presents program accomplishments to the board for their evaluation in light of goals and objectives. Therefore recreation boards and commissions are traditionally involved in step 2 and step 8 of the rational planning process.

The degree of participation by the board in any aspect of the program planning process is, of course, a delicate balance that is the hard-won result of a concerted effort at two-way communication by board and professional. It is not easy to determine to what degree the board should be involved in program planning. Do they merely add a stamp of approval to the staff-chosen program goals and objectives, or are they actually key decision makers in what these program goals should be? Ideally the program planner has provided the board with the data from research of the problem phase (step 1), so that the board can work with the planner in accomplishing the policy formulation phase of step 2. From here the board would merely be kept updated on the progress of steps 3 through 5 and then would assume a greater responsibility in the evaluation step. There are more variations on this "ideal" in reality than there are similarities. In small recreation agencies (such as a private agency in which there are no paid professional staff), the entire planning function may need to be carried out by the board or commission itself. This is a difficult mode of operation because, among other things, rational planning is based on data gathering and comprehensive research, and a policymaking board may find this too time consuming a task as well as one for which they are not technically prepared.

Specifically, the function of a board or commission in recreation program planning may include the following:

1. Defining the goals and objectives of recreation program services
2. Defining the responsibilities and standards of program planning staff and being involved with the process of employment proceedings (hiring, firing, and promoting)
3. Maintaining a useful liaison between the agency's programming efforts and other community agencies and influential officials
4. Interpreting the role of the recreation program services to the constituency and in turn relaying constituency reactions and wishes back to the program planning staff
5. Overseeing an adequate fiscal basis for the program services and reviewing and giving final approval to budget requests
6. Reviewing, evaluating, and studying the program services on a regular basis in regard to overall program policies and objectives

How to devise the details of the involvement of the board or commission in program planning depends on the unique situation and personalities in the agency.

In general, the role of staff persons is not to make policy but to administer policy determined by the managing authority of the agency: the board or commission. Since the professional staff is responsible for seeing that the agency moves forward efficiently and effectively according to its stated purposes, the staff will usually be the caretakers of the planning process in behalf of the policymaking board.

Recreation and park agency staff

All types of recreation agencies must develop logical and useful internal structures. A functional structure delineates the various divisions and levels of work responsibility within the agency, ranging from the top administrator to the part-time or volunteer instructor. Traditionally, three broad levels of responsibility exist: the executive or administrative level, the supervisory level, and the direct-leadership level. Most agencies find it useful to subdivide these hierarchial levels into categorical types of responsibility. For example, some common divisions are areas and facilities, program services, construction and maintenance, public relations, and services to special populations. Some large recreation and park departments may even have divisions that specialize in personnel, planning, and research.

Fig. 2-1 represents a typical organizational structure for a hypothetical large recreation and park agency. The figure shows a simplified internal hierarchy in which the Director of Recreation and Parks, at a top executive level, is responsible for administering two major supervisory division: parks and recreation. In another type of agency these supervisory positions could be any major subdivision of the department's work. Kraus and Curtis (1982) suggest that many recreation agencies have identified five major functional responsibilities and established a division for each. These divisions are programs, special facilities (such as a rifle range), construction and maintenance, business and finance, and public relations. In Fig. 2-1 each of the major functional responsibilities is under the supervision of its own director. The park and recreation divisions are then subdivided into additional functional units that operate at the direct-leadership level of responsibility. Note from the illustration those authority levels that are usually responsible for program planning (indicated by an asterisk). The figure also briefly indicates the relationship between the two major divisions at the direct-leadership level. For instance, if leader A notices a large and dangerous hole hidden in the grass at playground 1, he or she notifies the director, who communicates the problem to the playground grounds superintendent, who sees that the problem is remedied by one of the playground maintenance staff persons.

In other types of recreation agencies, such as therapeutic or voluntary organizations, the internal organizational structure may have labels different from those in Fig. 2-1, but the structure remains basically similar in the flow of authority, responsibility, and action. In every recreation agency there is always at the top a policymak-

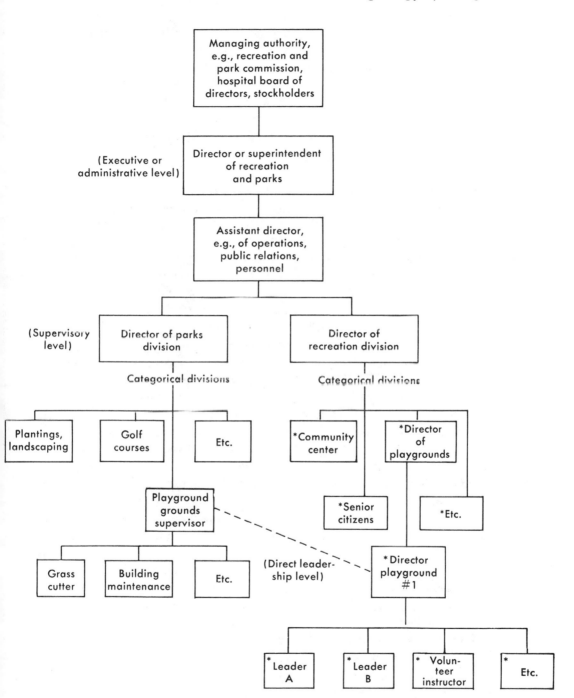

Fig. 2-1 *Typical organizational structure of a recreation agency.*

ing managing authority that depends on an executive director to see that the agency's goals are met. The executive director in turn subdivides this task into functional divisions and then additional divisions. From top to botton in the hierarchy, the level of responsibility becomes smaller and more specific in scope, but ultimately everyone in the agency is working toward the accomplishment of the same goals. The director of playground 1, for example, must apply the rational planning process in a way that complies with overall department program goals and prescribed avenues of authority.

Because of the very nature of an organizational hierarchy (and the popular notion of the "Peter Principle"), those who do a good job as program planners and producers at the bottom of the hierarchy will be rewarded by being promoted up and up the ladder until they are no longer involved with program planning! This is unfortunate for the status of program planning because it implies that planning is a starting place rather than a professional responsibility with its own importance.

It is important for the program planner to remember that there are usually other planners operating in the agency. Depending on the size and form of the agency, these professionals could include facility planners, fiscal planners, and research planners, in addition to program planners. Interdivision coordination among a recreation agency's staff is an essential ingredient for successful program planning. In addition to coordination, professional respect and cooperation are necessary. Often, because of hierarchical specialization and departmentalization of areas of responsibility (particularly in recreation vs. park divisions), staff find it easy to get into nonconstructive disagreements or to built up overprotective feelings of domain.

One attempt at internal integration and coordination of structure is currently being tried by the Park and Recreation Management Division of the City of San Diego, California. As Fig. 2-2 indicates, San Diego is divided into three geographic subdivisions. Within each subdivision the management of parks and facilities is combined with the management of programs and considered a joint comprehensive service. For example, in the Coastal Division the supervisor for District III (Community Park and Recreation) is responsible for overseeing both facility and program functions for the locations listed. These locations include all those services physically located along the coast, regardless of size or scope. The supervision of the city's lake recreation services, on the other hand, is in the Eastern Division because that is where the lakes are located. The supervisor of District XI, therefore, is responsible for both maintaining and programming the city's recreational lakes. San Diego hopes that through this new internal structure comprehensive planning will be less a philosophy and more a reality.

Such agency attempts at internal coordination, mutual respect, and cooperation are vital for the future health of the leisure service field. A comprehensive view of recreation planning is necessary to meet the multidisciplinary, integrative, holistic approach to service provision predicted for the future. The program planner must be

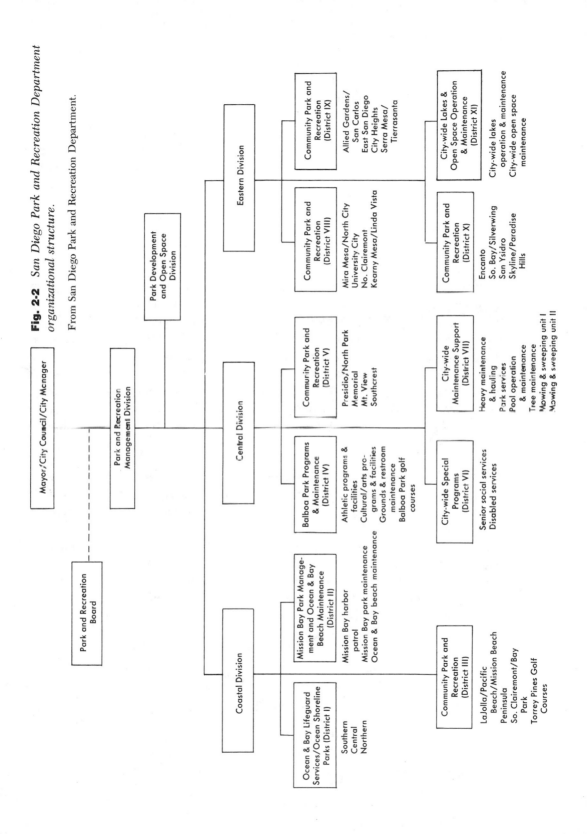

Fig. 2-2 *San Diego Park and Recreation Department organizational structure.*

From San Diego Park and Recreation Department.

Mayor/City Council/City Manager

Park and Recreation Board

Park and Recreation Management Division

Park Development and Open Space Division

Coastal Division

Ocean & Bay Lifeguard Services/Ocean Shoreline Parks (District I)

Southern
Central
Northern

Mission Bay Park Management and Ocean & Bay Beach Maintenance (District II)

Mission Bay harbor patrol
Mission Bay park maintenance
Ocean & Bay beach maintenance

Community Park and Recreation (District III)

LaJolla/Pacific Beach/Mission Beach Peninsula
So. Clairemont/Bay Park
Torrey Pines Golf Courses

Central Division

Balboa Park Programs & Maintenance (District IV)

Athletic programs & facilities
Cultural/arts programs & facilities
Grounds & restroom maintenance
Balboa Park golf courses

Community Park and Recreation (District V)

Presidio/North Park Memorial
Mt. View
Southcrest

City-wide Special Programs (District VII)

Senior social services
Disabled services

City-wide Maintenance Support (District VIII)

Heavy maintenance & hauling
Park services
Pool operation & maintenance
Tree maintenance
Mowing & sweeping unit I
Mowing & sweeping unit II

Eastern Division

Community Park and Recreation (District VIII)

Mira Mesa/North City
University City
No. Clairemont
Kearny Mesa/Linda Vista

Community Park and Recreation (District IX)

Allied Gardens/San Carlos
East San Diego
City Heights
Serra Mesa/Tierrasanta

Community Park and Recreation (District X)

Encanto
So. Bay/Silverwing
San Ysidro
Skyline/Paradise Hills

City-wide Lakes & Open Space Operation & Maintenance (District XI)

City-wide lakes operation & maintenance
City-wide open space maintenance

able to work with, as well as understand the work of, other planners in the agency to serve the constituency comprehensively.

When organizing for program planning, it is best to be prepared for possible conflicts that arise automatically from the structure of agency hierarchies. For example, perhaps the simplest resolution will do: when the planner and the playground program staff sit down each year to work through the planning process, the grounds superintendent of the playgrounds could be included as a member of the planning group. Any step that guards against division conflicts and contributes to constructive cooperation will make the planning endeavor more worthwhile and productive.

The program planner

The success of any organized recreation program ultimately depends on the professional staff persons who plan and conduct programs. Qualified, trained, and experienced programmers form the very foundation of a recreation service (Meyer and Brightbill, 1956). In the hierarchy of recreation agencies the persons who perform programming functions are labeled and classified differently, have varying job descriptions, are paid both well and poorly, and may or may not have other responsibilities. Some recreation programmers will need to score well on extensive written and oral examinations to get the job, whereas others will volunteer or be drafted. In the recreation and park profession there is no distinct, officially labeled or recognized position of *program planner*. Who the program planner is—his or her qualifications, salary, or job description—depends on the type, scope, and size of the recreation agency.

A list of job titles of those involved in program planning for all types of recreation agencies would be long and confusing. Professional positions in governmental recreation and park agencies, for example, vary considerably. Typically, a medium-size city would have both direct-leadership and supervisory personnel assigned to program responsibilities in categories including (1) specific program areas such as arts and crafts, music, aquatics, or sports; or (2) specific facilities such as a park, playground, nature center, or community center. Such persons might or might not have other, nonprogramming functions. In nongovernmental agencies, such as voluntary and commercial ones, personnel standards generally allow much more diversity and flexibility in the job description or role of their program planners. These agencies might ask the programmer also to be involved in planning and carrying out the agency's total recreation services.

Traditionally program planning responsibilities in most recreation agencies have been the jurisdiction of three broad levels of jobs:

1. *Managerial-supervisory level.* Here professionals function under the general direction of a top executive; depending on their degree of responsibility, they sometimes exercise substantial control over the programs under their jurisdiction. At this level are job titles such as supervisor of music, recreation center director, hospital

---

**SAMPLE JOB DESCRIPTION FOR PROGRAM PLANNERS,
CITY OF SAN DIEGO**

**Class specification
San Diego City Civil Service Commission**

Recreation Center Director III

Definition: Under direction, to plan, organize, and supervise a comprehensive and varied recreation program at a large recreation center or athletic facility; to plan, organize and supervise a comprehensive recreation program at a medium size recreation center requiring very difficult and sensitive community liaison work; and to perform related work.

*Typical tasks: Initiates, develops, implements, and directs a wide variety of recreation activities for all segments of the community; determines community needs and interests in developing recreation programs and activities; performs difficult and sensitive community liaison work in the promotion and development of a comprehensive recreation program; provides information on programs and activities to the public and prepares necessary material for publicity; plans, organizes, and supervises special events and solicits community support and assistance; prepares program submittals and evaluations; supervises programs at satellite playgrounds, gymnasiums, and related facilities; provides direct program leadership, as necessary; participates in organizing and supervising district leagues and events; meets with recreation councils, community groups, business organizations, and other bodies on the center's activities; supervises a large subordinate staff and plans work schedules, makes work assignments, provides training, deals with disciplinary problems, and evaluates and rates their work performance; supervises and monitors contract staff activities; prepares a variety of reports; schedules the use of the facility, issues use permits, and applies fee schedules; ensures the proper maintenance and security of the facility.

**Employment standards: Equal to college graduation with a Bachelor's degree in recreation or a closely related field and one year of professional level recreation experience. Additional professional level recreation experience may be substituted for education lacked on a year for year basis.

---

*Typical tasks are examples of duties performed by employees in this class. The list may not include all required duties, nor are all listed tasks necessarily performed by everyone in this class.

**Employment standards are a guide for determining the education, training, experience, special skills, and/or licenses which may be required for employment in the class. These are re-evaluated each time an examination is opened.

From City of San Diego, Park and Recreation Management Division.

ward director, program coordinator, golf course manager, and supervisor of athletics. Among other supervisory duties, the program planning role at this level could include coordination of a specific program activity or specialty, administration of programs according to geographic area, and/or supervision of other program personnel.

2. *Direct-leadership level.* Recreation leaders are in positions that require direct contact with the program constituency. These are those wonderful people who call the directions in a square dance, count out the motions in jazzercise, and hold the bike of a beginner. Usually the leader has responsibility for planning, organizing, and directing a specific event, activity, sport, or part of a larger program. In addition to being involved with program planning, recreation leaders are more specifically responsible for aspects of program implementation (publicity, officiating, record keeping, and teaching).

3. *Activity-specialist level.* This is the technical expert whose skills and experience are particularly proficient in one specific program activity. The specialist position involves the planning and/or conducting of this one activity and usually allows for considerable freedom in both areas. The position may require actual leadership in the activity, or it may consist of only organizing and initiating the activity.

See the box on p. 47 for an illustrative job description from the City of San Diego, Park and Recreation Management Division. Which of the three job levels does this description represent?

Volunteers

In a discussion on the program planner's responsibility for planning within the organizational limitations of the agency, it is important to consider the volunteer worker. Volunteers are actually a major part of the history of the recreation program movement itself. In fact, most early program planning and implementation was done solely by volunteers who were simply believers in the values of planned recreation. This same motivation causes volunteers to continue to be extremely valuable to the entire recreation movement and particularly to recreation programs. Because volunteers are there primarily because they wish to help fill a need, to share a skill, or to serve those who need to be served, they can bring to a program dedication and sincerity. Yet many times the volunteer occupies a position in the agency that is misunderstood, mismanaged, or—worse—ignored. This usually results from a lack of management skill on the part of the professional staff person in charge. Program planners would certainly be wise to make sure they understand volunteer attitudes in order to use volunteer skills and interest efficiently. Volunteer assistance in meeting recreation program goals is a natural part of the profession. You either learn how to work well with it toward the betterment of services, or you do not—to the detriment of services.

Volunteers can hold a wide variety of responsibilities. Often they carry out routine, unchallenging, time-consuming tasks that offer little excitement but must be done. In other cases volunteers undertake more responsible or more challenging tasks. Within the program services division of recreation agencies, the volunteer can assist in the following valuable ways:

1. Working as activity implementers for specific facilities or groups, including playgrounds, senior citizen centers, special population groups, and youth clubs
2. Serving as planning advisers on projects that require special expertise, skills, or interest such as a light opera guild or a community ecology league
3. Providing clerical assistance by helping with such tasks as program advertising and evaluation reports
4. Performing study, research, or survey tasks necessary to determine program areas of need and program goals and objectives
5. Providing an emotional ingredient, such as a fresh outlook, new enthusiasm, and interest, that regular staff often cannot match
6. Serving as a special link between the community or neighborhood and the recreation agency

Some recreation agencies use volunteer help more frequently and in more areas than others. Volunteers are a means of extending program services beyond what the agency budget can provide. For instance, early in my career I was asked to conduct programming in girls' athletics, family fitness, dance, and children's crafts at a community center. Through the recruitment, training, supervision, and recognition of volunteers from the student body of a nearby college, these areas were provided for much more extensively than if I had planned and implemented them all on my own.

The supervisor of volunteers in a recreation agency is challenged with a double programming duty: to provide services that may be possible only with volunteer help and to enable the volunteer to have a recreative experience through volunteering. This duty may be viewed either as a burden or as a golden opportunity for creative programming. Volunteering must be meaningful, relevant, and compatible with the organization's goals, just as other activity programs are. Recruitment and the design of relevant tasks, therefore, become essential elements in a volunteer program. Using volunteers is no simple matter; a serious effort at recruitment, training, supervision, and recognition is a must.

Volunteers must be recruited in a systematic, purposeful manner. In general the most effective volunteers are those recruited for their special talent, training, or interest in the program area. Therefore the most useful sources for enlisting volunteers are organizations with an interest in recreation programs, such as church groups, special interest or hobby organizations, or college undergraduate programs. My volunteer leaders in the example above were mostly college physical education majors who had expertise in sports and athletics and were interested in gaining real experience in their field for later use on job resumes.

Volunteers should be recruited for a specific aspect of the program. Early in program planning, the planner should determine those functions that can be performed best by volunteers. Many programmers have found it advantageous to assign to volunteers the functions and tasks that enhance the program planning effort rather than those that determine its basic operation.

There are numerous ways of communicating a call for volunteer help; some examples are newspaper ads or notices, speeches before club or class meetings, notices on club or school bulletin boards, and city or school volunteer referral services. One of the easiest methods of recruiting is to watch for potential leaders in already-existing program activities and to encourage these participants to become volunteers. Such volunteers would have the advantage of being preoriented to the agency and the programs. Recruitment of volunteers for program planning or implementation should not be handled casually. Some recreation agencies have found it useful to make the recruitment and supervision of volunteers the responsibility of a specified person. These organizations employ volunteer coordinators to develop and implement a volunteer program for the entire agency. In agencies choosing this option, the individual selected should be in close touch with community groups and thoroughly knowledgeable about the program objectives and needs of the agency.

All volunteers should have exact arrangements discussed with them at the time of recruitment. These should include a job description, a time commitment, and the exact duration of the volunteer's service. A volunteer should receive on-the-job orientation and training, for both the program and the agency, on a par with that of paid employees. If sufficient numbers are involved, many programmers have found it useful to hold special volunteer training institutes or workshops. Practice in working with volunteers has indicated that special training emphasis should be placed on safety and legal liability, discipline, and limits of authority. Typically, the following areas should be covered in orientation meetings with new volunteers:

1. Introduction to the physical layout of the agency or facility where they will be working
2. Introduction to the staff and the other volunteers with whom they will be working, including an overview of their functions
3. Review of the agency policies and program objectives
4. Instruction in the specific tasks, functions, and responsibilities of the volunteer
5. Orientation to the program clientele according to such factors as background, limitations, and personal characteristics
6. Review of rules and regulations of safety, discipline, accident procedures, first aid, and other legal considerations

The supervision of volunteers is similar to that of paid employees; it must be adequate and helpful. Volunteers should be observed regularly and assisted by their supervisor. Such supervision indicates to the volunteer that his or her contribution is being taken seriously. In order to maintain a good volunteer-agency relationship, one key role of a supervisor of volunteers is motivation. The only sincere methods of ensuring volunteer enthusiasm and interest for the assignment are to help develop a sense of satisfaction in the specific assignment, a belief in the program, and a feeling of worth. It is important to keep in mind that volunteer involvement must be consistent and dependable, but at the same time there are limits to which an agency should rely on volunteers. Above all else, volunteers should have meaningful areas of responsibility that challenge their capabilities.

Finally, it is vital to both the satisfaction of the volunteer and the health and effectiveness of the program that volunteers know that their efforts are making a valuable contribution. This can be accomplished in many of the same ways that an employee is recognized, except of course through a pay raise. Because of this difference, special consideration should be given to congratulating volunteers for a job well done. Simple verbal reinforcement, mention in reports and news articles, praise at staff meetings, and special ceremonies are all methods designed to award the work of volunteers. Some agencies, such as the American Hospital Association, have "volunteer recognition days" when they single out all those who have contributed volunteer assistance to their programs throughout the year.

In program planning you can choose to use or not use volunteers; neither option is absolutely necessary. Tillman (1973, p. 56) had something quite determined to say about not using volunteers:

> . . . three dimensions are shut off for your program. First, growth and expansion will always be limited by the dollars available. Secondly, an excellent staff recruitment opportunity is denied. And thirdly, many people who receive their greatest fulfillment from serving others will be denied that fulfillment.

With the changes that have occurred in society over the past decade, it is evident that volunteerism is coming into a new age. Recently, more and more recreation and park departments have begun actively to promote volunteerism as a positive way of involving citizens and as an effective way of stretching program dollars.

Citizen participation

Participation by constituents in planning recreation programs reaffirms America's basic democratic principles and ideals. Such participation provides an opportunity to initiate programs and to effect changes in existing ones so that these programs will more completely meet participant needs. Philosophically, citizen participation may be viewed as a commitment to reversing social, economic, and political disengagement. Although involving citizens from all sectors of community life in recreation services is a traditional practice, there will no doubt be an even greater need for and interest in citizen participation during the 1980s. Because of rising inflation and continued competition for decreasing tax dollars, recreation program services will need to be closer to the people. Likewise this will necessitate a close working relationship between policymakers, professionals, and participants if program opportunities are to have relevancy and be considered a community requirement.

Nonetheless, citizen participation in program planning in recreation and parks has had a variable reception and its use has been spotty and confused. As Arnstein (1971) has written, "the idea of citizen participation is a little like eating spinach—no one is against it in principle because it is good for you." It does seem difficult to argue with the principle that citizens have a right to participate in and influence the development of plans that will affect their lives. In spite of the extra effort, time, and expense often required, it is my contention that the ultimate effectiveness and survival of any recreation or park agency depend on the involvement, cooperation, and effort of many individual citizens and civic groups.

When does the recreation agency program planner find it advantageous to integrate constituents into the planning process? And once they are involved, how does the planner organize and thus maximize their contribution to the planning process?

Historical basis

The concept of using and organizing the consumers of social services for planning began in earnest in the early 1960s, operating primarily as a fringe outside the major and governmental social institutions. Before this time small developments had been initiated. Around 1949 the federal government began to provide money for communities to develop overall plans for urban renewal. To obtain funds, cities were obliged to use rational planning in preparing master plans, with citizen involvement being a required ingredient. The same concept was embraced in planning practice again in the 1970s. By this time governmental and other major agencies were emphasizing consumer participation. In fact, since the mid-1960s there has been no piece of federal social legislation that does not charge government with the responsibility for fostering and supporting grass-roots participation in decision making about social programs. The same has been true for a great deal of state and local legislation. The federal government's shift to general revenue sharing in the early 1970s also included mandates for citizen participation in planning. Government, therefore, has assumed a determined stance for using and insisting that others use citizen participation in planning (Specht, 1978). Some private agencies have also adopted this position.

One of the most visible examples of the growth of citizen participation in government in the late 1970s and early 1980s was the citizen-initiated taxpayers' revolt to limit government spending in California. Other examples include the dramatic expansion of public interest groups, consumer groups, environmental groups, and neighborhood organizations. This growth is not surprising because the ideal of citizen participation in their own governance is deeply rooted in U.S. law and tradition. Americans not only have a predisposition to participate; they assume it is their basic right.

Recreation and park agencies have also been a part of this history and this tradition. Among the more active agencies have been those of urban governments. In the early 1970s increases in the demand for recreation services came from inner-city slum residents, particularly minority groups. Black and Spanish-speaking residents in particular confronted urban recreation agencies, demanding fuller participation in policy development, improved facilities and programs in their neighborhoods, and expanded hiring of local people. In response to these pressures, a number of recreation and park departments in major cities took bold steps to promote citizen participation in the planning and conducting of local services.

Perhaps the most visible and studied example was the use of the advisory council technique for representing citizens in the planning of the Philadelphia Department of Recreation. The recreation advisory councils were established as part of a council system that included approximately 70 local councils, a few district ones, and a city-wide recreation advisory council. The purposes of the local councils were to:

> . . . provide a means for the interpretation of public opinion to the recreation staff as well as the interpretation and support of the recreation program to the community. These important councils are the bridge between the neighborhood and the recreation facility and are geared to the needs of the community. (Philadelphia Department of Recreation, 1968, p. 1)

The specific duties of the councils included the following:
1. Interpreting recreation needs and desires
2. Studying and evaluating existing programs
3. Developing plans to improve recreation resources
4. Advising planning staff so that the program is developed in accordance with the plan
5. Acting as a clearinghouse for suggestions
6. Making the staff aware of local traditions and recreation usage patterns
7. Publicizing programs
8. Investigating criticisms
9. Raising funds
10. Recruiting volunteer leadership
11. Assisting staff in understanding public reaction to programs
12. Providing transportation for trips (Philadelphia Department of Recreation, 1968, p. 2)

In 1972 Geoffrey Godbey reported the findings of a study of Philadelphia's recreation advisory councils. The data were analyzed according to representativeness and effectiveness of the councils, council member participation in decision making, and the effects on the councils of the socioeconomic status of geographic areas within the city. It was concluded "that citizens participate on recreation advisory councils both within and outside poverty areas, but that there are systematic differences in that participation" (Godbey, 1972, p. 31). In general, the study concluded that in poverty areas participatory management of urban recreation agencies was not achieved effectively by using advisory councils because the citizens tended to participate less in negotiation, joint planning, shared policy and decision making, and delegation of planned responsibility. On the other hand, the study found that the degree of benefit obtained by such councils was far greater in middle- and upper-class neighborhoods. Whereas advisory councils in nonpoverty areas were primarily concerned with improving, expanding, and altering existing programs, councils in poverty areas too often were forced to protect the status quo, the very existence of the recreation facility and its programs. This example illustrates well the complexity of employing citizen participation in program planning.

Designs for citizen participation

Although local planners often see citizen participation as an additional burden to the already hectic and cumbersome job of planning, it is now common practice for many local agencies, planners, and citizens to work together. The term *citizen participation* is a generalization often simply defined as providing citizens with opportunities to take part in decision making or planning processes. Neither the term nor its definition provides any suggestion as to how such participatory events might be structured or what might be expected in terms of results. In fact, historically many attempts at citizen participation have met with failure because little or no attention was given to structure or desired purpose. Let us now look at specific designs for making citizen participation happen within the planning process.

Five general objectives of citizen participation can be identified as information exchange, education, support building, decision-making supplement, and representational input (Glass, 1979). See Table 3 for a distinction between the objectives according to their definition, perspective, degree of citizen involvement in planning, and appropriate techniques. As the table indicates, there are two basic views on the real purpose of citizen participation: one is the citizen perspective and the other is the administrative perspective. The administrative purpose is to involve citizens in planning to increase their trust and confidence in the agency, making it more likely that they will accept the agency's plans and decisions. The purpose of the citizen perspective, on the other hand, is to provide citizens with a voice in planning to improve the delivery of services.

Determining which techniques of citizen participation match which objectives is the crucial task for the planner, because not all techniques will yield the same results and thus provide the attainment of the same objectives. Again, consult Table 3 for an outline of the specific techniques according to objective.

Unstructured techniques refer to an informal means of participation and are designed to produce face-to-face contact between the planner and the citizen. These techniques offer planners exposure to large numbers of citizens in order to create an

Table 3 *Objectives of citizen participation*

Objective	Definition	Perspective	Planning Involvement	Mechanisms
Information sharing	Bringing planners and constituents together for sharing ideas and concerns	Planner	Does not involve citizen directly in the program planning process	Unstructured, e.g., drop-in centers, neighborhood meetings, agency information meetings, public hearings
Education	Extending the information sharing objective, with an additional educational supplement aim	Planner	Does not involve citizen directly in the program planning process	Structured, e.g., citizen advisory councils, citizen review boards
Support building	Creating a favorable climate for proposed preset plans or the resolution of conflict	Planner	Does not involve citizen directly in the program planning process	Structured, e.g., citizen advisory councils, citizen review boards
Planning supplement	Providing citizens an increased opportunity for input into planning; seen as supplement because it provides the planner with another dimension to consider along with the normal agency staff input	Citizen	Involves citizen directly in the program planning process	Active, e.g., Nominal Group Process, analysis of judgment
Representational input	Identifying through representation the views of the entire community on particular recreation issues so that later plans will reflect community desires	Citizen	Involves citizen directly in the program planning process	Passive, e.g., citizen survey, Delphi process

Adapted from Glass, J.J. *Journal of the American Planning Association*, 1979, 45, 180-189.

opportunity to exchange information and attitudes on a direct basis. This category includes drop-in centers (permanent locations established throughout the city where planners and citizens can interact informally), neighborhood meetings (a series of meetings held throughout the community to produce reaction to particular plans or programs), agency information meetings (one-time-only meetings held to inform the constituency about a particular agency program), and the traditional public hearings (meetings usually held in compliance with a legal ordinance or statute).

Structured techniques, on the other hand, afford planners some control over how many and which citizens will participate, because citizens are usually previously selected by the planners. The Philadelphia Department of Recreation's citizen advisory councils are an example of this technique. Structured techniques are used appropriately when education and support-building objectives are desired. Planners are able to work with citizens either to educate them about a proposed planning effort or to gain their support for a new program. Participants are then encouraged to educate the citizens they represent and in turn to gain a broader support in the community for the program plans. Techniques in this category include citizen advisory committees or councils (groups of citizens permanently affiliated with an agency), citizen review boards (similar to advisory committees, but provided with more authority), and citizen task forces (groups formed for a specific purpose and then dissolved).

Active techniques, which are more difficult to organize and manage, are those efforts in which participation occurs through a well-developed process; citizens are directly involved in specific phases of the planning process. As with structured techniques, planners have control over who and how many will participate, while also having control over exactly how participation will occur. For example, Nominal Group Process is a step-by-step procedure resulting in a selection of ranked recommendations; analysis of judgment policy uses mathematical models of policy positions to produce an assessment of problems; and value analysis is a process that produces ranked consequences of various proposals. (The Nominal Group Process is explored in depth in Chapter 3.) Active techniques such as these are designed to extract information from citizens and thus are most useful in achieving the supplemental decision-making objective.

The final technique, the *passive* approach, includes the Delphi method and the citizen survey. These passive techniques are highly structured and follow well-developed methodologies. The Delphi method produces information that can be viewed as a consensus of the participants, and the citizen survey yields researched data that can be generalized to an entire community. These methods are considered passive because citizens have no direct contact with planners; nor are they actively participating in the planning process. Because generalization is possible, this technique is appropriate to the objective of representational input. This technique will be considered more carefully in Chapter 3.

San Diego
Lawn Bowling
Club

BOWLERS WELCOME
Games every afternoon
except Mondays.

RAY BELLAROSA

The fact that there is no one technique capable of satisfying all five of the citizen participation objectives draws us to conclude that there is no single technique that is the best alternative. Instead, the best technique depends on the community situation and the planning objectives sought. The planner's decision to use citizen participation must include, therefore, a detailed identification of the desired objectives so that the appropriate techniques can be selected. Furthermore, because no one participatory technique can meet all the objectives, and if a firm commitment to citizen participation exists, then what seems necessary is the development of a continuous, multifaceted system of citizen participation that employs several of the techniques.

Costs and benefits

Citizen participation, in reality, is very complex. Often its ultimate effectiveness is foggy and unverified. This difficulty occurs when participation is not assessed by all concerned (politicians, planners, citizens) at the outset in terms of how it should contribute to the achievement of predetermined, clearly articulated objectives. Ambiguity in citizen participation programs serves only to protect planners and citizens alike from being accountable, and its results can be costly, time consuming, ineffective, and frustrating.

Before determining the desirability of citizen participation in a program planning situation, the costs and benefits should be considered. The costs of citizen participation include the following:

1. Takes significant amounts of time and money
2. Works against administrative efficiency
3. Arouses the expectations of the citizens involved
4. Raises questions as to the rational nature of planning when emphasis is placed on the end product of consensus
5. Makes it difficult to determine who "citizen" is
6. Requires sustained citizen training and technical assistance

On the other hand, citizen participation has these benefits:

1. Allows exercise of a basic democratic right
2. Offers an opportunity for checks and balances
3. Assists the agency in setting priorities
4. Develops indigenous leadership
5. Solidifies community issues into "hot" or "cold" ones
6. Develops an awareness of issue politics
7. Assists in aligning agency efforts with constituency needs
8. Constitutes affirmative activity by offering program consumers a chance to mobilize their energies into production of service
9. Sometimes actually works to solve community problems

Even after a careful evaluation of the costs and benefits of citizen participation, further warning is necessary: if it is not done correctly and seriously, it will not work. Before the planner attempts to integrate citizen participation into a program planning process, further reading and study is advised. (A list of resources for further reading is provided at the end of this chapter and in the appendix.) Advance consultation with experienced professionals in citizen participation from municipal recreation and park agencies, such as those in Philadelphia, Washington, D.C., and Boston, also would be wise.

Planning committees

In addition to involving agency staff and citizens in recreation program planning, consideration should be given to involving professionals from other disciplines. This can be a vital ingredient for successful planning. Because of specialization, planning committees made up of representatives from related professions, other recreation agencies, technical assistance firms, and elected officials will benefit from a broader base of knowledge and cooperation. Today the program planner of leisure services often requires the input and expertise of many professionals from outside the recreation and park field; planning program services can no longer be the insular concern of the recreation program specialist.

A basic problem that can develop, however, with multidisciplinary planning committees arises from placing diverse professionals together as co-workers. For example, having community residents, professionals, and representatives from private groups and agencies serve on a planning committee will not bring about results if there are tensions among professionals or between professionals and lay persons in the group. Nor will the results be useful if the committee members are not skilled or knowledgeable enough in the logistics of planning or of recreation programs. For these reasons, participation in planning, without some preliminary understanding of what is expected of the expert and what is hoped for from the citizen through adequate training, is foolish and even dangerous (Bannon, 1976).

When soliciting and managing a program planning committee, the planner must have a workable understanding of the group process and the dynamics of getting work done through a committee format. The nature of the group experience itself influences the way in which individuals relate to the work to be done and their effectiveness at committee problem solving. In a group such as a planning committee—which is concerned with exploring problems, making plans, developing recommendations, or carrying out other planning tasks—the planner who is responsible for leading the group needs to perform certain group leadership functions. These functions include the following:

1. Helping the committee members to define the limits of the problem(s) and determine the aspects with which they intend to deal
2. Encouraging each committee member to express his or her ideas
3. Maintaining an atmosphere in which tensions are reduced and cooperation is enhanced
4. Keeping the committee efforts focused on the planning work to be accomplished
5. Helping the committee to move steadily from theoretical considerations and professional or personal attitudes to realistic outcomes and practical steps
6. Helping the committee to evaluate its decisions, goals, and procedures by testing for consensus

Outside planning consultants

A final consideration in organizing for planning is the opportunity for employing professional planners. Even though it has been uncommon for a professional planning consultant to be called in for assistance in recreation program planning, it is important to know that this option is available. Recreation program planners faced with programming problems that require the expertise of a consultant must first understand, however, what a consultant can and cannot do and then know how to locate the right one. Basically, a good planning consultant diagnoses the problem, prescribes the proper program solution, and maintains contact to determine the effectiveness of the recommendation. A consulting fee is charged for this service.

As a result of frequent and intense immersion in daily operations and their related problems, program administrators and planners often are unable to see the basic, underlying nature of the problem; instead they identify and deal with only symptoms. Outside consultants, who are less involved and who have been exposed to many similar situations in other agencies, thus are frequently best able to assist in step 1 of the program planning process. They are most capable in helping their clients to identify and define the nature of the problem to be solved with proper programming.

Most consultants actually provide this problem diagnosis free of charge, when presenting the initial bid. Therefore planners can bring in the opinions of more than one consultant early during the problem definition phase of the process. An obligation to pay for the advice begins only after the agency reaches agreement with the consultant on the specific assignment. Once a consulting arrangement begins, the consultant will apply his or her knowledge, experience, abilities, and time to the task assigned and ultimately will develop analyses and recommendations that appear to be most useful and appropriate to the agency.

When selecting a consultant, therefore, the planner can make only a subjective judgment in advance. Great care must be exercised in this choice because consulting services can be expensive. The best way to minimize the risks is to maximize the choices available and the planner's preliminary exposure to them.

Once an assignment agreement has been reached and a contract has been made with the consultant, the primary means of communicating recommendations for problem solutions will be a written proposal submitted by the consultant. (At this point, the importance of defining the scope of the proposed work in advance becomes clear; failure to do so can be not only costly but disappointing in the end.) The proposal should include a clear statement of the problem, relevant objectives to be achieved, and the nature of the program to be implemented to achieve these objectives. The proposal should also provide a definite estimate of cost and time for program implementation and should tell precisely how the project is to be staffed and who will manage the entire proposal.

As a purchaser of consulting services, the planner can minimize risks by pinning the consultant down precisely, *in writing*, as to exactly what the consultant's responsibility will be for implementation of the recommendations. There are some differences of opinion, even among consultants themselves, about the nature of the product that the agency is buying. Some consultants maintain that their obligation ceases once they have diagnosed the problem and have designed appropriate recommendations to solve it. The planner may not wish to settle for this definition. Depending on the agency's resources for implementing recommendations, the planner may need to insist that the consultant follow through to completion of the program solution; if so, this stipulation must be included in the consulting agreement. Unless the planner and the consultant are in complete agreement as to the specific purposes of a consulting project, the project has slight chance of success.

As noted earlier, consultants can cost money. Just how high consulting fees can go depends on how many consultants are required and how many days will be needed to do the job. The fee is usually payable in a single lump sum that represents a total of the daily billing rate plus an overhead expense fee. The agency should insist that the estimated fees not be exceeded unless the scope of the project is enlarged (under a special agreement drawn up in advance). Regardless of the price, the best way to get one's money's worth from planning consultants is to place great interest in selecting them wisely. After proper selection of a consultant has been made, the second best way to ensure value for the price is for the planner and the staff to become involved in the consulting process as actively as possible and with an attitude of cooperation and helpfulness.

RAY BELLAROSA

In summary, Buttimer (1976, p. 22) has organized a list of items the planner and the agency should know before making a commitment with a planning consultant:

1. The objectives and scope of the proposed work, what the end products will be, and that the end products include an implementation plan
2. The approach that each consultant will take to the work
3. The time required for the project and how much it will cost
4. Who will manage the work and the group of consultants from which it will be staffed
5. Whether the consultants will provide any assistance needed and desired in implementing their recommendations

As a purchaser of consultant services, the client agency should keep in close touch with the consultant's work as it progresses. If the agency administrator or program planner cannot do this personally, a key member of the staff should serve as a liaison between the agency and the consultant. Periodic oral or written progress reports from the consultant should be requested so that the planner can check for adherence to project objectives and schedule and deal with any problems the consultant may have encountered.

Consultants can be a waste of agency money, but when selected wisely for problem determination and resolution services not available from within the agency, they can be a genuine assistance in planning. Wilbanks (1974) conducted a study of the use of private consultants by municipal park and recreation agencies located within a 300-mile radius of Lexington, Kentucky. The study found that private consultants were more likely to be employed by small and medium-size community agencies. Reasons for utilization differed according to the size of the agency. Medium-size agencies, for example, tended to hire consultants to make up for deficiencies in skill or qualifications in their own staff. All agencies studied used private consultants for technical rather than nontechnical services. Wilbanks noted that the problems most frequently encountered in the use of consultants were failure of the consultant to meet deadlines and the cost overrun of projects.

CONCLUSION

The program planner—no matter how large the agency or what type it may be—has numerous options available when embarking on the planning process. The planner's decision of whether to incorporate and utilize other members of the agency staff, concerned citizens, professionals from other disciplines, and planning consultants in the planning process depends on their ultimate contribution toward the effectiveness of the end product—the programs. This level of contribution depends on the unique planning situation, as well as the agency and community environment. Careful consideration of these options, nonetheless, should be a part of the preparations for program planning.

References

Arnstein, S.R. A ladder of citizen participation in the U.S.A. *Journal of the Town Planning Institute,* 1971, *57,* 176-181.

Bannon, J.J. *Leisure resources: Its comprehensive planning.* Englewood Cliffs, N.J.: Prentice-Hall, 1976.

Buttimer, J.W. Tips on using management consultants. *Parks & Recreation,* 1976, *11:11,* 19-22, 38.

Crompton, J.L., & Van Doren, C.S. Changes in the financial status of leisure services in thirty major U.S. cities: 1964-1974. *Journal of Leisure Research,* 1978, *1,* 37-46.

Glass, J.J. Citizen participation in planning: The relationship between objectives and techniques. *Journal of the American Planning Association,* 1979, *45,* 180-189.

Godbey, G. Recreation advisory councils and the poor. *Parks & Recreation,* 1972, 7, 28-31, 41-43.

Kraus, R.G., & Bates, B.J. *Recreation leadership and supervision: Guidelines for professional development.* Philadelphia: W.B. Saunders, 1975.

Kraus, R.G., & Curtis, J.E. *Creative management in recreation and parks* (3rd ed.). St. Louis: C.V. Mosby, 1982.

Meyer, H.D., & Brightbill, C.K. *Recreation administration.* Englewood Cliffs, N.J.: Prentice-Hall, 1956.

Murphy, J.F., & Howard, D.R. *Delivery of community leisure services: An holistic approach.* Philadelphia: Lea & Febiger, 1977.

Philadelphia Department of Recreation. Community organization for recreation. Mimeographed, 1968.

Rodney, L.S. *Administration of public recreation.* New York: Ronald Press, 1964.

Sessoms, H.D., Meyer, H.D., & Brightbill, C.K. *Leisure services: The organized recreation and park system* (5th ed.). Englewood Cliffs, N.J.: Prentice-Hall, 1975.

Specht, H. The grass roots and government in social planning and community organization. *Administration in Social Work,* 1978, 2:3, 319-334.

Tillman, A. *The program book for recreation professionals.* Palo Alto, Calif.: Mayfield, 1973.

Wilbanks, J.E. An analysis of the use of private consultants by municipal park and recreation agencies, M.S., University of Kentucky, 1974.

Part Two

The rational planning process

The planning process

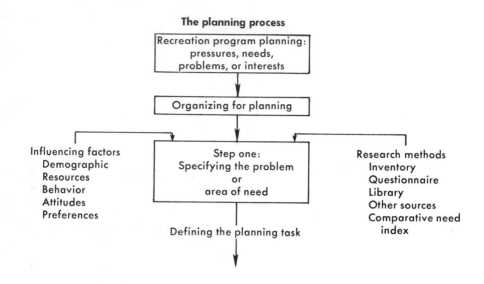

Chapter 3

STEP 1

Specifying the problem or area of need

Has your teen center disintegrated into a drop-in center, and nobody drops in? Does your recreation commission or director of recreation still equate successful programs with attendance figures alone? Has your preschool tiny tots program become merely a baby-sitting service? You are sure that athletics and sports are not the only answer for young people. But what socially acceptable, inexpensive, exciting activities can compete with attractions such as drugs, auto cruising, and drinking?

Fundamental to the idea of providing recreation program opportunities is the existence of a condition of need for such services. Therefore the program planning process should emanate from the needs, problems, and interests of the program constituents. The program planner's first step is to determine these factors through research. Research provides new information that can lead to constructive solutions or a better understanding of current problems. From a broader perspective, the recreation professional has always aimed at improving the quality of life by contributing to the pleasure derived from free time. Thus the professional has relied on research as an essential tool for furthering recreation services. Program services are no exception; research in program planning is absolutely necessary.

In spite of the importance of research, recreation professionals have not always used their findings for planning. Not until around 1960 did professional recreation practitioners, and educators as well, become interested in research as a foundation for and a vital aspect of recreation and park services. Thus only recently has there been any real interest in using research to develop more effective operational procedures and program services. Professionals now realize that for recreation to be an effective field, oriented to meeting the leisure needs of those it serves, it must have a valid approach to those needs. Research is the key to such an approach. By helping to ensure against establishing recreation program policies and services on the basis of invalid assumptions, research contributes to the provision of relevant, cost-effective programming. This chapter, which focuses on the research done by the program planner, is illustrated with the findings of actual research from the field.

The first planning step

Identification of the needs, interests, and problems of the program constituency is a logical place to start the planning process. This assessment remains the most fundamental aspect of program planning. Step 1, therefore, entails the analysis of leisure behavior patterns and recreational preferences in order to provide an informative and objective foundation for making program decisions. Information gathered in this step is used to set program goals and priorities and to establish program form and content; ultimately it influences the effectiveness of program services. Basically stated, documenting problems justifies the development and implementation of specific new programs. In a similar way, the research of step 1 determines the continuing validity of the goals, objectives, and services of an existing program.

The efforts of the planner in this initial stage of the planning process are crucial and pivotal because step 2, the adoption of program objectives, will depend on how the problem or concern is defined. Furthermore, research is the way to get answers to the questions that must be asked during all the steps of the planning process. Because this first step is a foundational one, research ultimately informs the planning function at every stage in the planning process. Research provides the data that are used by the planner to develop realistic options for objectives and programs and to weigh the advantages and disadvantages of each. Research is getting the answers to questions; planning is using the answers in an organized series of steps to accomplish something.

Step 1 of the planning process is often called *situation definition*. At this stage questions such as the following are frequently asked by the planner or planning group:

- Is this problem our problem, or is it more suitably the concern of another agency in our community?
- Is this problem our concern alone, or should we encourage others to share it?
- Is this problem timely? Is it important to us now?
- Is this apparent problem the real, underlying concern or merely a symptom of a deeper, more basic concern—or a different but related problem?

A good illustration of this last question comes from De Boer (1970). A church that for many years had enjoyed a reputation in the community for having an outstanding youth recreation program put "ability to work with youth" high on its list of job specifications for a new minister. As one new minister went to work and the years passed, it seemed that the entire youth recreation program was deteriorating. Each year there were fewer young people participating in the program, and the quality of the program itself seemed to be declining. The governing board took note of these things and tried to solve the downward trend by allocating more money to the program. But all to no effect. The number of participating youths continued to drop. There was some discussion about the inability of the new minister to relate to young people as effectively as his predecessor. The church was almost ready to engage an associate minister whose job would be to give major time to this type of work.

At about this same time the church joined other local churches of the same denomination in making a self-study of its membership, programs, and community environment. One of the things it was required to do was to compare the percentage of its own members in various age groups with the percentage of the city population in these same age groups. Much to the church's surprise, it discovered that the percentage of young people in its youth recreation program was almost twice that of young people in the city population in this age group. In other words, the church had done an excellent job of attracting young people, but the total number of young people in the community had been dropping. On the other hand, the church discovered that proportionately it was reaching a far smaller percentage of older persons than that of the same age group in the city population. In summary, the church had been succeeding in the area where it thought it had been failing, and it was failing (relatively) in an area it had not even recognized.

In-depth research into the situation caused the church to redefine its problem or area of need. Instead of hiring an associate minister whose expertise was in youth work, the church requested a person with demonstrated ability in serving older persons. The redefinition of the problem resulted in a different objective: to serve older members. This illustration shows that adequate and relevant research is dependent on delineating the correct or most appropriate problem or area of need.

A note is in order here. Although the identification of a constituency's recreation needs seems a logical place to start the planning process, few recreation agencies systematically attempt to collect the necessary data. Instead they often rely on tradition and past experience in the formulation of program services. Commenting on this problem, Murphy and Howard (1977, p. 186) state that "while the collection of 'need' data can be complex and time consuming, providing recreation services solely on the basis of professional consideration without regard to clientele input can be a hazardous practice." Murphy and Howard have described two reasons for their strong support of research-based programming. First, an assumed or supposed knowledge of a constituency's needs and interests is fruitless because recreation as a profession does not have available (to date) a systematic, historic measurement of the impact of its services on which to base such assumptions or suppositions. Second, in a period of economic scarcity it is becoming increasingly difficult to "justify expenditures for more recreation on the basis of emotional appeals, based on what the recreation administrator 'feels' the community needs in the way of leisure opportunities" (Murphy and Howard, 1977, p. 186).

Types of concerns, issues, problems: what research tells us

What specific kind of data or information is sought in step 1? The planner is usually concerned with five distinct types of information:

1. *Demographic data.* This information describes the composition of the con-

stituency according to such variables as age, sex, income, education, and family size. The precise information that should be sought depends on the specific program constituency. If it is adults, for example, the most vital data would include marital status, income, occupation, and presence of children. For youth, appropriate data would include grade in school, allowance or earnings, and after-school schedules.

2. *Available resources.* These are the community resources, both current and potential, available for meeting the recreation needs of the constituency. They include facilities (such as golf courses, swimming pools, craft huts), staff, programs, and funds.

3. *Recreation behavior.* A more difficult type of data to assess, leisure behavior is concerned with which activities people participate in and how often, when, and where they take place. Determination of the recreation areas most used is also an important indicator of leisure behavior.

4. *Attitudes and opinions.* What is the level of satisfaction people have about the programs already available to them? This information focuses on such matters as people's attitudes toward the involvement of local government in providing recreation programs, reasons why people do not participate in activities they consider desirable, general attitudes toward recreation for their own lives, and whether community residents would be willing to increase their financial support for recreation services.

5. *Expressed interests and needs.* Such preferences reflect what a person would like to do rather than what he or she actually does. This area of information also tells what types of program services the constituency would like to have provided.

Factors that influence the demand for programmed recreation

By considering all factors that can influence the planned recreational program, the planner assumes the most effective position possible in developing the comprehensive program. Let us now examine these factors more closely.

Demographic factors

Demography, the study of human population, is one of the most crucial factors that can influence considerations of programming recreation services. The number of people in a specific geographic area and their density or dispersion with reference to resources are the main elements of demography (Shivers, 1978, p. 251). Other demographic factors that directly affect programming include cultural, economic, vocational, educational, residential, and political association. The variety, emphasis, magnitude, and type of recreation activities enjoyed by people stem from the joint impact of these factors.

Culture   An analysis of the cultural factors that directly influence the provision

RAY BELLAROSA

of recreation programs is required if social pressures are to be understood and balanced by appropriate recreational opportunities. One of the most vital cultural factors the planner must take into account is tradition. Specific regions of the United States have traditional activities. For example, the Southwest is noted for the rodeo, the Southeast has a tradition of cotillion dances, the Midwest emphasizes state fairs and community festivals, and boating is particularly popular along the Atlantic and Pacific coasts. Regional differences in climate, terrain, history, economy, and industry have played a large role in shaping the form of recreational activity that is traditional to a particular geographic area. These traditions are so ingrained in the people of these regions that they must be considered in planning recreation programs. To ignore them is to fail to meet the interests of the constituency.

This same consideration for tradition should be given to program constituents who are members of various ethnic groups. Blacks, Mexican-Americans, Native Americans, Chinese-Americans, and other subcultures reflect certain beliefs, values, customs, and life-style patterns that have particular cultural meaning that pervades their interests, needs, and behavior. Given an expected increase in these subcultures (Toffler, 1970), it is important for program planners to come to understand and appreciate their nature and their application to recreation program plans.

A research study by Miles (1976) investigated participant attitudes toward recreation programs as a function of race. The subjects for the research were adult participants in both structured and unstructured recreation programs in six recreation centers in Dallas, Texas. The study results revealed a significant difference among three ethnic groups in attitudes toward various program elements. For example, a significant difference existed among the whites, Mexican-Americans, and blacks in preference for games, sports, and athletic programs. The blacks preferred these programs considerably more than the Mexican-Americans or the whites did, and the Mexican-Americans expressed a stronger preference for them than did the whites. This study also found that blacks preferred music and drama programs more than the other two groups did, with Mexican-Americans preferring them more than whites did.

These and other research results show the need to understand cultural diversity and ethnic identity when planning the delivery of program services. Otherwise the planner might be in the position of "throwing a party and nobody came."

Residence   Residence is one of the most important factors that shape an individual's personality; people also tend to select places of residence based on their own personality and life-style. To determine the residential factor of a given constituency, two basic scopes can be considered. One is the nature of the area. Is it urban, suburban, or rural? Rural residents offer a distinct contrast to urban residents. Sparsity of population, a high degree of cultural homogeneity, and a sense of vocational, social, and territorial permanence are associated with the rural person. Restricted social and political contact, resulting from the sparseness of population, produces a conservative, traditional outlook. Those individuals living in a downtown, city-center area tend to be concerned with their job and consumerism; in general they are more liberal and adventuresome in their outlook. The suburban resident is a composite of rural and urban traditions, mores, and economics.

The effect of population density on recreation programming is considerable. Urban dwellers tend to prefer and expect more diverse and comprehensive programs than rural dwellers. Likewise there is a greater probability that the city will have large facilities and elaborate programs to offer its constituency. In rural areas no real organized and continuing program offerings may exist. There are exceptions to this broad generalization, but rural programs of recreation are usually characterized by reliance on routine and time-honored programs. Rural-urban differences also are

apparent in outdoor recreation. Typically, urban and suburban dwellers are represented much more frequently in many forms of outdoor recreation (principally camping, hiking, and skiing). It is interesting that metropolitan residents usually have to
go the farthest to enjoy outdoor recreation, but they make the effort because of their
need to "get away from it all." According to the 1974 data of the Department of the
Interior (p. 207), 69% of all outdoor recreation activity is performed by people living
in the major metropolitan areas.

Another residential factor to consider is housing style. In a research study conducted by Michelson (1973) in Toronto, Canada, indications were that people select
housing according to their own personality, life-style, and recreation preferences.
The study found that persons who choose high-rise apartments, for example, tend to
exhibit more passive leisure behavior (such as reading or TV watching) than those in
single-family houses. The study also found that apartment residents spend more
recreation time outside their dwellings, whereas homeowners are more likely to
spend their leisure time at home. High-rise apartment dwellers, it was also concluded, tend to pursue leisure either alone or in very small groups, whereas those
living in houses tend to engage in more and larger group activities.

Age One of the more important demographic factors influencing recreation
planning is the age of the people in a given constituency. The program planner is
usually aware of age-group characteristics that will affect the kind and gradation of
organized recreation experiences. For example, the national outdoor recreation
study conducted in 1974 by the Department of the Interior found that youthful vigor
probably accounts for more kinds of outdoor recreation participation than any other
element of human makeup. Outdoor leisure activity is greatest during the teen years
and holds up well into the forties. Then the more demanding, youth-oriented activities have to be given up (however reluctantly) for the more leisurely paced forms of
outdoor recreation. See Table 4 for a more precise statistical presentation.

The characteristics associated with age are often dangerously stereotypic, ignor-

Table 4 *Age and outdoor recreation participation*

Percent of all outdoor recreation occasions	Age of participant (years)
21	Under 12
26	12-17
13	18-24
23	25-44
13	45-64
4	65+

From U.S. Department of the Interior, *The recreation imperative.* Washington, D.C.: U.S. Government
Printing Office, 1974, p. 205.

ing individual differences, but they are basic and pervasive enough to warrant careful attention by the planner when programming. Therefore it is helpful to summarize the age-related characteristics of the child, the teenager, the adult, and the elderly and their influence on recreation needs and behavior.

Play is the child's world. Play is the research by which the child explores the self and the self's relationship to the world. Childhood, with its fusion of work and play, is a time for nurturing intellect and molding personality, for developing potentialities, for discovering life and experiencing it. For the child play and learning are a continual and integrated process. A child plays without waiting for specific times or places to play. Therefore, the challenge for organized recreation programs is to provide for play in a way that does not set up a single, predetermined, or limited pattern. Every child needs to express himself or herself and have an effect on the surrounding environment. A traditional example of meeting this need is found in the playground sandbox. Sand is one of the few program media in which children can release their imagination and leave their world different from the way they found it.

The teenager is no longer a child and not yet an adult. He or she is likewise

RAY BELLAROSA

betwixt and between in terms of recreation program planning. While looking for his or her own identity, the teenager also relies highly on peer opinions and acceptance. Teenagers are competitive and have tremendous intellectual, physical, and sexual energy. Teenagers are misfits seeking adventures in a world that offers adventures in increasingly stereotyped ways. They are fond of role playing—trying on various possibilities in new situations and with new people. As a group, teenagers want to be with one another and away from the scrutiny of adults. The easy approach to programming for teenagers—providing a few athletic facilities and hoping that the appropriate activities will take care of themselves—is no answer. The need is for activities that are meaningful to teenagers themselves, not simply diversional. Program experiences must be adventuresome and involve risk; they should be carried on within a social group of peers, with the participants having some say and control.

It is easier to develop recreation programs for the adult age group because they are self-sufficient and mobile. But adults, no less than any other age group, need programs that enrich their lives on many levels and answer the complex needs of their life-styles and life situations. Within this broad age grouping there is great diversity, and recreation program needs vary accordingly. Adults with children, for example, need recreation opportunities close to home that include as well as exclude recreational contact with the children. Adults without children, on the other hand, are more likely to look for social experiences; they will spend more time and money traveling away from home for recreation as well as patronizing commercial establishments such as restaurants and movies.

The challenge of organized recreation for the adult is planning for the whole personality that is the adult. The adult, particularly the urban adult, learns to respond selectively and narrowly to the way the environment badgers and abrades the senses. If the problem with children is to stimulate them, with adults it is to keep them aware. It is therefore increasingly important that recreation programming involve people more directly in the life around them. Ken Dewey, the environmental artist, organized a small program in Stockholm several years ago that illustrates this point well. In the program a bass fiddler got off a bus and suddenly began to play in the middle of a park square. Simultaneously a ballerina arrived by taxi and joined him with dance. When they had finished, they left—in the same way they had arrived. The people watching were stunned. For days afterward they were far more alert and sensitive to their environment, waiting for another "happening."

The elderly are the product of their past, of a time when work was honored and leisure was not. For the elderly of today, productivity and diligence are still primary goals. Dignity and self-sufficiency are more sought, yet increasingly difficult to retain. The average retiree today finds it an adjustment to relax and enjoy a life of leisure. (This will undoubtedly change as leisure-educated groups advance to retirement age.) The elderly person must have a productive place in society—a functioning place in the physical, economic, and social sense. Such a place can be forged only after a realistic evaluation of today's elderly: who they are and what they need. One major and well-recognized problem of old age is loneliness. The traditional answer to this problem has been to create places and experiences that induce the elderly to come together and socialize. But this well-known recreation need should not over-shadow other important needs. For example, although their energies are limited, the elderly are still interested in physical activity. In many cases the recreation needs and interests of this age group are the antithesis of what we usually think.

To plan recreation programs effectively, the planner must be well aware of the age distribution of the constituency and the associated age-group characteristics, without running the risk of making gross stereotypic and unverified generalizations that will result in noncreative programming.

Educational level   Although educational levels are less significant when plan-ning for children, they have greater significance in planning for adults. Varying educational levels and intellectual experiences create diversity of interest, ability, and skill that must be allowed for in organized recreation programs. In a recreation group where participation is motivated by a common interest in the activity, educa-tion levels alone have little effect on participant compatibility. However, choice of activity type, form, and frequency are often influenced by the education factor. In the outdoor recreation study conducted by the Department of the Interior (1974), the statistics clearly indicate a correlation between educational attainment and outdoor recreation participation. Generally the study found that the more educated the per-son, the better equipped and the more interested he or she is to fill leisure time with outdoor recreation. The highest rate of participation was found for high school grad-uates and those with some college education. Surprisingly, those with 4 years of college or more had a slightly lower participation rate than did those with 8 years or less education.

Occupation   Occupational identity frequently serves as an organizational basis for recreational activity groups. Social involvement with others who are employed in the same job, within the same profession, or especially within the same company is typical and appears to be a natural result of the work environment. Occupational identity also frequently serves as an indicator of recreation interests and preferences. The occupational variable is so closely related to income level, education level, and social status that an attempt to determine its direct influence on recreation program planning is meaningless. It is one additional conditioning factor that represents the total demographic composition.

Social status   The system of social status that operates in the United States is closely correlated with economic level, residence, family background, and education. Social status distinctions serve to position people in certain social places, and there is no doubt that people are influenced by the standards and values of their particular places. Social situations mandate attitudes, opinions, behavior, and interests, and this applies indeed to recreation. For example, the leisure of the lower-middle class is typified as spending much free time around the house in family-related activities, watching television, working on cars, drinking beer, bowling, car camping, and playing cards. In this social class there is usually little attention given to civic activities (Murphy and Howard, 1977). It has also been noted by Le Masters (1973) that a certain segment of men within this social class tend to deviate from the normal trend of working-class leisure patterns and spend most of their free time away from their families, frequenting taverns, drinking, playing pool and cards, and talking with their buddies. Likewise, Dishon (1975, p. 23) observed:

> For those who are its regulars, the Oasis bar functions much as a country club does for middle- or upper-class persons: it is the center of social life, the major locus for leisure activities. The tavern draws into itself not only the male workers who form the core of its clientele, but their wives and families as well. It is a public drinking place which has become, in many regards, a private club.

Social status can affect organized recreation programs not only from an activity preference point of view but also from a political viewpoint. Some people think that they cannot participate in certain programs because people from another social class are also in attendance. This can work two ways: the upper classes can look down on participating with lower classes, and the lower classes can feel uncomfortable participating with people from the upper classes. Such deep-seated bias prohibits these persons from joining any recreation program, regardless of interest or enjoyment in the activity, when those whom they consider socially different are also participating. Some social scientists claim that with upward mobility and greater opportunities for more education and better paying jobs, this aspect of social life is gradually disappearing. However, social class remains a demographic factor that requires the attention of those who plan recreation programs.

Family life-style The family exercises a powerful influence on its members and offers certain behavior and attitude norms that determine which recreational pursuits are considered desirable and worthwhile. Different family types will encourage their members to participate in different kinds of leisure pursuits and provide training in those skills and knowledge necessary to participate in them. Good downhill snow skiers usually come from skiing-oriented families, for instance. It is probably safe to claim the reverse: family recreation involvement also influences family life-style and structure. Orthner (1974), for example, suggests that within a family the ability of recreation participation to stimulate social interaction has important consequences for marital structures and relations. He maintains that there are three patterns of recreation participation that can be used to characterize families: parallel, joint, and individual. According to Orthner (1974):

> Parallel activities are individual expressions which occur in a group setting providing little direct communication, such as television viewing or going to a theater. Joint activities require a higher degree of interaction for successful completion of the activity,

and make the individuals involved more aware of new communication opportunities as expressed in picnics, for example. Individual activities are pursuits in which communication with others is not required and actually may interrupt successful completion of the activity.

Parallel and joint family activities will obviously have a primary impact on marital communication because they directly reinforce family member interaction and thereby influence the needs of the marital relationship. On the other hand, individual activities reinforce personal needs and usually operate outside the marital or family relationship.

The presence and number of children within a family unit can also have an impact on the life-style pattern and in turn on recreation interests and needs. For example, families with three or more children are more likely to be interested in outdoor recreation activities than those with one or two children. Families with any number of children are twice as likely to participate in outdoor recreation as singles or two-person families (Department of the Interior, 1974).

Religious affiliation   In a nation where religious domination of the social and cultural life of the people is rare, church and sectarian associations still offer some influence on social customs and moral values. Religious affiliation plays a large role in shaping the nature of some recreational events. The best examples are holidays such as Christmas, Yom Kippur, St. Patrick's Day, and Mardi Gras. These basically religious occasions have been modified over many years to meet the social flavor of the times, and many organized recreation opportunities have been stimulated by these occasions.

It is helpful for the planner to know the values and customs of constituency religious affiliations to avoid mistakes in programming for their recreational needs. Some religious groups in the United States do not participate in certain recreational activities. For example, although the Southern Baptist Convention officially has been an initiator of church-based recreation programs, there are some Baptist congregations that prohibit dancing and card playing. Thus the program planner would be wise to heed local religious customs in planning programs for religious holidays and events.

Resource factor

In step 1 of the rational planning process an investigation must be made of the existing program service resources that are aimed at the same constituency that the planner's efforts are directed toward. The planner should systematically gather data relating to:

1. Currently available activities offered by all recreation agencies operating in the community; these programs include those offered by voluntary, commercial, public, and private agencies
2. The availability of outdoor and indoor recreation areas and facilities, includ-

ing structures that exist for potential development in serving the planner's constituency

3. The future program plans of all other recreation agencies within the constituency community
4. The nature of existing constituency recreational participation, classified according to type of involvement and location of involvement

One very common problem in the provision of recreation program services is overlapping in some activity areas and complete, yet unintentional, absence of offerings in other areas by those agencies designated to serve a particular constituency. A thorough survey of what is already available from other agencies can aid the planner in determining meaningful and comprehensive program goals for his or her own agency.

Once the planner makes an effort to be aware of the available program resources in a given community, lines of communication are initiated and avenues of coordination for program services are made possible. For example, a municipal recreation department that is considering an outdoor recreation program for handicapped youth may discover, through a review of other outdoor programs available for this group, that the local ski area is considering starting a ski lesson program for handicapped children. This discovery could (and probably should) lead to a cosponsorship of the ski instruction program. If the planner discovers, on the other hand, that the ski resort is already conducting an instruction program for the same target constituency and that this program is adequately meeting recreation needs, he or she should consider other activities in outdoor recreation.

The program planner for a public or governmental agency is concerned with the promotion of recreation program services throughout a community. Knowing what program service resources exist in that community better enables the planner to fill in gaps, supplement the offerings of other agencies, and provide an overall coordinated service. The planner should not compete with existing programs, but should work with or around them and, when appropriate, join them in a cooperative effort.

Recreation behavior factor

What does the planner know about the current recreation behavior of the constituency? On a typical Sunday afternoon where are they and what are they doing? What kinds of books do they buy in the local book shop? What hobbies do they engage in at home?

The U.S. Bureau of the Census has been charting participation rates for selected recreation activities since 1960 (see Table 5). It reports (1979) that amateur softball participation for adults increased from 16 million participants in 1970 to 29 million participants in 1978. The number of golfers grew from 4,400,000 in 1960 to 12,655,000 in 1978. There has been a tremendous leap in participation in tennis since 1960. What does this suggest for the planning of organized recreation programs? A

Table 5 *Participation in selected recreational activities, 1960-1978*

Activity	Year				
	1960	**1965**	**1970**	**1975**	**1978**
Softball (amateur)					
Adults	NA	NA	16,000,000	26,000,000	29,000,000
Youth	NA	NA	255,000	450,000	550,000
Golfers	4,400	7,750	9,700	12,036	12,655
Tennis players	5,000	NA	10,655	NA	31,217
Bicycle riders	2,600,000	4,600,000	5,000,000	10,100,000	7,500,000

From U.S. Department of Commerce, Bureau of the Census, *Statistical abstract of the United States.* Washington, D.C.: U.S. Government Printing Office, 1979.

Table 6 *Participation in selected outdoor recreation activities, 1977*

Activity	Participants		Participation	
	Number (million)	**Percentage of population**	**Five or more times (million)**	**For first time (million)**
Camping				
Developed areas	51.8	30	21.0	1.9
Undeveloped areas	36.0	21	15.0	0.7
Hunting	32.6	19	24.5	0.3
Fishing	91.0	53	61.9	1.9
Riding off-road vehicle	43.6	25	33.8	2.0
Hiking	48.1	28	28.1	1.9
Other walking and jogging	116.1	68	96.7	4.1
Bicycling	79.4	46	66.1	1.5
Horse riding	25.2	14	13.5	1.0
Water skiing	26.8	15	13.1	2.7
Sailing	19.1	11	7.8	2.0
Canoeing, kayaking	26.9	15	9.0	2.6
Other boating	57.3	33	34.3	1.5
Swimming, pool	107.4	63	83.5	0.9
Swimming, other	77.9	45	59.5	0.3
Scuba diving	0.2	>1	0.2	0
Golf	27.1	15	18.9	2.4
Tennis, outdoor	55.7	32	40.9	7.0
Other games or sports	94.8	55	73.1	2.6
Going to outdoor sports events	104.3	61	75.5	0.9
Visiting zoos, parks, etc.	123.6	72	66.1	0.9
Sightseeing	106.5	62	61.7	1.2
Picnicking	123.8	72	84.0	0.3
Pleasure driving	118.3	69	97.9	0.7
Skiing, downhill	11.9	7	7.3	2.0
Ice skating	27.8	16	15.7	0.9
Sledding	35.5	20	20.8	0.5
Snowmobiling	13.8	8	7.8	1.5
Parachuting	0.2	>1	0.2	0.2
Rock climbing	0.2	>1	0	0
Gardening	3.4	2	2.7	0.2
Skateboarding	0.2	>1	0.2	0.3

From U.S. Department of Commerce, Bureau of the Census, *Statistical Abstract of the United States.* Washington, D.C.: U.S. Government Printing Office, 1979, p. 238.

comprehensive table of participation statistics based on a telephone survey in 1977 and presented by the Bureau of the Census (1979) is shown in Table 6.

The program planner is interested not only in what type of activities are participated in but also in how frequently. A community recreation participation study reported by Cheek and Burch (1976), for example, looked at activity rates by the week and also by the month. When considering adult participation in certain recreation activities during a one-week period, they found the most frequently participated in weekly activities to be:

1. Reading a newspaper   87%
2. Watching television   84%
3. Visiting friends   75%
4. Reading for pleasure   73%
5. Listening to music   54%
6. Driving for pleasure   53%

When the researchers asked the same adults to judge how frequently they participated in the same list of activities during a one-month period, slightly different results were obtained:

1. Reading a newspaper   90%
2. Watching television   88%
3. Visiting friends   86%
4. Reading for pleasure   75%
5. Driving for pleasure   66%
6. Dining out   65%

Greater differences in participation rates were noted by the researchers in more active, organized activities. For instance, picnicking, going to the movies, water sports, and going to the zoo or park were much more likely to be done on a monthly rather than weekly basis.

Recreation behavior is an important influence on program planning. Not only does it provide an indication of present recreation activity preferences and attitudes, but it also allows the planner to make predictions about possible future preferences and attitudes. For example, recent research studies report that early childhood recreation participation does influence adult participation patterns. Much of recreation behavior in adult life stems from the recreation values, attitudes, and behavior of parents and groups in which the individual has been a member. They predict that in the future youths will have fewer opportunities to participate in hunting and fishing activities when, because of limited resources and changing attitudes, parents will have substantially reduced their involvement in these pursuits. One certain consequence of this reduction will be a proportional decline in participation in these activities among all future adults.

A word of caution about what recreation participation data cannot tell the program planner. This information is not always accurate in revealing participant needs, motivations, or preferred behaviors. Unfortunately, participation types and rates often reflect only available program and facility resources and not desired or needed program services. Furthermore, different people may derive the same benefits from participation in different activities. For example, one individual's need for competition may be satisfied through participation on a field hockey team, another's through chess, and yet another's through boxing.

An understanding of what is behind the recreation behavior is vital if the planner is to know the true value of the commodity he or she is providing. What type of person demonstrates a certain kind of recreation behavior? People can be categorized according to their different types of behavior. Studies in psychology have shown that some people are more leisure oriented than others. In addition, different types of people prefer to participate in different types of recreational activities. Some are outdoor oriented, while others are drawn to the fine or performing arts; some prefer activities that put them in the company of many people, while others enjoy activities that offer solitude and tranquility. Through a research technique known as *factor analysis*, Duncan (1978) has identified five different types of recreation behavior. These types represent a one-dimensional continuum ranging from a high-energy, creative, challenging type of recreational orientation to one that is passive and spectator-like. For instance, type A is primarily an orientation toward such activities as water sports. Type D includes gardening, conversation, entertaining, and cooking for pleasure.

What type of person is most likely to be oriented to which recreation behavior type? Recreation research has progressed beyond merely describing the types of activities engaged in by people and counting their participation rates. At last researchers have realized that planners need more information if they are to plan intelligently. As a result, the most recent studies have attempted to identify and label the characteristics of persons engaging in various activities. One such study, done by Granzin and Williams (1978, p. 123), found that patterns of recreational preferences relate to patterns of behavioral characteristics.

> [The study] has demonstrated that there are groups of persons who are somewhat homogeneous in their preferences for sets of related activities and in the relative emphases they give these activities. Furthermore, these participants favoring a given activity pattern can be characterized in terms of parallel, multidimensional sets of related demographic, self-concept, interpersonal orientation, and behavioral measures.

In abbreviated form, basic recreation activity and behavioral patterns portrayed by this analysis were:

1. Strenuous and/or sociable activities appealing to robust, younger participants
2. Relatively sedentary, culturally broadening pursuits for self-indulgent persons
3. Passive recreational alternatives associated with individuals of higher social class

4. Varied and less vigorous activities for persons seeing themselves as fragile
5. Water-related and hobby pursuits linked to easygoing life-styles
6. Skiing interests appealing to those with carefree, solitary life-styles
7. Physical fitness associated with the behaviors of innovativeness and nimbleness

This and other research has direct implications for program planning. Those designing recreation programs could decide which activity pattern and participants they could provide for, learn about the participants by determining their pattern of behavioral characteristics, and base the program package around these patterns.

Attitudinal factor

Reduction in the length of the workweek and alternative work schedule patterns are signs that the shift toward a leisure-oriented society is now taking place. Is it appropriate, therefore, for the planner to assume that there is a corresponding development of positive attitudes toward leisure and a decrease in emphasis on the work ethic? For many years the recreation service professions have planned and conducted programs and provided facilities on the assumption that they were contributing to the development of positive leisure attitudes. Leisure attitudes, in turn, have played an integral part in the process of selecting recreation activities.

Recent research has attempted to answer such questions as whether participation in recreation programs enhances attitudes toward leisure and general life satisfaction, whether individuals with a positive attitude toward leisure compose the largest number of participants in organized recreation programs; and what recreation program planners should do to promote the development of positive concepts of leisure. One such study looked at the correlation between leisure attitudes and recreation activities in a sample of college students (Mobley and others, 1976). Overall the students' responses to the questionnaire reflected a high degree of work orientation and a lower score in attitude toward leisure. For example, the students indicated that they could "stand" a "life of leisure" for about 1 year (an earlier sample of adults with full-time jobs indicated 2 years). What did the study conclude about the relationship of these predominantly positive work attitudes and participation in recreation activities? It claimed that, in general, active participators saw leisure as "fuller" and were more satisfied with it, whereas less active participators saw work as more fulfilling and important. (It is interesting that "doing nothing" had a somewhat more negative value than did "consuming alcohol" and only a slightly more positive value than "taking habit-forming drugs.") The study also concluded that the person who prefers nonstructured recreation activities tends to be more oriented toward vacations and free time than toward work; a person preferring structured recreation activities tends to look for achievement in these situations because of stronger orientation toward work.

Because the United States is a melting pot, practitioners need to recognize the pluralistic nature of our attitudes. Some of us value leisure, others value work; some of us value nature and the environment, others value productivity and progress; some of us value traditions and stability, others value change and new ideas. Diverse orientations in attitude were reflected in the work done by Clark (Clark and others, 1971). The research findings suggested that campers and managers of campsites disagreed about the types of activities needed because of differing attitudes toward camping. The authors attributed this conflict to the gap between the urban, fast-paced attitudes of the campers and the more traditional, natural environment orientation of the campsite managers.

These and other research studies on the relationship between an individual's attitudes and choice of leisure interests have indicated that there is a strong correlation. O'Connor (1970) found, for instance, that hikers showed significantly higher attitudinal orientations toward achievement, change, dominance, autonomy, and exhibition. Hospital volunteers, on the other hand, exhibited significantly higher scores in positive attitudinal orientation toward affiliation.

It therefore seems that participants in recreation programs select the type of program according to their own attitudes toward life, themselves, work, and play. Program planners thus should view their obligations for providing program services in light of individual differences in attitudes; any research conducted at step 1 of the planning process should consider the attitudes that precede the recreation experience.

Preference factor

When the program planner considers the preference or interest factor in step 1, he or she is taking into account what members of the constituency say they would like to have offered in the program. In the process of developing recreation programs, this factor is the most traditional starting point. Some communities or agencies rely heavily on checklists of participant activity preferences for trying out or justifying new program features. In many hospitals and voluntary agencies it is customary to have patients or members fill out an "interest survey" as a regular admission procedure.

But does what people say they prefer to participate in really indicate to the planner what they do participate in? Is there a sound correlation between recreation activity preferences and actual participation? A research study reported by Chase and Cheek (1979) compared stated recreation activity preference with actual participation in an effort to answer this question. Their findings maintain that there is a relationship between interest and behavior. The researchers cautioned, however, that this preference-participation relationship is confounded by intervening variables such as amount of free time, geographic location, and availability of appropriate facilities. For example, if I were asked at this moment what my favorite recreation activity is, my answer would be cross-country skiing. But there is no correlation between my expressed desire for this activity and my actual participation in it because I currently live in southern California, about 10 miles from the Mexican border. Thus for me geographic location is a very active intervening variable.

The Chase and Cheek findings have shown that activity preference can be a useful concept in explaining actual leisure behavior. See Table 7 for the study results in comparing preference for specific recreation activities with participation in those activities. As the table indicates, activities such as fishing, hunting, golf, and tennis have a preference-participation correlation that is rather high. These findings suggest that for these activities a need estimation based on stated preferences would be appropriate for the program planner.

•   •   •

All the factors just discussed—demography, resources, recreation behavior, attitudes, and interests—directly influence the need for programmed recreation. The specifics of these factors must be actively sought and understood by the planner at this first step of the planning process so that the planner will recognize problem or need areas for target by program services. This logic assumes that recreation programs can fulfill certain needs and resolve certain problems for both the individual and the community. The professional in the field of recreation and parks has always been supported by the premise that recreation services benefit society and satisfy certain human needs. (Review Chapter 1 of this text.) Much has been written to both tout and verify this justification.

In fact, Kass and Tinsley (1978) considered this very issue. In their study the need-satisfying characteristics of 10 commonly selected recreation activities were

Table 7 *Correlation of preference for a recreation activity with participation in that activity*

Activity	Percent participating*	Activity	Percent participating*
Golf	63	Basketball	45
Fishing	61	Camp	45
Hunting	61	Pleasure boat	41
Swim	57	Picnic	36
Tennis	55	Baseball	34
Ride horse	53	Football	32
Ride bike	48	Hiking	31
Water ski	47	Pleasure walk	31
Volleyball	46		

From Chase, D.R., & Cheek, N.H. *Journal of Leisure Research*, 1979, *11*:2, 92-101.
*Of those who expressed a preference for this activity.

investigated. The investigators focused on a particular recreation activity and a particular need and asked the following questions:

- Do participants believe this need can be satisfied through participation in this activity?
- Do male and female participants differ in their estimation of the need-satisfying properties of this activity?

The methodology was simple: persons participating in an activity were asked to rate the extent to which each need was satisfied by that activity. Scores on 33 of the 45 needs were significantly related to the activity in which the participant was involved, and sex of participant was not significantly related. Therefore the study supported the premise of professionals that many human needs are recreation-activity specific. In other words, certain needs can be satisfied to a greater degree through participation in certain recreation activities than by participation in other activities. The Kass and Tinsley study specified that the human need for catharsis, independence, advancement, getting along with others, reward, understanding, activity, ability utilization, exhibition, sex, and supervision appear to be particularly recreation-activity specific. This means that certain needs are satisfied by certain recreation activities. Other researchers in the field (Bishop and Witt, 1970; London, Crandall, and Fitzgibbons, 1977; and Tinsley, Barrett, and Kass, 1977) also have reported differences in recreation activities in terms of the needs that they fulfill.

The influencing factors of demographic data, available resource data, behavior indications, attitudes, and stated interests help the program planner not only in determining the need for organized recreation programs but also in deciding what types or forms of recreation programs are needed. This chapter, and this entire book, will stress the importance of assessing program needs of participants and potential participants to determine which form of activities will satisfy and be meaningful. In the 1980s those who provide monies for programs are concerned with the need for demonstrating accountability. The recreation program planner must be able to verify that the needs of his or her constituency are being met.

Needs are an integral part of the process of selecting and organizing recreation programs. In spite of this, program services personnel have tended to follow other traditional guidelines in planning recreation programs rather than basing their decisions on definitive research findings. The reasons for this are numerous. Perhaps the most widespread and obvious one is a general lack of ability in conducting applicable research. To aid the student planner in step 1 of the planning process, the following section describes some common methods for gathering data.

Research methods

High population density, accelerating economic changes, expanding technological developments, transportation problems, and increasing leisure time have combined to place a premium on effective recreation services. Therefore it is important to repeat that recreation programming must reflect the requirements of the constituency served. Step 1 of the planning process entails a comprehensive understanding of the needs and capabilities of actual and anticipated program users, coupled with the systematic application of this knowledge to program plans. But exactly how is this understanding obtained? Where and how does the planner begin? What research methods should be used? A study of MacArthur Park in Los Angeles (see Byerts and Teaff, 1975) may help to illustrate the use of research methodology.

This research study was initiated by city planners because of a need to reevaluate park planning, present park policy, and current programming in the park. The research methodology involved collecting historical, physical, and demographic information; taking inventory of existing park facilities; and interviewing and observing park users. The study then related the research findings to park design and program recommendations.

MacArthur Park is located in the Westlake district of Los Angeles. This is an older, once-fashionable neighborhood in the central part of the city. The intensive commercial establishments that border the park include cut-rate shopping facilities, small manufacturers, B-grade movie theaters, bars, cafeterias, medical clinics, a nursing home, apartments, boarding houses, and retirement hotels. A comparison of the demographic data of the Westlake area to that of Los Angeles shows that the area surrounding the park is approximately three times denser in population than the city-wide average and is mainly white. Local residents are 12 years older than the average city residents, earn two thirds of the city resident's average income, and are composed of one third more single people. Crime statistics show this area to be among the worst districts in the city.

The study's inventory of existing resources in MacArthur Park includes a bandshell with fixed seating for 100 and open lawn seating for 200, a snack bar, shuffleboard courts, a horseshoe pit, table and card game area, and two toilet facilities. This 32-acre site also has many scenic bench-lined paths and a lake. Except for boating, active recreation is confined to a large open field. Many Hispanic youths use it for weekend soccer. The card and game areas are used mainly by older adults. A tot lot, surrounded by benches, serves as a center for children's activities.

A field interview and observation technique was used to gather more specific information on the users of MacArthur Park. A sample of 35 adult park users who make two or more visits to the park per week was interviewed. The sample consisted of 28 men and 7 women and had an age range of 23 to 85 years. Of the sample, 8 members were foreign born; 30 were white, 3 were of Mexican-American origin, and there was 1 Native American and 1 black. Most members of the sample were of working-class background, with 11 currently employed and 24 retired. The average length of residence in the area was 12 years. Self-reported park usage by the 35 interviewees indicated that 22 were daily park users; 22 spent their time there alone.

Reasons given for going to the park were to get away from home, to exercise, to be in a natural setting, to be with and make friends, and "nothing else to do."

To compare the respondents' stated activity patterns with actual behavior, the interview sample was observed unobtrusively over a 2-month period. Individual respondents did appear to be generally following their own reported patterns of movement within the park, patterns of activity, and social relations.

An analysis of the research information led Byerts and Teaff (p. 63) to make the following conclusions about the needs and problems of MacArthur Park:

> While [the park] is used by a broad segment of ethnic, economic, and age cate-gories, the majority of the regular older, adult users are working class, male, and elderly. Declining health, low socio-economic status, fixed incomes, few family ties, and reduced mobility are all major factors that appear to narrow recreation options for these inner-city residents. They are limited to the park as a source of inexpensive recreation. . . . MacArthur Park has evolved into a satisfactory and well-used, passively oriented recrea-tion space. A range of options are provided within differing landscape arrangements and include activity areas for individuals, small groups, and large groups, as well as settings for individual relaxation. Within this "successful" park, however, there is need for experi-mentation and improvement. A new range of alternatives reflecting user needs should be added to MacArthur Park. At MacArthur Park, the real and perceived needs seem to be for more security, increased options, revitalization of facilities, and comfort (especially for those spending long periods of time in the park).*

Let us investigate more carefully the MacArthur Park research methods as well as other methods for assessing problems and needs for program planning.

The inventory

Although certainly less scientific than research, a simple exploration of existing and planned recreation programs, areas, and facilities and of staff expertise is a tool that can aid the planner in determining need. The inventory method requires the planner to list or to map out the situation in terms of existing recreation program services. This inventory of what *is* helps to define or redefine the planner's starting point for determining the area of need. By reviewing and stating what currently exists early in the planning task, the planner is later better able to define what is expected. The question here is one of available resources. It helps to determine where the planner begins; on what scale he or she can realistically plan; what monies, buildings, programs, and personnel expertise are at hand or soon to become avail-able.

The questionnaire

The questionnaire is basically a printed form delivered, handed, or spoken to a respondent who answers the variety of questions on the form and returns it to the

---

*Reprinted from the **10:**1 (1975) issue of *Parks & Recreation* by special permission of the National Recreation and Park Association.

sponsoring agency. The questionnaire is probably the most widely used method for determining the need for recreation services; some professionals in the field have estimated that as many as half the research studies conducted use a questionnaire.

There are a number of initial assumptions the planner makes when choosing to use a questionnaire. Bannon (1976, p. 137) describes the typical assumptions:

> [that] respondents are a competent source of information; that they will provide information willingly; that they understand the questions in the questionnaire; and that they will answer questions in the form intended and with candor.

The appropriateness of the questionnaire would have to be questioned if these assumptions do not hold true.

There are generally five areas of questioning that a questionnaire can include. First is the area of activity interests or participation rates. To collect this information, the questionnaire usually provides a long list of recreation activities, and the respondents are encouraged to indicate those in which they actively participate or have interest. The results from such a questionnaire are simple to tabulate but can be difficult to interpret accurately. For example, respondents will not be able to indicate interest in activities to which they have never been exposed. Therefore the planner will not be able to readily determine whether "lack of interest" in a particular activity truly represents lack of interest or whether it represents only lack of introduction or exposure.

Second, the questionnaire could survey general, descriptive information about the constituency already participating in the program. Items in the questionnaire would include questions on age, income level, transportation means, and hours of participation each week. This type of questionnaire focuses on those who are already being served by the program so that a profile of those attracted to the program offerings is possible.

A third direction for a questionnaire is to solicit attitudes and opinions on existing program services. The questions asked would have the respondent evaluate the program according to factors such as crowdedness, safety, and satisfaction. The respondent is asked to make a value judgment or state a viewpoint.

A profile of the nonparticipant is the focus of the fourth type of questionnaire. The intent here is to seek data on dissatisfaction or reasons for noninvolvement. The questions can be either open ended or multiple choice. Usually the more options offered for response, the more specific and helpful the answers will be to the program planner.

A fifth type of questionnaire is one that solicits and assesses constituency opinions about proposed future services or future program priorities. Usually this means presenting the choices to the respondent and requesting a reaction.

The questionnaire can be administered in one of three ways: mail, personal interview, or hand delivery. Self-administered questionnaires (those delivered by hand or through the mail) are used most often when person-to-person interviews with the constituency are not feasible or necessary. A mail-delivered questionnaire is the most common means of distribution, though frequently questionnaire forms are hand delivered to constituency homes or given out at meetings or events. In terms of reliability the personal interview method is preferable to a mail questionnaire. When an interviewer asks a question directly, he or she can obtain a reliable answer by controlling the question meaning and eliminating any misconceptions. The choice between conducting a personal interview questionnaire or a self-administered one is usually based on the costs involved and the appropriateness of the situation.

There are a number of conditions that determine the appropriate delivery and retrieval system. In a large community, for example, it is impractical to use the hand-delivery and hand-pickup method because of the large number of people needed for delivery. In a smaller community, on the other hand, where the size of the constituency is smaller and, more important, where community awareness and interest are greater, this method may be preferable.

There is some disagreement in the recreation field about the desirability of the questionnaire distributed by mail. The controversy centers around the belief that mail questionnaires fail to bring adequate response rates. This is sometimes true, but many considerations need to be taken into account when trying to increase the return rate of mailed questionnaires. According to a study on the mailed questionnaire reported by Wendling (1980), several procedures can be used to control and reduce nonresponses. Wendling's study found these procedures useful: approval for conducting the study by respondents' superiors, pretesting the questions, notification of respondents before initial mail-out, questionnaire appearance and neatness, use of colored paper, cover letters emphasizing the importance of the study, letterhead stationery, use of first class mail, inclusion of stamped and return addressed envelopes, and follow-up reminders. Interestingly, a study of Igo (1971) concentrated on the importance of nonresponses and found no significant differences between respondents and nonrespondents. Igo claims that predictions based on a partial response to a mail questionnaire can be assumed to provide a valid representation of the needs, preferences, and behavior of a given recreation population.

The design of the questionnaire can be tricky and difficult to construct. Two common pitfalls are asking inappropriate and unimportant questions and omitting questions that the planner really needs the answers to. Perhaps the greatest pitfall is assuming that people understand the questions and know what is meant by professional terms such as *teen center* and *recreation commission*. Much information on questionnaire construction is available from books, and the newcomer should consult these in depth. The planner should also solicit help from research experts and professionals before designing a questionnaire. Although published questionnaires are available to the program planner, every situation presents new and different circumstances; to adequately determine the area of program services need, a great deal of advance reading, design, testing, and community involvement is required for questionnaire construction.

The precise questions used depend on what kind of information is being sought. In wording the questionnaire the planner must consider whether he or she wants facts or attitudes. Much advance care in formulating questions is required to better guarantee that responses are reliable and meaningful. Although care is important in phrasing questions for factual information, even greater care is necessary when opinions and attitudes are being sought. The reason for stressing the necessity of clear, unambiguous, and meaningful wording of questions is to ensure that reliable and meaningful responses are received.

The questionnaire is becoming increasingly popular for determining constituency need. As an application of sample survey research, it can (if effectively designed) also gather evaluations of existing program services and views on agency policies and program goals. As long as the correct procedures of probability sampling are employed, questionnaires provide the advantage of yielding information that may be generalized to the entire community. Because of the need for correct sampling, some technical expertise in questionnaire design and implementation is required. Great attention must be given to the size of the sample required, random selection of respondents, design of the questionnaire, supervision of data collection, and interpretation of results. Although resource materials on the construction and implementation of the questionnaire are available in the library, this method is best employed with the advice or assistance of an expert in survey research.

The library

The planner should not overlook the neighborhood library, the city or county library, the agency library, the hospital library, and the college or university library as sources of pertinent data on constituency need. Source material is usually scattered throughout the various library divisions, but an initial chat with the reference librarian and an exploration of what sources are available will help the researcher decide which items in the library will be most fruitful. The library can make its greatest contribution in two areas of the planner's research: it houses documents that contain local, county, state, and national demographic data; and it offers journals and books that report the research already performed by others in the recreation field.

When interested in demographic data, the planner should ask the reference librarian for the city or county fact book, the city or county documents collection, or the census data compiled by the city, county, or state planning department. Contact with the librarian at the city planning department itself could yield additional demographic information about the constituency.

The planner should consult certain published sources in the library to locate other recreation research that is applicable to the planner's study. Journal and periodical article indexes, journal abstracts, and published bibliographies are located in the reference room of large libraries. These direct the researcher to published research reports according to specific topics. Professional journals such as *Research Quarterly, Journal of Leisure Research, Parks & Recreation, Therapeutic Recreation Journal,* and *Leisure Sciences* report only recreation research findings, so the planner may wish to survey them directly.

Other research sources

Gone are the days when the recreation planner could find everything about constituency needs in one place or in one book. Today's information explosion makes manual search and review of all knowledge in an area an overwhelming and impossible task for the researcher. Fortunately for the student, educator, practitioner, volunteer, and researcher, there are organizations whose sole purpose is to retrieve, catalog, and disseminate information.

The list below (see box) has been assembled as an aid to identifying and using information sources relevant to recreation program planning. The information base of these resources may include all, a combination of, or only one of the following: journal articles, unpublished research reports, masters theses, doctoral dissertations, scholarly books, government documents, project and conference reports, and bibliographies. When the planner requests information from such an organization, the output might be a list of citations, an annotated bibliography, or a complete literature packet with actual article reprints. Access to the actual cited materials would then be through a direct request to the author, through the library, or through direct purchase from the information resource.

As in many social service fields, much of the recreation program knowledge base is so embedded in research literature that often it has little òr no impact on the work of program practitioners and on the programs themselves. The practitioner's use of the research literature has been hampered by two major factors:

1. The tremendous increase in the amount and variety of written work available
2. The lack of translation of research findings into usable implications for everyday program functioning and planning

To counteract these factors, a list of retrieval sources of recreation research findings is presented (see boxed material, pp. 93 to 95).

Constituency-initiated research methods

The two methods presented here for determining program need require an active, and many times initiatory, role by the program constituency. The Nominal Group and Delphi processes both assume the premise of citizen participation (introduced in Chapter 2): meaningful constituency participation in planning requires effective communication among planners, agency officials, and service users at every step of the planning process. That means inclusion in step 1.

Nominal Group Process The Nominal Group Process (NGP) is a method for

---

OTHER SOURCES OF RELEVANT RESEARCH

Educational Resources Information Center (ERIC)

ADDRESS: National Institute of Education
Dissemination Task Force
Code 401
Washington, D.C. 20202

TELEPHONE: (202) 755-7666

PURPOSE: Designed and developed by the U.S. Office of Education and operated by the National Institute of Education, Department of Health, Education and Welfare, to keep educators and social scientists abreast of significant findings from current education research and developmental activities.

CHARACTERISTICS: Publishes *Research in Education,* a monthly abstract of recently completed research projects, descriptions of outstanding programs, and summaries of other documents of education significance.

Microform Publications

ADDRESS: Microform Publications
School of Health, Physical Education and Recreation
University of Oregon
Eugene, OR 97403

TELEPHONE: (503) 686-4116

PURPOSE: Serves fields of health, physical education, and recreation as authorized by the National Microcard Committee, a joint committee appointed by major American library associations. This nonprofit service provides microform reproduction of materials with major emphasis on unpublished research materials, early professional and scientific journals and scholarly books now out of print.

CHARACTERISTICS: All microform publications issued are cataloged and periodically indexed in *Health, Physical Education, and Recreation Microform Bulletin,* which is sent to most college and university libraries. As of Volume 3 of the *Bulletin* (October 1972) all publications are in microfiche form. To order send title and author's name to Microform Publications. Publications are available to individuals as well as institutions on three different payment plans.

National Clearinghouse for Mental Health Information (NCMHI)

ADDRESS: National Clearinghouse for Mental Health Information
National Institute of Mental Health
5600 Fishers Lane
Rockville, MD 20852

TELEPHONE: (301) 443-4513

PURPOSE: Established to identify mental health sources from all over the world, collect information, and process this information for dissemination to meet individualized needs of research scientists, professional practitioners, educators, administrators, students, and concerned citizens.

Continued.

OTHER SOURCES OF RELEVANT RESEARCH—cont'd

Psychological Abstracts Search and Retrieval (PASAR)

ADDRESS: Psychological Abstracts Information Service
American Psychological Association
1200 Seventeenth Street, N.W.
Washington, D.C. 20036

TELEPHONE: (202) 833-7600

PURPOSE: Provides search of all records published in *Psychological Abstracts* starting in 1967; references supplied in overlapping subject areas to satisfy specific behavioral and social science information needs. Requests for a search should be submitted on a special PASAR Request Form. A computer printout listing citations and abstracts is returned in about 2-3 weeks. Charges are based on a $15 processing fee for each request, plus $2.25 per minute computer time.

Therapeutic Recreation Information Center (TRIC)

ADDRESS: Therapeutic Recreation Information Center
Department of Recreation and Leisure Studies
University of Waterloo
Ontario, Canada

TELEPHONE: (519) 885-1211, Est. 3667

PURPOSE: Literature and document storage and retrieval system that indexes and abstracts published and unpublished articles, books, conference proceedings, and other materials to aid those interested in therapeutic recreation service. At present there is no charge for the service.

University Microfilms

ADDRESS: University Microfilms
300 North Zeeb Road
Ann Arbor, MI 48106

TELEPHONE: (313) 761-4700

PURPOSE: Publishes doctoral dissertations on microfilm and compiles and indexes abstracts of both doctoral dissertations and master's theses.

Bibliography of Theses and Dissertations in Recreation, Parks, Camping, and Outdoor Education 1970

ADDRESS: National Recreation and Park Association (NRPA)
1601 North Kent Street
Arlington, VA 22209

TELEPHONE: (703) 252-0606

PURPOSE: Compilation of titles of theses and dissertations in the areas of recreation, parks, camping, and outdoor education.

OTHER SOURCES OF RELEVANT RESEARCH—cont'd

Completed Research in Health, Physical Education, and Recreation

ADDRESS: AAHPER Publications—Sales
1201 Sixteenth Street, N.W.
Washington, D.C. 20036

TELEPHONE: (202) 833-5550

PURPOSE: Compilation of abstracts of master's theses, doctoral dissertations, and a bibliography of selected published research from periodicals in the fields of health, physical education, recreation and allied fields. Published annually since 1958.

---

conducting structured group meetings. A nominal group session is a method of citizen or constituency participation that can be directed by planners so that participants respond to a specific question, such as "What are the most pressing recreational needs of the community?" Through the use of NGP, not only will all concerned participants have an equal opportunity to respond to the question, but by the end of the meeting the planners will have the group's opinion on the most important problems in order of priority.

Developed by André Delbecq (1975), NGP consists of a series of steps, centered around a specific question, that lead to definite results. The steps include a period of written responses to the specific question posed by the meeting leader; a round-robin recording of each participant's responses; a small group discussion of each response; a voting period when each meeting participant ranks the top five responses; and a vote tally. Those responses receiving the most votes are considered to be the consensus of the group, although sometimes a second period of small group discussion and vote is added if necessary. The NGP can be used with constituency groups of any size as long as subgroups do not exceed 10 members.

The advantages of NGP are that everyone interested in recreation program services can participate; domination by the most vocal persons is controlled; and a definite conclusion to the meeting is achieved. NGP is most useful in obtaining input before solution exploration. For example, the planner might ask a group of citizens to identify problems, desired goals, or service delivery needs. Such information would provide another dimension to the data gathered in step 1 of the planning process.

The Delphi technique   The Delphi technique is also a group process that uses written responses. Like NGP, it is a means of collecting the judgments of the constituency to improve the quality of program planning. However, unlike NGP, it does not require the participants to be together in a meeting setting. Because Delphi does not require face-to-face contact, it is particularly useful for involving experts, users, resource managers, and agency administrators who cannot or should not come together.

Delphi is essentially a series of questionnaires. The first questionnaire asks individuals to respond to a broad question. Each subsequent questionnaire is built upon the responses to the previous questionnaire. The process stops when consensus has been approached among the participants or when sufficient information for planning has been obtained. Like NGP, Delphi can be used to help identify problems and needs, set goals and priorities, and even identify problem solutions.

However, three critical conditions are necessary to complete Delphi successfully:

1. Adequate time
2. Participant skill in written communication
3. High participant motivation

Delphi should not be used unless about 45 days are available for the procedure. Delphi should not be used with groups that have difficulty in reading or expressing themselves in writing. Finally, the quality of responses is greatly influenced by the interest and commitment of the participant; Delphi requires high participant motivation because no one else is present to stimulate and maintain enthusiasm for the process. Details on specific implementation of the Delphi method are presented by Delbecq (1975).

Comparative need index

A final method for identifying needs in determining program planning priorities is through a device called by professionals the *comparative need index*. This method seeks to integrate demographic, attitudinal, available resource, behavioral, and preference data (obtained through many of the research methods already discussed) and come up with a numerical comparative priority figure of need for recreation program services. It is important to realize, however, that this method is most useful in determining which groups within a constituency most need program services attention rather than what type of program services are needed. The use of this method for determining need is based on the belief that people do not have an equal need for program services.

The comparative need index works via a mathematical assessment of social factors as compared to available recreation resource factors. The social index is then subtracted from the resources index and a comparative priority value for the need is obtained.

The planner first selects those social factors that have the most bearing on the planning situation. These factors can include any of the following examples:

1. Population
   a. Total population
   b. Segments of the total population, such as youth population 5 to 19 years of age or those 65 years of age and over
   c. Population density per square mile or per square acre
2. Residential
   a. Number of dwellers in single-family housing, apartments, or condominiums
   b. Number of dwellers in public housing projects or substandard housing
   c. Density of occupants per room
   d. Number of homeowners vs. renters
3. Social disorganization
   a. Delinquency petitions per 1,000 youths
   b. General crime rate
   c. Number of recipients of welfare or Aid to Dependent Children
4. Social status
   a. Average income range
   b. Occupation
   c. Educational level
5. Religious affiliation
   a. Percentage Southern Baptist
6. Ethnic background
   a. Number of whites, blacks, Hispanics, etc.

The factors comprising the resources index can include any of the following examples:

1. Recreation areas
   a. Acreage of neighborhood recreation sites per 1,000 persons (or some other population/acreage standard)
2. Recreation facilities
   a. Number of sports facilities per 1,000 persons
   b. Number of swimming pools per 1,000 persons
   c. Number of any facility type per any population standard
3. Personnel
   a. Number of recreation centers with one or more full-time staff per 5,000 persons
   b. Number of playground leader hours per 1,000 children per summer
4. Program
   a. Number of tennis classes per 1,000 youths between the ages of 7 and 12
   b. Number of any program type per any population standard number

5. Monies
   a. Expenditures per capita
   b. Amount of grant money earmarked for following year

Other research methods need to be used to gather the data required by the above examples. For instance, factors of the social index could be defined by a trip to the library or planning department; factors of the resource index could be learned through the inventory method.

After the program planner has selected and defined the appropriate factors for both the social and resource indexes, a comparison of the indexes will yield a priority of need. The general formula used to determine this comparative priority of need is represented in Fig. 3-1. The formula subtracts the social index from the resource index to equal the need index. When the recreation resources are greater than the social conditions, the result will be a positive number. On the other hand, when the social factors are greater than the resource factors, a negative number will result and the comparative need will be greater. Let us rethink this relationship by studying a simplified example.

Let us suppose we have just received some additional program monies earmarked for youth programming. We want to determine which of four specific neighborhoods in our community needs more or better recreation programming the most. Suppose for each neighborhood we research these resource factors: (1) number of recreation programs for ages 7 to 16; and (2) number of full-time program staff per 1,000 persons between the ages of 7 and 16. On the other side of the formula, for each neighborhood suppose we research these social factors: (1) juvenile delinquency rate (measured by number of arrests for those aged 7 to 16); and (2) median family income. The results of our research are shown in Table 8. Next, let us rank the data, awarding a score of 4 to the highest and a score of 1 to the lowest. Therefore for juvenile delinquency, neighborhood *A* is ranked number 4 and neighborhood *B* is ranked number 1. The rankings for each neighborhood and for each factor are represented within parentheses in Table 8. Then we correlate the numerical rankings separately with the need index formula presented in Fig. 3-1 for each neigborhood. For neighborhood *A*, for example, the formula is as follows:

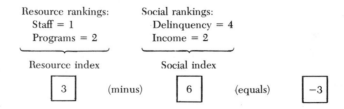

Resource rankings: Social rankings:
 Staff = 1   Delinquency = 4
 Programs = 2   Income = 2

Resource index   Social index

 | 3 | (minus) | 6 | (equals) | −3 |

Thus for neighborhood *A* we derive a comparative need index of −3. When the rankings for resource and social factors are likewise added and then applied to the

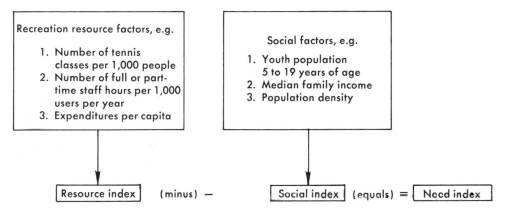

Fig. 3-1 *Formula for determining comparative priority of need.*

Table 8 *Sample results of research in example of comparative need index*

	Neighborhood			
	A	**B**	**C**	**D**
Social factors				
Delinquency rate	32 (4)	5 (1)	28 (3)	19 (2)
Median income	$9,400 (2)	$12,000 (3)	$8,500 (1)	$22,050 (4)
Resource factors				
Number full-time staff per 1,000 youths	2 (1)	3 (2)	5 (4)	4 (3)
Number recreation programs for youth	19 (2)	21 (3)	18 (1)	22 (4)

formula, a comparative need index can be calculated for each neighborhood. When this is done for our example, we find that neighborhood $A = -3$, neighborhood $B = +1$, neighborhood $C = +1$, and neighborhood $D = +1$. Therefore in our sample community it is obvious that neighborhood A has the most urgent need for program funds and services at this time, and in the planning process the youth of this neighborhood should be given first consideration.

Although the comparative need index has certain philosophical and conceptual limitations, its use in determining comparative priorities is worthy of the program planner's consideration.

A note on sampling

It would be ideal if the planner could ask every resident of the program services community what his or her recreation needs and problems are, but such a procedure is economically and logistically prohibitive. Unless the program planner is working with a small group, it is almost impossible to examine every member because of numbers, distribution in the community, and time limitations. In most research situations the planner must be content with looking at only a part of the whole; that part of the whole is called a *sample* of the population. When the planner asks questions of a sample to make judgments of need or priority for an entire population, the mathematical realm of sampling enters the picture.

Therefore in research methods such as the questionnaire great care must be given to the selection of the sample and its size. If there is any particular aspect of step 1 in the planning process that is usually beyond the knowledge and skill of the recreation program planner, it is sampling. This procedure is the job of a trained statistician. But the program planner should not despair. Help is available.

Many universities and research centers have research laboratories that offer assistance to practitioners as part of their community services. If they do not conduct the research themselves, they usually offer free or inexpensive assistance to agencies undertaking the project. Commercial marketing research firms, which charge a fee, are also available to assist with or completely conduct the survey type of research required in step 1. Also, if an agency has hired a planning consultant, he or she will have access to research technicians. Finally, there are some very good library references on sampling techniques, but this approach is often tedious for the program planner.

Samples and the need for validity and reliability in their selection can be maintained only by someone skilled in sampling techniques. Knowing the difference between what the program planner can do on his or her own and what requires the supervision of a sampling expert is the key to effective determination of constituency need.

Defining the planning task

The real needs of the program population, which are always subject to change, are seldom systematically and periodically investigated by current practitioners in the recreation field. The great challenge is to ask the right questions and relate the answers to program design. Even the most modest research program, based on any of the methods discussed in this chapter, could help a program services agency provide better service.

This is the effort of step 1 of the rational planning process: What is the problem or area of need? Problems to be solved or needs to be satisfied must be isolated, and a priority must be established to indicate which problems or needs are most critical. To do this, the planner must know how to gather the facts that are relevant and realistic to the planning situation; to take into account varying viewpoints; and to ultimately define the planning task. The planner's most serious decision, and perhaps major contribution to recreation programs, is what may be called the formulation or definition of the planning task. Everything else in program planning follows from this decision. Ideally the definition of the planning task must be as free of speculation, bias, and assumptions as possible. The need to draw on as much relevant and accurate information as possible cannot be overemphasized.

At the outset of planning it is important to put the definition of the planning task in writing. This keeps the planner on the proper course and helps to keep the focus clear for the remaining steps in planning. Some examples of statements of planning tasks follow:

1. Although adequate funds are being spent on recreation center programs, adults have been reluctant to participate.
2. The local school district has just converted to a year-round school schedule that causes the YMCA summer day camp program to be unused.
3. The city council of a small community has just allocated additional monies for senior citizen recreation program services.
4. The wave of vandalism in the county park has not only destroyed valuable and irreplaceable areas and facilities but also caused participation in park programs to decrease dramatically.
5. The aquatics director has made it clear to this summer's staff that the boating program should be more exciting and challenging to attract more participants.
6. Because of increased neighborhood violence, the parents of the members of Girl Scout Troop 197 have requested that the weekly meetings be 1 hour longer than usual so that they have time to pick their children up after work instead of allowing them to walk home.

CONCLUSION

Planning begins because there is a complaint, tension, disagreement, dissatisfaction, bright idea, conflict, suffering, need for choice, a bill enacted by a legislative body, some combination of these, or a dream. As these actions and feelings are researched and their rationales are formulated, the planner emerges with a statement of the planning task.

Armed with a problem statement, which is the result of the process of verifying and stating the issue, concern, problem, or need, the planner moves into the process of defining program objectives. To know that a program is the right one to select, the planner needs something to measure it against: objectives. In general, an accurately defined planning task leads to accurately chosen objectives.

References

Bannon, J.J. *Leisure resources: Its comprehensive planning.* Englewood Cliffs, N.J.: Prentice-Hall, 1976.

Bishop, D.W., & Witt, P.A. Sources of behavioral variance during leisure time. *Journal of Personality and Social Psychology,* 1970, *16,* 352-360.

Byerts, T.O., & Teaff, J.D. Social research as a design tool. *Parks & Recreation,* 1975, *10:1,* 34-36, 62-66.

Chase, D.R., & Cheek, N.H. Activity preferences and participation: Conclusions from a factor analytic study. *Journal of Leisure Research,* 1979, *11:2,* 92-101.

Cheek, N.H., & Burch, W.R. *The social organization of leisure in human society.* New York: Harper & Row, 1976.

Clark, R.N., Hendee, J.C., & Campbell, F.L. Values, behavior, and conflict in modern camping culture. *Journal of Leisure Research,* 1971, *3:2,* 143-159.

De Boer, J.C. *Let's plan: A guide to the planning process for voluntary organizations.* Philadelphia: Pilgrim Press, 1970.

Delbecq, A.L., Van de Ven, A.H., & Gustafson, D.H. *Group techniques for program planning: A guide to Nominal Group and Delphi Processes.* Glenview, Ill.: Scott, Foresman, 1975.

Dishon, R.L. Inside the workers' tavern. *San Francisco Examiner,* March 21, 1975.

Duncan, D.J. Leisure types: factor analyses of leisure problems. *Journal of Leisure Research,* 1978, *10:2,* 113-125.

Granzin, K.L., & Williams, R.H. Patterns of behavioral characteristics as indicants of recreation preferences: A canonical analysis. *Research Quarterly,* 1978, *49:2,* 135-145.

Igo, A.J. *Recreation research mail survey techniques: Effects of self-administration and nonresponse.* Unpublished master's thesis, Michigan State University, 1971.

Kass, R.A., & Tinsley, H.E. Leisure activities and need satisfaction: A replication and extension. *Journal of Leisure Research,* 1978, *10:3,* 191-202.

Le Masters, E.E. Social life in a working-class tavern. *Urban Life and Culture,* 1973, *2,* 27-52.

London, M., Crandall, R., & Fitzgibbons, D. The psychological structure of leisure activities, needs, people. *Journal of Leisure Research,* 1977, *9:4,* 252-263.

Michelson, W. Discretionary and nondiscretionary aspects of activity and social contact in residential selection. *Society and Leisure,* 1973, *5,* 29-53.

Miles, R.G. *Caucasian, Negro and Mexican American attitudes toward recreation program elements within a metropolitan parks and recreation department.* Unpublished master's thesis, North Texas State University, 1976.

Mobley, T.A., Light, S.S., & Neulinger, J. Leisure attitudes and program participation. *Parks & Recreation,* 1976, *11:12,* 20-22.

Murphy, J.F., & Howard, D.R. *Delivery of community leisure services: An holistic approach.* Philadelphia: Lea & Febiger, 1977.

O'Connor, C.A. *A study of personality needs involved in the selection of specific leisure interest groups.* Unpublished doctoral dissertation, University of Southern California, 1970.

Orthner, D.K. *Toward a theory of leisure and family interaction.* Paper presented at Pacific Sociological Association Annual Meeting, March 1974.

Shivers, J.S. *Essentials of recreation services.* Philadelphia: Lea & Febiger, 1978.

Tinsley, H.E., Barrett, T.C., & Kass, R.A. Leisure activities and need satisfaction. *Journal of Leisure Research,* 1977, 9:2, 110-120.

Toffler, A. *Future shock.* New York: Bantam Books, 1970.

U.S. Department of Commerce, Bureau of the Census. *Statistical abstract of the United States.* Washington, D.C.: U.S. Government Printing Office, 1979.

U.S. Department of the Interior. *The recreation imperative.* Washington, D.C.: U.S. Government Printing Office, 1974.

Wendling, R.C. Mail questionnaires: Are they dependable? *Parks & Recreation,* 1980, *15:*3, 53-54.

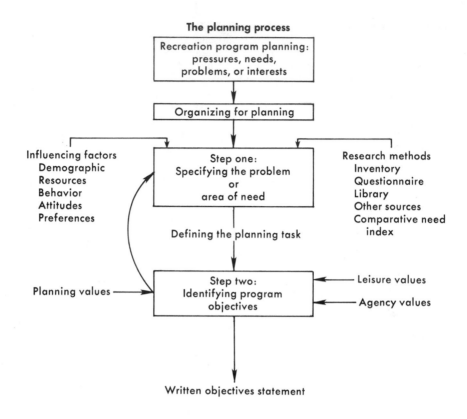

The planning process

Chapter 4

STEP 2

Identifying program objectives

The game of hopscotch began in ancient cultures as a portrayal of the symbolic act of advancing one's soul through a labyrinth, represented respectively by the stone and the design of the game course. For ancient players this game symbolized the effort and goal of life. Later, in Christian cultures, the game design was elongated to resemble the layout of a basilica. Then pushing the stone meant striving toward paradise (Fontana, 1978).

In ancient India chess was first played with four kings. Later the game spread to medieval Europe and came under the dual influence of reverence for the Virgin and courtly love. As a result, two of the kings were changed to queens, and the queens became the most powerful playing pieces in the game. Meanwhile the kings were limited to the quasi-passive role of figureheads (Fontana, 1978).

As these examples show, there is, and always has been, a strong relationship between recreation and the major social institutions: work, religion, family, and education. It is important to understand that the relationships among these social institutions have changed considerably, particularly during the past 80 years. At the turn of the twentieth century recreation was not recognized as a separate, distinguishable institution in American society. At that time the family assumed the prime responsibility for giving family members their play orientations, opportunities, equipment, and space. Although today the family remains the center of a child's recreation experience, society has taken on a greater responsibility for providing programs, facilities, equipment, and instruction for community members. With this increased responsibility comes a need for greater attention to values. Recreation professionals should be asking themselves: What programs should we be planning? How can we best meet the needs of our constituency? What societal, moral, or political values should be reflected in our program objectives?

To date the recreation services profession has been guided by principles, values, and practices initiated during the formative years of the American recreation movement. Today there is doubt about the relevance of these values in light of sociopolitical and technological changes that have left some recreation planners numb. Yet because of the new stature the recreation service field has achieved in the United

States, the practitioner, the educator, the student, and the participant must have meaningful guidelines to direct program services. These guidelines must be founded on sound premises of leisure. Such guidelines are called *objectives*. Adhering to the definition of the planning task established in planning step 1, program objectives need to reflect the philosophical values of planning itself, of leisure, and of the sponsoring agency. Before concentrating on the production of program objectives, let us first consider the effects of planning, recreation, and agency values.

Values

Opinions, beliefs, choices, and values are in the forefront in recreation program planning. Just as the planner cannot escape the matter of preference, there can be no rationality in recreation programs without decisions about merit. The concern is with values: what is most important, how needs are to be regarded, what sacrifices are justified for what objectives, and whose prerogatives are to be protected. *Values* are defined as patterns of behavior and beliefs we hold important to our way of life (Murphy, 1975, p. 127). Values are ideas of how reality ought to be.

Leisure expression is a part of our value structure; therefore the recreation activities the planner chooses to provide for a constituency result from that value structure. Today, as rapid changes are taking place in our society, new and fundamental issues about values are being raised. As a result, recreation services are being expected to provide new human experiences and alternative sources of life fulfillment. Leisure is being viewed as representing the whole life of a person.

Accordingly, recreation service agencies need to reflect current societal values by restructuring their program plans to recognize the importance of preference decisions. In planning recreation programs the planner deals with dynamic and sometimes conflicting values as he or she tries to determine what future conditions (objectives) the constituency wants and needs. At all stages of planning the issue of participant need must be confronted and weighed against current values.

When the planner advances to step 2 in the planning process—identifying program objectives—he or she must be aware of and accept the constant interweaving of the values of planning, recreation, and the sponsoring agency.

Values in planning

Planning is choosing. It is choosing that is reflected against research, evaluation, and feedback. The planner must constantly make assumptions about the future, such as the priority of agency policies, the maximum price to be paid for achieving objectives, the wishes of the public, and the criteria for measuring the achievement of objectives. Planning is a practice that openly invites the examination and debate of political, moral, and social values.

Even in rational planning the planner cannot act solely as a technician. The concept of values may seem out of place in a process that emphasizes analytical skills and rationality; planning is supposed to be as objective as possible. Yet values are critical in all planning because planning is a process of making social choices. Values enter into the planning process in several ways. They may be introduced to or reflected in the planning process through:

1. The planner
2. The constituency group
3. The way problems and needs are defined
4. The envisioning of the larger environment in which needs occur
5. The decision making involved in choosing the specific program plan

The planner is listed first because he or she represents the chief source of values in the planning process. The professional values to which the planner is committed, as well as the technical competence he or she claims, bring to the planning process predetermined values that affect plan choices. The program consumers also reflect their values in the planning process through their opinions of what reality ought to be. This is particularly true if their participation in the planning is actively solicited. Even the fulfillment of planning step 1—the type of research the planner chooses, the population data chosen as relevant, and the definition of the area of need—reflects the planner's values. Society's philosophy of and attitude toward such universal concerns as leisure, work, and morality bring values into the planning process; their role in the outcome cannot be ignored. If we as a society value "open space" or "freedom of space," for example, this will be reflected in planning choices. And, finally, decision making itself, which is inherent in each step of rational planning, involves making value-laden choices.

Along with the realization that planning reflects current values, the planner needs to recognize his or her resulting responsibility. The planner needs some basic planning guidelines to carry out this responsibility successfully. Although it is doubtful that any set of planning guidelines could cover all possible cases and their circumstances, the following list presented by Kahn (1969, pp. 104-106) is instructive and merits attention:

1. *The principle of impartiality.* There should be no prior specification of groups or persons who will receive greater planning attention, unless the research of step 1 advocates it. Discriminatory treatment of some portions of the constituency, either positively or negatively, only because they are the people that they are has no place in responsible recreation program planning.

2. *The principle of individuality.* Values are to be assessed as having their primary locus in the individual. Program planning should be directed at the needs of the individual and not at the needs of the agency, the city, or the corporation. This attention to serving the individual (even in commercial recreation) also mandates flexibility in dealing with individual differences.

3. *The principle of "maximin."* This principle advocates that planners strive to

upgrade the planned services for those with the least rather than extend to greater achievement the planned services for those who have the most. In other words, the achievement of a program is appraised by its minimum (or lowest) level of success, not by the height of its peaks.

4. *The principle of distribution.* This principle dictates that the more people who have a good thing, the better. It is that aspect of democratic philosophy that gives weight to the majority: we can never have too many enjoying a particular good.

5. *The principle of continuity.* No merit is attached to a break with established patterns and practices merely because it is a break. However innovative program changes are, their worth lies in the substance of the changes.

6. *The principle of autonomy.* Planning is to do for people only what people cannot do for themselves. This is another component of basic democratic theory.

7. *The principle of urgency.* The rate of progress toward planning objectives is to be maximized. The attention in planning should be toward the future, but only after dealing with present needs.

Careful attention to such planning guidelines can sensitize the planner to the possible implications of programs being planned and guide the planner in interpreting the complexity of values that enter the planning process. Professionals in recreation program planning have a responsibility to plan with wisdom, fairness, continuity, propriety, and urgency.

Values in recreation

In addition to the values inherent in the process of planning, the planner must recognize the values held sacred in the recreation service field itself. These values determine what recreation is expected to do for people, what recreation behavior and enjoyment are supposed to be like. Does the recreation professional think that recreation's value lies in its ability to entertain, to instruct, to relax, or to challenge the participant? Or is recreation's value viewed as holistic; that is, as meeting the total social, psychological, and physical needs of human beings? What about deviant behavior—such as drugs, illegal gambling, vagrancy, and prostitution? Is it recreational? What are good, effective, and worthwhile recreational pursuits, and what are not? The way the professional sees recreation's role in reality and the way the participant sees it will have a strong impact on the program services provided by recreation agencies.

For example, it is expected that in the United States leisure-oriented life-styles will become more common in the years ahead, as people begin to attach a greater value to the contribution recreation can make to their life rhythm. Recreation service agencies will need to reflect this change by broadening the base of service delivery, by incorporating a multidimensional approach, and by accommodating more varied life-styles. But in the meantime American leisure rhetoric is still rooted in the virtues of hard work and occupational achievement rather than those of contemplation, self-expression, and leisure. As a result, recreation pursuits reflect these values: games should have winners, craft projects should be completed, and recreation should be active. This prevailing value system has had a profound effect on the organization and management of recreation programs. This can be verified by studying the following list of recreation program guidelines gleaned from several respected texts in the field:

1. *Skill levels.* Recreation programs should have an interrelationship and allow the participant to progress from one level to another.
2. *Participation.* Recreation programming should be organized so that maximum involvement is possible for all.
3. *Available resources.* Recreation programs should be designed to use all facilities and areas available.
4. *Democracy.* Recreation programs must be geared to promote the values of a democratic society.
5. *Variety and balance.* Recreation programs should entail balance and variety both in type and in organizational form.
6. *Appropriateness.* Recreation programs should be compatible with the economic, social, and physical abilities and potentials of the participants.
7. *Leadership.* Recreation programs should be conducted and supervised by competent, adequately trained leadership.

Beyond these well established recreation program goals is the increasing attention being devoted to recreation's main value: the fostering of overall human development. Recreation has always been recognized for its ability to promote each person's potentialities as a unique and whole individual. Recreation is valued for its role in the development of positive self-image, self-respect, and relationships with others. Therefore recreation programs must be seen in their totality—a totality in which the participant can explore and take advantage of opportunities for human development, growth, and self-fulfillment. This is why another program guideline should be added to the above list.

8. *Human development.* Recreation programs should seek to develop people emotionally, physically, intellectually, socially, and spiritually.

Recreation service personnel should be aware of the total individual and give full consideration to how each person can be fulfilled at his or her own level of development.

Values in recreation agencies

In addition to planning values and recreation philosophy values, the values of sponsoring agencies are interwoven and reflected in the determination of program objectives. These values are frequently labeled *agency policies, service delivery models,* or *administrative objectives.* Whatever the label, these officially established agency values govern all agency operations and ultimately specify program decisions.

They have been stated in many ways. National organizations in the recreation field have issued formal documents outlining the social objectives or value systems that ought to underlie the provision of recreation services. National conferences and meetings have drawn up statements of national recreation and park priorities. Individual communities and agencies have developed similar policy statements and documents. Typically, recreation agency annual reports state policies in at least one of the following areas:

1. To enhance the quality of life
2. To provide a balance between the environment and people
3. To meet the interests and needs of the constituency

Such formal statements of values or policies are both administratively important (to guide day-to-day operational decisions and staff functioning) and philosophically important (to clarify the agency's position to others and express the basic conviction of the agency). Policies are usually adopted by the governing board of the agency and, if well devised and kept up to date, should serve as the foundation for the administration of the agency. An agency should have policies governing every aspect of its operation, including administration, finances, public relations, personnel, program, and maintenance. These policies are normally written down in the form of a policy manual. In some cases a policy manual may contain the most minute details of administrative practice.

Policies, like any value decisions, are reversible. When agency philosophy or circumstances change, so do (and should) policies. Many times policies are changed to allow a more flexible course of action. In some cases special policies must be developed to deal with fluid problems and unanticipated emergencies. Because of the need to keep agency operations flexible and to be creative in problem solving, such policies rarely are recorded in policy manuals. Nonetheless they continue to influence the establishment of program objectives.

The dominant value system of this country has been a definite influence on the policies of recreation and park agencies. For example, typically agencies have used a direct service approach to service delivery; this approach involves a commitment to provide leadership, facilities, programs, and equipment *for* participants. Such agency policies have been to assume responsibility for determining which programs will be provided, for which constituency, when and where they will take place, and even with what stance. According to this general policy, recreation agencies establish the overall basis for determining and implementing a series of program opportunities that they hope will facilitate recreation behavior. To date, this direct service policy has been the dominant delivery method in recreation. As Murphy and Howard (1977, p. 105) have stated:

> [the direct service approach] typically has resulted in the operation of leisure service programs on a chain-link fence philosophy. This facility oriented concept views leisure

service personnel to be primarily concerned with surveillance of the grounds or operation of the recreation center, community center, or playground; developing a master program plan for the facility; assuring superiors and the community that compliance with rules, safety and proper use of facilities is being met; and coordination of maintenance activities of the facilities.

Murphy and Howard offer an alternative service delivery policy that is on the other end of a continuum from the direct service approach. They term this policy the *enabling, referral-coordinated approach.* The opposite of a direct approach, this policy "recognizes the agency's commitment to serve as a catalyst and assist people to implement their own desires and interests through programs and facilitate their needs through a comprehensive service offering" (p. 105). This policy emphasizes the agency's role as an offerer of recreation opportunities rather than a provider of prepackaged activities. Table 9 illustrates the program delivery policy continuum. All recreation agencies have policies that lie at some point on this continuum.

The direct service approach determines, or makes assumptions about, the constituency's recreation needs and interests and then makes available ready-to-use programs and facilities. The enabling approach, on the other hand, recognizes a broader, more holistic responsibility and helps people to implement and satisfy their own desires within the network of human activity. Most agencies tend to be located at the extremes of the program delivery policy continuum. Recreation agencies usually have employed the direct service approach, but recently there has been much debate on varying the approach to make program delivery more responsive to the times and to the constituency.

For the program planner this policy debate remains an important one. Do the

Table 9   *Changing policies in program services delivery*

Direct service approach ⟶		Enabler, facilitator service approach
Present service delivery model	**Shifting service delivery model**	**Possible future service delivery model**
Measurement assessed in terms of attendance	Individualization of activities	Self-determinism
Standardized recreation programs	Diversification of programs	Agency-nurtured individual potentialities, allowing each
Facility orientation	Serving people where they are	individual to find own life
Recreation is expression of earned, unobligated time; a	Psychological-personal time recreation is an expression of	solution—in work and leisure
relief from dissatisfaction	self; positive, reaffirmation	Recreation occurs when one
Leader directed and organized activities and programs	of internal needs, inner satisfaction	feels it exists
	Self-initiated activities and programs	Fostering of spontaneity, autonomy

Adapted from Murphy, J.F. *Recreation and leisure service: A humanistic perspective.* Dubuque, Iowa: William C. Brown, 1975, p. 95.

agency's official policies reflect the determined needs of the participants and the context of the broader society within which they operate? Is it more realistic for the agency to be providing recreational opportunities for people, or should the agency be helping them provide for themselves? I view this policy discussion as one that will require increasing attention from professionals in the future.

The next planning step: establishment of objectives

Armed with an understanding of the impact planning, recreation, and agency values have on recreation program planning, the planner is now ready to move on to step 2: identifying objectives. Once the area of needs has been specified (step 1), it is possible to adopt specific objectives in response to it. Schematically (see diagram at beginning of this chapter) it is simple to describe the development of objectives as a direct linear descendant of the definition of the planning task. Following formulation of the planning task, the program planners, their advisory or planning committees, and sometimes the constituents involved consider objectives in light of the researched data obtained in step 1. They formulate and reformulate possible objectives until there is an outcome that represents a good "fit" in light of all these considerations. Depending on the specific planning situation, the identification of objectives can be an elaborate or a simple process.

What exactly are objectives? As defined by Theobald (1979, p. 24), *objectives* are observable, measurable, and attainable ideals or values to be sought. An objective is an aim or an end of action—a definite point to be reached. Usually expressed as a written statement, an objective is the desired program outcome.

There are two types of objectives that the recreation program planner formulates at this planning step. These are termed *program objectives* and *performance objectives.* It is important for the planner to distinguish between objectives that describe outcomes, or the measurable end products of the program (performance objectives), and those that define processes, or the means for accomplishing them (program objectives). Performance objectives are sometimes called *ends objectives*, while program objectives are also referred to as *means objectives.* Let us consider each objective type separately.

Program objectives are the means (materials, leaders, facilities, organization) used to operate the program. This type of objective also may be labeled *operating objective* or *production objective.* Program objectives involve three basic factors: leadership, facilities, and administration.

Leadership is the most important factor in operating a recreation program. To specify program objectives for leadership, the planner must consider the desired number of leaders, their job description, and minimum skill levels. For example, in planning a program for hospitalized children, the planner may state a program objective this way: This program plan has as an objective the use of two part-time staff persons who are trained in therapeutic recreation and have particular skills and interests in working with children.

Program objectives that consider areas and facilities are concerned with specifying the type and quality of physical resources necessary to operate the program. For example, in planning a program for inner-city youth, the planner may state a program objective this way: This program plan has as an objective the acquisition and use of a centrally located drop-in site that has a casual, noninstitutional atmosphere.

Finally, how the program is to be organized and administered is another of the planner's concerns in stating program objectives. This objective involves the technicalities of conducting a program, such as planning, organizing, directing, and controlling. A program objective for administration might be concerned with a deadline for the start of the program, the amount of involvement by agency directors or supervisors, the size of attendance, the degree of citizen participation, or the level of constituency independence in running the program. At this step in the planning process written statements of program objectives should be as precise and as definite as possible. Not only should they contain specific expectations for the conduct of leaders, facilities, and administration (the program process itself) but also definite expectations for the minimum level of accomplishment.

Performance objectives, on the other hand, are not concerned with the conduct or process of the program. Instead they are directed toward the outcomes of the program. In simple terms, program objectives reflect the amount of effort to be extended, and performance objectives detail the return expected on the investment of personnel, resources, and effort. Performance objectives are impact objectives. They focus on this basic question: What happened to the participant as a result of experiencing this program? Performance objectives (also called *behavioral* or *instructional objectives*) describe the behavior or attitude that the program's target constituency should demonstrate at its conclusion—some skill, attitude, or knowledge they did not have before.

Because performance objectives are relatively new to the recreation program planning field (program objectives such as attendance counts are more familiar), and because writing them correctly is critical for later evaluation, the following extended discussion is devoted to their construction.

Any performance objective must be stated in clear, specific, and measurable language. According to Theobald (1979, p. 109) there are four distinct parts to a well-defined performance objective:
1. It is stated in terms of the person(s) or thing involved.
2. It specifies a certain behavior that can be counted, verified, or otherwise measured.
3. It specifies the conditions under which the behavior must occur.
4. It specifies a minimum level of accomplishment or performance.

Theobald describes a good, specific performance objective in terms of good

RAY BELLAROSA

sentence structure: "Who is to do something relates to the subject of the sentence; what is to be done relates to the sentence verb; what was done relates to the sentence object; and how it is to be done relates to the modifier in the sentence" (p. 112). This implies that the planner's expectations for the program participants are satisfied in varying degrees, which can and should be measured. Performance objectives appropriate to the rational planning process therefore focus on a specific group and a specific action or behavior. Interpretations of such objectives usually are not variable or subjective.

The first part of a well-defined performance objective specifies the target (who or what) of the objective. In recreation program planning this could either be the participants (such as 12-year-olds, elderly residents of a nursing home, or college students) or the program (such as a recreation center summer program or day camp program). How specific this part of the statement of objective is depends on how much the planner knows about the planning task from step 1 of the planning process. Examples include:

1. The participant
2. The day care students
3. The elderly park users
4. The citizens of Charleston
5. The swimming class

The second part of a well-defined performance objective, according to Theobald, specifies what the program or participant will be able to do when mastery of the objective is demonstrated. Because it is impossible to see into a person's mind, the planner can only estimate the level of a participant's knowledge, skill, or enjoyment by observing some aspect of his or her behavior or performance. This behavior may be verbal or nonverbal. The participant may be asked to respond verbally, to demonstrate an ability to perform a certain skill, or to solve certain kinds of problems. Whichever method is used, the planner can only infer the state of behavior by observing performance. Thus the most important characteristic of a useful performance objective is that it identifies the kind of performance that will be accepted as evidence that the program (or participant) has achieved the objective.

For example, consider the following objective: "To develop an understanding of the operation of the ham radio." This statement does not tell what the program participant will be able to do when he or she demonstrates that the objective has been reached. The word that comes closest to describing what the planner wants the participant to be able to do is *understanding*. Yet is is doubtful that any two people would agree on the meaning of this term. A better way of stating this objective is: "When the participant completes the program, he or she will be able to identify by name each of the parts and controls located on a ham radio."

The way to write a performance objective that specifies behavior is to concentrate on what the participant is able to do to demonstrate that the objective has been achieved. Here is another example: "To develop an appreciation of music." What will the participant do to demonstrate achievement of this objective? As presently stated, the objective does not give the answer. Because this objective neither precludes nor defines any behavior, any of the following behaviors would be acceptable as evidence that the program participant "appreciates" music:

1. The participant sighs in ecstasy while listening to Mozart.
2. The participant buys a stereo system and $500 worth of albums.
3. The participant correctly answers 50 multiple-choice questions on the history of music.
4. The participant writes an eloquent and thorough essay on the meanings of five operas.
5. The participant says, "Oh, how enjoyable!"

I am not suggesting that "to develop an appreciation of music" is not an important or worthwhile objective. The point is that when an objective is stated so vaguely it fails to communicate the planner's intent. Performance objectives must specify the behavior or performance expected.

To communicate program intent, the planner will sometimes need to define the behavior further by stating the conditions for demonstrating mastery of the objective. Simply specifying the performance may not be enough to prevent misunderstanding. Stating the conditions under which the behavior is to occur is the third item in Theobald's four-part objective. Examples include:

1. Given a standard set of fishing tackle
2. Without the aid of matches
3. Within a 5-minute time limit
4. Without touching the side of the pool

Specifying the conditions under which the behavior should occur ensures that other behaviors will not be mistaken for the desired, intended behavior. Regardless of how they are presented, performance objectives will define the behavior more sharply if they contain words that describe the situation (conditions, allowances, or restrictions) in which achievement of the objective is accomplished.

Theobald's fourth requirement of a performance objective, which increases its preciseness, is the specification of a certain level of performance. If the planner specifies at least the minimum acceptable level of performance for each objective, a performance standard for evaluating the program is established. This criterion of acceptable performance will later be an accurate means of determining whether programs are successful.

To indicate what the acceptable level of performance will be, the planner adds words that describe the criterion of success. One of the most obvious ways of doing this is to specify a time limit when one is appropriate. "To be able to run the 100-yard dash within 14 seconds" includes a time limit performance criterion. Another way to specify a level of successful performance is to state the minimum acceptable skill. For example, the percentage of base hits, the number of holes-in-one, and the proportion of gates skied through all specify skill levels in various sport activities.

In summary, the planner can write clearer, more complete performance objectives by testing draft statements against the following questions:

- Does the statement of objective specify to whom or what (person or program) the objective is directed?
- Does the statement of objective describe what the person or program will be doing, what action or behavior is to occur?
- Does the statement of objective describe the conditions under which the person or program will be expected to demonstrate competence?
- Does the statement of objective indicate how the program or person will be evaluated? Does it describe at least the lower limit of acceptable performance?

For example, test the following statement of performance objective against the above four questions.

> The members of Girl Scout Troup 127 will be able to demonstrate fire-starting ability by starting three fires each with the use of one match per fire.

In planning step 2 the planner is concerned with suggesting appropriate objectives in response to a given concern or area of need. Objectives are shaped, on the one hand, by the needs they are designed to fill and, on the other hand, by the limitations of the available resources and the values of the agency or the planner. Although this text presents the establishment of objectives as following the definition of the planning task, the two steps are tightly connected and interrelated in the reality of planning; they are often done simultaneously.

In formulating specific, measurable program and performance objectives it is often helpful to develop a working pyramidal hierarchy of objectives, beginning with the broadest statement of intent and backing it up with a series of sub-objectives and sub-sub-objectives that become increasingly specific and thus more measurable. See Fig. 4-1 for an illustration of how the planner might use a pyramid type of thought process to establish both kinds of objectives. The intellectual process of continuing to reformulate basic statements of the planning task into increasingly specific objectives can yield measurable and usable statements of program intent. If necessary, sub-objectives and sub-sub-objectives may be formulated to narrow the field where program action is proposed. Indeed, planners have found that at this planning stage it is a good idea not to worry about precision or scope but instead to set down a broad statement of goals. Sub-objectives within the broader goal are then identified and set down. This procedure of setting down objectives within objectives can be continued until the desired degree of precision is obtained and working objectives are reached.

For example, consider this general performance objective: "Participants will become more knowledgeable about the application of democratic principles." To make this statement more specific and measurable, it could be worded this way: "At

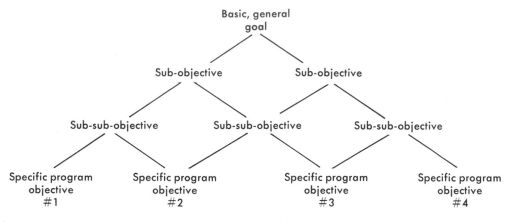

Fig. 4-1   *Deriving specific objectives.*

the end of the program the children will be able to select their game leaders through democratic means such as the vote." The success of meeting this more specific objective can now be measured. The sequence of developing objectives begins with a broad statement of goal or direction in which a recreation program planner wishes to move; this general goal is restated and restated to narrow the focus of the program intent. The examples found in Table 10 illustrate the difference between broad statements of goal or direction and specific, measurable statements of objectives.

There should be no guesswork in understanding what the planner's objectives are meant to be. Clarity in setting objectives is not rigidity but a necessary prelude to a smooth flow through the rational planning process. In stating the planning task in Chapter 3, a broad objective was incorporated into the definition of planning task itself. This was not unintentional, since any well-formulated definition of planning statement specifics at least one objective in its broad initial form. The requirement of specificity was not a concern during the first step as it is in the second.

To write, clarify, and rank program and performance objectives, the planner must also deal with the overall objectives of the recreation agency as stated in its official policies, the values and ethical standards of planning, and the broad societal goals of recreation. The planner must consider the many intangible variables that play a role in determining program and performance objectives. Many times these are unwritten or implicit policies that have been developed over the years and that are an inherent part of the agency or the profession. Although the value judgments, expertise, and opinions of all concerned are important in the establishment of pro-gram and performance objectives (and cannot be counted on to vanish during pro-gram planning), the strongest determinants must be analytical. The planner must aim

Table 10   *Examples of specific objectives*

Broad direction of program	Specific objectives
Program outcome	**Performance objectives**
To make children safe while in or near the water	Each first-grade child will be able to successfully complete the Red Cross Beginner Swimming course.
To enhance the quality of urban life	At the conclusion of the program, each participant will be able to identify flower species within a one-block radius of his/her home.
To encourage socialization among the psychiatric patients	The psychiatric patients will demonstrate interaction with others by conversing with another patient twice during the rest break of the bicycle trip.
To develop psychomotor skills for kindergarten children	Each child in the kindergarten class will be able to perform the skills of running, walking, skipping, and galloping in different directions.
Program operation	**Program objectives**
To increase the number of scouts in the Boy Scout Council	There should be a 10% increase in the number of Cub Scouts, an 8% increase in the number of Boy Scouts, and a 5% increase in the number of Explorer Scouts in this district in the next 2 years.
To provide adequate leadership for the program	The program will maintain a minimum of two staff persons, devoting at least 3 hours per week.

RAY BELLAROSA

for precision in setting objectives because this is the most imprecise yet most vital step in the rational planning process.

Objectives serve as standards of program success or failure. Vague and general objectives lead to vague and general evaluative conclusions that cannot be measured empirically. To reach meaningful, definitive conclusions about program success or failure, objectives must be clear, specific, and related to concrete outcomes that can be objectively recorded, measured, or observed. Without the opportunity for such empirical measurement, objectives serve no purpose.

One of the basic concerns of step 6 in program planning, evaluation, is the determination of whether a particular program is accomplishing what it was intended to do in the manner that was intended—that is, achieving its objectives. Determining whether a program's objectives have or have not been met provides an excellent chance for the program planner to look at the objectives themselves. It is possible that some objectives for a program have not been accomplished because the program leaders and participants did not identify them as their objectives. In such a case accurate program and performance objectives may not be developed until the evaluation step; then the evaluator would take the initiative in redefining or modifying the stated objectives. This relationship between objectives and evaluation is a reminder that the processes of planning and of evaluating programs must be considered as circular, each constantly supporting the other as new information on program effectiveness and efficiency is discovered and accumulated.

Programs without clearly defined objectives are impossible to evaluate. Yet recreation planners often implement activities without considering what they want to accomplish by them. This is a mistake. When program and performance objectives have been adequately determined, an evaluator needs only to gather the data necessary to determine whether or not the objectives have been met, and thus whether or not the particular program is successful. "Evaluating recreation programs without first knowing what the objectives are is as futile as trying to determine if someone has been successful in life without knowing what success means to that person" (Theobald, 1979, p. 109).

CONCLUSION

A program's objectives are written intentions about the desired outcome of the program and the desired means toward that outcome. They must be precise so that the program's success or failure can be measured. An objective is a statement of what the planner wants the program to accomplish. Once the planners, leaders, or administrators of recreation programs have determined what their specific objectives are, they have a foundation on which to base the important decisions that lie ahead in the program planning process. They can select from a vast assortment of activities those that are most likely to help achieve the objectives. They also can select the equipment, facilities, staff, and schedules that will allow the greatest potential for objective achievement. Therefore, in addition to providing the basis for later program evaluation, objectives provide the basis for deciding what activities and resources are required. The next step, therefore, is to explore the ways in which the program planner can select from the variety of activity types and forms and choose those arrangements that will best meet the objectives. The discipline of setting objectives and refining them lays the groundwork for good decision making.

References

Fontana, A. Over the edge: A return to primitive sensations in play and games. *Urban Life*, 1978, 7:2, 213-229.

Kahn, A.J. *Theory and practice of social planning.* New York: Russell Sage Foundation, 1969.

Murphy, J.F. *Recreation and leisure service: A hu-manistic perspective.* Dubuque, Iowa: William C. Brown, 1975.

Murphy, J.F., & Howard, D.R. *Delivery of community leisure services: An holistic approach.* Philadelphia: Lea & Febiger, 1977.

Theobald, W.F. *Evaluation of recreation and park programs.* New York: John Wiley & Sons, 1979.

The planning process

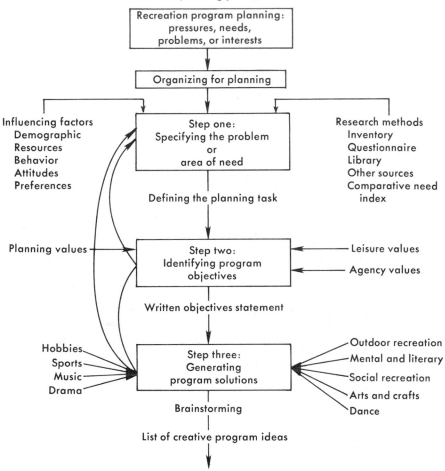

Recreation program planning:
pressures, needs,
problems, or interests

↓

Organizing for planning

Influencing factors
Demographic
Resources
Behavior
Attitudes
Preferences

Step one:
Specifying the problem
or
area of need

Research methods
Inventory
Questionnaire
Library
Other sources
Comparative need
index

Defining the planning task

Planning values

Step two:
Identifying program
objectives

Leisure values

Agency values

Written objectives statement

Hobbies
Sports
Music
Drama

Step three:
Generating
program solutions

Outdoor recreation
Mental and literary
Social recreation
Arts and crafts
Dance

Brainstorming

List of creative program ideas

Chapter 5

STEP 3

Generating program solutions

In the early 1960s the Boeing Aircraft Company conceived and projected a very large airplane to meet the anticipated needs of the 1970s and 1980s. The company's projection was based on a vast increase in air passenger and cargo traffic. Thus the Boeing 747, the first of the "jumbo jets," went into planning in August 1965, when a preliminary design group was established. Originally projected as a double-decked, larger version of the 707, the 747 went through 50 design variations on the drawing boards before the idea of a single-decked airplane was considered. The engineers then explored more variations of the single-decked version before deciding on the one that finally rolled off the assembly line on the last day of September 1968. After the design goal (a larger airplane) had been adopted, immense planning effort went into exploring all possible design alternatives. This exploration of alternatives is an important part of the planning process.

Now that the problems or areas of need have been specified in step 1 and the program objectives identified in step 2, the planner needs to find out what different kinds of programs are possible for meeting the results of these steps. Therefore step 3 of the planning process, generating program solutions, requires the most imagination, the most adeptness in associative thinking, and the most creativity. This step asks for any and all points of view to be placed on the "drawing board" for consideration. A later planning step (step 4) concentrates on such details as budgeting, scheduling, and staffing, but in step 3 it is necessary only to consider estimates of cost, constraints of time, and personnel requirements to develop useful and creative program ideas.

The concern of this planning step is creativity. The development and optimum use of a creative imagination are the keys to using knowledge successfully. The knowledge derived from creatively understood practical, everyday problems is the most beneficial knowledge available to the planner. Such knowledge is what links creativity and practice in a wholesome and dynamic manner (Bannon, 1980).

The challenge of this planning step is to combine good judgment (which oftentimes hampers novel and innovative ideas) with creative thinking. For some professionals in recreation and parks, judgment may actually take the place of imagination.

To them creative thinking is often thought of as the opposite of good judgment. This is both unfortunate and inaccurate. Creativity is the key to success in any profession, and recreation program planning is no exception. The ability to generate creative program alternatives to meet constituency needs and program objectives is a valuable professional skill. The ability to see possible program solutions from various angles, different viewpoints, and alternative sources is a skill in which recreation planners should receive training and practice.

For the recreation program planner to develop and maintain his or her own creative abilities and to encourage this in program staff or constituency-based planning groups, many times great odds must be faced. Agencies are often structured so that they inhibit creative thought. Rules and policies often exist because of tradition or habit, not because they provide for the most efficient operation; such restrictions can inhibit the creative thinker. In an agency the price of creative thinking can be high. The recreation professional who looks for new ways, suggests the untraditional, or otherwise "rocks the boat" may find that such innovation is not appreciated by either supervisors or colleagues. In general, agency philosophy and administrative practices have failed to emphasize a positive approach toward generating creative program ideas. And it shows: a close look at recreation and park programs across the United States reveals that many offerings are identical to those provided in the 1940s. The thesis that creative thought is the sole domain of the inventor, the artist, or the musician is no longer valid or desirable. As the 1980s unfold, and the planner is faced with new social problems, scarce dollars, changing values, and an accelerating pace of life, the ability to produce new ideas may become the planner's most important professional skill.

The agenda of program planning in step 3 is to generate and list all the program ideas that can possibly answer the objectives established in step 2. There are several means of doing this. They range from a simple reconsideration of the program topics offered previously to the more complex procedure of brainstorming. Brainstorming is a commonly used means of generating creative program alternatives. In brainstorming, ideas—new, old, unusual, different, similar—are listed as potential programs to be critiqued and implemented later. Because of the increasing use of brainstorming by recreation programmers, this chapter will give extensive attention to its use and operation.

Brainstorming

Brainstorming is a technique that is particularly useful in enabling a planner or group of planners to consider a wide range of possible solutions to a problem or ways of reaching an objective. In brainstorming sessions a group of persons (usually a small group) sit around a table and are presented with the statement of planning task and the program objectives. Then everyone is asked to say anything that comes to mind as a possible program solution. The group may face a pad of newsprint or a chalkboard where the program objective under consideration is written. During a set period of time (such as 10 minutes) a session leader writes down all the ideas as rapidly as they are spoken. The ground rules call for the ultimate use of imagination and creative thinking. No overt judgments are allowed at this point; no one is permitted to scoff at or applaud any idea that is suggested. No negative thoughts are encouraged. In listing the various ideas no consideration is given to such factors as feasibility or cost. The object is to stimulate thinking so that one idea may trigger another and many creative minds may respond to and build upon each other. Remember, the impractical ideas will be eliminated later.

Principles of brainstorming

Brainstorming is a way of producing more and better ideas than is possible when judicial evaluation is allowed to comment on creative imagination. It is simply a practiced technique that encourages a planner to stick out his or her neck so that new and novel program ideas can be produced. It asks the brain to "storm" for ideas with no limitations. Therefore judgment is suspended for a time so that ideas can flow freely. According to Bannon (1980), the basic precept of brainstorming is a principle known as deferred judgment. Deferred judgment, Bannon observes, alternates creative thinking and judicious thinking instead of applying both types simultaneously.

Bannon states that research has indicated that applying the principle of suspended judgment in brainstorming not only results in good ideas but also produces a greater quantity of ideas, and ultimately these ideas are of greater quality than those generated under more conventional means. By deferring judgment for the time being, the planner will have many more ideas from which to choose later, when judgment is applied. Quantity can yield quality in brainstorming. The greater the number of ideas generated, the greater the likelihood of coming up with new and potentially effective program alternatives.

Another key principle of group brainstorming is its multiplying effect. Even though brainstorming can be done alone, it is the combination with and improvement on the ideas of others that causes the technique to be so creative. In addition to contributing ideas of their own, brainstormers are urged to suggest how the ideas of others and themselves can be turned into better and new ideas, or how two or more ideas can be combined into still a newer, additional idea. This hitchhiking—one idea with another—often results in program alternatives that probably would not be thought of otherwise.

In summary, the major principles of brainstorming are:
1. *Deferred judgment.* Critical evaluation of ideas is postponed to allow the flow of creativity.
2. *Quantity breeds quality.* The more numerous the ideas suggested, the better the likelihood of achieving new and worthwhile program alternatives.

3. *Group thinking.* Combination and improvement of individual ideas are encouraged in group effort.

Setting up and conducting brainstorming sessions

The nature of the planning task and the program goals determines who should be asked to participate in a brainstorming session. Most of the literature on brainstorming advocates that the group consist of between 5 and 12 persons (however, with skilled leadership, effective sessions can be conducted with larger or smaller groups). Also, as mentioned earlier, the brainstorming method can even be used successfully by one planner if the proper precepts are applied.

The composition of the group should vary according to the nature of the planning task and the nature of the programming agency. Ideally it should include an assortment of those directly concerned with program planning and those participating in the program. Because the purpose of the session is for ideas to flow easily and naturally, the mixing of people of extremely diverse personality types should be avoided. Using a congenial mix of people avoids the danger that the session will focus on the differences among group members rather than on the problem itself. Ideally the brainstorming group should also be made up of persons of similar levels in the agency but with differing types of job descriptions. The presence of high-ranking supervisors sometimes can inhibit the free flow of ideas. Whatever the composition of the group, the emphasis should be on the contributions of participants with varied expertise and viewpoints.

The leader of the brainstorming session should be trained and practiced in advance to ensure success of the endeavor. The brainstorming literature also advocates that the session take place in a location different from the normal working environment. Such a setting can be more conducive to creativity and an uninhibited exchange of ideas. Brainstorming schedules should not call for marathon sessions. No more than 2 hours overall devoted to brainstorming is suitable. The mood of the session should be informal but serious. To ensure a free-wheeling yet productive atmosphere, the skill and role of the session leader are crucial. Room arrangement and participant seating also should be controlled to add to the serious yet creative nature of the occasion. Whatever the session leader thinks will enhance a group's cooperation, relaxation, and productivity should be done.

In coordinating and preparing for brainstorming the leader might find it useful to adhere to the following "to do" list adapted from Bannon (1980):

1. Review the statement of planning task and program objectives (planning steps 1 and 2) to ensure that there is adequate specificity and clarity.

2. Send a summary one-page memo to those selected to participate in the session. This memo outlines the background of the planning task, states the program objectives, and gives "starter" ideas of the type to be sought in the session. This memo should be sent with enough advance time to encourage participants to prepare.

3. Prepare a list of stimulus ideas or leads for idea generation for use in case the session becomes bogged down. (A list of idea-spurring questions is presented in the box below.) The leader may wish to list these on a blackboard or large sheet of newsprint for greater ease in encouraging the group toward creativity.

4. In the beginning of the session an orientation to the brainstorming method should be provided. This orientation should include the principles of brainstorming and a warm-up period on a hypothetical planning case. Warm-up sessions should be simple and last for no more than 2 minutes. Such questions as "What or how many uses can you brainstorm for an apple?" or "What various means can you brainstorm for two people to cross a river?" can often serve to warm the group up, as well as illustrate the principles of the methodology.

5. After the orientation and warm-up, the leader calls for program ideas that could satisfy the actual planning task. Only one idea should be offered by any one person at a time. The leader encourages group members to voice ideas that are directly sparked by a previous idea.

6. A group secretary should be appointed to write down all suggested program ideas. Some agencies have found it useful to tape-record brainstorming sessions as a backup to the list compiled by the secretary. Visual stimulation for participants is also attained if the essence of the idea suggestions is recorded on a blackboard or sheet of newsprint.

7. From time to time during the brainstorming session, the leader may need to ask idea-provoking questions if the session pace slows down, or refocus the participants on the planning task and program objectives if they stray from the subject.

IDEA-GENERATING QUESTIONS FOR BRAINSTORMING

1. *Put to other uses?* New ways to use as is? Other uses if modified?
2. *Adapt?* What else is like this? What other ideas does this suggest?
3. *Modify?* Change meaning, color, motion, sound, odor, taste, form, shape? Other changes?
4. *Magnify?* What to add? Greater frequency? Stronger? Larger? Plus ingredient? Multiply?
5. *Minify?* What to subtract? Eliminate? Smaller? Lighter? Slower? Split up? Less frequent?
6. *Substitute?* Who else instead? What else instead? Other place? Other time?
7. *Rearrange?* Other layout? Other sequence? Change pace?
8. *Reverse?* Opposites? Turn it backward? Turn it upside down? Turn it inside out?
9. *Combine?* How about a blend, an assortment? Combine purposes? Combine ideas?

Modified from Osborn, A.F. *Applied imagination.* New York: Charles Scribner's, 1963, pp. 229-285.

8. The leader concludes the brainstorming session by summarizing the nature and quantity of the ideas generated and thanking the participants for their contribution.

9. Postsession ideas can also be sought by seeing or phoning all participants the following day. Sometimes valuable ideas can be obtained in this way.

10. The secretary should prepare a neat listing of all the program ideas suggested during and after the brainstorming session; the list is then edited for clarity, and the various ideas are grouped according to logical categories.

The evaluation of these ideas and the subsequent selection of the best takes place as soon after the brainstorming session as possible. At this point the planner applies the judgment of ideas that was deferred during brainstorming. This is the topic of the next chapter and the task of step 4 of the planning process.

Recreation activity areas

The great variety of activities and endeavors that occupy the free time of people is usually referred to in the field as *recreation*. Indeed, the ever-expanding profession of recreation and park services is limitless, and the specific activity type and format are defined only by the imagination of the program planner. Because recreation covers a wide range of activity opportunities, and because of the varied backgrounds of people, agencies responsible for providing recreation program services have had to develop planned programs many times as broad as human interest itself. This is not meant to dismay the student planner but instead to encourage the creative use of the recreation activity media. Recreation activities may require differing skill levels, take place at different seasons of the year, have a complex or simple organizational structure, take place indoors or outdoors, require formal or informal participation, be highly competitive or passive and reflective, and be conducted with or without a leader.

Because of this variety, recreation professionals have found it necessary and desirable to catalog and measure recreation behavior into an activity set. Therefore it is common for the program planner to plan for the recreational experiences and the emotional states discussed in Chapter 1 around a recreation activity list. When you ask a person what he or she typically does for recreation, the answer is usually in terms of some set of specific activities. Participants generally do not see recreation as an attitudinal experience but rather as a specific activity. As a result, recreation planners have organized program services around sets of activities. But in order for the program services to be an efficient and effective contribution to the leisure consumer, the planner must not only understand the mechanics of activities but also watch for the result or meaning of participating in these activities.

Classifying the experiences that offer recreational meaning and value is a difficult task. The media are limitless, and the means of classification are arbitrary. For example, programs can be ordered according to: low organization/high organization; individual/group; active/passive; indoor/outdoor; or by age, skill level, cost, inherent activity characteristics, or season of the year (Pierce, 1980). The recreational activities programmed by the planner are currently classified by most recreation and park agencies according to a categorical grouping of activity types.

This classification, as used in this book, is portrayed in the following outline.

1. Sports and games
   a. Individual sports and games
   b. Dual sports and games
   c. Team sports and games
   d. Fitness and calisthenics
2. Hobbies
   a. Education
   b. Collecting
   c. Creative
3. Music
   a. Vocal
      (1) Performance
      (2) Listening
      (3) Instruction
      (4) Composition
      (5) Study/practice
   b. Instrumental
      (1) Performance
      (2) Listening
      (3) Instruction
      (4) Composition
      (5) Study/practice
4. Outdoor recreation
   a. Camping/outdoor living
   b. Nature-oriented activities
   c. Conservation
   d. High-risk activities/adventure
   e. Outdoor sports
5. Mental and literary recreation
   a. Reading
   b. Writing
   c. Speaking
   d. Analysis
   e. Study
6. Social recreation
   a. Parties
   b. Eating events
   c. Social dances
   d. Clubs
   e. Meetings
   f. Visiting/conversation
7. Arts and crafts
   a. Drawing and sketching
   b. Painting
   c. Sewing and needlecraft
   d. Jewelry making
   e. Leatherwork
   f. Weaving
   g. Printing
   h. Woodworking
   i. Paper
   j. Sculpture
   k. Candle making
   l. Model building
   m. Cooking/baking
   n. Photography
   o. Scrap crafts
   p. Pottery/ceramics
   q. Metal
8. Dance
   a. Folk
   b. Modern/interpretive
   c. Social/popular
   d. Acrobatic
   e. Tap
   f. Ballroom
   g. Ballet

h. Children's rhythms
i. Country/square
9. Drama
   a. Creative dramatics
   b. Film/television

c. Formal plays
d. Pantomime/mime
e. Puppetry/marionettes
f. Dramatic readings
g. Storytelling

This outline is what recreation professionals have come to label for planning communication purposes *recreation activity areas*. Although this classification cannot be all-inclusive, it at least sets a basis for discussing the planning process. A great deal of debate has raged in the recreation field about the "proper" nomenclature of recreation activities. Perhaps it is the very breadth of recreation opportunities that makes them elude "official" classification. Therefore for the past 60 years the professional literature has reflected a variety of means for categorizing recreation activity. The terms employed in this text represent a composite of the predominant forms found in the literature.

This book does not attempt to present the full range of activity types or format possibilities that could be offered to the program participant. Instead it focuses on planning and agency resource considerations, giving specific examples within each activity category, so that the program planner will have a better grasp of all the tools necessary for the effective and efficient provision of recreation program services. The intent here is to discuss each recreation program area in a manner that will enable the planner to judge, select, implement, and evaluate appropriate activities according to the planning task. (For additional information on specific recreation activities, see the bibliography in the appendix of this book.) In addition, it is assumed that those who actually lead the programmed activities have the necessary leadership knowledge and skill; this instruction is not within the scope of this text.

Sports and games

Growth in sports and recreational games, probably the single largest recreation program area, represents one of the most remarkable trends in recreation during the past several decades. As proof, it would be difficult to find one household that does not have at least one golf club, one basketball, one tennis racket, a pair of running shoes, or some other sport paraphernalia.

In terms of participation the sharpest increases have occurred in running, tennis, softball, and racquetball. Track, volleyball, golf, horseback riding, and skiing have also shown significant growth recently. Soccer, rugby, and ice hockey are currently booming at the local level in certain regions of the country. "New Games," which involve total group participation as well as noncompetitive game formats, recently have received enthusiastic programming attention in some recreation agencies. However, most Americans still support the vicarious enjoyment of spectator sports, with baseball and football being the most widely attended and viewed.

Because of the great popularity of sports and games, many recreation profession-

RAY BELLAROSA

als complain about the overemphasis on sport and athletic programming in recreation and park agencies. In modern society sport has many facets that lead to dispute and controversy. Sport is institutionalized, professionalized, commercialized, and organized to the extent that it often becomes difficult to distinguish between the various sport levels and arenas. For example, some people have difficulty in making the distinction between the conduct of play in the American and National Leagues of professional baseball and that of the Little League of recreational baseball.

Every evening millions of Americans arrive home from work, plop into their special chairs, and read the newspaper. Day after day front pages attack them with news of an approaching war, the demise of the dollar and the general sickness of the economy, the collapse of Western civilization, along with the possible extinction of the human race itself. Most readers skip such depressing news and turn straight to the sports page. What makes sport and game activities so engrossing for both the participant and the spectator? Why do all those millions of people watch the World Series on television? Why are recreation agencies being confronted with greatly increased requests for tennis courts, ball fields, golf courses, and other sports facilities? Why is membership in commercial athletic and fitness centers soaring? Tillman (1973, p. 86), offers an understanding of this phenomenon:

> Sports are the experience of challenge, man against animal, the elements or other men, with physical exertion its primary identifying characteristic. In some instances habit activates the participation, with sports as a substitute for survival activities, or as a reminder of the physically demanding life of our forefathers. Time and a new, less physical world are making sports the only means for adults to keep fit and healthy and to join the youth who have accepted sports as an important component of life.

Values   Program planners for recreation agencies are rarely involved in planning for professional or spectator sports. More frequently they are charged with the sports programming for the amateur participant—children and adults, you and me. Sports and games offer their highest potential for satisfying participant needs through physical activity. Muscles strengthen, reactions quicken, and heart rates improve as exercise and sport develop and keep healthy the human body. Team or group sport involvement adds the opportunity for social interaction, security, and a sense of belonging. The sense of belonging is strongest during highly competitive team play, whereas social interaction is most prevalent in less competitive situations. The social interaction value of sport and game programs can be illustrated by the "New Games" movement. Originating in San Francisco during the mid-1970s, New Games encourages group cooperation rather than competition among players. The emphasis is on total group involvement and enjoyment rather than winning.

Sport offers the opportunity for fulfilling dominance, creativity, or mental activity needs. The team captain, the individual athlete, and the coach have a high potential for experiencing these values because of the leadership roles they assume.

Sports and games also contribute toward the socialization of children and young adults into society and its institutions. Current research (Kando, 1980) views sport as a microcosm in which learning, rehearsal, and preparation for adulthood or the real world take place and recognizes it as an important aspect of human development.

Because sports offer the participant a physical and emotional challenge sometimes made keener by competition, they are notorious for providing an opportunity to "let off steam." By engaging in physically vigorous competitive play, many individuals can express their aggressive or combative tendencies. People seem to need to compete with others, the environment, and themselves; playing to win seems unavoidable in modern society. Many times this natural emphasis on winning results in overemphasis at the expense of other important values for the participant. The cathartic value of sports can also be extended to those who observe rather than participate in sports. For its spectators, sport has often been said to be a legitimate outlet for the pent-up frustrations that could otherwise lead to serious violence.

The place of competition in sports and games is well established. The success of competitive sports programming depends on the soundness of the planning and the ability of leaders, coaches, and officials to maintain proper emphasis on all values of sport for the participant. This presents a challenge to the program planner; the task calls for selecting from an extremely large offering those activities and formats most appropriate for the constituency.

Planning considerations   Planning and operating procedures for sport and game activities vary with local conditions, different agencies, geographic location, and type of activity. Staff, budget, and facility parameters also help to define the planning of sports programming. The widespread interest and participation in sports make its program planning a difficult task. It is important for the planner to remember that the atmosphere in the recreation setting should promote physical well-being, fun, and fellowship. Through sports, recreation planners should seek to open the door to joyous physical activity.

The values of sports, such as the social interaction and sense of belonging that come with team participation, should be reflected in planning. Assignment of staff and facilities, as well as budget allocations, should include consideration of sport participation values. These values can be maximized by adherence to the following planning principles.

First, sports programs should consist of various activity levels. Activities should not be designed for only the highly skilled, nor should the individual participant be slighted. (Because of the demands for numerical participation, team activities are often easier to plan.) If one skill level is overemphasized, other levels will automatically reflect a diminished value. This principle requires that the professional effectively reflect the constituency served by matching planning efforts to all ability levels. It suggests that sports programming select activities within the playing ability of the participant by making lead-up skill progression available.

The second planning principle advocates that athletic programming reflect a wide selection of lifetime sports. The American hierarchy of sports—football, baseball, and basketball—is really useful only for the school-age participant. When the participant reaches adulthood, it becomes difficult to continue in such sports because of lack of facilities and opportunities. Lifetime sports such as swimming, tennis, bowling, cross-country skiing, badminton, bicycling, jogging, and archery offer continuing opportunities for participation instead of forcing the player into the vicarious role of spectator when his or her "career" is over.

The third planning principle focuses on safety. The nature of sports—pitting oneself against unpredictable obstacles and placing oneself in physical jeopardy—calls for the organization of experiences according to sound health and safety practices. What practices? The rules of the sport or game should be consistently followed, and sport or game play should be overseen by responsible officials. Athletic facilities should be inspected constantly for safety hazards, and these hazards should be corrected before play is allowed to resume. The need for continuous care and maintenance of equipment and facilities is paramount, not only for safety but also for a better and fuller enjoyment of the sport activity. Sandlot ball and street athletics have produced thousands of crippled veterans. If controls such as rules, officials, and hazard-free facilities are lacking, the health of the participant will be in jeopardy.

Types of sport and game activities The categories below indicate the broad scope of the sports and games program area and help to refine our thinking about each sport activity for planning purposes. No attempt is made to include every possible activity under each category; the limits depend on the creativity of the program planner. In selecting from the categories below, the planner should pay close attention to the results of planning steps 1 and 2.

Traditionally sports are categorized according to how many people are needed to make the performance of an athletic or mental skill into a game. Most sport skills can be practiced by an individual alone, but the greatest potential for need fulfillment lies in participation with others.

Individual sports and games are those activities in which a single individual can find a game situation possible. A game takes place when a player uses his or her skill according to specified rules in overcoming physical or mental obstacles to achieve certain goals. In this category an opponent is unnecessary; the challenge is created by a target, goal, or previous record. This is not to say that any of the sports classified as individual are exclusively individual, only that they can be engaged in as a game experience by one player. Refer to the box on the opposite page for specific activity suggestions under the heading of individual sports and games.

A wise and creative program planner can scale any sports activity up or down the range from individual to team play. Individual sports play is usually most appropriate when the interest and need are for pure, undistracted concentration, such as an opportunity to get close to nature or one's own body or mind. Participation in an individual sport provides a high potential for fulfilling the needs of dominance, recognition, and solitude. Individual sport play is one person performing the complete execution of a skill within a game context without the assistance or necessary involvement of a partner or teammate.

Dual sports and games are those activities that are most enjoyable when at least two people oppose each other within a game situation. As with individual activities, dual sports and games allow participants to direct their participation with little formal structure necessary. One-on-one play situations yield a high potential for intense social interaction; therefore an alert programmer structures the play so that emotions are controlled and constructively confined to the game itself. The program planner can also ensure that uneven abilities are equalized, so that contests are not so unbalanced that they depress one player and bore the other. Perhaps the greatest value in dual sports lies in the opportunity for combining boys and girls, men and women in co-recreational activities. See the box opposite for sports designated as dual.

One of the fastest growing and most significant forms of both individual and dual sports is the computer and video game phenomenon. A computer system such as PLATO, in addition to its primary learning component, provides a means for people to play chess and other games while at a physical distance. Home video games have been big sellers for the last several Christmases, and video game arcades continue to attract profits. And now, instead of going to swim camp or tennis camp, some children spend their summers at computer camps learning the basics of computer science and spending engrossing hours playing highly sophisticated computer games.

Team sport and game activities require participants to play in clearly defined groups. Because the rules of participation are rigorous and team organization and leadership can be volatile, the programming of team sports is a complex and challeng-

TYPES OF SPORT AND GAME ACTIVITIES

Individual sports and games

Archery
Auto racing
Bat ball
Baton twirling
Biycling
Boating
Bowling
Canoeing
Casting
Darts
Diving
Dungeons and Dragons
Fishing
Golf
Gymnastics
Hopscotch
Horseback riding
Ice skating
Jacks
Marbles
Pinball
Power weight lifting
Roller skating
Rope jumping
Running
Sailing
Scuba and skin diving
Shooting
Skydiving
Sledding
Snow skiing
Surfing
Swimming
Track and field
Trapshooting
Video games
Water skiing
Weight training

Fitness and calisthenics

Aerobic dance
Jazzercise
Jogging
Karate/martial arts
Parcourse
Rope jumping
Trampoline
Walking
Yoga

Dual sports and games

Backgammon
Badminton
Billiards
Boxing
Checkers
Chess
Croquet
Curling
Darts
Dodge ball
Fencing
Follow the leader
Foursquare
Frisbee
Handball
Horseshoes
Judo
Racquetball
Shuffleboard
Squash
Table tennis
Tennis
Tetherball
Video/computer games
Wrestling

Team sports and games

Baseball
Basketball
Crew racing
Dodge ball
Field hockey
Football
Ice hockey
Kickball
Lacrosse
New Games
Polo (water and field)
Rowing
Rugby
Soccer
Softball
Volleyball
Water ballet

ing task. The great value of this programming effort is the potential for fulfilling the participant need of belonging. For those who seek or accept team leadership roles, the need for dominance also can be fulfilled.

Perhaps the most difficult function for a program planner is putting the team together and keeping it together. Each sport requires a specific number of participants for official play. Often it is necessary for the planner to adapt play to smaller, non-regulation-size team play. Two-player touch football and three-player basketball are such adaptations that have grown into highly sophisticated programs in their own right in many recreation agencies. (Refer to the box on p. 135 for team sport and game ideas.)

Fitness activities differ from the previous categories in two ways. First, the number of participants is irrelevant. Second, the goal is not to win a game but to achieve better physical fitness and a higher level of health. The program planner needs a great deal of technological expertise to ensure a safe, beneficial contribution to the participant's health and fitness. Future program planners can expect an increasing demand for activities that emphasize fitness and health. One such development is the programming of activities that merely prepare a person to participate in a sport. The boldest example comes from commercial recreation agencies: dry-land ski schools for beginners and conditioning classes for veteran skiers. In southern California, for example, cross-country ski schools have new skiers practice their techniques on the sand at the beach. (The box on p. 135 lists some sport activities engaged in primarily for their fitness value.)

Summary   It is easy to become exhausted trying to keep up with the dynamic area of sports and games. Success in its programming depends on not only keeping up with the enormous fluctuation of interest in sport activities but also staying one step ahead of it.

Competition, which allows the play to be interesting, challenging, and constantly changing, contributes to the dynamic nature of sports programming, making the program planner's task a complex one. It also suggests certain cautions for the planner. According to one recreation professional, all is lost if "in the process of motivating participation, we carelessly allow built-in failure and loss of self-esteem to exist. The programmer must use competition as a fine surgical tool, adapting it carefully so that no physical or emotional harm comes to any participants" (Tillman, 1973, p. 109). While rules of play, court or field dimension regulations, and officials give discipline to sport activities, it takes a creative and thoughtful program planner to ensure that sport and game programming provides a fulfilling experience for all participants.

Numerous changes in sport interest, sport domain, and sport forms can be expected in the future. It seems likely that sports will strive for greater professionalism; that technological and physiological research will create better athletic participants and equipment; that people will expect sports to fulfill the human need for risk and adventure at an increasing rate; and that land available for the construction of sport areas, fields, and courses will become more scarce. Therefore the program planner must be alert for new trends and changes, must be able to adapt to such changes, and—most important—must stay one step ahead and capitalize on them to provide better, more relevant programming.

Hobbies

Hobbies are often misunderstood or ignored in recreation programs. Not all books on recreation program planning even mention hobbies, and some people think they have no appropriate place in the organized program offerings of recreation agencies. *Hobbies* is an old-fashioned word from old normal school pamphlets, antique *Reader's Digests*, and craft kits. It is derived from the word *hobbyhorses*, meaning things to get on and ride with intense involvement. This state of "intense involvement" is what defines a hobby activity today. It is a recreation activity usually pursued on an individual basis over an extended period of time. A hobby indicates a deep and committed interest in the activity; this interest usually does not depend on an organized program schedule but permits the hobbyist to start and stop the activity as chosen. The range of hobby activities is as broad as a list of recreational activities itself. Gardening is probably the most popular American hobby and also one of the most expensive.

Hobbies are a more important program area than most recreation and park program planners realize. When researchers asked what Americans do with their average of 35.67 weekly hours of leisure time (Kando, 1980, p. 127), the answers always included hobbies. For example, an early study reported by De Grazia (1964) asked a national probability sample of more than 5000 Americans over 15 years of age what recreation activities they had engaged in the previous day. Answers were as follows (Kando, 1980, p. 127):

57% watched television
38% visited friends or relatives
33% worked around the yard or garden
27% read newspapers
18% read books
17% drove for pleasure
14% listened to records
11% attended meetings
10% engaged in special hobbies
 8% went out to dinner

A later study (Szalai and others, 1972) compared free time involvement in the United States with 11 other countries. These findings indicated that Americans watch a great deal more television and read more newspapers than the citizens of the other countries. But this study and other recent studies indicated a typical American pattern for recreational use of free time. After television viewing, the top 10 activities generally include visiting, gardening, reading the paper, and various other hobbies. What people do with free time and what they prefer to do with it may be two different things. To make this distinction, Faunce (1959) asked a group of automobile workers how they might use a hypothetical increase in free time. Their answers, as summarized by Kando (1980, p. 128), were as follows:

96.8% would work around the house
76.8% would spend more time with the family
53.6% would travel
48.8% would go to ballgames, fights, hockey games
42.4% would fish and hunt
25.6% would engage in other hobbies
24.8% would engage in some form of athletics
24.8% would read more
19.2% would go back to school or learn a trade
17.6% would be active in school boards, PTA
16.8% would get another part-time job
15.2% would join more social clubs
12.8% would engage in more political action work
11.2% would rest, relax, loaf
 4.8% would swim, boat
 2.4% would work on car
 1.6% would engage in church activities

Values   A hobby offers the individual an intense and continuing interest in an activity without requiring much outside stimulation. Hobbies possess an element of independent exploration that gives the hobbyist a chance to know self and the world around better. Because hobbies tend to be individualized pursuits, the same hobby activity can satisfy different needs for different people. The choice of a particular hobby is determined by an unconscious need to fulfill certain social and psychological desires that are not being met through everyday responsibilities.

For most people hobbies are a means of relaxation and emotional separation from the frustrations of work and daily survival. For others, hobbies help combat boredom by making daily life more enriching. Like most activity media, hobbies meet the needs of participants in numerous ways. Some of the values of hobbies are (1) an opportunity for creative expression, serving as a means of compensation (excelling in a hobby to compensate for mediocrity on the job); (2) acquiring knowledge and learning skills; (3) an opportunity for solitude and contemplation; (4) a good way to try out career interests; and (5) a temporary relief from frustration. For many people a well-chosen hobby growing from their own desires, needs, and abilities can make a joyful contribution to the art of living.

Planning considerations   Hobbies are fundamentally an individual pursuit. The selection and maintenance of a hobby are up to each person. However, it is often desirable for program planners to offer beginning instruction, continued motivation, and sometimes even materials to those with hobbies. Much of the assistance a recreation agency provides the hobbyist is indirect, but some planning considerations can be applied directly.

One way is to provide instructional programs for the beginner. This assistance should include learning about the scope of the hobby activity, information on how to get started in a hobby, and materials on what sources of help are available for continuing interest. The beginning hobbyist needs to be introduced to hobbies and then assisted in learning the basic skills necessary for pursuing the activity. Many hobbyists start by participating in introductory classes, viewing demonstrations or displays, going on field trips, listening to other hobbyists, or having a friend or relative who is involved in a hobby club. Program planners can help the potential hobbyist by programming such introductory opportunities.

Recreation agencies also have encouraged and supported participation in hobbies by sponsoring clubs or other group activities for those with a common hobby interest. This can take the form of providing leadership, but more often it simply involves furnishing a place where such groups can hold meetings. For some groups the provision of a meeting space can become involved and expensive. For example, the provision of a darkroom and equipment for photography hobbyists, a room and facilities for radio amateurs, or a field for the operation of model planes requires serious planning and sizable budget allocations. Hobby shows and exhibits, demonstrations, and displays also afford the program planner an opportunity to support the hobbyist past the introductory stage. The main intent is to help the hobbyist come in contact with other hobbyists in the same field.

Types of hobby activities   This book classifies hobby interests for convenience in considering the wide scope of activities. Because hobbies are as broad as human interests, their classification is difficult. Hobbies mean different things to different people. Here hobby pursuits are subdivided into educational, collecting, and creative categories. But these categories are not meant to be exclusive or distinct. For example, art can be a creative hobby for the person who paints the landscape on a Sunday afternoon; a collecting hobby for the person who collects the works of one artist; or an educational hobby for the person who studies a certain artist or period of art. The classification of a hobby depends on the nature of the participant's interest and how the interest is pursued. Nonetheless, whether a hobby is creative, educational, or collective is not nearly as important as what it does for the participant—the value derived from involvement.

Educational hobbies concentrate on the acquisition of knowledge and the learning of skills. The two most common rewards of participation in educational hobbies are exploration and adventure. Creative hobbies constitute one of the most effective means of satisfying the creative urge in all of us. To create, to make, to construct is a basic human drive. Although every hobby offers some opportunity for creative expression, some are richer in this value than others. A collection hobby can be a serious, sophisticated art or a mere accumulation of odds and ends that are meaningful only to the collector. Collection hobbies are practically unlimited in scope; anything that comes in at least two different appearances can be collected.

A list of specific hobby activities arranged into the three categories is presented in the box below. Most hobbies have characteristics from several categories. For example, a stamp-collecting hobby is obviously of the collecting category. But it also offers a creative reward to the collector who arranges and organizes the collection; likewise it includes educational value for the collector who studies related historical, geographical, economic, or artistic aspects of the stamps. Therefore the lists of hobbies in each category are not complete.

Summary   Hobbies do not fit neatly into recreation program areas for two reasons. First, hobbies mean different things to different participants. Therefore the programming of hobbies toward a specific end result or value is difficult. The mere mention of raising orchids, breeding dogs, or collecting steamboat whistles may bring a glint of enthusiasm to one person's eyes, while causing another to shrug his shoulders. Second, most hobbies fall into one of the other program areas discussed in this chapter, such as sports, outdoor recreation, music, dance, or arts and crafts.

TYPES OF HOBBY ACTIVITIES

Educational	**Collecting**
Archeology	Antiques
Astronomy	Autographs
Beekeeping	Automobiles
Entomology	Books
Meteorology	China
Ornithology	Coins
Reading	Dolls
Science	Gems and rocks
Travel	Glass
	Guns
Creative	Indian relics
Calligraphy	Marbles
Cooking (gourmet and specialty)	Matchbooks
Gardening	Paintings
Knitting	Postcards
Model making	Recipes
Photography	Seashells
Woodworking	Stamps
Writing	Toys

Hobbies are considered separately in a program plan because oftentimes the intensity and the lifelong quality of participation distinguish them from other program areas. Despite these difficulties, the program planner cannot ignore the enthusiasm of hobbyists. Today they are legion. Individually and in groups hobbyists follow their interests with a dedication that often resembles a mania, complete with a unique body of literature and an esoteric language.

Almost everyone can find personal enjoyment and life enrichment in a wisely selected hobby. In fact, some people insist that a person cannot be happy without a hobby. It is true that in a decade in which leisure hours exceed work hours, in which societal problems weigh heavily, and in which individual psychological complexity has increased, hobbies are more important than ever. Recognizing hobbies as a means of enriching life and achieving personal worth and recognition, recreation agencies can do much to offer these benefits to program participants.

Music

In every culture and nation of the world music is an integral part of life. Sometimes called the most universal of the arts, music stimulates emotional responses that give people great pleasure and rewards. The pleasures of music in its many forms have been appreciated by every culture from the beginning of time. "From the pagan rhythmic chants to the latest popular tune, music has dynamically demonstrated its ability to blend human beings in the participation at hand" (Carlson and others, 1972, p. 445). Primitive songs and chants, ancient Greek choruses and hymns, melodic madrigals of the Renaissance, sacred chants of the medieval church, the impact even today of world-renowned composers such as Beethoven, Bach, and Mozart—all testify to the enduring force of music in influencing the cultural lives of people all over the world.

The influence of music in the United States is widespread and strong. At last count there were 46 million active amateur musicians, with 20 million pianos, 4 million guitars, and 3 million violins (Statistical Abstracts, 1975) performing in 1,470 symphony orchestras and 956 opera companies (Statistical Abstracts, 1979). It is rumored that there are more piano players than fishermen! Indeed, the number of amateur musicians has grown from the 19 million reported in 1950 to over twice that many today. These musicians spend over $850 million annually for musical instruments. Symphony orchestras are by far the longest lived performing organizations in the United States. The first major American orchestra, the New York Philharmonic, was founded in 1842 (Kando, 1980, p. 146).

Music is a way of expressing mood through sound. It is a combination of sounds that stir our emotions, please us, or upset us. These sounds do not have any useful purpose; instead they appeal directly to the emotions. People feel music rather than think it. That is its basic function. Therefore the majority of those who participate in the various forms of music do so for recreational reasons.

Values   In music the values to the performer and to the listener are numerous. Music can act as a soothing agent, an invigorator, an arouser, a revitalizer, or a unifier. As in other program areas, people vary in the values they find in music. However, most recreation program planners do identify one set of values as particular to the music experience. The planner should consider music programming when it is necessary or desirable to:

1. Control behavior
2. Develop group or team unity and cooperation
3. Have a background for other recreation programs
4. Provide therapy
5. Express feelings, beliefs, or thoughts
6. Make the environment more pleasing

For example, music has the power to move people deeply. It can build moods that ultimately influence action. Therefore the programmer can use music to slow down overzealous play, stop roughhousing, or end lethargy. Carefully chosen songs can quiet boisterous laughter around the campfire and prepare campers to match the somber mood of the dying embers. Band music and fight songs can whip sport fans into a cheering frenzy. Snappy hiking songs can make the last mile of a hike easier.

Through music the program planner can create a group experience. Music seems to have a unifying effect on people, whether they are performing or listening. It can calm hostilities, unify spirits, and integrate purposes. It is difficult to hate the persons you are joining in song. The planner can use music to harmonize program participants. The fellowship derived from involvement in a chorus or orchestra provides an emotional integration that identifies the participants as part of a group.

Because of music's mood-setting ability, it is often used to set the tone or provide the background for other recreation activities. What would a dance performance, a water ballet, a movie, a party, an evening campfire, the rising curtain on the stage be without music!

The field of music therapy has developed from a recognition of the value of music for the physically ill, the emotionally disturbed, and the mentally ill. Research that documents this value is still under way, but evidence to date is sufficient to verify the inclusion of music in therapy programs. This therapeutic advantage is based on music's ability to contribute to a sense of personal well-being. This comes from the wholeness of response and the release of tensions that bring an easier flow of energy and a lift of spirits. Even people who are not ill can benefit from the therapeutic value of music. The driver who turns the radio on while going home from work and the student who studies while playing the stereo are experiencing the therapeutic value of music.

Through music one can express joy, sorrow, love, enthusiasm, or reverence. Music is valued for its contribution to communicating emotions and ideas. Participants are able to express themselves, to tell their story.

Music is valued by the program planner for its ability to make the recreation setting pleasant. It is that "little extra" in life that makes living more pleasurable. Because music can be enjoyed for its own sake, the planner can use it for no reason other than to appreciate its form, line, color, balance, and rhythm.

Planning considerations Music in planned recreation programming has not kept pace with its dominant role in our lives. In spite of music's values and universality, recreation agencies have not felt any desire or pressure to program for this interest. The temptation has been to use music programming as a spillover for people who are not interested in athletics or crafts. Even for these participants music programs usually have not advanced past elementary levels—singing games, listening rooms, rhythm bands, and community singing. Therefore music's role is comparatively small in recreation agency budget, staff, and facility allocations. Even though music is a major aid to other planned programs, it has no major role as a separate programmed experience.

This is a result of one important planning consideration: recreation music leadership requires technical knowledge. No other activity area so disturbs the generalist leader. This lack of confidence often deters programmers from offering exciting or demanding musical opportunities. It also explains why music programs are most likely to be launched only after someone with musical expertise has been hired. Perhaps this situation will have to be accepted because the degree of technical knowledge and ability required for leaders in music is important. In order for the participant to enjoy and be satisfied by the music experience, the leader must be able to achieve a certain level of results. Thus qualified leadership is a must for music programs. However, its absence from an agency's staff should not deter the planner from programming for music. There are various other leadership options, as discussed in Chapter 6.

This leads us to another planning consideration. Music programming should use as many available community resources as possible. Recreation agencies need to tap into and coordinate with existing music programming. Both private special interest organizations and commercial establishments have extensive instructional and performing music programs; the manufacturers of instruments and sheet music are anxious to promote their products; and the schools provide more formal opportunities in both choral and instrumental programs. The resourceful program planner can develop specific ways of using these resources in conjunction with his or her own agency's music programming. Particularly in small agencies—where expertise or budgets may not allow a broad range of options for listening, singing, or playing— cooperation with educational institutions, other recreation agencies, and commercial firms can provide a progression of creative musical outlets.

Because music appeals to almost everyone, planners of music programming should attempt to serve all interests. Unfortunately almost everyone has a different taste in music. Good music connotes classical string quartets to one individual and country and western fiddling to another. As in any recreation activity area, the planner must be sensitive to the tastes of the constituency in order to select, organize, and introduce appropriate music experiences.

Likewise, music programming should not deny opportunities because of skill level. This is a difficult planning consideration because in no other area of recreation programs does the failure of one individual so detract from the quality of the experience for all. Therefore the planning dilemma becomes one of providing adequately for matched skill levels. Those programmers who have wrestled with this problem suggest that because there are no adequate lead-up programs (in contrast to sport), the planner winds up with one music program and numerous ability levels. What usually results is a music program that really is not a meaningful experience to anyone. Such large group events as voice choirs and guitar bands, which are organized to satisfy everyone by seeking a common talent base, often become the first and only group music experience for most participants. To be viable in a competitive program arena, the music program must extend its services to include challenges for those of higher skill levels who enjoy more demanding musical opportunities.

Types of music activities   As indicated earlier, the types, extent, and range of music program opportunities depend on the availability of qualified leadership and the interests of the participants. The list in the box opposite suggests the variety of planned musical activities classified as vocal or instrumental. This list is by no means all-inclusive. Any of the activities can take place in a wide range of settings and can be organized to meet the needs of different talent levels.

These activities also can be distinguished by the degree of planning and organization required: informal activities with little organization or formal activities that require more organization. Even in their simple form, such informal activities as singing around the campfire, musical games in the playground, and listening to the stereo in the senior center can offer a satisfying means of self-expression. Individuals or small groups often turn to music with little or no stimulation from program planners or activity leaders. On the other hand, playing an instrument or singing with others often requires planning. Barbershop quartets, string ensembles, opera study groups, glee clubs, and special performances require more advance planning consideration.

Summary   The popularity of music for group and individual expression will continue to fluctuate over the next decade. What will future trends demand? Will small jazz ensembles and country and western stomps continue to be popular, or will there be a renewal in folksinging and a new appreciation of classical music?

Since the impetus given to music as a part of recreation programming by the Federal Arts Project of the Depression years, many recreation agencies have seen the benefit of including music in their offerings. Today most music programming continues to be offered by school, church, and private recreation agencies. Public recreation agencies, unfortunately, tend to stay away from music programming.

TYPES OF MUSIC ACTIVITIES

Vocal	**Instrumental**
Performance	Performance
Glee clubs	Rhythm bands
A cappella choirs	Orchestras
Madrigal groups	Rock bands
Music theme festivals	Ensembles
Christmas caroling	Talent shows
Barbershop quartets	Mobile stages
Listening	Jazz clubs
Records and tapes	Listening
Concert attendance	Records and tapes
Television viewing	Concert attendance
Trip to opera	Live performances
Park concerts	Television viewing
Instruction	Downtown noon mini-recitals
Voice training	Instruction
Song-leading workshops	Guitar classes
Composition	Piano lessons
Interpretive singing games	Flute lessons
Song writing	Composition
Musical charades	Improvisation jam sessions
Study/practice	Study/practice
Singing in shower	Practice rooms
Children's singing games	Bach society
Opera study groups	New Wave appreciation classes for
Fan clubs	parents
Songbook making	

When they do offer music programs, they typically do not go beyond the rhythm band for children or the city symphony orchestra and chorus.

Perhaps the greatest role music plays in recreation programs is in combination with other activities. Without the organ music at a baseball game, music for dancing, music to announce the rising curtain at a dramatic performance, and music for the social recreation party, the sport, the dance, the play, or the party would not be the same experience. Some would argue that without music these activities would not even be possible.

Outdoor recreation

The outdoors is a great laboratory for learning, a museum for study, and a playground for wholesome fun and enjoyment. It affords a special kind of fulfillment not available in any other recreation setting. Because outdoor recreation has become a vital part of American life, this area of organized recreation service has expanded dramatically during the past two decades. On all levels and in every possible setting, new areas, facilities, and programs have been developed. Most significant is the expansion of organized outdoor recreation programs. Yet it was only recently that outdoor recreation resources became available to the majority of Americans. As many urban centers became uninhabitable, as suburban sprawl merged suburb and city into an unwieldly megalopolis, and as pollution and population continued to devour natural resources, Americans developed a deep concern for the quality of life. It was from this concern that the demand for outdoor recreation rose.

Thus, despite shrinking space, an overwhelming majority of Americans want to participate in some form of outdoor recreation. In fact, according to the U.S. Department of the Interior (1974), participation is increasing and is expected to continue to increase at a rate of 10% each year. Most outdoor recreation occurs close to home, after work, after school, and on 1-day outings. The findings of the Department of the Interior (1974, p. 203) show that:

> 75% of all outdoor recreation occasions are close to home and on 1-day outings
> 12% are on overnight recreation trips
> 13% are on vacation excursions away from home

With increased energy costs and inflation in the 1980s, the responsibility for outdoor recreation program planning rests with those agencies located where the people are. In spite of the important legacy offered by national parks and forests, these and most other resources for outdoor recreation are not located where most of the users are. For example, the total U.S. public recreation estate is 491 million acres, yet less than 3% of these lands are available for day use for the majority of the U.S. population (U.S. Department of the Interior, 1974).

Exactly what is outdoor recreation—as distinguished from just playing out-of-doors? Should a game of checkers played on a park bench, a concert performed in a bandshell by the river, or a game of football on a grassy outdoor field be considered outdoor recreation? Although some recreation philosophers would disagree, I think that outdoor recreation must have a meaningful and intentional relationship to the natural environment. According to Jensen (1977, p. 8):

> [Outdoor recreation is] resource-oriented recreation. It is defined as those recreational activities which occur in an outdoor (natural) environment and which relate directly to that environment.

Therefore under the heading of outdoor recreation come the diverse pursuits related to the use, enjoyment, and understanding of the natural environment. Because outdoor recreation is resource-oriented recreation, it includes activities that depend strongly on the use of natural resources. It means fishing in the pounding surf, skiing across a snowy meadow, camping among the pines in a state park, listening to a bird sing, clinging to the face of a rock, or gathering wild chestnuts from the forest floor.

Choice and ability play a major role in shaping outdoor recreation. How people pursue their recreation in the out-of-doors reflects varying personal attitudes and physical, social, and economic differences. Almost every American engages in one or more outdoor recreation activities. The fewer the cost or energy requirements or the less exacting the performance standards, the more people will partake of the activity. Conversely, where the requirements of an activity are many and demanding, the fewer the participants. For example, picnicking calls for a minimum of skill and advance preparation. Over 100 million people go picnicking each year (U.S. Department of the Interior, 1974). Mountain climbing, on the other hand, is physically risky and taxing, requires many practiced skills, and calls for courage. Consequently even though their numbers are increasing at a rapid rate, mountain climbers total barely one hundredth of the picnickers.

Today walking for pleasure and picnicking rank as the most frequent outdoor activities. Ranking low in actual participation but high in attraction potential are sailing, scuba diving, skiing, and rock climbing. See Table 11 for statistics on participation in selected outdoor recreation activities. Even though there are many more outdoor recreation activities, those shown in Table 11 account for well over 90% of total participation. This ranking tends to reflect (in inverse order) increases in the number of resource or skill requirements each activity demands of its participants.

In summary, the three major points of this introduction are:

1. Most outdoor recreation areas are inaccessible to the majority of participants.
2. Because of increased financial and energy restraints, most participants will continue to seek outdoor recreation in their own communities.
3. Participation is greatest in the simplest outdoor pursuits.

The challenge for the program planner is to provide opportunities for outdoor enjoyment while lessening the abuse of outdoor areas. This means offering meaningful outdoor experiences for all participants—even the new generation of urbanites growing up with only superficial contact with the out-of-doors—in spite of increasing obstacles.

Values   Outdoor recreation offers some unique values. Besides having meaning and significance for individuals, it offers benefits to society and the nation. In America the time has finally come when the use of natural resources for recreation purposes is as important as their practical uses. Outdoor recreation is now recognized as a great national asset.

Specific cultural values are being appreciated in scenic study, nature photography, scene painting, and bird watching. As a result, recreation agency priorities are reflecting such values: a sense of responsibility for the preservation, care, and wise use of the natural environment; an understanding and appreciation of America's heritage of outdoor living, skills, and pursuits; and good outdoor citizenship. Learn-

Table 11 *Participation in outdoor recreation activities*

Activity	Participants (in millions)
Picnicking	114
Driving for pleasure	110
Swimming	104
Sightseeing	100
Pleasure walking	77
Attending sports events	66
Playing outdoor games or sports	65
Fishing	57
General boating	52
Bicycling	41
Sledding	29
Attending concerts and plays	26
Nature walking	25
Camping	25
Hunting	19
Ice skating	17
Horseback riding	16
Hiking with pack	14
Water skiing	10
Bird watching	9
Canoeing	6
Snow skiing	6
Sailing	5
Wildlife and bird photography	3
Mountain climbing	1

From U.S. Department of the Interior.*The recreation imperative.* Washington, D.C.: U.S. Government Printing Office, 1974, p. 201.

ing to keep camp and picnic areas clean, to avoid marring the landscape, and to be considerate of the rights and enjoyment of others are important social attributes, and they are rapidly becoming more important in outdoor recreation because of the tremendous increase in participation.

The outdoors has greatly influenced America's history and character. But perhaps its greatest value is its contribution to the health and sanity of the American people. By counterbalancing the artificialities of modern life, contact with nature satisfies deeply felt human needs and contributes to the physical, mental, and emotional well-being of the participant. Outdoor recreation pursuits help the individual become more resourceful, self-reliant, and adaptable. In addition, many outdoor interests allow the participant to engage in them throughout life. Unlike such recreation pursuits as team sports, outdoor activities can be pursued regardless of physical vigor. In fact, those who regularly participate in outdoor activities generally improve their overall fitness. Finally, one of the great comforts of contact with nature is an awareness of the beauty and reason in the balance of nature. Everyone needs beauty for the soul.

Planning considerations   In the outdoor recreation field certain activities make more demands on planning expertise than others. Although much of what is included in this program area takes place in informal situations, there is still an important need for recreation agencies to make planned provisions to serve the needs of their constituencies. For example, physical outdoor resources and access to these resources are essential if certain program opportunities are to be available. Also, those who conduct outdoor recreation programs often must have special skills and knowledge. Many activities require special training in safety procedures or an educated acquaintance with the natural sciences.

In the 1970s interest mushroomed in what has come to be known as adventure or high-risk programs. Because this type of outdoor recreation programming probably requires the most stringent attention to planning, it will be given special attention here.

Social, educational, correctional, and leisure service agencies all have begun to conduct programs that include such activities as extended backpacking or canoe trips, rock climbing, white-water rafting and kayaking, orienteering, adventure running, winter camping, and cross-country skiing. Teenagers, an age group usually difficult to program for, especially may benefit from adventure programming. Demanding outdoor programs such as rock climbing or extended wilderness ventures, however, should be undertaken only after extensive planning and forethought.

The following guidelines are for any agency or private enterprise interested in developing outdoor adventure programs. Although large and remote outdoor areas may not be accessible to many agencies, some activities can be adapted to urban settings. In developing an outdoor adventure program, the first major ingredient is enthusiastic, interested, and competent leaders. Whether they come from one agency or from a variety of agencies and backgrounds, the leaders will establish the goals and purpose of the outdoor program, the needs it hopes to meet, and ultimately its success.

Competent outdoor leaders should be the basis of any outdoor program. Although the need for certification and outdoor leadership training is now under national debate, there is still confusion as to the desirable qualities of an outdoor risk leader. All members of the outdoor adventure staff should (1) be skilled and certified in the program's particular skill or activity as well as first aid, water safety, and CPR; (2) have outdoor teaching experience; (3) understand group dynamics; and (4) show sound judgment in stress situations. The program's director and staff also should have a basic knowledge of outdoor rescue and evacuation procedures. In general, outdoor adventure activities require significant technical skills for instructing the activities, strong safety skills, and sharp judgment. There may already be someone in the planner's agency with the necessary skills. If not, these leaders will have to be trained in the agency or sent to an outdoor school such as Outward Bound or the National Outdoor Leadership School in Lander, Wyoming. The former places more emphasis on the personal and group experience, and the latter deals more with specific outdoor skills.

Another primary consideration is program design. If professional outdoor staff or consultants are brought into the planning process, the resulting program will probably provide a better organized and safer experience. An outdoor adventure program should be designed for accessible locations such as forests, lakes, and rivers. A base of operations should be established, and the question of a mobile program as opposed to a highly centralized one, or a combination of both, must be settled. Other questions must be answered: Will activities be for all seasons? What will the size of the groups be? Will the courses run after school, on weekends, during vacations, or for extended periods?

A complete familiarity with logistics—based on area guides and maps, planned area reconnaissance, safety procedures, and emergency planning—should be a primary consideration before outdoor adventure trips are begun. Local terrain and outdoor areas available might determine the type of activities offered. This restriction may be especially important during the first year of the program if long-distance travel of 2 hours or more is impossible owing to financial restraints.

All participants should be covered by an insurance policy that covers at least medical expenses. Participants should also complete a standard medical form, a course application, and an acceptance of risk statement. Such statements indicate the participant's knowledge of the high-risk nature of the activity and his or her intent to follow all rules and regulations of the program. These statements in no way free the program from liability. Safety and liability are major issues when considering an outdoor program, but they need not be a total hindrance. See Chapter 6 for liability and risk management considerations.

Some additional thoughts for planning an adventure-based program, as adapted from Storms (1979, pp. 24-27), are the following:

1. An exploration of current literature and research related to outdoor adventure programs should be undertaken. One good source for such materials is the Colorado Outward Bound School, which maintains a series of publications on this program area. Write the school at 945 Pennsylvania Avenue, Denver, Colorado 80203.

2. Develop a knowledge of existing programs related in activities or goals to your program plans. This includes a survey of existing agencies within your area concerned with outdoor and personal growth experiences. A directory of existing outdoor adventure programs can be obtained from Outdoor Experiences Incorporated, Box 1055, Mankato, Minnesota 56001. Included in their booklet is a nationwide listing of outdoor risk programs with a content description on each. Questions about adventure programs within your geographic area can also be directed to the Association for Experiential Education, Box 4625, Denver, Colorado 80204.

3. Identify other groups or agencies that might lend aid or support or in some way coordinate efforts. Many local agencies such as schools, recreation departments, scouting organizations, churches, police, mental health agencies, and local industry and business may offer aid through sponsorship, limited funding, office space, program supplies, transportation, referrals, or promotion. Although some agencies, such as a school district, may not be willing to become directly involved in adventure activity because of liability questions, they might be willing to offer promotional help that includes visits to classrooms, publicity in school publications, and dissemination of information and program schedules to students.

4. Determine the availability of professional consulting services. There is no substitute for people who can give technical or administrative consultation and have had considerable experience themselves in operating adventure programs. In addition to consultation services provided by Outward Bound Schools, the directory of programs already mentioned may give a local consultation source.

The reasons for establishing an outdoor adventure program are many. Primary goals are (1) to promote positive interpersonal interactions, (2) to gain therapeutic rewards, (3) to offer an alternative to traditional programming, (4) to teach certain concepts, and (5) to satisfy the increasing constituency demand for adventure programs. However, the most important planning consideration is to first decide on the specific goals or purposes of the program and to gather as much information as possible about similar programs already in operation.

In summary, it should be remembered that outdoor programs with stressful and challenging activities involve a commitment of qualified staff, finances, and time. Careful planning and thought must precede the establishment of any adventure program. Intensive and thorough planning should maximize the rewards of the experience and minimize the risk factors. Large-scale adventure programming may not be for every agency, but many such programs can be modified to provide challenging leisure experiences throughout the year.

Types of outdoor recreation activities The goal of outdoor recreation programming includes both learning about the environment and learning how to behave in the environment; to know how to enjoy and use it while preserving it. Outdoor recreation programs that strive for these goals are usually located in day and resident camps, playgrounds, commercial resorts, nature centers, and schools. Agency provisions for outdoor recreation programs vary greatly. Some programs emphasize understanding of the natural environment; others emphasize camping, outdoor living skills, and outdoor sports. What is planned usually depends on the natural resources, the man-made facilities, the needs of the constituency, and even the interests and abilities of the leaders. A few agencies are traditionally and specifically oriented toward outdoor programs. For example, the Girl Scouts, the Boy Scouts, garden clubs, sport clubs, and conservation clubs devote a great deal of programming effort to the out-of-doors. Such popular enterprises as guest ranches, vacation farms, and ocean-science camps represent privately sponsored outdoor recreation that is totally oriented toward such programming. The variety and breadth of outdoor recreation activities available for the planner are suggested by the box below.

Camping simply means living in the out-of-doors. This usually means that the camper assumes some responsibility for his or her own food, shelter, and travel and engages in activities related to the immediate camp surroundings. Activities in natural science invite the participant to learn about the wonders of the natural environment, whereas conservation activities stress preservation of our natural endowment. High-risk adventure activities such as rock climbing and glider soaring provide challenge and excitement not possible through any other medium. Outdoor sports refer

---

TYPES OF OUTDOOR RECREATION ACTIVITIES

Camping/outdoor living

Fire building
Map and compass
Outdoor cooking
Picnicking
Tool craft and care
Backpacking
Hosteling

Conservation

Landscaping
Conservation study
Planting for wildlife
Building plant and wildlife sanctuaries
Weather observation
Bird census
Erosion control projects

High risk

White-water kayaking and canoeing
Mountain climbing
Rock climbing
Hang gliding
Glider soaring
Spelunking

Outdoor sports

Bicycling
Hunting
Fishing
Boating/sailing
Snow skiing
Water skiing
Orienteering
Horseback riding
Scuba diving
Hiking
Surfing
Snowshoeing
Snowmobiling

Nature oriented

Nature print casting
Nature crafts
Nature games
Animal husbandry
Tree/plant identification
Stargazing
Terrarium making
Nature walks
Discovery trails
Outdoor photography
Weather prediction

to those outdoor physical activities that do not rely on playing fields, courts, or stadiums, but instead depend on natural land or water areas for their full enjoyment. For the most part, outdoor sports may be engaged in on an individual basis.

Summary   Outdoor recreation is as old as the human race, but it was not always considered recreation. In earliest history outdoor pursuits were often indistinguishable from the primary business of surviving, and as recently as the settling of America outdoor skills were essential to living. This heritage, in combination with the increasing complexity of modern life, causes us all to have that urge to establish contact with the land—to plant, to harvest, to learn the secrets of nature, to fish, to hunt, to paddle a canoe, to pitch a tent, to build a fire and cook our meal. The tremendous number of users of national, state, and local parks; the vacation industry; the organized camping movement; the outdoor programs of museums, libraries, schools, and recreation agencies; the special purpose clubs; and the number of people sitting on the bank of the river this very weekend all attest to this interest in the out-of-doors. A return to the world of nature with its order, its challenge, its beauty, and its meaningfulness serves as a balance to the materialism that threatens the human spirit.

Mental and literary recreation

Few recreation activities could be discussed in this chapter that in no way involve mental perception, linguistic ability, or communication mechanisms. Puzzles are worked on camping trips, skits are written for dramatic performances, literary hobbies are undertaken, and mathematics is encountered in music. However, there are recreation experiences that should be considered separately and programmed for their own worth as mental, linguistic, or literary activities.

Even though mental and literary offerings currently occupy a small place in the comprehensive program, such activities may become an increasingly vital part of programs if the cultural explosion continues. For example, Kando (1980) states that book sales and library circulation have soared three times more rapidly than the population since 1950. From 1958 to 1978 annual retail sales of general books (excluding college texts) increased from $275 million to approximately $1.8 billion (*Time*, 1978). *Time* labeled this phenomenon a "rambunctious revival."

As for the future, Alvin Toffler in his book *The Third Wave* has chosen the gloomier phrasing of "mental maelstrom." Toffler's claim is that "never before have so many people in so many countries—even educated and supposedly sophisticated people—been so intellectually helpless, drowning, as it were, in a maelstrom of conflicting, confusing, and cacophonous ideas. Colliding visions rock our mental universe" (Toffler, 1980, p. 306). This does sound like a valid theory, since every day brings some new life-style fad, religion, scientific finding, or pop psychology manifesto. Toffler continues: "Nature worship, ESP, holistic medicine, sociobiology, anarchism, structuralism, neo-Marxism, the new physics, Eastern mysticism, tech-

RAY BELLAROSA

nophilia, technophobia, and a thousand other currents and crosscurrents sweep across the screen of consciousness" (p. 306).

The recreation program planner will undoubtedly need not only to sift through all these trends but also to reflect them in program offerings.

Values   A person who has cultivated a love of reading may travel to the ends of the world without actually leaving the window seat. The person who spends free time writing short stories enjoys the thrill of creative achievement. The person who masters a foreign language finds stimulating mental exercise. To explore all the ways in which lives can be enhanced through stimulation of mental abilities would be an overwhelming task. Primary values in this area are creativity, sharpening of mental skills, and exploration and discovery.

Reading, writing, and speaking, although among the oldest activities in the recreation field, have not been developed to any great extent. Yet they offer participants the values of becoming more articulate, more creative, more widely read, and analytically sharper so that they can more effectively contribute to making the world a better place to live.

Planning considerations   Many mental and literary activities require no audience, no teammate, no partner, and no special facility. In fact, study, research, creative writing, reading, and contemplation can be enjoyed best in solitude. Some mental and literary activities may require other persons and special equipment; such activities involve the desire to communicate, to show off new skills or knowledge, or to compete.

Reading, writing, speaking, and analytical activities have a desired place in a well-rounded recreation program for several reasons. In addition to appealing to a wide range of constituency, they are relatively inexpensive to both the participant and the agency. The demands on leadership and physical properties are reasonable and limited; however, leaders must be knowledgeable and experienced in the specific literary activity. Facility and equipment needs often include only a quiet corner or room, tables, chairs, and pillows.

Types of mental and literary activities Numerous program offerings can be considered for the area of literary activities. The activities can be divided into the subcategories of reading, writing, speaking, analysis, and study. For many people books are the greatest and most satisfactory of recreations. Reading activities for organized recreation programming include book clubs, Great Books seminars, vacation reading contests, and bookmobiles. Writing activities can lead to programs that share talents with others, such as plays, poetry readings, and contests; or they can instruct in popular aspects of creative writing, such as seminars on greeting-card verse writing or short story writing. Almost everyone has at least once aspired to write the Great American Novel; recreation agencies can offer an outlet for such aspirations.

There is a universal urge among people to be seen, heard, and understood. Speaking activities can take the program format of public speaking clubs, debates, broadcasting, storytelling, and foreign language clubs. Analytical experiences include word puzzles, game board activities, card playing, and mathematical challenges. Programming these activities is often very simple because all the programmer must do is set out the game or puzzle on a table. Yet creative programmers can see the potential for other directions. For example, I have had great programming success with Dungeons and Dragons play days and tournaments.

Although the exploration of any given topic by an individual or a group is not usually the concern of the recreation program planner, stimulation for such pursuits can be provided by the recreation agency. Study programs can include offerings such as topical group discussions, wine-tasting evenings and vineyard tours, resource libraries (such as at camp), genealogy study groups, and study field trips. See the box on p. 156 for program suggestions in this activity category.

Summary Mental and literary programming can be based on differing rationales and can take various forms of expression. For example, one of the easiest and most successful programs I have designed was a series of poetry readings in a large retail bookshop. The store was anxious to have the increased foot traffic (meaning increased sales); the featured poets (most were published) were pleased to have their poems read in public and at no charge. The readings were held monthly. On two separate months an "open reading" was held, and any community member who had written poetry was invited to read before an audience. Attendance figures showed that even a small town can support such a program.

If program services are to achieve the broad scope of leisure satisfactions necessary in this challenging decade, the area of mental and literary activities cannot be ignored.

TYPES OF MENTAL AND LITERARY ACTIVITIES

Reading

Bookmobiles
Book review clubs
Vacation reading contests
Reading to others
Dramatic readings
Speed-reading classes
Mystery reading clubs

Writing

Letter writing clubs
Pen pals
Poetry readings
Instruction in creative writing
Essay contests
Play writing

Speaking

Storytelling hour
Foreign language clubs
Toastmaster's clubs
Recording tapes for visually impaired
Debates
Television and radio production

Analysis

Puzzles
Board games
Card games
Computer games

Study

Topical group discussions
Study trips and tours
Resource libraries
Rare manuscript study

Social recreation

The label *social recreation* describes recreation program experiences that bring people together for relaxed sociability and friendly interchange in group settings. These activities hold as their main objective the creation of a spirit of fun, fellowship, and sociability. People need people. The late-night prison movie on television has made it clear that there is no punishment worse than "solitary." All people have a need for the informal and sociable experience basic to social recreation. The children's birthday party, banquet, college fraternity party, senior citizen social, and evening of bingo at the church are examples of events whose goal is primary social interaction—offering the fullest potential for good feelings. Thus the task of the social recreation programmer becomes one of mixing the right people in the proper doses in the best setting. The common bond of interest in the social situation is for desirable companions.

At its best the social recreation situation is a relaxed one in which the desire to win or excel is minimal. Although there are competitive elements in many party games and other social activites, they are low key and never the main goal of participation. Unlike many other recreation activity areas—in which challenge, achievement, skill practice, or entertainment is primary—social recreation tends to consist of the ordinary and the familiar. If skill or knowledge becomes important in social programming, then its main value slips away. Most social recreation programs require only simple skills with few rules and oftentimes improvised equipment. In addition, there is no emphasis on distinguishing between age levels or skill differences. For example, the dramatic social recreation experience encourages the talented thespian and the novice alike to have equal opportunity for group fun in dramatics.

Social recreation relies on all other program areas to achieve its social interaction objective. A party may include aspects of sports, drama, music, crafts, dance, and the out-of-doors, but in the social setting these experiences usually are secondary to cooperation, friendship, and enjoyment. Occasionally a social recreation activity is organized so that the goodwill created by socialization enables other recreation activities to function better. A tennis club that has members bickering, complaining, or losing interest could plan a dinner dance that gives them a chance to know each other as individuals rather than just as competitors.

Values The very title of this program area states its top-echelon value: socialization. Well-conducted social recreation programs help people build desirable social relationships. Participants can learn positive group skills, respect for others, awareness of themselves as group members, and the value of democratic group participation.

In addition, social recreation provides a strong potential to fulfill the needs for security, recognition, and new experience. Social programming often involves nonroutine activities and differing group configurations. Most people tend to repeat social contact with old friends, family, business associates, and work companions. However, in situations where new social contacts predominate, the possibilities for new experiences are valued highly. The development of new friendships, as well as the maintenance of old ones, is usually the most frequently cited reason for social get-togethers. Social programming also serves to attract new members and to add variety to an organization's or a company's regular business.

Social recreation experiences also afford the value of recognition. Even though being part of a group requires some conformity, being a member of a group gathered for a special reason offers some distinction. Social recognition can become very important for those who are unsuccessful in the more structured aspects of their lives. By identifying with others in a friendly, supportive setting, the social participant gains feelings of security and a sense of belonging.

Planning considerations In planning social recreation events certain factors should be considered. The most important planning factor is appropriateness. What is the group, and why are we asking them to be sociable? The organizational patterns for activities must be geared to the answers to these questions. For example, is this the first gathering of strangers, or is it the assembling of people with already established relationships? In some cases programming involves only providing the place and the accessories (such as food and decorations), setting up, and then letting the interaction begin. In other cases social recreation programs should be highly structured according to a set pattern of progression.

Programmers have often suggested that a social recreation event should follow a "social action curve." This means that there should be a low level of excitement as the participants arrive for the event, and it should build to a higher level about midway through. Then toward the end of the event, the level of excitement should decline. This social action curve advocates a definite beginning and an end for a social event.

Adherence to an excitement level curve depends on the degree of formality and preplanned structure desired or its appropriateness for the occasion. A highly structured social recreation event (such as a square dance for sixth graders) is planned according to a widely recognized format; the event should include first-comer activities, ice breakers, mixers, active games or dances, and quiet activities. First-comer experiences are designed to involve participants as soon as they arrive. They are actions that can be entered into or departed from at any time without disturbing the flow. Such activities can be enjoyed individually or in small groups, and they may be competitive or noncompetitive. Ice breakers occur next to announce that the social recreation event has begun. They are actions that involve all participants for the purpose of initiating sociability. Next are mixer activities, which offer participants an opportunity for direct communication. Active games involve more vigorous interaction and are followed by the calming influence of quiet closing activities.

The more a social planner knows about the people with whom he or she will be planning social events, the more intelligently the degree of structure can suit. Age of the participant is one of the most important factors in determining appropriateness. Children, for example, come to a party on a rather high emotional level and have less need for activities to stimulate social interaction than adults do. However, they often require a carefully planned sequence of events to control the emotional pitch of the group.

The second planning consideration is leadership quality. The social recreation leader must be personable and dynamic enough to motivate large groups, yet sensitive enough to appeal to smaller gatherings. The trained leader knows how to study the situation, feel the pulse of those involved, and recognize when to insert direct stimulation or control and when to allow the natural flow of events to occur. The leader must also be proficient in human relations and group processes and well versed in motivational techniques. The quality of the leadership is a vital element in social recreation program planning because participant enjoyment of the experience often hinges on this element.

Types of social recreation activities   What kinds of experiences are typically provided in social recreation programs? Whether choosing activities for 100 couples or a 25-member Brownie troop, the planner can offer numerous types of socialization experiences. Too often social recreation is thought of only as parties with decorations and refreshments. Yet it includes dances, banquets, covered-dish suppers, picnics, holiday celebrations, costume competitions, club meetings, coffee houses, and other festive occasions. For more examples, see the box below.

TYPES OF SOCIAL RECREATION ACTIVITIES

Parties

Co-recreation sports nights
Party games
Pageants
Circus and fairs
Card parties
Birthday parties
Hayrides
Masquerades
Scavenger hunts
Treasure hunts
Holiday parties

Clubs

Drop-in centers
Coffee houses
Senior citizen social clubs

Eating events

Coffee/tea hours
Banquets
Dinners
Picnics
Eating out socially
Barbecues
Potluck suppers
Clambakes
Ice cream socials
Cookouts
Taffy pulls
Receptions
Brunches
Fund-raisers

Meetings

Political
Charitable
Cultural
Social

Social dances

Amateur nights
Square dances
Formal dances
Club dances

Visiting/conversation

Visiting hours
Receptions
Visiting shut-ins
Shared television viewing
Open houses

The social recreation program area has tremendous variety because much of its activity crosses over into other program areas. For example, some of the more creative party games include dramatics; a club may be organized around a particular hobby; and social dances naturally revolve around dancing.

Parties occur more frequently in social programming than any other activity type because they are popular and because they can happen easily—at any facility, with any group, and for any occasion. Clubs, families, agencies, schools, churches, businesses, and industry identify the party as an immediate means of socialization and goodwill. Parties are usually planned around a special need, theme, or celebration (seasonal holidays, birthdays, and anniversaries). The element of surprise is frequently and successfully used to make a party different. Do the unexpected: hire a palm reader to lightheartedly tell the guest's fortunes.

If it were not for the expense of energy and funds in food preparation, the eating event would be the most frequently used means of initiating socialization. Food has an ability to bring people together in a congenial manner like no other piece of recreation equipment. The social recreation programmer uses the eating event in many forms—the pot luck, the picnic, the coffee, the tea, the box social, the reception, the progressive dinner, the cookout, the coffee break, and the taffy pull. These events all rely on food as the magnetic center for conversation and activity.

The social dance uses dance much as the eating event uses food. There is activity and physical contact (usually), with music as the motivating force. The social dance has always been one of the most difficult of program areas in terms of guaranteeing success. Social dances continue to follow a mercurial pattern—from great success to great failure and vice versa almost overnight.

The club approach is one of the best organizational tools for bonding people together socially on a more-than-temporary basis. Because clubs emerge out of a common and established interest, they often aid the programmer by having members in ready reserve to support a class, special event, or league in their interest area.

The meeting—whether it be for a charitable cause, a business decision, or skills and knowledge training—deserves special consideration as a social event. In practice many participants in special interest meetings enjoy these encounters so much that their relationships extend beyond the meeting setting to other situations. In fact, some planners use the meeting format to bring people together for more involved social interaction.

Socialization is the very basis of visiting friends and relatives, conversing with neighbors over the back fence, chatting while in the sauna, and talking on the telephone. The programmer (although not actually a controller here) should try to encourage conversation as a recreational activity.

Summary People of all ages and situations have a need for social recreation. Its primary value in a total recreation program is the contribution to the social health of the participant. Social recreation is usually organized according to an informal, appropriateness-conscious approach that is adapted to the interests and abilities of the participants. Emphasis on skill and winning is minimized; group cohesiveness, fun, and enjoyment are far more important. Social recreation rarely stands alone; it is that extra polish that is often applied to another purpose. For example, it is used to end a crafts program, start the basketball season, introduce a new employee, celebrate a holiday, or express thanks for a job well done.

Arts and crafts

Arts and crafts provide an outlet for human expression and creativity. Creativity is a universal human need; many view it as closely linked to establishing an individual's very identity. In decorating each fish in Fig. 5-1, the urge to create has carried this young student beyond the limitations of the classroom assignment. In reviewing the history of arts and crafts, beginning with the uninstructed but vitally felt cave drawings of primitive people, one cannot escape the conclusion that arts and crafts are a basic and necessary human activity. This is evident when a child begins to draw; the drawings reflect the child's spirit and natural response to color, rhythm, form, and texture. Unfortunately, as the child advances into adulthood, the lessons of society blunt this responsiveness, and he or she develops a greater appreciation for accuracy and realism than for a beautiful color, a bold line, or a vibrant texture.

According to Tillman (1973, p. 155), "Arts and crafts as a process is self-indulging; it becomes creative when something is produced that positively adds some dimension, small as it may be, to society." Historically art and craft experiences have contributed to the development and enrichment of the creative personality, and in doing so they have ultimately contributed to the positive worth of community life. Since the arts and crafts programs of woodworking, sewing, and weaving for children in the Boston Sand Gardens of 1885, recreation agencies have continued to explore program avenues through which people can understand their own creative capabilities and realize that they can paint seascapes or design silver jewelry.

To some programmers it is important to distinguish between arts and crafts in order to better serve the needs of the participant. Crafts may be viewed as the use of materials to make items that have utilitarian value. Art may be identified as the use of materials to demonstrate a symbol, concept, or perception. Why people engage in the experience may be the best means of further distinction. People engage in crafts to create something for themselves or for others or to test their creative potential. For the participant art seems to mean a calculated involvement to succeed—to produce an object that will contribute to the aesthetics of the environment or to achieve acclaim over other works in an exhibition. Historically, crafts have emerged from the utilitarian needs of a society: furnishings, food vessels, clothing, and utensils. Art has sought to create the refinements and ornamentations for an otherwise dull world.

Values   People not only need to express their creativity; they also need to communicate it to one another. Communication is one of the primary values of arts and crafts. As a person creates a sculpture out of a gnarled piece of walnut or a

Fig. 5-1 *The urge to create.*

From Wankelman, Willard F., and Philip Wigg, Arts & Crafts: A Handbook of Arts and Crafts for Elementary and Junior High School Teachers, 4th. ed. Copyright 1968, 1974, 1978 Wm. C. Brown Company Publishers, Dubuque, Iowa. Reprinted by permission.

sweater out of a ball of yarn or a scene out of canvas and acrylics, that person is taking an opportunity for self-expression. Therefore the object created reflects his or her personality and culture. The object itself allows the person to communicate a personal emotional expression. Although certainly not every arts and crafts program participant has the capacity to become a celebrated artist, he or she can make a personal expression that is valid for that person. Using one's hands to express a culture or an individual personality in an object relates to the origin and growth of life itself. This channel of communication has been and will continue to be a vital record of civilization.

Modern society is responsible for replacing the human role in making the necessities of everyday life. The urge to manipulate, control, or mold something with one's own hands—to touch good wood, to fold paper, to cause clay to turn colors under heat, to melt glass—is strong. In crafting an object or developing an artistic expression, the participant is the dominating, motivating factor in the final outcome. Manipulative art and craft experiences are a valuable part of a child's learning. For example, some educators see manipulative activities as directly contributing to the development of linguistic expression. During childhood, learning to associate verbal dialogue with thought expression is transferred from the expression of thought manifested through handicrafts (Benson and Frankson, 1975).

"I made it!" The pride of accomplishment is a vital value of arts and crafts programming. The 50-year-old woman who watercolors her first portrait not only has an opportunity to revel in the pride of accomplishment but also enjoys the compliments of viewers.

Arts and crafts has objectives beyond the personal rewards of creativity, communication, manipulation, and accomplishment. These more utilitarian values are aesthetic development and therapeutic aid. Although the primary emphasis of this program area should be placed on enjoyment and the satisfaction of creating, the planner should constantly aim toward the development of aesthetic good taste and appreciation of beauty, form, and design. The development of an appreciation for attractive color and shape ultimately affects the beauty of the environment in which we all live. Craft experiences have also been used to reduce emotional tensions and to bring about desirable psychological reactions and behaviors. This value has been labeled *art therapy,* and its usefulness has been documented in many different therapeutic settings.

Planning considerations   Participation in arts and crafts can be individual or it can involve joint participation. Unlike certain forms of sports, drama, or social recreation, its enjoyment does not necessitate the involvement of others; nor is there usually a need for a specifically designed area or leader. However, this does not eliminate the need for rational planning and critical forethought. Certain planning considerations are particularly applicable to art and craft programming.

Perhaps the most creatively useful consideration is the use of crafts in other areas of recreation programming. Crafts can be an effective part of dance, drama, music, social and outdoor recreation, and hobbies. For example, craft projects and instruction can be incorporated into the stage sets, costumes, and makeup for a dramatic production. The integration of crafts with activities in the natural environment can enhance the appreciation of the beauty of the natural setting, or it can lead to the development of outdoor living utensils. Social recreation experiences can be complemented by craft projects such as table centerpieces, handmade candles, gift wrapping, or stitchery work on table linens. This correlation is not meant to suggest that arts and crafts are a service or crutch for other program areas. On the contrary, if art and craft experiences are not planned to enhance other program areas, they should not be planned.

Art and craft programs that are planned for their own sake are greatly influenced by the scope and adequacy of the leadership, the material and equipment resources, and the skill levels of participants. The degree of simplicity or complexity should be determined by these three factors. Programs may range from finger painting to batiking, from embroidering to loom weaving, from papier-mâché to wood carving.

An arts and crafts specialist or leader is just as important to the effectiveness of a crafts program as a coach is to the success of a basketball team. However, multiskilled arts and crafts leaders are sometimes difficult to locate. This need not be a deterrent because an effective program can be developed by using several single-skilled, part-time or volunteer instructors instead of one or more full-time persons. The major role of the leadership, nonetheless, is to stimulate careful and quality workmanship, stress creativity and originality, encourage free expression, and provide constructive guidance. Respect for the individual and his or her ideas is a cardinal code of conduct for the leader who expects a genuine and sustained interest from program participants. The most meaningful art forms have been born and nurtured in an atmosphere of freedom. Leaders must remember the importance of recognition of

RAY BELLAROSA

TYPES OF ART AND CRAFT ACTIVITIES

Drawing and sketching

Calligraphy
Graphics
Pencil
Charcoal
Pen and ink
Computer terminal free-form sketching

Jewelry making

Lapidary
Silver molding
Bead weaving

Printing

Block printing
Silk screen
Stenciling
Vegetable printing

Sculpture

Clay modeling
Papier mâché
Wax sculpturing
Soap carving
Sand casting
Dough art

Painting

China painting
Finger painting
Oil
Sponge painting
Batiking
Water colors
Building murals

Leatherwork

Leather tooling
Carving
Dyeing

Model building

Boats
Airplanes
Automobiles

Cooking/baking

Cakes
Pies
International menus
Canning
Gourmet
Dough art

Photography

Developing
Picture composition
Matting
Filmmaking

Woodworking

Carving
Picture frame making
Furniture making

Pottery/ceramics

Pouring molds
Painting glaze
Pottery wheel
Coil method
Pinch pot

Sewing and needlecraft

Knitting
Puppets
Embroidery
Crewel
Quilting
Crocheting

Weaving

Chair caning
Macramé
Rug hooking
Tapestry weaving
Baskets

Paper

Christmas cards
Origami
Foil sculpture
Paper making

TYPES OF ART AND CRAFT ACTIVITIES—cont'd

Candle making

Beeswax candles
Hand dipping
Molds

Metal craft

Tin craft
Copper enameling
Silver molding

Scrap crafts

Collage
Mosaics
Nature crafts

---

participants. The younger the participants, the more emphatic the recognition should be. The wise leader sees the best in each person's efforts and uses this understanding to guide and inspire.

Arts and crafts projects can be conducted in the janitor's closet on a card table, squatting on the playground asphalt, or on a cot at camp. Adaptability to place is one of the most attractive aspects of this program area. However, the more appropriate the environment, the more meaningful the craft experience. Some crafts do require attention to special facilities and equipment. In ceramics, for example, the pleasure is lost if there is no kiln, sink, or worktable or if enough glaze colors, molds, or brushes are not available for creative free expression. The desire to establish a regular arts and crafts workshop emerges when there is extensive, sustained interest in certain activities and an ongoing program is maintained. When a workshop is available, it should be well lighted and have adequate work, storage, and exhibition space. Inclusion of reference materials is also desirable. Clean-up facilities should include sinks, running water, soap, and towels. Safety considerations include proper storage for flammable materials, adequate ventilation, fire extinguishers, segregated areas for power tools, and a first aid kit.

As art or craft experiences become specialized and complex, the participants' levels of skill should be predetermined and evenly balanced for program effectiveness. Novices should experience simple projects with easy-to-use materials; skilled artisans should be challenged so that their skills will continue to develop. (Remember that projects developed by highly skilled participants and by beginners should be measured solely by the personal satisfaction that comes from the doing.) A good community recreation program normally has arts and crafts programs operating at many different skill levels. It is important for the planner to realize that no arts and crafts activity can remain static but must continuously provide the participant with a link to new and increasingly significant fields of expression.

Types of arts and crafts activities The preceding box illustrates the numerous categories for grouping activities in arts and crafts. Like other program areas, it is as broad as there are individuals or groups of people and as varied as there are different types and combinations of materials. What craft or art projects are planned within these categories is determined by leadership, resources, and participant competency. For example, under the sculpture category the activity may range from sandbox castles to bronze life-size sculptures; weaving may vary from string belts to draperies; woodworking may range from a whittled marshmallow stick to mahogany furniture.

The most commonly planned arts and crafts projects for children have been paper crafts, clay modeling, leathercraft, weaving, drawing, painting, woodworking, metal crafts, ceramics, needlecraft, and plastics. The most frequently planned projects for adults have been ceramics, painting, leathercraft, drawing, and needlecraft (Weiskopf, 1975, p. 234). Whether this planning has been based on determination of need (according to the process of planning as advocated in this book) is doubtful. An arts and crafts program may be as broad as the materials available. It is restricted only by the abilities and vision of its leadership and by the expressed needs of its constituents.

Summary Art and craft experiences are a major source of human expression as well as human release. The art experience has been traditionally used by program planners as the most predictable way of fulfilling identity needs through creativity. As Albert Tillman (1973, p. 155) has aptly said: "Only someone who has entered the arts and crafts arena and felt the pangs of endeavor can meaningfully pay hundreds of dollars for a handcrafted carving that is also available for $1.98 in molded plastic."

Art and craft experiences seem to exist in current programming because (1) they are expected; (2) they help fill the cultural gap created by an overemphasis on sports; and (3) making things with your hands is universally appealing. To some degree this statement is well taken. Art and craft programs have been victims of habit, and they have had to compete for participants and budgets with more demonstrative program areas. But there are signs suggesting that art and craft programming may be coming into its own.

Participants seem to be taking arts and crafts more seriously and are increasingly interested in developing craft talents and skills. Sand castles at the beach have become a serious art form; high-level crafts such as glassblowing and stained-glass design are increasingly being requested from agencies. Increased competition among artisans is also coming into vogue despite conscientious efforts by program planners to make success an individual evaluation. The growing number of arts and crafts shows that involve cash awards can meaningfully serve the talented, and the student planner needs to learn to handle them professionally and effectively.

Dance

Throughout the years, dance has gained both favor and disfavor as entertainment and recreation. From the ancient ritualistic dances of the Egyptians to the occupational dances of the Middle Ages, from the courtly dance pace of the Renaissance to the frenzied Charleston of the twenties, from the earliest American hoe-downs to the rockabilly steps of the eighties, dance has been alternately praised and condemned. We Americans have been particularly fickle in our attitudes toward dance. George Washington, for example, greatly admired the artistry of dancer John Durang, the son of a soldier of the American Revolution and the first professional dancer of note to be produced by the new United States (Terry, 1980). By the end of the nineteenth century, however, the lingering Victorian attitude of American audiences totally rejected the free-spirited dance innovations of Isadora Duncan, who is now considered an important founder of modern dance.

Dance is a form of expression through movement; it is an active response to rhythm. As such it can have strong appeal to both spectator and participant. Dance may be a tightly woven group or social recreation experience or a highly individualized art form. Dance is the primordial urge to move in rhythm. Infants cry for the cradle's rocking motion, and adults move their bodies in a pattern than matches their moods. Each of us listens to our own private drumbeat, plugging it into our emotions, and accompanying our rhythmic body motions with music. This dance movement conveys feelings and ideas; communication is its goal.

Dance has played a central role in the activity of life in all societies. It has been intimately related to the human traditions of religion, war, love, occupation, and celebration. In fact, dance is made up of the fundamental human movements—jumping, running, darting, turning, sliding, and stretching. Although modified by social, political, religious, and popular influences throughout history, the spontaneity of dance, as initiated by the feelings and needs of the people, is a strong factor in its long survival.

During the last several decades there has been a significant increase in the number of persons and groups participating in dancing as recreation. In some communities a close relationship has been established among schools, recreation agencies, commercial and private dance studios, and private special interest clubs. This cooperation has paved the way for an interchange of leadership, program ideas, and dance techniques that has resulted in a higher level of appreciation and participation in community events.

Values   Dance can be a successful program experience in a variety of settings and for a wide range of spectators or participants. Depending on how it is used by the programmer, it can match a long list of need fulfillments. According to the type of dance, the values and rewards range from a simple opportunity for free expression to the satisfaction of accomplishing exacting movement patterns.

A prime value of dance is its contribution to the physical fitness of the participant. Physical activity in dance can equal participation in the most vigorous sport. Dance is a versatile exercise that aids muscle tone, weight control, gracefulness, and general body control and health. A second important value of dance is the opportunity some forms offer for social interaction. The atmosphere of folk and social dance, for example, allows participants to concentrate on each other rather than on performing for an audience or meeting skill specifications. When dance is programmed for socialization, emphasis must be diverted from concern for the critical eye of others to physical and emotional exuberance.

Recreation authors have listed creativity, aesthetics, cultural understanding, relaxation, self-confidence, and new experience as other values applicable to dancing. Because dance can be programmed to serve many functions, it offers a variety of values. Certainly its greatest program potential is as a physical means for self-expression. Dance also can be vital as a vehicle for permitting people to relate to each other in group situations.

Planning considerations Organized recreation programming has done its best job with children, especially at the younger ages and at the introductory level of participation. In recreation programs most dancing consists of instructional classes. The classes are usually highly structured and culminate in recitals before an audience of family and friends. Another common programming use of dance is to bridge social gaps. Dance has been used as a reason for getting people together and providing a communication bridge between people in various social recreation programs.

Program planning considerations for the dance experience are not very different from those of other recreation program areas. Attention to participant needs, interests, and skills remains a primary consideration. Planning principles that are particularly pertinent to dance will be presented in the form of five broad areas: (1) leadership, (2) equipment and facility, (3) community resources, (4) performance outlets, and (5) role of competition.

The recreation agency that undertakes sponsorship of dance activities for its constituency should first consider that successful dance programming is based on competent and experienced dance leadership. Particularly for instructional groups, the trained dance teacher is essential. The dance teacher should be able to present, adapt, coach, and control a program of quality without forfeiting the element of fun and enjoyment.

As with sports programming, dance programs depend on a minimum standard of equipment and facility. A well-ventilated area with good acoustics and adequate floor space and surface is essential. Too small an area makes movement difficult and destroys the quality of the dance experience. In socially oriented dancing too large an area destroys group cohesiveness and breaks the spirit of the gathering. The condition of the floor surface is perhaps the most important facility consideration; the degree of slickness desired depends on the type of dance. For instance, both traditional ballroom dancing and disco dancing require a hard, smooth surface such as hardwood or linoleum tiles. On the other hand, popular rock dancing can be programmed for almost any flat surface—even a sandy beach or a carpeted living room. Adequate musical accompaniment—whether it be records, a pianist, or a large dance band—is an absolute must. Sufficient amplification is also a consideration; the success of a square dance program depends, for example, on being able to hear the calls.

Dance programming should constantly try to use all available community resources. Incorporation of dance experts, dance teachers, choreographers, and dance professionals from other agencies or from independent community organizations should be considered by the programmer. However, it is important to avoid competition with private studios or dance clubs that are already successfully meeting certain constituency needs. The program planner should seek to fill service gaps rather than duplicate what is already being offered.

Dance programming, particularly for instructional dance, requires periodic performance outlets. It is an ideal concept that one should be totally inner directed and uninfluenced by outside recognition. Our social training mandates that we have at least some dependence on others for shaping our evaluation of ourselves. The "end of the program" performance event is the way the program planner rewards and highlights the time and effort of the participants. The planner can use this performance outlet to structure the participant's whole dance experience, to guide future efforts, and to offer fulfillment beyond self-expression—cooperation, recognition, and reward.

A final planning consideration is to design cooperation rather than competition into dance programs in order to encourage the most effective participant fulfillment. As Tillman (1973, p. 172) states, "When dance is used to emphasize an individual's expression more is gained if everyone wins to some degree. Cooperation leads to achievements of a different dimension than the individual dancer can accomplish alone." Although it is occasionally desirable to use well-thought-out competition in dance programming, by tradition and practice dance has served the participant as a cooperative, expressive effort.

Types of dance activities   Many listings and classifications of dance and rhythmics have been proposed by planners. The types of dance experiences that are most frequently found in recreation programs are shown in the opposite box.

According to the Athletic Institute (1963), folk dancing consists of those movement experiences that are the outgrowth of the everyday lives of people and have survived to become a part of the traditional social custom of the culture. Folk dance programming provides an opportunity for people to costume themselves and imagine through dance their own and others' folk heritage. Part of the enjoyment in folk dancing is learning how the various dance patterns depict the environment in which people lived, their occupational roles, the major events of their lives, their religious beliefs, and the customs of their social lives. Folk dancing has enjoyed much popularity in playground, recreation center, and camp settings, particularly in the format of pageants and festivals.

Early in this century there evolved in America a new kind of dance that, for want of a better name, was labeled modern or contemporary dance. Modern dance is the art of total creative expression and communication of ideas through movement. It

---

TYPES OF DANCE ACTIVITIES

Folk

International folk dance festival
Ethnic dancing
Romanian dance club
Instruction

Social/popular

Teen dances
Dance mixers
Sadie Hawkins dance
Dance contest

Tap

Instruction
Performance
Parent nights
Show dancing
Tryouts

Ballet

Performance attendance
Instruction
Performing
Clinics with professionals

Modern/interpretive

Instruction
Conditioning and free exercise
Performing
Performance attendance
Clinics with professionals

Acrobatic

Baton and drill teams
Talent shows
Belly dancing
Instruction

Ballroom

Formal dances
Instruction
Ethnic dance forms
Waltz club

Children's rhythms

Free rhythms
Identification rhythms
Rhythm games

Country/square

Square dance clubs
Clog dancing
Competitions
Learning to call

---

came into being out of an aesthetic necessity. Its originators were rejecting the rigidities of ballet and the thematic material rooted in fairy tales and fanciful dreams of butterflies, flowers, and sugarplums. Education in the art of story or idea communication through improvisational body movements is often necessary for both spectator and participant enjoyment of modern dance.

Social or popular dance experiences are offered by more recreation agencies than any other type of dance. As a co-recreational activity, social dancing has a great attraction for people of all ages and environments. It is also one of the few dance activities that involves a minimum amount of planning. Perhaps more than any other type of dance, the social dance portrays the spirit of the times.

A spin-off of dance activity is the widely popular area of acrobatic dance. This is usually programmed as baton twirling, drill teams, and floor exercise in gymnastics. Tap dancing involves the mastery of intricate foot maneuvers and is enjoyed because of the sound patterns resulting from the shoe taps. A large percentage of the participants who choose acrobatic or tap dancing are, it seems, interested in the ultimate goal of performance.

Ballet requires a technical regimen of classical movements. The ballet offered in the recreation program is often modified from the classical style but still requires well-trained leadership. Ballet training has been considered beneficial in developing poise, grace, and self-assurance in young children, as well as professional football players.

Creative rhythmic movements typically have been used to introduce small children to music and dance. Children can participate in rhythmic experiences as if playing games; the movements are informal, unpressured, and largely interpretive. Rhythmic experiences also are presented to children as a way of exploring fundamental motions such as walking, running, galloping, striding; as a means of understanding space; and as a way of learning responses to various sounds and stimuli.

Although they derive their origins from Europe, square dancing, clogging, reels, and running sets are the only true American folk dances. Square dancing is probably the simplest form of group dancing available for programming; the basic shuffling step used throughout is relatively easy for most people. All that remains is to listen for the formation instructions from the caller. Square dancing has particular social appeal because of the constant change of partners and intermingling of couples.

Summary   In recent years evidence has pointed to the importance of and need for larger and more varied programming in dance. Television and film presentations of all kinds of dance have offered people a greater exposure to this program area than was previously available. As a result, more schools include dance in physical education classes, more dance curriculums are now available at the college level, and there is a stronger national emphasis on dance as a performing art. These developments will continue to stimulate a greater demand for dance experiences from recreation agencies. Intelligent and sensitive program planning is needed to promote dance as a truly expressive recreation outlet.

Drama

Our universal attachment to the experience of drama is apparent in our daily life: in the make-believe play of little children, in our fascination with movies and television, and even in the little stories we tell about ourselves to colleagues over morning coffee. Drama allows us to interpret our environment and our feelings to others through techniques and styles that both entertain and communicate. The need to share thoughts and emotions must have developed as soon as it was realized that people had them. Drama is an imitation of life. It is the most personal and direct way of passing on our culture.

What distinguishes programmed recreational drama from life's drama is the player's option to walk away from a role. Drama, which of all recreation activity areas is the most direct copy of life, is designed to fulfill needs for self-expression without pressure for survival. In dramatics, performers and audiences can try out new personalities, thoughts, and relationships without serious consequences.

At the first known American theater performance in Virginia in 1665, the participants were arrested. From then until the opening of the John Street Theater in New York City in 1767, dramatic activities were severely suppressed by Puritan influences. It was not until the nineteenth century that drama became the nation's foremost mass cultural activity. By the mid-1960s, on an annual basis over 100 million people attended almost 500,000 theater performances, performed and produced by over 25,000 groups (Kando, 1980, p. 148). There were more theatergoers in America than boaters, skiers, golfers, and skin divers combined.

By the mid-1970s, despite the astronomical growth of amateur regional theater, the total annual number of tickets sold was estimated at only 62 million (*U.S. News and World Report*, 1977). The drama experience so widely available through television is probably the most significant factor in this change. Television viewing is by far the most popular and most time-consuming recreational activity in the United States. Today the average television set is turned on for 6 hours every day. Because a qualitative discussion of television as a dramatic medium is not in the scope of this book, it is sufficient to say that there are those who see a lot of good in it and those who do not. I think that the value question boils down to whether television is fulfilling its artistic and intellectual potential and whether it is adequately meeting the participant needs for dramatic experiences.

Both spontaneous and planned drama programs can be experienced today in most community recreation and park programs. Drama activities can be as simple and unpretentious as a children's story hour or patient television viewing in a hospital, or they can be as elaborate as an annual pageant involving hundreds of skilled performers or a professional production by a national company.

Although ticket purchases to formal dramatic performances are declining, other attendance figures report that more and more people are practicing the dramatic arts and becoming participants/performers rather than just members of the audience. New community programs are being started under alternative auspices; adult education has taken on a larger role in improving skills and appreciation; and there has been closer cooperation among diverse recreation agencies and recreation settings for the creative provision of the dramatic experience. See the box on p. 174 for a delightful illustration of this new emphasis on alternative dramatic programming.

Values   Drama activities offer participants the opportunity to express them-

SAD MR. LION AND HIS LOST HAPPY SONG

by John R. Sharpham

Take a large local park, a group of 50 children, several creative drama instructors, a warm spring morning, and an idea, and what might result? Using the entire park as a play area the children developed a two-hour dramatization around a simple story line suggested by the instructors.

The story started the moment the children entered the park. The instructors had borrowed theater costumes and were dressed as a lion, Lorax, a bird, Mother Nature, a clown, Timothy Ugly, and a princess. As the children arrived they were greeted by Mother Nature and her helpers and led into the pavilion. When all the children had arrived they were introduced to Mr. Lion from the small zoo next door and were told that he was sad because the wind had stolen the four lines of his happy song and hidden them all over the park. Would the children help him find his song and make him smile again? The children chorused "Yes!" and filed outside to look for clues.

On the pavilion balcony they discovered a large bird-like creature who eventually confessed to having the first line of the song. He was persuaded to give it up, but only after the children had answered some riddles and told him some of their jokes. In return he taught them the first line of the song and then led them to the playground where the Lorax was waiting. She had a clue which she surrendered after teaching the children a complicated dance step leading them through the trees and back to the pavilion. There in a shadowy corner sat Timothy Ugly who thought himself so ugly that he would not talk to the children for they were all prettier than he.

The children were led quietly away, and Mother Nature suggested that they make the ugliest masks possible so that Mr. Ugly would talk to them and help them find the song. All the materials for the mask making were laid out on the floor, and the young people worked for about 40 minutes designing and making their ugly masks. Then they all crept down to the corner with their masks on and called out to Mr. Ugly. Reluctantly he turned and, delighted with what he saw, talked to the children and gave up the second line of the song. He then led the children out of the pavilion down to a bridge where a pretty princess helped them search for the third line. A great roar went up when it was discovered beneath a weeping willow. The children, led by the students, sang and danced their way back to the pavilion seeking the final line. After a thorough search it was found by a group of small children still wearing their masks.

The children put the four lines together and sang the song. Only then did they realize the lion was missing, saddened by the loss of his song. After a quick search he was discovered in his cage in the zoo (by arrangement with the friendly curator who thought the whole thing was a marvelous idea). The children streamed to the cage and asked Mr. Lion why he was there. Supported by the background roars of other lions, he explained that he felt so miserable because the song was lost. Delighted by this, the children produced the four scrolls and proceeded to sing him the song, several times and quite loudly. The lion was released, and the happy youngsters returned to the pavilion for cookies and lemonade.

Reprinted from the 9:6 (1974) issue of *Parks & Recreation* by special permission of the National Recreation and Park Association.

selves through imaginative and interpretive play. Every individual has the tools necessary for this expression: a voice and a body. The values derived from the creative use of these tools can be numerous and often very personal.

The primary value, and thus the major motivation for participation, is that involvement in the dramatic arts can extend the horizons of the participant by stimulating the imagination and by providing an opportunity to be something else temporarily. Well-programmed drama includes the chance to achieve a very personal, original, or escapist expression without the pressure of reality. For the professional performer or for any participant concerned with the pressures of audience criticism, the recreational value of escape, fantasy, and make-believe may be impossible.

In addition to fulfilling creative needs, drama is valuable as a means of interpersonal exchange and group interaction. The creative processes of drama may be personal and individual, but they also invite interplay between people: performer-performer and performer-audience. Informal dramatics and dramatic games, for example, are frequently programmed for social recreation purposes.

Understanding others is another positive value afforded by dramatic experiences. It helps people to better understand their own life-styles and to appreciate life-styles and cultures different from their own. Drama requires sensitivity to others whether the audience is viewing the role of a particular character or a performer is relating the role to others. Empathy is stimulated by drama in another way. Being part of an enjoyable dramatic undertaking creates a sense of belonging and cooperation as much as any team sport does. The drama experience depends on people working together.

Appreciation and development of body movements and voice tones as art forms are other possible values of the drama experience. Children and adults alike can develop poise and self-control from training and involvement in drama. Many other diverse talents and abilities can be incorporated into drama programming. People can sharpen other creative talents or skills by participating in such support functions as costuming, set design, script writing, and directing.

Drama has also been one of the most successful recreational therapies. When handled correctly, dramatic involvement offers the opportunity to express all emotions and to release hostility and anger under the protective shield of make-believe. Psychodrama is one of the most powerful examples of such therapy.

Planning considerations   Dramatic communication, whether a game of charades at a party or a stirring portrayal of Lady Macbeth, provides a rich area for recreation programming. There is no community, agency, or recreation group so lacking in talent or interest that, if stimulated, cannot initiate dramatic programming.

Planners of dramatic programs should understand that drama as a recreative experience needs to offer broad goals for the talented as well as interesting horizons for the uninspired. Each participation or each attendance at a performance should provide a step in a progression of dramatic opportunities that range from the simple to the sophisticated. A program's success is not necessarily dependent on attaining a goal such as a play production and performance. The basic creative elements of storytelling, dramatic games, and skits can serve to prepare young persons for more highly developed and formal productions, but these simple elements should also be emphasized and enjoyed for their own sake.

A similar planning consideration is for programmed drama to provide both passive and active formats. Drama offers the flexibility for quiet, thoughtful, introspective activity or for energetic and vigorous action. The planner deals with a wide range of mental and physical involvement for tailoring the drama experience to meet various individual and group needs. Community recreation programs should give particular attention to providing complementary areas, facilities, and leadership for the broad range of dramatic activities.

There is another great range in the nature, size, and organization of facilities for drama programming. The most demanding requirements are made by the formal production; yet highly complex presentations have been conducted with many kinds of accommodations. Dramatic experiences can take place anywhere: a private home, community center, vacant store building, church, steps of a public building, terrace, park, garden, lake, swimming pool deck, river bank, gazebo, patio, or mobile van.

In spite of this flexibility there are minimum requirements for dramatic presentations (Athletic Institute, 1963, p. 85):

1. A performing area that is in full audience view
2. A performing area large enough to accommodate the performers and the action that is the play
3. Easy access to the staging area for players and scenery
4. Elimination of the noise and distraction from adjacent activities

Even though these facility requirements are minimal, enjoyment of the drama experience is heightened by good facilities. I have often viewed a drama group rehearsing on the stage of an all-purpose room while basketball practice was being conducted on the gym floor. Although the quality of the basketball experience was not affected seriously, the drama experience became nearly impossible.

Informal dramatic activities make simple demands on facilities. A classroom or an activity room, gathering around a picnic table or crowding together in a tent during a rainstorm are all suitable for imaginative play or games. These areas should be free from distraction and offer good visibility for all participants.

In the last decade mobile units have come to serve a number of functions for community drama programming. Trucks or vans equipped with facilities for puppet shows, children's theater performances, talent shows, and even professionally produced productions are transported to various sections of the community. Often the programming format is to bring in a traveling unit equipped with a portable stage and a trained nucleus of talented staff persons around whom the local participants can perform in peripheral but meaningful roles.

Staging equipment (scenery, lighting, sound equipment, costumes, and makeup) is brought into the drama experience to provide a setting for characters and to assist them in telling their story. Such equipment can run the gamut of complexity and expense. The preparation of scenery and costumes constitutes a recreational activity in itself. Commercial stage equipment companies furnish catalogs and details to help drama groups better enjoy this aspect of the experience. For productions that require elaborate staging, the planner should first check with local authorities for approval of electrical and wiring changes and installations, check safety recommendations for fireproofing scenery, know proper safety precautions for handling rigging, and become familiar with other local safety controls.

Costumes and makeup are a primary joy of putting on a play or even of telling a story. They help both the performer and the audience feel the illusion of the characters and the setting. The vitality of costumes in children's dramatic activities is especially important, even if the costuming is simple. If costumes are made of good, durable fabric and according to classic designs, they can be varied through the addition of accessories and thus used many ways, many times. Makeup may be a simple or a skillful, complicated procedure. Because makeup is an art, the assistance of an expert is recommended for a large formal production. Clown craft has become a successful program in some innovative recreation agencies. In addition to developing clown stunts and routines, clown craft programs devote considerable attention to the portrayal of emotions through makeup.

In addition to those qualities considered important for any recreation leader, certain interests, attitudes, and abilities are particularly desirable in the drama leader. A specialist trained in drama is, of course, an advantage. However, most general recreation leaders can become proficient in conducting dramatic programs if they receive special training in the philosophy and techniques of acting, play production, and informal creative dramatics. For the regional or community theater, professional leadership is essential to ensure the quality of the experience. The local college drama department is usually a good source for recruiting drama specialists; students majoring in drama find community theater an excellent opportunity for gaining experience. Some remuneration is usually expected.

The leader for a children's drama program, in addition to being able to work well with children, should have a knowledge of creative dramatics and children's literature. The successful drama leader should also possess an ability to improvise and create a lot out of a little. The leader of adult programs is usually required to have some experience as actor, stage manager, and director.

Types of drama activities   The various types and forms of drama make a conclusive list of dramatic activities difficult to compile. The scope or type of dramatic programming will depend on the sponsoring agency's philosophy and objectives, as well as on constituency needs and available facilities, budget, and leadership. The activities listed in the box on p. 178 offer a sampling of ideas common to the recreation program.

In creative drama the performers improvise their own lines and movements. It

TYPES OF DRAMA ACTIVITIES

Creative dramatics

Skits and stunts
Games
Nosebag drama
Shadow plays
Talent shows
Experimental theater

Formal plays

Musicals
Operettas
Pageants
One-act plays
Play tournaments
Opera
Playgoing clubs
Children's acting classes

Puppetry/marionettes

Finger puppets
Mask making
Stick puppets
Marionette acting classes

Radio/film/television

Production
Viewing
Movie mobile

Pantomime/mime

Charades
Story narration
Musical pantomime
Interpretive mime
Clown craft

Dramatic readings

Choral speaking
Play reading clubs
Monodrama
Monologue

Storytelling

Story plays
Storytelling
Dramatization
Imitative stories

is the performer's enjoyment, not the audience's, that is the prime purpose. Much of the dramatic programming for children is made up of creative drama activities. Creative drama for children uses the natural play of children in an educational way: to explore the possibilities of life in an imaginative setting. In creative drama participants are not trained to be actors or even to act; rather they are led to explore their own uniqueness and to expand their imaginative faculties. Scenes and costumes are used infrequently and audiences are incidental.

Formal drama refers to the production of specific dramatic events with lines to be memorized, rehearsals to be practiced, staging to be set, and an audience to be invited. The main ingredient of formal drama is the play, a story acted by players on a stage before an audience. The play itself and the means of preparing for its presentation provide unlimited opportunities for a drama program. Formal productions can provide the peaks in ongoing drama programs, but they need not always be considered the ultimate goal.

Often a participant who is timid about performing on a stage will find it more enjoyable to project through a puppet or marionette. For the child, the interests and skills developed through performing with a finger puppet may progress one day to the intricate art of constructing and handling a string marionette or Muppet. Puppetry programs, like formal drama, usually culminate in presentations before an audience.

The film, television, videotape, and radio category offers two different program formats. First, participants can be involved in viewing of films or listening to radio shows. Second, magnificent program potential lies in the production of films or radio and television performances. For example, amateur cinematography groups that produce drama on 8-mm film are becoming increasingly popular.

Pantomime is the visual expression of an idea or emotion without reliance on the voice. Thoughts and moods are conveyed only through facial expression, body position, and body movement. This medium is secondarily an excellent means of developing fundamental formal drama skills. Some dramatic games also use elements of pantomime.

Dramatic readings involve the reading aloud of dramatic pieces. The reading can be performed either by a single performer or by a group, with or without staging, and for the primary enjoyment of either participant or audience. This most flexible drama activity includes such events as choral speaking, monologues, and monodramas, which offer unique opportunities for interpretive expression. Excerpts from novels or plays, short stories, song lyrics, epic and narrative poetry, and essays can all be read aloud to create a dramatic effect.

The ageless art of storytelling provides excellent recreation for young and old. Stories that begin with action, move forward in terms of clear-cut situations, and build in excitement to a climax are best for both storytelling and story dramatization. Story plays are activities in which the listeners, in groups or as a whole, react with the story line on cue from the storyteller. "Going on a lion hunt" is a favorite illustration of imitative story participation, with the group imitating the actions or words of the storyteller.

Summary   The integration of the drama program area with other program areas is an advantage in creative program planning. For example, the experience of drama can incorporate dance choreography, scenery construction, costume design, musical score composition, and singing as well as the performance of the actors.

The trend in drama programming is toward innovation. Drama productions in the park, actor-audience interactions, amateur film festivals, and commercial mime are all trends likely for the future. The "drama workshop," once an innovative experiment, has developed into more permanent programming. And this is a good idea. When neither staff nor facilities are capable of supporting a sophisticated youth or community theater, the workshop approach invites a guest specialist (often someone of renown) to run a limited series of sessions to expose untrained but enthusiastic participants to the drama experience. Today the drama workshop is an activity in itself, instead of being a preparation for or a mini-version of the theater.

Drama, in its broadest interpretation, caters to one of the most universal of human interests. A sense of the dramatic is as important for a full and rich life as is a sense of humor. The sense of release that comes from pretending to be someone else and the vicarious thrill of identifying with others who are performing are worthy experiences for recreation programming.

Creativity: nontraditional solutions

Recreation program professionals are faced with a dual challenge: to offer programs that meet the needs and interests of their constituency and to help establish new and invigorating trends of leisure pleasures. This dual function requires not only astute constituency research and preplanning but also a spark of creative vision. Nontraditional program solutions are brought into the planning process by the planner at this step only through a capacity to be creative: to be able to improvise, to relate seemingly unrelated concepts, to listen, and to not settle for mediocrity. Gold-panning expeditions, hot-tub construction workshops, hot-air balloon races, fitness programs downtown at noon, gourmet eating clubs, and marathon training clinics are recreation programs that reflect innovation, creativity, and attention to changing life-styles.

How does creativity happen? Can creative planning be developed and practiced? The nurturance of creativity, the capacity to brainstorm new ideas, to improvise, and to relate seemingly unrelated objects or concepts is within the grasp of every thinking person. Creative people are not all eccentric, bohemian, wild-eyed artists. Creativity is a large part of the success of teachers, business executives, doctors, lawyers, and even insurance salesmen. Curtis (1979, p. 123) describes creative people in the following way:

Creative people are usually collectors of information, especially observant, bright but not brilliant, often having average to below average scholastic records; visionary, seeing pictures, relationships, and patterns in everyday things; capable of holding many ideas "juggling" about at the same time; generally vigorous, interested in life, "joie de vivre" types; livers of more complex lives than average; very often self-conscious and quite self-critical; and more primitive and more cultured, more destructive and more constructive, crazier and saner, than the average person.

Creative planning means assembling new concepts or ideas from old, familiar, unrelated ones. It does not mean making something out of nothing. As noted in the discussion on brainstorming (Chapter 5), new and creative program solutions are typically the combination of two or more previously unrelated program solutions. A creative planner brings familiar ideas, notions, or functions into close proximity so that they will ignite and affect one another. The result is a new way of seeing the planning task and its solutions.

If the planner wishes to enhance his or her capacity for creative behavior, Curtis (1979, pp. 123-124) offers six steps for practice:

1. *Read.* Read a variety of books and periodicals on a wide range of subject areas that include both professional and nonprofessional information.
2. *File.* Develop a way to file both mentally and literally the array of significant or interesting material your reading uncovers.
3. *See.* Pay attention to what is going on around you; be a student of popular culture; look under, behind, above, and below the obvious; look at what others overlook.
4. *Listen.* Listen to what is going on around you; ask questions; seek clarification; rethink what you hear in a new manner.
5. *Meet people.* Talk to others and tolerate and cultivate their originality; study their life-styles; appreciate their hobbies.
6. *Juggle.* Learn to assemble and reassemble many ideas simultaneously.

Creative programming starts with not only knowing the constituency but also trying to view their needs and interests in varying ways. For example, the planner might go to a busy game store and ask what customers are buying. Can his or her program offer instruction in a popular game or even provide playing space? Where do single adults go to meet other single adults? There are a variety of recreation programs that have traditionally attracted single adults (drop-in volleyball, auto mechanics courses, and gourmet cooking and eating classes). Do these ideas offer solutions to the planner's program plans? In practicing the steps to creative thinking suggested by Curtis, the planner should think in terms of projects people are already doing at home. What home repair or construction projects occupy their interests? What games are children playing in the vacant neighborhood lots or in the streets? What products are people buying? Would they like to learn to make a product themselves, or use it better, or know other owners of the same product? Flipping through the yellow pages of the telephone book will suggest program ideas to the planner who is open to creativity. After rediscovering and revisualizing existing community resources, the planner can put them to work in setting new program trends.

To help ignite the spark of creative vision the following section will relate some recent trends in recreation program solutions that are the result of planners who juggled old, familiar ideas to come up with something new.

Shopping Centers Becoming Social Centers*

You can shop for anything from diamond earrings to disposable diapers, from fur coats to furry critters. Or maybe you won't shop at all. Maybe you'll go to ice skate or dance, or challenge your mind at the electronic game arcade, or visit the folk art museum, or take a college extension course, sit in on a gourmet cooking class, or listen to a poet read his own work, or send your children over to listen to a costumed story teller. Perhaps on your way to an information both on crime prevention you'll pause to enjoy a free performance of the local community theater troupe.

In what recreation center are you likely to find all of these services and programs? A shopping center using the increasingly popular "mixed-use" sales approach is becoming a shrewd business blend of department store slickness and old village square geniality. The mixed-use concept is a relatively new effort by shopping center planners to draw customers into a kind of community focal point by mingling recreation programs with retail stores—all in one spot—within easy access to a large population of people. And the bottom line is that recreation oriented shopping centers also have proved to be an effective way of boosting sales.

In fact, University Towne Centre, which opened four years ago in San Diego, California, is acknowledged in real estate circles as perhaps the best example of mixed-usage in the country. The center has an impressive 17 percent of its leasable space dedicated to non-retailing, community-related attractions. Six community meeting/programming rooms are provided rent free, as is space for an art museum, and a preschool day-care center. A sand castle construction competition, tied into a Renaissance fair theme, was one of the recreation program activities designed to entertain customers this past year at Mission Valley Center, also in San Diego. In The Vineyard Shopping Center in Escondido, California a recreational participant on any given Saturday can choose between listening to live jazz in the bookstore, attending a cooking class in the cookware shop, learning off-loom weaving in the crafts supply shop, drinking 25¢ beer and listening to a German band on the patio of the delicatessen, learning calligraphy in the artist supplies store, practicing needlepoint in the yarn shop, or viewing a camping equipment exhibit put on by the sporting goods store.

New Program Vistas Through Age-Old Mime†

In a 4-H camp in Illinois, a creative program planner used mime both as an entertainment for campers and as a teaching tool for the key concepts of ecology. By encouraging the campers to pantomime various parts of the ecosystem, the complex relationships of plants, animals, and the environment became clearer. In San Diego, a special program for hearing-impaired children developed into a sophisticated mime company composed entirely of children with total hearing loss. The results have been very impressive. A

*Modified from *San Diego Evening Tribune,* September 24, 1980.
†Modified from Olson, E. Open new recreational vistas with mime. *Parks & Recreation,* 1979, *14:6,* 27-28, 56.

program of social recreation planned and conducted for senior citizens in Carbondale, Illinois used mime as an effective mixer activity.

Recreational mime differs from formal mime and even pantomime. Pantomime and mime are dramatic techniques that require some advanced training and are used primarily to entertain an audience. Recreational mime is done for mainly the participant's pleasure and capitalizes on his or her natural ability to move, to gesture, and to express fantasy.

Self-Awareness Programs For Leisure Casualties*

Our society has many leisure casualties. These are persons who are unaware of their leisure needs and incapable of putting their free time to meaningful use. One form of assistance that recreation agencies can offer these leisure illiterates takes the form of leisure self-awareness clinics. Such clinics have in the past delved into such concerns as boredom, relaxation, stress, loneliness, and lifestyle planning. In addition to providing information they have allowed for interpersonal sharing as well as instigated inspiration and motivation in participants to produce results.

There are several subjects for self-awareness clinics that have met with success and may serve as the basis for a more permanent programming trend. One clinic idea is "Leisure Lifeline to the Teleholic." This clinic was designed to help "teleholics" break away from a dependence on television. Subject content consisted of one-on-one discussions on personal feelings when too much television had been watched. The group also was exposed to the different aspects of balanced lifestyles. "Reaching Out to Recreation" is another clinic idea that involved a bus tour of the city's recreation opportunities for new residents. Adult education centers, recreation centers, parks, and commercial facilities were all visited. A briefing on cultural opportunities, service bureaus, night spots, and athletic events preceded the taking of a leisure interest test. The clinic "Rendezvous in Relaxation" offers a panel discussion by a psychologist and a medical doctor on stress—what it is and what it does to you—as well as the practice of such relaxation techniques as progressive relaxation, autogenics, breathing, sensory awareness, music therapy, and yoga.

These self-awareness clinics may represent a rather radical departure from regular programming to many recreation agencies, but the growing interest in this idea may characterize the future. The recreation profession needs to become as interested in tensions as it is in pools, in boredom as it is in bats and balls, and in loneliness as it is in facilities.

An Inventor's Expo on Your Program Calendar?†

In 1978 the Baltimore County Department of Recreation and Parks received a request by a member of their service area to sponsor an exhibition for inventors. The idea was instantly appealing to the department inasmuch as invention is a creative process and they viewed creativity as an integral part of the recreation experience. This event, which was heralded as a welcome alternative to the well-worn arts and crafts show, was geared toward providing an opportunity for inventors to display their inventions and to give the public a chance to see them. A round table discussion was a featured activity at the expo with the participants including an independent inventor, a patent attorney, and an indus-

---

*Modified from O'Connor, C. Self-awareness programs: A new frontier in recreation. *Parks & Recreation*, 1979, *14:10*, 43-45.
†Modified from Wells, E.W. Liven up your special events calendar with an inventor's expo. *Parks & Recreation*, 1980, *15:1*, 77-84, 97.

try specialist in marketing. Fifty-nine exhibit tables presented an array of new individually and industrially invented objects including sports safety equipment, consumer home products, games, energy saving devices, aids for the disabled, etc.

CONCLUSION

The basic desires to express, to create, and to enjoy are present in all of us. These appetites can be more than satisfied; they can also be developed and nourished if the program planner develops program alternatives generously and intelligently. The natural desire to give expression to various psychological and physiological needs results in numerous forms of recreation activities. The actual form that the recreation program eventually assumes is influenced by many factors. Available leadership, facilities, and budget are interfaced with agency goals, participant interests, political atmosphere, and many other internal drives and external conditions. All these factors enter into the decision-making process, which is the next step in the planning process. At this juncture the main point is that whatever programs are to serve the recreational needs of a particular constituency must be broadly conceived and must encourage a wide freedom of choice, flexibility of selection, and continuity of opportunity.

References

Athletic Institute. *The recreation program.* Chicago: The Athletic Institute, 1963.

Bannon, J.J. *Problem solving in recreation and parks* (2nd ed.). Englewood Cliffs, N.J.: Prentice-Hall, 1980.

Benson, K.R., & Frankson, C.E. *Arts and crafts for home, school, and community.* St. Louis: C.V. Mosby, 1975.

Carlson, R.E., Deppe, T.R., & MacLean, J.R. *Recreation in American life.* Belmont, Calif.: Wadsworth, 1972.

Curtis, J.E. *Recreation theory and practice.* St. Louis: C.V. Mosby, 1979.

De Grazia, S. *Of time, work, and leisure.* New York: Anchor Books, 1964.

Faunce, W.A. Automation and leisure. In H.J. Jacobson & J.S. Roucek (Eds.), *Automation and society.* Westport, Conn.: Greenwood Press, 1958.

Jensen, C.R. *Outdoor recreation in America.* Minneapolis: Burgess Publishing, 1977.

Joseph, G. Shopping centers becoming social centers. *San Diego Evening Tribune*, September 24, 1980.

Kando, T.M. *Leisure and popular culture in transition.* St. Louis: C.V. Mosby, 1980.

Kraus, R. *Recreation today: Program planning and leadership.* Santa Monica, Calif.: Goodyear, 1977.

O'Connor, C. Self-awareness programs: A new frontier in recreation. *Parks & Recreation,* 1979, *14:10,* 43-45.

Olson, E. Open new recreational vistas with mime. *Parks & Recreation,* 1979, *14:6,* 27-28, 56.

Osborn, A.F. *Applied imagination.* New York: Charles Scribner's, 1963.

Pierce, R.C. Dimensions of leisure III: Characteristics. *Journal of Leisure Research,* 1980, *12:3,* 273-284.

Rambunctious revival of books. *Time,* October 30, 1978, p. 124.

Sharpham, J.R. Sad Mr.Lion and his lost happy song. *Parks & Recreation,* 1974, *9:6,* 69-70.

Storms, J. Guidelines on adventure programming. *Parks & Recreation,* 1979, *14:4,* 24-30.

Szalai, A., and others. *The use of time.* The Hague: Mouton, 1972.

Terry, W. An effort to save the masterpieces of modern dance. *Smithsonian,* 1980, *11:7,* 61-69.

The Culture Boom. *U.S. News and World Report,* August 8, 1977, pp. 50-53.

Tillman, A. *The program book for recreation professionals.* Palo Alto, Calif.: Mayfield, 1973.

Toffler, A. *The Third Wave.* New York: William Marrow, 1980.

U.S. Department of Commerce: Bureau of the Census. *Statistical abstracts of the United*

States. Washington, D.C.: U.S. Government Printing Office, 1975.

U.S. Department of Commerce: Bureau of the Census. *Statistical abstracts of the United States.* Washington, D.C.: U.S. Goverment Printing Office, 1979.

U.S. Department of the Interior. *The recreation imperative.* Washington, D.C.: U.S. Government Printing Office, 1974.

Wankelman, W.F., Wigg, P., & Wigg, M. *A handbook of arts and crafts.* Dubuque, Iowa: William C. Brown, 1974.

Weiskopf, D.C. *A guide to recreation and leisure.* Boston: Allyn & Bacon, Inc., 1975.

Wells, E.W. Liven up your special events calendar with an inventor's expo. *Parks & Recreation,* 1980, *15:1,* 77-84, 97.

The planning process

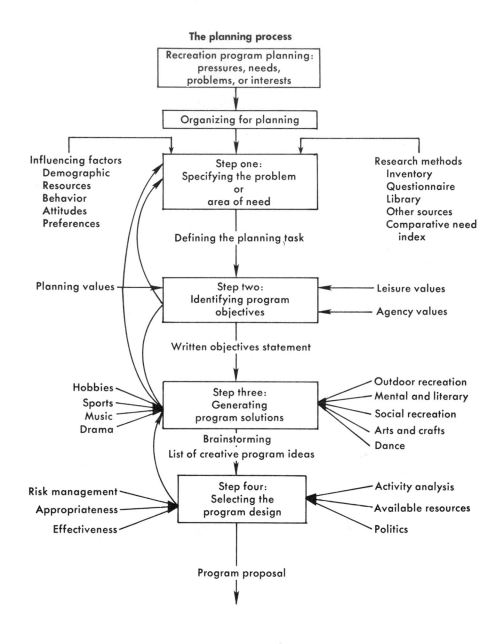

Chapter 6

STEP 4

Selecting the program design

At last we have arrived at the planning step that allows us to consider all the data gathered at previous planning steps in order to make a decision. At step 4 in the planning process the program or programs are selected in terms of the best match with the nature of the planning task, objectives, and other criteria of appropriateness. To decide which of the brainstormed program ideas are best, the planner weighs one program alternative against another until those that "fit best" are selected.

Thus the stage has been prepared for program development. Each of the previous planning decisions must now be translated into operational terms. Details of scale, staging, staffing, and budgeting must be worked out. So demanding is this planning phase that some recreation planners see it as the entire scope of planning. Policy must now be translated from general principles into program specifics and practice.

The diagram at the beginning of this chapter shows that step 4 begins as the planner considers the input from all previous steps and then analyzes the various options according to details of the current agency situation, such as budget, available leadership, adequacy of facilities, local politics, and safety measures. This means that at this phase the program design is determined in light of the researched needs of the constituency, the recommended objectives for meeting these needs, and any other relevant research. To accomplish this the planner must establish a list of decision-making guidelines that specify the absolute or desirable characteristics of any selected program alternative.

Decision making

The task of the recreation program planner at step 4 is therefore decision making. Yet decision making can be studied as a separate skill, one that is a part of many other endeavors. Tests and professional articles often use the terms *decision making* and *problem solving* interchangeably because the skills applied are virtually the same. I will allow this. However, although the planner has been making decisions all along the program planning process, decision making and program planning are not identical functions. For the purposes of the planning strategy taught in this text, decision making is a separate subcomponent of planning. I am labeling this step *decision making* to highlight the point at which the planner makes the *major* decision.

As decision maker, the program planner must apply all the expertise and information available to decide which of the brainstormed program alternatives is most likely to succeed. Through the precise procedures of decision making one of these alternatives, or perhaps a combination of several, will be selected for the planning task. It is the judgment of the decision maker that this choice will be successful and appropriate for the situation at hand.

What is decision making?

Let us first consider the nature of decision. What is a decision? A common phrase is an accurate answer: "make up your mind." To decide is to make up one's mind. Or, as Fishburn (1972) says, the making of a decision is the same as the fixing of a belief.

A more scholarly response is that a decision is a deliberate act of selection, by the mind, of an alternative from a set of competing alternatives in the expectation that the resulting actions will accomplish certain goals. The skill of decision making consists of choosing the most relevant alternative based on the information at hand.

However, no alternative is likely to be the absolute best. Any program design will be a compromise between what the planner would like to achieve and what is possible to achieve. The program chosen will be the best relative to the constraints the planner faces: those of budget, staff, and facilities. Likewise, the program alternative that is finally selected will never permit a perfect achievement of the objectives, but it is the one that the planner judges to come closer than any other. Only after performing step 6 of program planning, evaluation, will the planner know exactly how good the fit is.

Compromise in decision making should not carry the connotation of loss. On the contrary, it is a realistic awareness of what any recreation program can achieve relative to the objectives. The planner does not compromise on the planning objectives, only on the means for achieving them. If the planner has accomplished planning steps 1 through 3 conscientiously and if the program decision does represent the best fit in terms of the constraints involved, the planner can feel confident that the program alternative selected for implementation will be as effective as possible.

As a well-thought-out commitment to specific actions or inactions, a decision is not irreversible. As the back-tracking upward arrows in Fig. 1-1 indicate, many of the decisions in the program planning process, both before and after implementation, can be replaced by new decisions made in response to changing circumstances, needs, or desires. Along with the phrase "make up your mind" is the other familiar one, "change your mind." In fact, the planner's decision could consist of a broader set of decisions; for example, to implement an interim program or only half of the total program now and to later complete the program design with the final preevaluated decision. Such interim or partial decisions do not demonstrate a lack of planning responsibility; they are a recognition of the restraints planning realities force on the planner.

What sort of skills and characteristics must the person who makes program design decisions possess? The decision maker is the person who ably and willingly assumes responsibility for the choice. A decision maker is therefore a knowledgeable risk taker. Even if the decision is made by a group, the final responsibility and risk rest with the person in charge of the program. It would be unrealistic to ignore the impact of personal drives and needs that affect the decision maker's perspective; however, the planner has a responsibility to strive for rationality and to reduce emotional responses.

How to make the program design decision

The process of reduction helps to make decision making less confusing and more successful. This major effort calls for program ideas to be reduced to the best by judicious evaluation. The critical judgments suppressed during the generation of program alternatives phase should now come into full operation. The planner must be critical and ask which ideas are the most valuable. This evaluation, which results in the elimination of many alternatives, requires decision-making behavior that ranges from an intuitive rejection of some ideas to an in-depth, researched judgment about others.

Before considering each idea, the planner makes a list of the ideas that resulted from brainstorming and classifies them. This is an editing chore that serves to combine comparable ideas, to eliminate ones that at first glance will not meet the planning objectives, to weed out obvious idea duplications, and to combine and rename others. This editing can be done by any means that is most useful. For example, ideas could be classified according to recreation activity areas, the facility employed, how long it would take to implement, relative cost, or level of creativity. By doing this idea editing, the planner can begin to visualize and manipulate the alternative program solutions that can be chosen.

The planner then makes an initial screening of the classified list and decides which ideas seem most promising. This first selection should not rule out farfetched ideas simply because they are farfetched. Sometimes an unconventional idea can be manipulated and developed into the best idea. During this first evaluative look, the planner may wish to restate and combine comparable ideas in order to obtain better formulations of related program ideas. This initial critical analysis should result in no more than 10 selected program ideas so that the next step in decision making will be manageable.

Next the planner needs to decide what evaluative criteria will be used for judging the remaining program ideas. This list of criteria represents the dimensions of plausible alternatives. Although the list can be diverse, it should be specific to the unique planning situation of the agency. For example, one agency may specify that "time to implement" is an important decision criterion, whereas to another agency it is not; "degree of favorable community image" may be an important criterion to neither or to both. A sort of brainstorming must occur at this point to develop appropriate and meaningful judgment criteria.

Most planners agree that to be truly desirable the selected program should involve the least cost, have the least undesirable consequences, and present the most desirable advantages. What criteria the planner uses to determine this choice depends on what is important to the planner. The next section of this chapter will discuss the following decision criteria:

1. *Activity analysis.* What activity forms are best?
2. *Available resources.* Is there adequate staff, money, and space for this idea? Is it a wise use of resources?
3. *Alternative resources.* If not, are other configurations possible?
4. *Politics.* Do the broader community and other support systems consider the program desirable? Does it have a favorable public image? Will the constituency support it?
5. *Risk management.* Is the program safe and healthy and does it allow for legally prudent program conduct?
6. *Appropriateness.* Is it suitable for the constituency?
7. *Effectiveness.* Will the program accomplish what is intended?

Other criteria (not discussed below) that the planner might use as evaluation parameters include the following:

- Is the idea simple?
- Is it timely?
- Is it easy to implement?
- Can it be integrated into the scheme of future program ideas?
- Will it require changes in already-existing programs?
- Can it be sold to the board or council?
- Will it be accessible to the target constituency?

These criteria should not prohibit an idea from being evaluated, but they should show what parameters a program alternative must favorably encompass as it is evaluated. Criteria should be considered as different from objectives in that criteria present a desired framework within which program ideas can be judged, whereas objectives constitute a constraint for the ultimate measurement of the program implementation (Bannon, 1980, p. 119).

When the final list of program alternatives has been completed, each option must be evaluated against the decision criteria. The intensity of this judicious evaluation increases as the program ideas are narrowed, and it is highest at the time of the final decision.

As the planner begins to weigh and reevaluate the consequences of each program idea in view of the decision criteria, he or she needs to indicate which consequences are untenable within the criteria established. If, for example, the planner cannot spend over $1000 per year on the program, this is a distinct limitation on the budget criteria. When first testing to see if several program alternatives meet a given requirement, the decision maker may wish to limit the inquiry to whether each one falls above or below a minimum cutoff point. This helps keep the decision making from becoming cumbersome at this point. Later, as program ideas are reduced to three or four in number, the decision maker may need to make an evaluation that shows the magnitude of the pros and cons according to the relative importance of each criterion. This allows for an intense scrutiny of the final considerations that will lead to a final decision.

One means of making such an evaluation is to construct a profile for each program alternative in tabular form as illustrated in Table 12. This type of table simplifies the tasks of eliminating programs that do not meet the requirements of the decision criteria. As much space as desired can be used in each column to describe relationships to the various criteria. For example, in Table 12 program alternatives have been reduced to four. Each of these ideas is listed in a cross-tabular mode against the decision criteria. The spaces between are used by the planner to evaluate each idea's advantages or disadvantages according to each criterion. Granted, the comparisons are subjective because the planner can only estimate the relationships

Table 12 *Table for comparing advantages of various alternatives*

Criteria	Alternatives			
	No. 1	**No. 2**	**No. 3**	**No. 4**
Starting date (must be by Nov. 1; Sept. 15 is preferable)	Nov. 1	Oct. 1	Sept. 15	Sept. 15
Budget (must not exceed $1000 per year; lesser amount is preferable)	$500 annually	$1000 annually	$800 annually	$800 annually
Personnel required (involvement of program director not to exceed 4 hr per week)	2 hr/wk plus 2 volunteers	1 hr/wk plus 1 volunteer	4 hr/wk plus 2 volunteers	4 hr/wk plus 1 volunteer
Image in community (how much does the alternative enhance this image?)	Good	Fair	Excellent	Good
Safety (degree of legally prudent program conduct)	Excellent	Good	Good	Excellent
Feasibility (what chance does the alternative have of reaching the objectives?)	Good	Fair	Excellent	Good
Other criteria	—	—	—	—

between program and criterion. Yet the final decision will represent the program that is best for the given circumstances and time, and that is what the planner is after. According to the hypothetical comparisons presented in the example, which program idea should the planner select for implementation?

There is a risk in rejecting a program alternative as well as in selecting one. It is possible that for some yet unknown reason (or criterion), a certain program idea would be worth inaugurating; it might even develop into exactly what the constituency wants. But because it was not compared against other, perhaps more significant criteria, it was eliminated. So there is risk in saying no as well as yes. Therefore as the decision maker discards the few remaining program ideas, he or she must not only be certain that what is selected is the best under the circumstances but also that the circumstances themselves have been adequately considered.

Ultimately the planner has to make a final decision. Decision analysis must be stopped at a point when all the available information has been evaluated appropriately, when the planner's professional judgments have been wise, and when a careful analysis of the alternatives has been made according to the established criteria. To go beyond such a point is no longer advantageous for making a good decision.

Criteria of the decision

Using a predetermined set of evaluative criteria is helpful in deciding which of the brainstormed program alternatives is best for implementation. Exactly which and how many criteria are established depends on the unique circumstances of each planning situation. The following section discusses the criteria that should be considered, at least minimally, when performing step 4 of the planning process. The program that is finally chosen for implementation in step 5 should offer a positive response to each of the following decision criteria.

Activity analysis

On what basis should activities be chosen? If the planner is considering a crafts program, a logical concern would be the desirability of one type of craft over another. For instance, on what basis should a leather craft activity be chosen over a ceramics activity? Although this question is most frequently encountered when planning recreation programs for therapeutic settings, it is certainly a relevant question in all settings. It may be important to know, for example, what physical skills and what degree of emotional maturity each activity requires to guarantee participant satisfaction. Because some activities allow for a wide range of skills and abilities, their implementation can be organized to meet many different individual needs. Other activities have a definite format and prerequisite skills that specify their potential for implementation.

In addition to identifying the needs and objectives for each constituency group, it is necessary in programming to analyze the structure and characteristics of each activity proposed. This has been labeled *activity analysis* in the recreation field. Activity analysis is a procedure for breaking an activity down into component parts and examining each part to determine its characteristics. At this stage in program planning, activity analysis calls for the examination of the variables of every proposed activity before one is chosen for the final program design. The purpose of activity analysis is to provide the planner with a means of matching the needs and interests of the constituency with the types of activities that will best contribute to them. In so doing, activity analysis provides an accountable system for designating activities. It also contributes to individualized programming.

Activity analysis is accomplished by detailed study of an activity's subelements. Although some methods advocate greater emphasis on certain activity elements, all focus on the recognition that activities can be broken down into elements that can then be studied to determine the activity's suitability for specific program designs. All recreation activities have four elements: purpose of action, procedure for action, rules governing action, and results of action.

First, all activity has a purpose or goal. In shuffleboard, for example, the goal is to move a round disk into a designated space; in running it is to move successfully over the terrain under one's own unaided locomotion. For meaningful participation in an activity, the purpose must first be understood. Second, for every activity there is a certain procedure. In some activities, such as television viewing, the procedure is simple; in others, such as playing rugby, the procedure is involved. The procedure for action describes what behaviors are necessary to accommodate the purpose of the activity. The third element found in each activity is a set of rules governing it. These are fixed principles of conduct (such as required number of participants, prescribed role of participants, and equipment/facility requirements) that set the standards for the action. They confine or limit the procedures for action. Finally, there is the element of results. Each activity results in something—a satisfaction, a reward, a fulfillment—that is the final evaluation of the purpose. A study of some or all of these activity elements is what is required in an activity analysis.

Analyzing proposed activities has been approached by recreation program planners in many ways and with different philosophies. Some planners have proposed a simple analysis according to the abilities and skills a participant must possess to engage in the activity; for example, playing baseball requires the ability to throw an object, and playing bridge requires the ability to remember which cards have been played.

Analysis according to behavioral domains—physical, intellectual, and affective—has been advocated by many practitioners, most recently Edginton, Compton, and Hanson (1980). This approach maintains that each activity can be studied according to all three domains simultaneously; that is, each activity requires a certain type and degree of physical behavior, intelligence, and emotional stability. The physical, or psychomotor, domain includes physical and neuromuscular skills. The cognitive, or intellectual, domain deals with the acquisition of knowledge, comprehension, and understanding. The affective, or emotional, domain involves feelings, value judgments, and emotions. An activity analyzed according to this system would possess varying degrees of each domain. For example, the activity of making a pot on a potter's wheel involves psychomotor skills in working the pot with the hands and pumping the wheel with the foot. But it also entails cognitive behavior because certain procedural steps must be remembered and followed and the design of the pot must be invented. The affective behavioral domain is present in the potter's pride and the self-expression afforded by the finished pot.

Therapeutic recreation planners have often been confined to a kind of kinesiological analysis. For instance, cycling requires a plantar flexion of the ankle and foot that involves the tibialis posterior, soleus, gastrocnemius, peroneus longus, peroneus brevis, plantaris, flexor digitorum longus, and flexor hallucis longus muscles.

Other modes of analysis that have been advocated are combinations of the above methods. They include study of the following types of elements: degree of body contact, time required, allowance for indigenous leadership, suspense or risk ingredient, kind and intensity of competition, chance factor, amount of ritual, mirroring of real life, degree of humor, interaction, movement of body parts, potency, and number of winners allowed.

The basic tenets for activity analysis adopted by Farrell and Lundegren (1978, p. 68) are applicable to a wide range of activities and incorporate most aspects of other analysis models. The dimensions proposed are:

1. *Behavior domains.* Which of the three domains (physical, emotional, intellectual) is primary, secondary, and tertiary for this activity?
2. *Interaction patterns.* What sorts of social relationship groupings are inherent in this activity? Does the activity take place, for example, within a person and involve no outside person, as with the activity of yoga?
3. *Leadership.* Does this activity require minimum or maximum leadership?
4. *Equipment and facilities.* Does this activity require certain equipment or facilities? How much?
5. *Duration.* Does this activity occur during a set time, does it have a natural conclusion, or is it continuous?
6. *Participants.* Does this activity require a fixed number of participants?
7. *Age.* Is this activity age specific?

All the systems for activity analysis presented above are useful to the planner in decision making. The planner should select a mode (or design one) based on what would best accommodate the specific planning situation. The program planner in the psychiatric ward of a hospital would find it most useful to analyze activities according to the three behavioral domains. The planner of programming for a private athletic club, on the other hand, might lean toward physical dimensions for analysis. Or the planner may find it best to determine his or her own means of analysis based on bits and pieces of other systems. To become proficient in this particular planning skill, further reading and practice are necessary.

A final caution: Although Chapter 5 of this text devoted attention to the values of the various recreation activity areas through such generalized statements as "strenuous physical activities or certain crafts activities are useful for the release of anger, aggression, and hostility" or "social recreation activities are advocated for isolated and lonely patients," it must be remembered that these are only generalizations. Therefore when I advocate activity analysis in program planning, I am not referring to a precise list of needs and their accompanying activities. Therepeutic recreation program planners must be particularly cautious of the hazard of universally ascribing a particular activity to a specific therapeutic effect.

In summary, the major benefit of activity analysis is the planner's ability to individualize programming through determination of the most appropriate activities. Other benefits may also be realized, including the potential for activity modification and substitution, activity clustering, and program format specification.

Activity modification and substitution Activity analysis can help to locate areas of the activity that may need to be modified or substituted. Activity modification is the changing of an element or elements of an activity so that it can be adapted to an out-of-the-ordinary participant limitation or need. For instance, many athletic activities have been modified to allow full participation by the disabled. Through equipment modifications in downhill skiing, the pleasures of gliding down a snowy slope can be experienced by an amputee.

Activity analysis can also aid the planner in determining what activities may be substituted for other ones while meeting the same needs and providing essentially the same recreation experience. Recreation professionals are currently interested in research on substitutability; the idea that a particular activity meaning can be met by different recreation activities has useful implications. For example, a person's need for adventure and risk-taking could be met by hang gliding, rock climbing, gambling, or even giving a first public performance. Through activity analysis, substitutability can discover the equivalence of meaning in different activities.

Activity clustering Another benefit of activity analysis is that it allows the planner to identify recreation types that yield similar benefits or that appear to belong together. Such compatible activity types are usually brought together by means of a technique known as factor analysis. Factor analysis is a statistical process in which the variables of one activity are correlated with those of other activities and the activities are then grouped according to similarity of correlation. Thus activities having a relatively high correlation among themselves and a relatively low correlation with activities outside this group are clustered together. Program planners are interested in this because recreation participants tend to confine themselves to certain clusters of activity.

The research of Bishop (1970) helps to illustrate activity clustering. Bishop identified three factors under which activities could be clustered: (1) active-diversionary, (2) potency, and (3) status. Active-diversionary activities involved the participant's watching, viewing, or doing something. For example, participating in sports, hiking, bicycling, and picnicking would be clustered here. Clustered under the factor of potency were the "virile" activities or those in which individuals attempt to prove themselves in rugged communion with nature. Such activities included fishing, mountain climbing, camping, vigorous sports, and hunting. Status referred to the level of sophistication that the individual had based on his or her participation in certain activities, such as skiing, sailing, reading, and attending symphony concerts.

Bishop also investigated the relationship between his clusters of activities and selected demographic variables. These included age, sex, income, and marital status. Bishop found that the diversionary pursuits were participated in primarily by younger individuals; that the potency activities were engaged in mainly by males; and that the status activities were engaged in primarily by higher income individuals.

Formats for program structure   A final benefit of activity analysis is that because the elements of the activity are broken down and understood, the best structure for each activity can be selected. Shall it be free choice, highly structured, a single event, or a long sequence of sessions? Each of the activity elements influences the type of program format that can be used and that is most suitable. For example, a birthday party is, by its nature and definition, a once-a-year event. In contrast, learning to play the guitar usually involves a long sequence of training sessions.

Program format is the structure through which the activity is presented. In some instances the activity will focus on an instructional format; in others competition or presentation may be the focus. Usually the planner has a choice between at least two formats. Thus through analysis of the activity, along with attention to the program objectives, the planner can make the wisest decision. Ideally, in large comprehensive services, the participant can select from a variety of activity formats. For example, the golfer would be able to choose from a golf tournament, golf classes, a golf club, or unstructured enjoyment of the golf course.

The most frequently used activity formats are clubs, competition, trips and outings, special events, classes, open facility, voluntary service, and workshops, seminars, and conferences. In each format a different environment is present for experiencing the activity. The following section concentrates on these formats and their characteristics for total program structure.

1. *Clubs.* Participants who wish to experience an activity in a congenial social situation are often attracted to clubs. A *club* is defined as a group of persons organized around the enjoyment or practice of a particular activity or purpose. Recreational clubs are normally established around an activity, but they may also be organized around some other unifying factor such as age. For example, senior citizen and teen clubs are common club types.

Activity-based clubs—the bridge club, running club, gourmet cooking club, needlepoint club, and ham radio club—are single interest clubs that offer not only the binding effect of socialization but also continuous opportunity and support for participation in an activity. In the club format diverse needs and interests can be met simultaneously. This format also provides a communication and inspirational contact point that helps to create and reinforce individual interest. Information is traded, challenges are generated, and collective group energies are able to construct other activity formats (for example, competition and outings) not put together so easily by individuals.

The organizational pattern of a club usually provides for self-direction by members within the bounds of bylaws or a constitution, with minimum direction from the sponsoring recreation agency. The agency often provides assistance in establishing the club, after which the various activities become the responsibility of the club's officers and members. Initial agency assistance may include the development of written agreements, selection of leadership, definition of financial needs, and setting of ground rules and overall purpose. The constitution and bylaws of a club are the written rules of the club's organization and function; they are the fundamental principles of club operation. Because the program planner may often represent the agency in activity club formulations, an outline of both bylaws and constitution is presented in the box below. The student planner is also advised to consult *Robert's*

OUTLINE FOR WRITING CLUB RULES AND PROCEDURES

Constitution

Article I	Name of club
Article II	Purpose or object of club
Article III	Membership, who members are and their qualifications
Article IV	Officers and their election
Article V	Meetings of club
Article VI	How to amend constitution

Bylaws

I	Membership details
II	Dues, how much and how collected
III	Duties of officers
IV	Duties of board
V	Duties and purpose of committees
VI	Voting rules
VII	Manner of conducting business
VIII	Source or authority
IX	How to amend bylaws

Rules of Order and other references on parliamentary procedure. A constitution is a formal document that declares what the club is, what its purpose is, and how it will operate. Bylaws include all the specific rules that are important to the club, with provisions for changing these rules if so desired by the members. If the rules of conduct are numerous and elaborate, it is better to separate the most important rules and place them in the constitution. A club may operate under both a constitution and bylaws or under one or the other.

The club format is an efficient way of providing programs; for a minimum amount of supervision and budget, a substantial amount of programming can be made available. This is made possible by the efforts of volunteers who share an interest in the activity. With the help of volunteers, the program planner and leader are relieved from formal club involvement and can direct their efforts to other activity areas. If a planner or leader is reluctant to turn over the activities of a club to its members, creative and effective use of staff will be greatly hampered and there will be limitations on the quality and amount of programming possible. As a general rule, a sponsoring recreation agency has the responsibility of seeing that membership in the club is open to all interested constituents and that club activities are conducted in agreement with the spirit and philosophy of the agency.

2. *Competition.* In the competitive activity format the participant's performance is judged and compared to the performance of another participant or an established standard. Competition may take many different forms. An individual may perform against self to improve on previously set standards, or an individual or a group may perform against another individual or another group. Two individuals or groups may compete against each other either in parallel or in face-to-face performances. Finally, an individual may choose the competitive experience that pits him or her against the environment, such as mountain climbing, white-water canoeing, and hang gliding. Competition in other activities, such as skiing, can be offered to include both environmental and personal opponents.

Although traditionally sports have dominated competition program services, the planner may find that drama, music, and even camping and literary activities also lend themselves to the competition format. The planner's goal in selecting this format is to provide the participant with a competitive experience, at a variety of levels. Competition is a complex concept, and the planner can be pushed to his or her ultimate in organizing potential. Two principles that I think are paramount to worthwhile competition program planning and that should be memorized are:

- The participant in competition should always be provided with similar skills or ability groups against which to compete.
- The participant in competition should always be provided with a fair and safe environment.

Competition can be like juggling two highly explosive bombs. For the competition experience in recreation programs to be fulfilling to the participant, the planner needs creative, organizational, and perceptual skills. To aid the planner there are some excellent mechanical patterns for structuring competitive activities.

Organizational patterns such as tournaments, contests, meets, and leagues are useful for this activity format. Tournaments are forms of competition that rely on specific organizational configurations for winning. (Figs. 6-1 to 6-7 illustrate the most frequently used types.) Determinations of who will compete with whom and when they will compete are prearranged details of the tournament. Signing up performers, setting up matches, seeing that the action is conducted by the rules, tabulating the scores, and determining the winners are chores that must be done accurately if the tournament format is to be successful.

The elimination tournament is a common form that includes both single elimination and double elimination. As Figs. 6-1 and 6-2 indicate, participants initially are drawn by lots and matched by pairs. In the single elimination the participant is eliminated after losing one game, and the one remaining undefeated is the winner. In the double elimination the participant must lose twice before being eliminated from

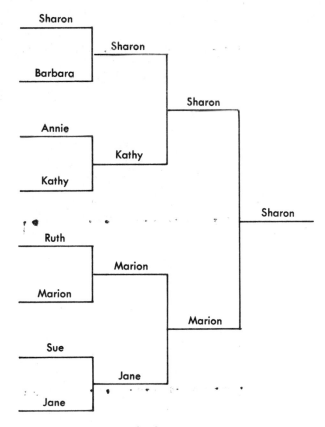

Fig. 6-1   *Single elimination tournament.*

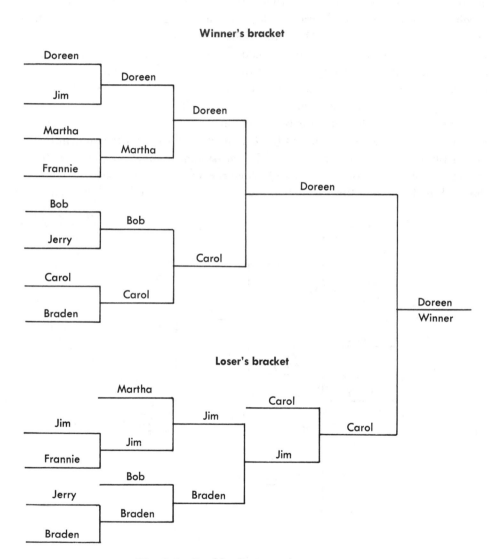

Fig. 6-2   *Double elimination tournament.*

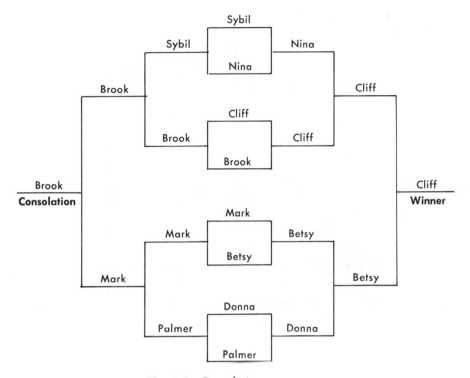

Fig. 6-3 *Consolation tournament.*

the tournament. In the consolation tournament (Fig. 6-3), another form of elimination tournament, two winners are determined by keeping first-round losers from being eliminated from competition. Still another form of tournament is the round robin (Fig. 6-4), which has traditionally been the favorite of recreation program planners. The reason for this is its potential for wider participation; in the round-robin tournament all competitors play successively every other competitor, they play the same number of games, and no one is eliminated from play. The ladder tournament (Fig. 6-5) preranks the participants according to ability. Those positioned on lower rungs of the ladder challenge those who are one or two rungs above, and the winners rise to the top. There are variations on the ladder tournament (for example, the concentric circle ladder and the pyramid ladder) that make it possible to adapt this format to larger numbers of participants (see Figs. 6-6 and 6-7).

Another competition device that permits individuals to try their skill against others is the contest. This format offers a comparison of ability through parallel performances, with a set standard usually determining the winner. Dance contests, spelling bees, and football pass-and-punt contests are all forms of competition in which the performance of one opponent does not affect that of another.

	Sandy	Doug	Butch	Lei	Gene	Ellie
Sandy	X					
Doug		X				
Butch			X			
Lei				X		
Gene					X	
Ellie						X

Fig. 6-4 *Round robin tournament.*

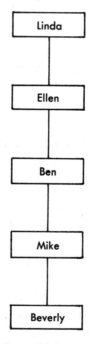

Fig. 6-5 *Ladder tournament.*

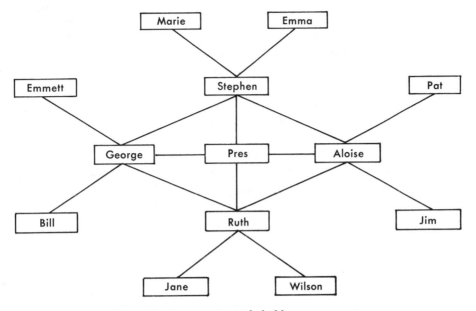

Fig. 6-6 *Concentric circle ladder tournament.*

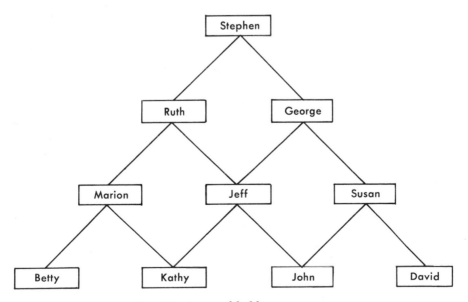

Fig. 6-7 *Pyramid ladder tournament.*

The meet, such as a track meet or a gymnastics meet, is a series of contests involving the measurements of skills against those of all participants. Often the scores of individuals are combined to show a total team score.

The competition format most in tune with the precepts of recreation is the league. Primarily effective with team sport programming, the league concept is based on the concept of "as much play for as many for as long as possible." In this format all teams are scheduled to compete against an equal number of opponents within their own league. The winner is determined by the most wins or the most points.

Competition in recreation activities has been the subject of controversy and abuse because the ability to compete successfully is generally believed to prove a person's worth. Yet the values that competition offers the participant are worth preserving; for example, competition can serve as a motivator for continued interest and improvement in the activity. However, preserving such values demands professional skills and attitudes of the organizers.

3. *Trips and outings.* The lure of going to see something new, unusual, or interesting is what keeps cars on the road. The possibility of getting away from the daily setting is another enticing experience. As a recreation activity format the trip or outing ranges from brief excursions to nearby places to more extended trips, for a weekend or longer, to distant places. With advance planning all recreation activity areas can be structured into this format to stimulate, revitalize, and add relevancy to programs. For example, the participants in the ceramics program could take a short trip to a professional studio, the modern dance program could hold a session in a nearby wooded area instead of the auditorium, the gourmet cooking participants could enjoy a continental meal in a five-star restaurant, or the drama program could journey to the Shakespeare Festival in England. Emphasis on discovery, coupled with capable and enthusiastic leadership, can make this activity format full of adventure. There is something in everyone that responds to going places, doing something new, finding out.

But the key is adequate advance planning and capable leadership. The trip format is one activity structure that cannot happen by itself. No matter how responsible or alert the participants, a group is sluggish unless it is led. Successful trips do not just happen; they require thoughtful planning. Some advice for careful planning is found in the following checklist.

Before the trip
- ☐ Encourage participant involvement in trip planning
- ☐ Decide date, time, initial gathering place
- ☐ Secure transportation
- ☐ Make necessary reservations
- ☐ Secure adequate leaders if appropriate
- ☐ Obtain publicity
- ☐ Get attendance commitments, sign-ups
- ☐ Outline travel schedule
- ☐ Provide participants with a list of what to bring
- ☐ Discuss the trip: what to look for, relevance to program, etc.

During the trip
☐ Be alert to whereabouts of all participants
☐ Be alert to safety practices

After the trip
☐ Send thank-you notes when appropriate
☐ Reinforce the trip through group discussion or related activity

Museums, planetariums, zoos, libraries, theaters, parks, and state capitols have been the traditional settings for trips and outings. The challenge to planning in the 1980s is to try new, untrodden roads for travel discovery. For example, the trip format need not always include actual travel. Travel literature, travel films, and armchair travel lectures are worthy planning options. One unique opportunity for recreation service organizations is to provide travel experience for those who cannot ordinarily travel on their own: a skiing trip for children, a theater excursion to the inner city for older persons, or an out-of-town visit to a major sporting event for the disabled.

4. *Special events.* Most recreation agencies rely on the special event format from time to time to add sparkle to their regular program services. Special events are activity formats in which a special treatment of the regular program is planned. The purpose of this format is to change the pace, ignite spirits, reward craftsmanship, announce new things, or honor old things. It is a different way of offering a recreation activity that departs from the normal program schedule and requires special planning attention. As one practitioner has pointed out, the special event is the single most powerful means to impress people that recreation programmers have.

Shows, play days, roundups, pageants, parades, olympics, exhibitions, fairs, and festivals are special event format tools that planners use to catch and focus attention. They are also used to unify different program activity areas and bring together people who are usually outside an agency's existing service area. Therefore this format usually involves larger participant groupings than normal. This creates an opportunity for not only increased exposure to the agency's services but also broader social interaction and a sense of community. Many special events, such as a crafts fair, are planned as a culmination of the efforts of participants in other regular program formats—in this case, the weekly crafts class. Demonstrating mastery of a skill and receiving recognition for it are of prime value for participant pleasure. In addition, special events allow the planner to feature seasons of the year, raise funds, promote a change in the routine, start something new, put an end to something ongoing, deliver a message, or recruit new participants.

One planning factor stands out when preparing the special event format: it is big. Bigness is what makes the event special. It also results in complex planning. Crowd control, multiple scheduling, provision of comfort facilities, and extra clean-up details are examples of related planning problems that programmers are not required to face on a daily basis, problems that require extra thought and energy. This means planning attention to the activity participant and to the audience as well.

Unlike program formats in which the participant's pleasure is the only concern, special events also cater to the enjoyment of the spectator. In fact, the spectator's presence is crucial to the success of special events. Can you imagine a parade with no one along the sides to watch?

The process of planning a special event usually (and wisely) goes beyond the single-handed efforts of the program planner. Various subfunctions should be assigned to separate committees while the professional coordinates all the work and decisions and guides the process toward the actual event. The more highly structured the event, the more likely that it will run smoothly and effectively. Adequate instructional signs for participants, roped-off areas for spectators, leaders who know what they are doing, score cards, extension cords, parking facilities, wheelchair access, foul weather options require list making, double-checking, and outside coordination. The planner should allow plenty of preplanning time and leeway for such details.

What program activity areas provide the best source of special event ideas? Activity analysis is useful in determining which activities need to be revitalized, featured, or announced. Most activity areas respond well to the special event format: hobby fairs, flower shows, folk dance festivals, science fairs, woodchopping exhibitions are well-worn examples. Special events may also cover activity areas not normally a part of regular program services. Take a dog show, for instance. Is there just one way to conduct a dog show? The box on the opposite page relates a heartwarming example of an alternative.

The seasons of the year or annual holidays are also excellent reasons for special events. For idea stimulation and reference, the box on p. 208 contains a list of seasonal and traditional holidays. Certain holidays are not included because they vary in schedule from state to state or year to year. A current year's calendar should be consulted for these.

Special events can also be related to the environment. Communities that specialize in certain agricultural products, enjoy special weather, or have heroes and heroines invariably are interested in these themes for festivals and pageants. Cherries, tulips, snow, and Paul Bunyan have provided unlimited special event options for planners year after year. And it is true that a successful special event is usually repeated. Today's special event can become tomorrow's routine. The tenth annual whatever has a recreational appeal all its own and is gladly incorporated into an agency's program services because of the ease of planning a program more than once. Participants and spectators both enjoy repeated special events; these events provide a performance or exhibition outlet that can motivate activity throughout the year.

5. *Classes.* Most organized recreation activity participation is found in the class format. As noted earlier, every activity is a different experience to every participant, and this is shaped by many variables such as age, needs, past experience, and skill

KIDS DOG SHOWS

This recreation program, jointly sponsored by the National Recreation and Park Association and Ken-L Ration since 1975, aims to teach young canine lovers the responsibilities involved in dog ownership. At the same time, it provides a chance for them to have fun parading their dogs and winning prizes in a variety of nonprofessional categories. Over a million children and their pets in some 1,100 cities and towns across the United States have taken part in Kids Dog Shows.

The spirit of the program is inclusive; the sponsors are anxious to get everyone involved. Pedigreed dogs and mutts alike all take honors. Large, well-staffed recreation departments (such as those in Los Angeles) as well as smaller agencies which might never have attempted a dog show on their own have had successful shows. A special Kids Dog Show kit was designed to provide local planners with all the materials needed to run a show for 50 participants. The kits were free to N.R.P.A. members and included a planning guide with detailed instructions on how to arrange for everything from radio publicity to water bowls for the cold-nosed competitors.

The success of the N.R.P.A./Ken-L Ration programs is easy to explain—everyone who participates emerges a winner. If a pup doesn't win in one of the eight award categories, its owner still gets a ribbon of merit and an educational 26-page booklet on "How to Care For, Train and Feed Your Dog." Breed, pedigree, and special credentials do not matter in a Kids Dog Show. This is insured by such judging criteria as: best trick dog, smallest dog, largest dog, best looking, best costumed, funniest, best behaved, and best of show. Children four to fourteen years of age could compete.

The Kids Dog Shows have been adopted as regular features in many park and recreation department summer programs. This special event seems to take on the personality of the sponsoring agency, many of whom have added to the judging categories. In Bend, Oregon, a special prize was awarded to the dog with the largest spot. In Fisherville, Virginia, the noisiest dog won a ribbon. In Lee's Summit, Missouri, a best-smelling category was included. The possibilities for dog awards are as numerous as there are doggy characteristics. At various shows, dogs with the most hair, least hair, longest tail, or shortest ears have all won special awards.

Other sponsoring agencies have broadened the scope of the event by including other pets, pre-show clinics, veterinarian check-ups, etc. In Yuma, Arizona, a pre-show complete with prizes for stuffed animals was held. Other clinics have been set up to describe local regulations regarding animal ownership, feeding, grooming, and training as well as the responsibilities of handling a dog in public. In Prince William County, Virginia, the recreation agency added a look-alike contest in which prizes were awarded to the dogs most resembling famous canines such as Benji, Lassie, and Rin Tin Tin.

Just as important as the educational opportunity given to thousands of youngsters through the program, of course, is the entertainment given to the spectators as well. Kids of all ages were smiling coast-to-coast as participants strutted proudly before the judges' table with their very own top dog.

From Carter, B.C. A big day for Rover. Reprinted from the *11:11* (1976) issue of *Parks & Recreation* by special permission of the National Recreation and Park Association.

TRADITIONAL HOLIDAYS

January 1	New Year's Day
January 15	Martin Luther King Jr.'s Birthday
January 24	Gold discovered in California
February 2	Groundhog Day
February 12	Abraham Lincoln's Birthday
February 14	St. Valentine's Day
February 22	George Washington's Birthday
February 29	Leap Year
March 17	St. Patrick's Day
March 21	First day of spring
April 1	All Fools' Day
April 18	Paul Revere's ride
April 24	William Shakespeare's Birthday
May 1	May Day
May 21	Charles A. Lindbergh flew the Atlantic
May 30	Memorial Day
May—2nd Sunday	Mother's Day
June 14	Flag Day
June 21	First day of summer
June—3rd Sunday	Father's Day
July 1	Dominion Day in Canada
July 4	Independence Day
July 14	Bastille Day in France
August 11	Fulton's steamboat
September 14	"The Star Spangled Banner" written by Francis Scott Key
September 17	Constitution Day
September 23	First day of autumn
October 12	Columbus Day
October 31	Halloween
November—1st Tuesday	Election Day
November 11	Armistice Day
November—last Thursday	Thanksgiving
December 17	Wright Brothers' first flight
December 21	First day of winter, shortest day of year
December 21	Mayflower landed at Plymouth Rock
December 25	Christmas

level. Recreational activity participation is likely to reach its fullest potential when skills and knowledge are equal to the endeavor. This is perhaps why the instructional class format holds a dominant position in most recreation programs.

The class format for activity programming is a highly structured learning situation in which a group of participants meet to study the same topic over a specified period of time. The purpose of this format is the learning, development, and improvement of recreation skill. This format specifies a high degree of leader control, a limited number of participants, a series of meeting dates and times, and a definite occupancy of a particular facility and equipment. In addition, it is increasingly common for a special fee to be levied for enrollment. Classes generally follow a regular form in which a series of short sessions are held on a quarterly or seasonal basis. Frequently they culminate in a special event, such as an exhibition or performance, that honors the participants' progress; or the recognition may take the form of qualifying for graduation to more advanced classes.

The class approach to recreation activity programming seems to suit American participants, who are already school oriented. We Americans identify classes with learning and learning with self-improvement, which makes for purposeful activity. One of the main philosophical dilemmas for recreational pursuit is that purposeful activity is valued more highly in our culture.

Even though incidental learning occurs during participation in all activity formats, in a class setting opportunities for teaching and learning are purposefully directed through predetermined lesson content. As a result, the participant is able to know in advance the approximate outcome of the experience. There are several means for presenting content in a class situation; some traditional methods are the lecture, lecture with visual aids, use of films, videotape feedback, demonstration, and class member experimentation and practice. It is the teacher's responsibility to choose the most appropriate one for the learning environment. Which method or methods are used depend on the characteristics of the class members, the size of the group, an analysis of the activity being taught, and the facility and equipment available.

There are some additional planning considerations for the class format. For optimum recreational value, class size should be kept to a reasonable number; 10 to 20 class members is ideal. Scheduling of class sessions should allow for time intervals to accommodate outside practice and skill contemplation. The most recent experience of programmers has been that the traditional 10- to 12-week course session is too long to sustain interest. The trend is now toward shorter, more intensive courses—for example, classes twice a week for 4 to 5 weeks.

Recreational classes differ from those conducted in a formal school atmosphere because the students are participating voluntarily and therefore possess more learning readiness and enthusiasm. Often participants are eager to start performing the activity as soon as possible with the least amount of traditional classroom ritual.

Therefore at times it is hard to keep them drilling on activity subparts, learning terminology, or practicing in mock participation. An appropriate dose of formal ritual should be blended with activity performance for a more enjoyable recreation experience. For many participants the class is the initial exposure to the recreational activity, so it may determine their continued pursuit of the activity. Consequently, sensitive planning is extremely important.

6. *Open facility.* Casual or drop-in participation in a recreation activity is a program format used to encourage spontaneous involvement. This format usually involves assigning a certain portion of time for a facility (or part of a facility) to be available for unstructured play. For example, "open recreational swims" are usually in the pool schedule several times a day, and gymnasium and game room facilities are normally opened up for free play on a scheduled basis. Driving ranges, ski slopes, tennis courts, ice rinks, bowling lanes, racquetball courts, and other sports facilities are readily available for drop-in use. Mobile recreation units often provide free-play participation, and certain craft facilities can be made available for open use when nothing else is scheduled.

Open facility activities do not usually require any commitment from the participant: no class to enroll in, no club to join, no team to compete against. Because availability of free time varies from person to person, the open facility format can provide a real service for the busy person by encouraging participation in an activity when it is convenient.

In practice the open use policy is usually what is left over before or after the scheduled programs; it is rarely given scheduling priority. It could be argued that a planner's conscientious emphasis on planned, structured use of facilities can result in too little time and space available for self-initiated recreation activity.

The open facility concept is often an overlooked or underplanned activity format. Activity analysis reveals, however, that certain activities are actually more meaningful to participants when they are approached from a casual participation viewpoint, and that planning for this can be just as important a service for an agency to offer as any other format. Structure is not always a criterion for enhancing recreation participation. Careful planning consideration must be devoted to the unstructured format as well.

It is advisable, for instance, to first evaluate a facility's use and determine when people are most likely to use it for drop-in activity participation. These times should then be reserved specifically for the free-play participant. This open facility schedule should be communicated widely, and the constituency should be encouraged to take advantage of these specially reserved hours. Many times agencies have found it advisable to provide supervisory staff to maintain order and ensure safety, as well as to provide assistance or information when requested. Occasionally users of open facilities are required to supply their own equipment or supplies.

This activity format is a difficult one to use effectively. Without alert attention to the needs and interests of the constituency and to rational planning efforts, the open facility format can live up to its reputation of being an impersonal, irresponsible programming style.

7. *Voluntary service.* A recreation activity format that is often overlooked by programmers is voluntary service. Many participants consider using part of their free time to do something for someone else as one of the highest forms of recreational activity. Volunteering skills and energy to teach swimming, coach soccer, call square dances, take the Girl Scout troop camping, read to a hospital patient, or assist in a bird-banding project often offers the same satisfactions that others receive from being participants in these activities plus the value of contributing to the pleasure of others. Thus the planner should not ignore the voluntary service format when making programming decisions.

Chapter 2 of this text discussed volunteering from a leadership or implementation perspective. It considered the value of volunteers to the efficiency and effectiveness of the agency. Here voluntary service, a part of any comprehensive recreation program, is viewed as a program format. In using volunteering this way, the program planner must keep in mind its recreation potential for the volunteer participant.

Most volunteer participants give service time that is outside their regular daily pursuits. However, the nature of the service may be related to a work skill or profession. A doctor may volunteer time in the health lodge of a children's camp; an accountant may volunteer to be the treasurer for a community theater; an athlete may teach batting skills to a Little League team. Lending time and energy to health services, social clubs, fund-raising projects, charities, and other civic causes often means not only the value of the doing but companionship and social recreation as well. There is a twofold recreational value in voluntary service: to the agency and to the volunteer.

Why do people volunteer? Although there are many reasons, three major ones are presented here. One of the most important motivations is the desire to discover one's identity. For some this can be done through recognizing the needs of others. The volunteer in recreation activity receives not a monetary reward, but rather an identity reward. A second motivation is the opportunity to pursue a recreation interest or skill in a more thorough, frequent, or meaningful way. Just to be around others who enjoy the hobby or sport provides an additional outlet for expression. A third incentive for volunteering is to enjoy the special privileges and benefits of being "a part of the staff." Volunteers are usually permitted to go behind the scenes, in the office, or in the back and to use agency equipment and materials.

Volunteers are recruited and used on the basis of their contribution to the agency. However, this contribution is only of value if the agency recognizes the value such an experience holds for the volunteer. Voluntary service enables the participant to perform skills and demonstrate knowledge in an activity he or she enjoys; it offers an opportunity to discover and encourage unpracticed talents or extend professional expertise; and it affords the enjoyment that comes from contributing to others.

8. *Workshops, seminars, conferences.* This program format is similar to the class format except that it specifies an intense subject content conducted over a short period of time. Like the class structure, this format is instructional in nature. Yet occasionally the recreation planner will employ the conference format for decision making or planning itself. In addition, when the planner needs to organize the constituency around a specific project or concern, this format is an excellent way of arousing public interest and gaining publicity.

Choosing to structure recreation activity in the workshop, seminar, or conference form is based on the planner's intent for the participants to become intensely involved and singularly focused on the specific topic. The learning experience is often enhanced when the individual can study the topic on a continuous, uninterrupted basis. The normally short duration of this format allows for scheduling ease for the agency and is suitable to busy participant life-styles.

In order to distinguish between the various formats discussed here, Table 13 summarizes their purposes and general characteristics. As the table indicates, each format organizes groups of participants differently to obtain specific goals. For example, certain formats include only one-way communication and are used primarily for instruction. Others are designed to encourage two-way, face-to-face communication and are therefore used to share experiences and resources so that participants can learn from one another. If a group, for instance, is attempting to solve a problem or make a decision, the characteristics of the conference format would make it an appropriate choice.

Table 13   *Extended meeting format options*

Format	Purpose	Characteristics
Workshop	Instruction and training	Includes both general all-group sessions and small interaction groups; participants are also resources and play large role in instruction
Seminar	Group of skilled people gather to share resources and experience	High interaction in small face-to-face groups; leader is both discussion leader and a content expert
Institute	Instruction and training	Includes both general all-group sessions and small interaction groups; staff provide most resources and instruction
Conference	Planning, fact-finding, or problem solving	General all-group sessions with some small-group interaction; high level of involvement from participants
Convention	Annual business, information giving and decision making	General sessions and committee meetings; report giving and voting
Clinic	In-depth involvement in one topic for training purposes	Participants usually in trainee role; strict training principles followed in coach-team relationship

As a summary, Table 14 shows the application of the various structural formats to the different recreation program areas. At this step in the planning process, decision making entails selecting the best format for a chosen activity. This selection is based on the purpose of the planning and the goals of the program. All program areas can be worked into any of the structure forms, but recognizing the desirability of one format over another is an important part of the planning decision at this step.

Analysis of available resources

Decision making at this step in planning in addition to activity analysis also includes a criterion of available resources. Can the agency afford—in terms of personnel, facilities, and supplies—to offer the program service being considered? Costs are usually the first decision criterion that planners tend to observe because today cost is a major concern to program agencies. Planners must be prepared to justify selected programs in terms of cost of both human and material resources. More than ever the program planner needs to face the fiscal realities of each program considered and justify its cost, make adaptations, or select another program. Appropriated fees, the general operating budget, and outside gifts and donations are all weighed against the cost of personnel, supplies, equipment rental, and advertising. The nature of the program will reflect these fiscal parameters.

The general monetary difficulties of the 1970s and 1980s seem to be putting disproportionate pressure on recreation services. Because recreation is frequently considered a nonessential or a luxury, the recreation profession is being required, more and more, to justify itself in strictly monetary terms. This has gone so far as the development of the economic equivalency index (Kando, 1980). This potentially dangerous tool attempts to apply monetary values to the rewards of recreational activities. Through elaborate formulas it seeks to indicate, for example, that an outdoor city-wide music program is worth more (or less) in dollar value than a children's craft program. If used with sensitivity, this research tool may, however, enable recreation agencies to compete more successfully for available tax dollars or other revenues.

The primary costs to consider at this step in planning include leadership, facilities, equipment, supplies, and materials. The projected costs of these resources are weighed against the estimated amount of revenue available, and thus a budget is established. In recreation program services revenues come largely from taxes, activity fees and charges, donations, and grants; a certain amount also comes from a combined general fund allocated to program services. The amount of resources that can be allocated for a particular program depends on a number of factors, some of which the programmer cannot control.

Leadership costs   In fiscal year 1980 the Monongalia County Consolidated Recreation Commission in West Virginia had a total operating budget of $743,000. Of that total, $387,872, or 52%, went for the salaries of permanent, seasonal, and

Table 14 *Applying formats to program areas*

Program areas	Club	Competition	Trips/ outings	Special events	Class	Open facility	Voluntary service	Workshops/ seminars
								Format
Sports/ games	Polo club	Men's league softball	Major league trip	Playground play day	Beginning swim class	Free swim	Coaching Little League team	Soccer coaches preseason clinic
Hobbies	Stamp club	Best-of-show iris contest	Museum trip for collectors	Hobby show	Coin investment class	Model railroad layout	Teaching beginning coin class	Hydroponics workshop
Music	Record club	Battle of the bands	Trip to symphony	Hammered dulcimer festival	Guitar lessons	Music listening room	Conducting youth band	Song-leading workshop for camp leaders
Outdoor recreation	Sierra Club	White-water canoe races	Backpacking on John Muir Trail	Campcraft exhibit	Mountain-climbing class	Campsites	Camp counseling	Conference on psychological effects of adventure trips
Mental/ literary	Book-of-the-Month Club	Debate	Visit to library	Rare book sale	Speed-reading class	Library	Reading to shut-ins	Toastmasters' convention
Social recreation	Thursday club	Ice cream eating contest	Fall foliage bus trip	Haunted house	Etiquette class for children	Lounge with fireplace	Cooking-for-seniors club	Party-game workshop for recreation leaders
Arts/crafts	Local artists guild	Best-of-show pottery contest	Visit with Williamsburg artisans	Art in the park	Copper/enamel class	Crafts room open	Guest lecturing at art conference	Scrap crafts seminar for playground leaders
Dance	Romanian folk dance club	Dance marathon	Visit to ballet performance	Dance recital	Children's tap dance class	After-class practice space	Assisting with preschool baton	Ballet clinic by celebrity
Drama	High school thespians	One-act play contest	Play attendance	Play production	Acting class	Television available	Directing children's theater	Junior theater workshop

part-time personnel (*Annual Report: 1980*, p. 2). In the recreation literature the presence or absence of qualified leadership is frequently referred to as the most important factor for program success. Thus concern about the cost of leadership should never overshadow the planner's effort to ensure that only quality leaders will be used. In determining leadership costs, consideration must first be given to the leadership needs of the program.

The elements critical to program leadership costs are:

1. The leadership knowledge and skill necessary
2. The availability of personnel with the necessary knowledge and skills
3. The potential for combining leadership needs with leadership resources

Since the relative costs of quality personnel represent a large chunk of the total budget, the process of determining and selecting appropriate leadership must be approached seriously. It has been said that a program is only as strong as its leader. There is no place in recreation services for bad or even mediocre leadership.

The first effort in applying the leadership criterion is analyzing the proposed program according to the skills and knowledge required for its effective leadership. This analysis usually results in a job description that tells what functions will be asked of the leader and at what proficiency level these functions must be performed.

The next step is to identify the person, persons, or source of personnel with the specified skills and knowledge required for leadership in the proposed program. Qualified leadership may come from within the staff of the agency itself; the planner may be the best choice; or it may be necessary to recruit a leader from outside. There are a number of sources for locating potential leaders: colleges and universities, social or service clubs, hobby or special interest groups, public school systems, volunteer organizations, or even government or private employment agencies. A card file of leader sources can be an effective tool. Hobbyists, athletes, schoolteachers, musicians, artists, magicians, square dance callers, stable owners, seamstresses, and gourmet cooks are samples of contacts that should be on file. An inventory of the skills available throughout the agency can also assist the program planner in assessing leadership resources. The creative planner is always able to maximize the leadership talents already available, but when proposed programs require talents beyond those of agency staff, that planner is also able to cultivate new sources.

Finally, the planner evaluates the agency's potential for securing the necessary leadership. Can the agency afford to hire new staff? Will it need to rely on volunteers? Would it be more cost effective to reallocate to this program the leadership skills already available within the agency? Because this final consideration usually involves the actual selection of program staff, it frequently pulls the planner into other decision-making strategies such as application review, aptitude testing, interviewing, and contacting references.

Whether looking for a multitalented playground leader or a highly skilled ceramics leader, the planner must carefully analyze leadership talent. If quality leadership is sacrificed, the program's potential for success is reduced. If at least minimum leadership criteria cannot be met, perhaps other program options should take higher priority.

Area and facility costs   It is too bad that program planners are not called in to advise recreation facility designers. Because they are not, recreation areas and buildings usually are not well designed for programs. Therefore at this step in decision making, the program planner often must make the proposed program fit the available facility resources. When a program is being considered for development, the planner should know if it will be feasible in terms of setting and equipment. Is it desirable to offer a white-water kayak adventure program in an area where the nearest stream rapids are 500 miles away? Should a racquetball program take place in a church basement? All program activities have minimum requirements for area, facility, and equipment in addition to those special considerations that enhance the experience.

The planner is concerned not only with the appropriateness of existing facilities, but also whether these facilities can be adapted to better fit the program. For instance, many facilities used primarily for other purposes can be creatively used for recreation programs if the facility and the activity are compatible. The format the activity will have is an important factor in such cases. For example, the facility required for an archery tournament is usually more demanding than that needed for an archery class.

Normally program planners are not encouraged by the agency to request costly areas and facilities to better suit their program goals; more likely they have to make do with what is available. (This does not negate my plea for programmers to be a part of initial facility design and planning so that these expensive settings might be more useful.) However, program planners do have a certain amount of freedom when it comes to requesting equipment; usually they are able to specify what equipment and supplies are needed to "fit" the proposed program. Thus equipment, in terms of what is needed and what is available, will also have a bearing on the program chosen.

The budget: costs and justifications   The planner's concern for the proposed program and for meeting leadership and facility criteria leads to a determination of what it will cost. Program costs are of increasing concern to the program professional today. Primary cost factors that must be considered when selecting a program include those involving personnel, facilities, equipment, and supplies. The amount of cost that can be incurred for a specific program is directly dependent on the amount of monies available. This sounds simple enough, but overspending remains one of the most frequent errors in both governmental and private agencies.

Thus the bottom line for program deliberation at this step in planning is often the consideration of financial resources. The program planner must be intimately aware of how the agency derives and allocates its fiscal revenues. Cost can be viewed as a barrier to programming on one hand and a stimulator on the other. Often a program's worth to the participant is judged by how expensive it is. But usually the planner is concerned with keeping costs at a minimum.

To better understand and control the cost of a proposed program, a budget is determined. There are many systems for preparing a budget, and each agency normally has its own guidelines for budget planning. In its simplest form a *budget* is defined as an estimated plan for the future that helps keep expenses in line with income. Budgeting may be considered as planning in financial terms. Perhaps the most beneficial way to approach budgeting for proposed programs is to estimate the cost of each separate program and then compare the results to some predetermined revenue standard. Usually this standard reflects the agency's programming philosophy in terms of how much they are willing to spend. Estimating the cost of each proposed program before selecting it for implementation is critical for wise decision making.

At this stage in planning the process of establishing a budget is to look at each proposed program and assign an appropriate expense to it. This expense is then weighed against the estimated revenue. If the estimated expense column adds up to be greater than the expected revenue column, the planner may need to scrap the program idea, determine additional sources of revenue, or find ways to cut expenses. The whole foundation of a budget is balance; expenses and revenues must be "in balance" with each other (unless the agency is a commercial organization, in which case the goal is for revenues to outweigh expenses). If the agency is a public one, it may wish to subsidize the programming at a loss, but the trend seems to be toward self-sustaining programs even for these agencies. Recreation and park agencies, whether profit or nonprofit, occasionally are forced to recognize the public relations dividends of deficit spending programs. They have found that certain programs are worth sponsoring at a loss to enhance public opinion, to gain support, or to increase foot traffic—all of which ultimately will cultivate overall agency financial backing.

The task of budgeting must pay attention to both direct and indirect costs. Indirect costs are those expenses that are only partially designated to a particular program. They include such items as the salary of the administrative program planner, utilities, janitorial services, mimeographing, office supplies, and secretary time. Because the total cost of these necessities is usually shared by several programs, it is distributed throughout the total programming budget. A particular program's share of indirect costs is predetermined on the basis of the total agency budget and agency philosophy. Direct costs are those expenses that result solely from a particular program; they include such items as the class instructor's salary, craft supplies, portable stage rental, and party decorations.

Fig. 6-8 illustrates a sample budget using the program idea of a beginner's swim class. In this program budget an estimate of indirect costs is applied.

At the point of budget determination the planner arrives at the soul-searching question of program efficiency. With the fiscal crises of the first part of this decade, planners are increasingly concerned about determining the efficiency of both proposed and long-standing programs. Program efficiency is the assessment of relative costs in achieving program objectives as it compares to the ratio of effectiveness-to-effort in terms of fiscal and time resources. This ratio is based on the extent to which

Date prepared _____4/17/82_____

Prepared by _Stephen C. Williams_

Program title _Beginner's Swim Class_

Group size limit _____10_____

Length _Summer 1982_

Number of hours/week _2 hour sessions, twice_ a week

Location _Community Pool_

To begin _June 10, 1982_

To end _August 27, 1982_

Anticipated expenditures:

1. Leadership
   a. Number of leaders required _1 instructor, 1 lifeguard_
   b. Salary for each _$4.25_ X No. hour/week _5_
      X No. weeks _10_ X No. classes = $425.00

2. Facility
   a. Portion of total facility expense = $119.00
      (lights, janitor, heat, etc.)
   b. Special rental of facility   =   -0-

3. Materials and equipment
   a. Expendable equipment purchases   =   -0-
      (glue, crayons, Gatoraid, etc.)
   b. Permanent equipment purchases   =   (new kickboards) $120.00
      (costumes, balls, scenery, etc.)
   c. Portion of existing materials used =   -0-

4. Publicity and advertising   = $42.00

5. Administrative
   a. Phones =   -0-
   b. Office supplies =   -0-
   c. Mimeograph = $2.15
   d. Other =   -0-

6. Travel =   -0-

7. Other =   -0-

                           Total expenditures = $708.15

Anticipated revenue:

1. Registration fee _$25._ X _10_ Participants $250.00
   X No. classes =

2. Reimbursements from _-0-_ In amount of =   -0-

3. Sales items sold _T-Shirts_ In amount of = $200.00

4. Contributions from _-0-_ In amount of =   -0-

                              Total revenue = $450.00

        Total expenditures $708.15
        Total revenues (-) $450.00
        Balance   (=)   <$258.15>

Fig. 6-8 *Sample budget for beginner's swim class.*

program objectives are, or probably will be, achieved when measured against the kind and number of resources considered necessary to achieve program goals (Theobald, 1979).

The concern for a program's efficiency, either before or after implementation, has resulted in the use and adaptation of principles basic to the retail business. Researchers and proponents of such principles use the labels of *cost benefit analysis, cost utility analysis, Program Planning Budgeting System (PPBS),* and *cost ratio analysis;* but the intent is the same in each: to efficiently use available or potentially available resources toward the greatest benefit.

When determining the efficiency of a certain program, the planner should ask the following questions:

- How economically does this program achieve its objectives?
- Could other proposed programs achieve the same objectives at a lower cost?
- Can the program under consideration be modified to increase its objectives effectiveness without increasing its cost?

Why be concerned with budgeting and cost-effectiveness? Why not just plan programs that meet constituency needs and planning goals no matter what they cost? Why not focus on the potential social and psychological values of the program that are so important? Why be concerned with costs? Because accountability has become a major challenge to recreation program professionals. More and more, planners are being held accountable for their decisions and actions. Diminished resources have created a cautious and sophisticated constituency that demands that dollars, tax or otherwise, be used in an effective and efficient way. Therefore programs must be able to meet public expectations and withstand public scrutiny. Planners must account for managing human, physical, and fiscal resources in a justifiable manner. One way of accomplishing this justification is to substantiate each program with a budget.

No budget can be followed exactly, even in business. Therefore the recreation program planner must remember that a budget is an estimate, a guess of what should happen. During the implementation of an ongoing program, financial operations should be checked regularly, at least monthly, to determine whether the budget is being followed. If the budget is not being met, it may be necessary to reduce some items of expense or find new ways of generating revenue in order to ensure adherence to agency standards.

Alternatives to lack of resources

Lack of money has always been an easy rationalization for not attempting program expansion, program improvement, or program creativity. To find a program planner with unlimited resources is a rare treat. Yet must the planner give up? Doing without program essentials or even program frills is not always the best device for overcoming a limited budget. A recreation program that is sincerely desired and based on clearly identified needs and rational planning can find financing in various alternatives. Such alternatives must be worked out within the framework of the agency's policies and instituted with the approval of the managing authority. The following paragraphs describe some of the common alternatives to a lack of resources.

Fees and charges   The most widely used alternative (and one of the most controversial) is the charging of participant fees to finance the program. This allows a program to operate on a partially self-sustaining basis, with those involved paying the expenses. Such monies include program registration fees, entrance charges, team entry fees, transportation fares, and a wide range of similar revenues.*

The total progam service package of a recreation agency is likely to include the use of fees in certain circumstances. Some basic program activities are usually offered free of charge; some popular and relatively inexpensive programs are offered on a cost-of-materials basis; more specialized progams or those that involve much equipment require participants to pay a major part or even all of the cost.

The charging of fees for recreation program participation is being used more and more to keep program quality high in spite of shrinking fiscal resources. However, the critics of the practice argue that:

1. Everyone is entitled to recreation, the disadvantaged in particular; fees and charges exclude those who need it most
2. Recreation is a basic right of humanity, like air, freedom, and dignity; therefore fees for such are inhumane
3. Charging fees stimulates a sophisticated, profit-making greed in recreation personnel
4. Fees and charges make an agency more vulnerable to legal liability suits than when recreation services are free

As summarized from Curtis (1979), proponents of fees and charges, on the other hand, believe that:

1. Fees and charges place the heaviest tax burden on the heaviest users, the lightest on nonusers
2. A system of fees and charges allows better control or discipline of the program participants
3. Fees enable the recreation program to expand and diversify
4. Fees and charges offer a hedge against inflation and the increasing cost of providing program services
5. Fees that do not lead to profits do not increase the agency's vulnerability to legal liability suits

The arguments tend to cancel each other out, and the decision returns to the program planner. I think that fees and charges are never harmful if used properly. Fees must be reasonable, reflect accurately the costs to the agency, and be dis-

---

*The relationship between fee collection and expenditure payments is usually not as direct as it appears. For example, in some municipalities the law requires that fee monies be deposited in the general fund rather than be isolated for direct payment of particular program expenses.

tributed fairly among participants. Accommodation for disenfranchised persons must be sensitively included in any fee structure so that fees remain a program asset rather than becoming a deterrent to broad constituency participation.

Many programmers have found that fees often serve as a motivator for participation. When a price is attached to a service, an accompanying value for that service is established in the minds of those involved. Therefore human nature requires many participants to place a higher worth on programs that require a fee than on those that are free. Although this is not always the case, many professionals have found this attitude to be advantageous when establishing a fee for a program.

Grant writing   Another source of alternative resources is organizations outside the service area of the agency. Requests for financial assistance for programs can be made to both governmental and private agencies. However, federal aid in the form of categorical grants is being phased out, and many other governmental awards are being replaced by revenue sharing. It seems that recreation and park agencies must look more to private sources for the additional funds required for establishing or maintaining a sound financial basis for programming. In fact, in some communities private funding alone is what makes program services possible. Such funding is usually channeled through foundations.

Private foundations are nongovernmental, nonprofit organizations that have a principal fund of their own, are managed by their own directors, and are established to give financial aid to social, charitable, educational, and religious activities that serve the common welfare. These contributions serve, in turn, as tax deductions for the foundation (Joyce, 1974).

Foundations have traditionally been categorized according to five different types:

1. *General purpose foundations.* This category includes all the large, well-known foundations (for example, the Ford Foundation) that operate under charters and support projects in health, education, and welfare.
2. *Special purpose foundations.* These are created by a deceased person's will or trust, rather than by incorporation, to serve the financial needs of a certain purpose.
3. *Company-sponsored foundations.* These are nonprofit, legally separate subsidiaries of a company set up to administer the charitable contributions of that company. Therefore their programs are apt to be restricted to those locations where the company has its offices or plants.
4. *Community foundations.* Such foundations function under community control and for the benefit of their own city or area.
5. *Family foundations.* This type is set up by a person or family in order to have a tax-exempt channel for donating money to worthy causes.

Careful preparation in applying to private foundations may mean the difference between obtaining substantial awards and receiving none. In general, two basic considerations are necessary to obtain financial assistance from any private foundation. The first consideration is for the preparation and presentation of the proposal request. The appeal must be made through the correct channels and be tailored to the interests of the foundation. The second consideration is for the right contacts between the right people to take place at the right time.

Grant making is big business. In 1975 alone America's 25,000 foundations awarded 400,000 grants totaling roughly $2 billion. Yet over 95% of all grant applications submitted to foundations are turned down (Hillman and Abarbanel, 1975, p. 9). Many of these rejections would not have occurred if the applicants had known some basic grant writing principles. Even though no two grant seekers use the same approach, there are some basic guidelines to follow. Grant seekers with experience seem to agree on 10 steps. The usual time span between steps 1 and 10 ranges from 6 months to 1½ years. The following set of guidelines can be adapted to fit each specific project at hand. This material has been summarized from Hillman and Abarbanel (1975, pp. 17-86).

1. *Define your goal.* Success in obtaining private foundation money depends largely on locating foundations whose goals match those of the planner's program. A well-defined goal is thus the necessary first step. A clearly defined goal is usually stated in no more than one or two paragraphs and includes answers to the following main questions:
  • What is the need?
  • What are others doing to solve the need?
  • Who is the target constituency?
  • What aspects of the overall need can the agency realistically attempt to meet?

2. *Assess your chances.* At this point the planner should objectively assess the chances for successfully obtaining private foundation assistance. In general it will be difficult to win a grant if (a) the agency does not have an IRS letter of exemption,* (b) the agency is politically oriented, (c) the field is not well funded,† (d) the aim is support for general operating expenses or capital improvements, and (e) the planner lacks a track record of proven capability.

3. *Organize your resources.* Appoint a grant coordinator for the agency; create and maintain good internal agency communications; know the community reference library; know the other organizations with similar projects that are also competing for funds; start building contacts with influential people.

4. *Identify your prospects.* The research task here is to identify those private foundations that have previously funded projects similar to the planner's in purpose, field of interest, size, and locale. This can be done by compiling a preliminary list of the most promising foundations, researching each foundation in depth, and then narrowing the list down to a few. This research can be aided by consulting the

---

*In practice, foundations give virtually all their money to charitable, educational, religious, scientific, and cultural programs by agencies with IRS tax-exempt status.
†Historically foundations have funded education and health activities more heavily than others.

reference library for the *Foundation Grants Index*, the *Foundation Directory*, or the Smithsonian Institution's cultural directory.*

5. *Research each selected foundation in depth.* Additional research of possible sources should lead to a set of priorities as to which to approach first.

6. *Make initial contact.* At this point the planner is ready to arrange an exploratory meeting between appropriate representatives from the agency and the foundation. Even though face-to-face meetings are much more desirable, if the foundation refuses to schedule an appointment, ask if a letter of inquiry would be welcomed. The major effort at this step is to gain a preliminary indication of the foundation's degree of interest in the planner's project.

7. *Meet with the foundation.* Although some foundations may not grant interviews, preferring to conduct dealings through the mail, this is the time to prepare to present the significant facts and details of the proposal. Whether in a meeting or by mail, this contact should be brief, friendly, and professional.

8. *Write the formal proposal.* This written document is likely to be the planner's only representative at the foundation's board meeting. Proposals written for foundations and those written for federal grants will differ markedly in final form. Private foundations usually require a brief statement; governmental agencies usually require the completion of an extensive array of forms plus the planner's statement of intent. There is no standard proposal format available, but it should at least contain a statement of:

    a. Introduction
    b. Problem statement or assessment of need
    c. Program objectives
    d. Methods or solution
    e. Budget
    f. Future funding
    g. Evaluation methodology
    h. Summary

Of course the objective should be a direct outgrowth of the need; the methods should be a function of the objective, and the budget should be determined by the methods. There are several good references for the actual writing of a grant proposal; consult, for example, the Human Resources Network's *How to Get Money for: Youth, the Elderly, the Handicapped, Women, and Civil Liberties* (1975).

9. *Submit the formal proposal.* When submitting the formal proposal, also include a cover letter and an addendum if necessary, and always send the original copy to the foundation. The proposal should be neatly typed and proofread. Attention should be paid to the name of the person who will receive the proposal and the

---

*To order, write to: Smithsonian Institution Press
      Washington, D.C. 20560

application deadline. The same proposal may be submitted to more than one foundation simultaneously, but protocol demands that the applicant inform each foundation that this has been done. After the proposal has been mailed or delivered, try to avoid contacting the foundation for a progress report (although seeking verification that the proposal was received is justifiable).

10. *Follow-up.* Relax; be patient. The results will be made known to you as soon as they are determined. If the response from the foundation is yes, write a thank-you letter immediately and continue to maintain a good report system with the foundation on the program's progress. If the answer is no, write a letter thanking them for their consideration and request approval to keep in touch. Exit gracefully.

The procedure for requesting foundation monies requires much of the same planner behavior and decisions as does rational program planning itself. If the planning model as outlined in this text is followed, applying for grants requires little additional effort. However, further reading and consultation with agencies experienced in the intricacies of grant seeking is advised. Consult the reference list at the end of this chapter.

Contract programming Contract programming applies more to a deficit in facility or leadership resources than to a lack in fiscal resources. Contract programming does carry a price tag. This option entails a legally sanctioned contract between a recreation agency and a commercial business firm. The commercial firm has a service it specializes in performing, and the recreation agency contracts to purchase it. The most prevalent examples are the contracts signed for concession services such as park restaurants, rowboat docks, marinas, park bus lines, and ice skating rinks. But advantages are also being found in contracting for regular program services such as tiny-tot day care, skiing instruction, marathon races, and outdoor adventure programming.

Such contracts are generally given to legitimate, profit-motivated business firms that bid on opportunities to conduct such program services. When handled wisely, contract programming can bring in revenue above the cost of the contract in addition to providing the service.

Joint sponsorship Because of increasing difficulties in maintaining adequate supplies of available program resources, it is becoming rare for activities to be programmed exclusively within a single recreation agency. Today program planners are tapping the resources of other agencies and citizen groups within the community. The cooperation of recreation agencies and other community organizations in offering certain programs is an important and growing concept in the recreation field. Advantages of joint sponsorships include more and better staff, expanded budget, additional facilities and equipment, and more creative ways of meeting constituency needs. Through such joint sponsorship, or cosponsorship, the programming capability of an agency can be greatly expanded.

The combination of two or more agencies provides personnel, money, and facilities for offering an event or program larger and better than either agency could do alone. The organization combinations are endless and present a creative programming challenge. Churches, temples, industries, small business offices, police and fire departments, professional sports teams, universities, schools, travel agencies, movie theaters, unions, veterans' organizations, service clubs, hospitals, nursing homes, city and county recreation departments, and state park divisions represent the enormous possibilities for joint programming.

One interagency effort that has proved successful is the Humanities Project in Arlington, Virginia (Dwyer, 1974). In this community the municipal recreation agency's performing arts section has worked with school administrators and a regional citizens group (Service League of Northern Virginia) to expand and develop an arts program in the county's school system.

The structure for a project sponsored by several agencies must reflect a joint philosophical basis so that each agency feels equally represented in program planning and policy setting. Arlington's Humanities Project achieved this balance by appointing coordinators from both the city's performing arts division and the county schools staff. A steering committee of representatives from all involved organizations was also developed to provide a forum for communication.

Programs offered through joint sponsorship should reflect not only the needs of the constituency but also the various relevant capacities of the agencies. To accomplish this, the Humanities Project steering committee members first assessed school needs and reviewed already-existing arts programs. A priority was then established to develop programs that complemented the existing programs. Opera and drama experiences were selected as new program areas, while dance and music activities were developed to supplement already-established programs.

Perhaps the greatest advantage of a cosponsored program is the opportunity to develop favorable community support and understanding. This support can operate as a buffer against possible budget cuts in the future. Through the Humanities Project program, teachers, parents, students, and other members of the community of Arlington developed a greater appreciation of the efforts of each involved agency.

Voluntary special interest associations Recognizing its budgetary limitations for arts programming, the Anaheim Parks and Recreation Department in California has been able to provide an ever-expanding arts program by focusing its attention on what arts groups can and do provide for themselves (Ray, 1974). In 1963 a group of artists met with the department's program planner in charge of cultural activities and discussed their desire to organize a voluntary art association. A board of directors was established that included a representative of the department. The department assisted the Anaheim Art Association in such areas as publicity, mimeographing a monthly newsletter, compiling bylaws, and providing resource contacts. The programming of actual events was, however, accomplished totally by volunteer association members, with the department providing equipment and leadership only as requested. As the association grew in membership and organizational stature, it became self-sufficient.

Many mutual benefits are derived from such an arrangement between a recreation agency and a voluntary special interest association. First, the constituency is served by an organization that is administratively and financially independent. Because the constituency is often also the association membership, attention is better focused on the needs of that constituency. Second, the agency's responsibility for the provision of special interest programming is minimized, thus liberating department resources for other programming areas. Third, the association can return the favor and provide special assistance to the agency in conjunction with other agency-sponsored programming. For example, the Anaheim Art Association has given generously to assist the department in programs such as free art classes for the culturally disadvantaged and participation in all community-wide arts activities.

Proposition 13. Proposition 13, state legislation passed by California voters in 1978, mandated greatly reduced annual property taxes for real estate owners. This "taxpayer revolt" caused the decimation of numerous state and local social services, including tremendous budget cuts for several public recreation and park agencies. Some of the most severe financial shocks to recreation services occurred in Berkeley (the total department was eliminated except for a skeleton staff operating out of the city manager's office); Alameda (40% cutback in the department budget); Redondo Beach (layoff of all programming staff); Escondido (all staff cut but one coordinator); and Los Angeles County (a 33% reduction in all budgeted positions) (Foley and Benest, 1980). Because recreation services were regarded by California taxpayers as important but not essential, public recreation and park agencies fared worse than other social services.

The example of the situation in the Los Angeles County Department of Parks and Recreation after Proposition 13 can be used to summarize the discussion on alternatives to lack of resources. Like other California public services, this recreation department has been working diligently since 1978 to find ways to cope with extreme deficiencies in financial and personnel resources. The following is an outline of what the department did to cope with Proposition 13 cutbacks as cited from Cryder (1980):

> 1. *Reorganized our thinking.* Immediately following the adoption of the budget, we reorganized our thinking and developed a new written philosophy for the department, including long-term goals and year-to-year aims and objectives, and we developed a new policies and procedures manual for implementation. All of these items were outdated by close to twelve years.
>
> 2. *Departmental reorganization.* We reorganized the department from the bottom up and vice versa, taking into consideration chain of command and unity of command regarding our functional units of operations. We made generalists out of our specialized staff; instituted a new inservice training program; and incorporated zero based budget principles. We also set up six major committees within the department to help with specialized areas such as revenue resources, risk management, inservice training, energy conservation, public information, and the Employees Recreation Council.

3. *Volunteer hotline.* Immediately upon the passage of Proposition 13, and at the suggestion of the Department Chair, we implemented a brand new volunteer hotline system to solicit individuals and groups to assist us in the operation and maintenance of many of the department's programs. To date we have solicited and used approximately 80 individuals in various areas, not to mention the volunteer groups such as the Docents for our nature areas, the Mounted Park Patrol Assistance Units in regional parks, and various other individuals and groups who have assisted us with Jesse Owens Track and Field, California Special Olympics for the Retarded, and so forth.

4. *Self-sustaining recreation programs.* The board of supervisors approved a self-sustaining recreation program which permitted us to charge fees to recover all of our costs for conducting instructional programs, sports and athletics, trips and tours, special events, and other specialized services that we offer through our recreation agency to the general public.

5. *Existing fees and charges.* We have reviewed all of the existing fees and charges adopted by the board several years ago which needed to be updated to meet the actual costs as affected by inflation.

6. *Private sector funding.* We have been working with the private sector, particularly with the Atlantic Richfield Company, Coca Cola, and Pepsi Cola, to establish ways and means for cooperative ventures that will include both financial and personnel resources to continue important activities that we no longer can support. Our association with the private sector will need to continue indefinitely since it represents a long-term cooperative venture.

7. *Park and recreation councils.* We have developed guidelines for the creation of park and recreation councils to be established for each and every one of our regional and local parks within the system.

8. *Contractual services.* With the passage of Proposition A rescinding the county charter restriction on contracting services in November 1978, we have established a task force in the department to look at all areas that might be conducive to contracted services wherein the benefit derived is equal to the services now provided by this department but at a lesser cost. Currently we have identified four specific areas that include security at the Whittier Narrows Regional Park and the Hollywood Bowl; grounds maintenance for Cerritos Regional Park; contracting for starter services at Mountain Meadows Golf Course; and grounds maintenance at one or more local parks. Beyond these areas, we will continually be looking at other areas that could provide us with the service and the cost savings as outlined under the county's policy.

9. *Cost saving areas.* During the past few months, we have been paying particular attention to a number of areas, primarily those in the department's service and supplies budget, in hopes of either holding the line on expenditures or saving money as a result of better control and management.

10. *Park and recreation foundation.* Since October 1978, we have been researching the possibilities of establishing a county-wide park and recreation foundation outside the purview of government that could operate with a separate board of directors to receive both real and personal property, as well as gifts and donations, that could be distributed to the county and to various municipalities within the Los Angeles corporate limits. In the next fiscal year we will be working with prominent citizens, both in the private and public sector, to outline the provisions and use of such a foundation.*

---

*From Cryder, R.S. L.A. County kicks the Prop-13 blues. Reprinted from the *15:3* (1980) issue of *Parks & Recreation* by special permission of the National Recreation and Park Association.

Politics

In making decisions necessary for selection of the best programs to offer, the planner also needs to consider the political criterion. In every community there are influential individuals and groups of individuals who play a major role in making decisions for that community. Support from these "power elites" or "economic notables," as they have often been labeled, can significantly enhance the development of recreation program services. Influential community members can make a significant difference in attracting favorable community sentiment for recreation program services.

Who are these power elites? Research results have concluded (1) that persons not elected to a public or official office, operating behind the scenes, play significant parts in making important community decisions and (2) that some persons, groups, or combinations wield a disproportionate share of this influence (Howard, 1976, p. 31). Despite the fact that the distribution of power appears to vary from one community to another, research has discovered that invariably business or economic leaders exercise a great deal of authority. The control that business leaders can exercise over the wealth and resources of a community is a major factor in the structure of power and influence. Politicians and bureaucrats are seldom as powerful as professionals and business persons.

Particularly in an era of image justification, it is essential that recreation program administrators gain the support of top community leaders. The active endorsement or assistance of these influential individuals can be important to the development and maintenance of an agency's programs. There are numerous ways in which the program planner can use such support, either behind the scenes or in the forefront. Community leaders can be encouraged to be judges in competitions, guest lecturers in instructional programs, or spokespersons in program advertising and promotion. Spearheading (as honorary chairpersons) special events, such as the annual Special Olympics or a 10,000-meter "fun run," has been the traditional type of support sought. The planner should also consider that the ability to generate community support seldom goes unnoticed by the community's political leaders, who often make allocation decisions concerning budget requests, grants, and revenue sharing. More important, not only can powerful people lend the weight of their prestige and status to the recreation program, but often the business know-how that a bank president or a corporation director can bring to the planning process is critical to its ultimate success.

With the barrage of issues and people making demands on community influentials, it will be necessary for the recreation professional to compete wisely for their favors and support. The first step is to identify those persons who play a major role in community decision making. This can be done by listing those holding formal positions of authority in economic, industrial, or religious institutions; by scanning the newspapers; and by asking knowledgeable community residents. However, since the power elite are not always those with legitimate, formal power, some sensitive inves-

RAY BELLAROSA

tigation may be required. Then, convincing community leaders of the importance of recreation program services to the vitality or economic worth of the community may be a difficult and time-consuming task. Making such an appeal can be made easier by using the influential's own rationale for being an influential. Banfield and Wilson (1966) state that those who exercise power from unofficial positions do so for four types of reasons: self-serving, own profession or business serving, group serving, and community serving. A group of business persons, for example, may endorse a particular recreation program for the community because of the ultimate benefit it may reflect on their companies, on the welfare of the community, or on their own image in the community.

The ability of the power elite to win the approval of proposals for community improvements has been well documented. For instance, in 1936 Frank Manley, then a public school physical education teacher, persuaded wealthy industrialist C.S. Mott to convert his concern for the youth of Flint, Michigan, into what is today the internationally celebrated and practiced community-school program. An important challenge facing recreation professionals is to cultivate the energies and interests of community leaders toward expanding recreational opportunities for their constituency.

Risk management and legal liability

Another decision criterion that all program options should be scrutinized against is safety. Is the environment of the program activity reasonably safe—that is, free of unreasonable risk and foreseeable harm? Not only is it the planner's professional and moral duty to manage risk but also a legal one. Lawsuits have become a way of life with Americans, and recreation programs often have been the target. A toy rocket launcher that took out a child's eye with impact "greater than a BB gun" resulted in a suit settlement of $100,000; the victim of a trampoline accident resulting in paralysis from the chest down was awarded a $575,000 settlement; the family of a boy who died after being hit in the head with a golf club swung by another class participant was awarded $53,570 (Frakt, 1979, pp. 44-46). Monetary awards like these are made when a recreation program or service breaks liability rules; that is, when it does not provide a reasonably safe environment for the participant.

The object of liability rules, as of other legal provisions, is to "influence human behavior in such a way as to secure certain modifications and to protect certain expectations of community and individual rights" (Rankin, 1977, p. 48). In other words, an individual has a right to expect to live in an environment that is reasonably free from dangerous interferences and threats. This means that a recreation programmer must legally protect the safety of a program participant. Failure to do so is termed a *tort*. Tort liability, then, is a legal wrong resulting from a lack of proper protection from an unsafe environment. This lack of proper protection may result from (1) failure to do something that one should do or (2) doing something wrong that results in injury to person or property. Unintentionally failing to do something one should do or doing something that results in injury is called *negligence*, and most tort liability suits against recreation agencies involve negligence. Negligence is the unintentional violation of a duty to take into consideration the interests of others that results in injury. Negligence is failure to act as a reasonable and prudent person would have acted under the same circumstances; that is, as a professional in such leadership position should act.

Examples of negligence in recreation include:
1. Failure to repair a broken playground swing on which a child is later injured
2. A camp leader's inability to control rowdiness that results in a fight injury
3. Programming of a white-water kayak program for participants who are too young to appreciate the risk involved, too small to reach the toe blocks in the kayak, or not strong enough to control the double-bladed paddle
4. A lifeguard leaving his or her post without permission, after which a drowning occurs
5. Ignoring fire department occupancy regulations at a crowded senior center, which results in fire casualties

Risk management is an effort to safeguard against negligent acts and to provide a play environment that is reasonably free from hazards.

According to van der Smissen (1980), in order to achieve a sound standard of care for recreation participants, three areas of reasonable and prudent professional risk management are required: (1) supervision of participants, (2) environmental conditions, and (3) manner of conducting activity.

The advice of risk management is clear: the best way to reduce liability is to examine programs carefully to determine which would pose a high risk of injury even if they were well supervised, were provided with appropriate and well-maintained equipment, and were subject to proper warnings and instruction. What must be emphasized is that most recreation program activities are not inherently dangerous. Large court settlements usually arise from injuries that resulted from poor professional judgment, lack of adherence to current safety standards, absence of inspections and repair of areas and facilities, and laziness in design of program formats and conduct. How do the programs proposed at this step in planning match up against these standards of care? Will it be possible to provide adequate supervision? Will the facility and the necessary equipment be in safe operating condition? Can the program be designed and conducted to allow reasonably safe participation?

Program supervision of participants entails a sound plan of location, number, and competence of program or facility leaders. It is the responsibility of recreation activity leadership to alert participants to dangerous conditions, control disruptive behavior, know first aid and emergency care, and be sure that participants understand and adhere to safety practices. A vital part of sound and prudent supervision is making participants understand the demands of the activity in terms of their own capacity—both skill level and physical condition.

Faulty environmental conditions are one of the most frequently cited causes of injury. This makes inspection and maintenance of equipment and facilities, as well as careful consideration of the initial design and layout of facilities, vital. The overwhelming majority of major suits have involved man-made or substantially altered activity sites, such as swimming pools with diving boards, prepared and groomed athletic fields, and prepared ski areas. In most cases the facility had a dangerous obstruction, defective equipment, or faulty construction.

Most pertinent to the subject of this text is the third standard of care: manner of conducting the recreation program. This standard includes the reasonable attention paid to the adequacy of instruction. Not only should activity instructors know and be able to teach the activity well; they should also offer lead-up skill practice, if appropriate, and instruction for safety. The format of the activity should match the maturity, skill, experience, and abilities of the participant. Program objectives should reflect the most up-to-date and best professional practices and should not be so far-reaching as to set the participant up for injury. Advertising of program content and goals should be a truthful representation of the program. The program should include warnings of potential dangers inherent in participating and employ protective devices (such as helmets and life jackets) when appropriate. Programs that involve complicated activities or that rely heavily on equipment should be organized specifically to maximize proper preinstruction and progression of experience. For example, before programming a week's backpacking trip in the High Sierra mountains, several overnight and weekend trial runs should be taken with the group, and adequate orientation to weather changes at high altitudes should be offered.

This text advocates the conceptualization and implementation of innovative programming and the grouping of activities into new and creative configurations. But the fact remains that accidents and resulting injuries will inevitably occur. Recreation professionals should realize that they may be sued. This is part of the attitude of our impersonal, economically tight times. The professional programmer in recreation and park services is not an ensurer of safety; he or she cannot prevent suits by eliminating certain activities from programs. The professional can, however, win negligence suits by keeping the likelihood of liability to a minimum.

In developing program options the planner must make sure that the activity meets or exceeds all safety standards, that an attempt has been made to anticipate problem areas and to detail a system of handling them, and that there is an appropriate balance of enthusiasm for the program and concern for the well-being of the participants. If the activity is considered especially hazardous, it is important to be doubly certain that the participant understands the risks involved. Both during the planning process and after the program has been implemented, the program planner should document the steps taken to ensure the safety of participants. This means not only keeping thorough records of accidents but also noting dates and content of regular safety checks of facilities and equipment involved in the program. In short, the programmer must use the special skills and knowledge of his or her training and experience to make informed judgments that will account for the participant's physical safety and the agency's freedom from litigation. This must be done without forfeiting balanced program opportunities that include challenging and innovative experiences.

Appropriateness

The appropriateness criterion refers to the recreational needs of the target constituency derived in step 1 of the planning process. This criterion demands that each program alternative be evaluated according to its appropriateness for the potential participant. Appropriateness of programming also suggests two subconcepts: relevancy and accessibility.

If program services are to be relevant, maintaining an awareness of the changing and differing tastes, values, and needs of the various participant groups is an important programming task at this stage. The planner must stay abreast of trends, changes in behavior, and new customs to choose program services meaningfully. In addition, the planner needs to guard against creating and distributing program services that arise solely from his or her own personal values or norms. To make meaningful

RAY BELLAROSA

choices, the program planner must first pay attention to the needs and values of the constituency the program service is intended to serve. This involves being aware of his or her own limitations when planning for the needs of individuals whose values are different and seeking appropriate advice when necessary.

Accessibility in an important factor to consider in choosing among program options. Physical or social barriers in programming cannot be tolerated. One example of a physical barrier is a facility with narrow doors that prohibit participation by the disabled group the program is designed to serve; another example is having a program location outside convenient reach by the target population. Social barriers that limit a program's accessibility might include a misleading communication or an activity format that is unattractive to persons of differing social class, income, or age. Social norms or values also create social barriers of prejudice and discrimination that can greatly reduce the accessibility of program to certain constituencies.

Effectiveness

Finally, the program planner should compare each of the proposed program alternatives according to their estimated ability to meet the planning goals established in step 2. Will this program option accomplish what the planner wants it to do? As discussed previously, recreation program objectives are planning goals that state desired changes that will occur as a result of the program. These changes may be in attitudes, behavior, skill, or knowledge.

An effective program is one that leads to these desired changes. The process is as follows:

Edward Suchman (1969) and Carol Weiss (1972) have suggested two possible reasons for ineffective programs: "Either the program itself did not initiate the process necessary to achieve the objective (program failure), or the program did initiate this process, but the process did not yield the desired effects (theory failure)" (Theobald, 1979, p. 119). In the case of the first reason, program failure, the:

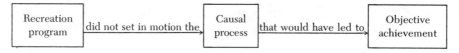

In this case the recreation program itself did not cause the appropriate action, and therefore planning goals were not obtained. However, in the case of the second reason, theory failure, the:

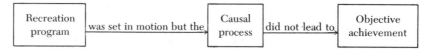

In this instance the recreation program caused something to happen, but the result did not accomplish the desired goal.

Therefore the success of a program depends on the effectiveness of the program itself as well as the effectiveness of the theory behind it. A professional estimate of such effectiveness is helpful at this stage in planning. A preliminary evaluation of each proposed program's ability to meet the established goals should be a criterion included in the decision making. The final program or programs selected must be the planner's best estimate for achieving the desired objectives.

CONCLUSION

The planner must now make a final decision. The deliberation of program alternatives must stop when the planner has optimized all the information available, his or her own intuitions about constituency need, and consideration of the program options. To delay beyond this point is no longer advantageous for making a good decision. As the program alternatives are reviewed, the planner must select the best—or maybe just the one with the fewest disadvantages—for implementation.

Frequently the planner will need to signify the completion of this planning step by preparing a report for submission to the agency director or the managing authority. Such a report should include a summary statement from planning steps 1 through 4 as well as a statement of prediction of results. Clearance for implementation of the selected program idea is in effect when the proposal has been approved. Then necessary equipment is purchased and dispensed, program leaders are trained and assigned, publicity is released, participants are registered, facilities are made ready—all leading to the implementation of a recreation program.

In most cases this completes planning step 4. However, sometimes it is determined advisable to recycle the effort back to a preceding step. For example, a detailed study of program alternatives according to the effectiveness criteria may indicate that an objective adopted earlier is impractical; therefore this objective must be changed or the planning need must be defined in a different way. One of the values of the rational planning process is that such recycling is not only possible but encouraged when it is necessary.

References

Banfield, E.C., & Wilson, J.W. *City politics.* New York: Random House, 1966.

Bannon, J.J. *Problem solving in recreation and parks* (2nd ed.). Englewood Cliffs, N.J.: Prentice-Hall, 1980.

Bishop, D.W. Stability of the factor structure of leisure behavior: Analysis of four communities. *Journal of Leisure Research,* 1970, 2:3, 160-170.

Carter, B.G. A big day for Rover. *Parks & Recreation,* 1976, 11:11, 29-30, 40.

Cryder, R.S. L.A. County kicks the prop-13 blues. *Parks & Recreation,* 1980, 15:3, 48-51.

Curtis, J.E. *Recreation: Theory and practice.* St. Louis: C.V. Mosby, 1979.

Dwyer, K. Interagency cooperation—The more the better. *Parks & Recreation.* 1974, 9:6, 59-60, 102.

Edginton, C.R., Compton, D.M., & Hanson, C.J. *Recreation and leisure programming: A guide for the professional.* Philadelphia: Saunders College, 1980.

Farrell, P., & Lundegren, H.M. *The process of recreation programming: Theory and technique.* New York: John Wiley, 1978.

Fishburn, P.C. Personalistic decision theory exposition and critique. In H.S. Brinkers (Ed.), *Decision-making: Creativity, judgment, and systems.* Columbus: Ohio State University Press, 1972.

Foley, J., & Benest, F. Viewpoint. Proposition 13 aftermath—A crisis in recreation and park leadership? *Parks & Recreation,* 1980, 15:1, 86-87.

Frakt, A. Putting recreation programming and liability in perspective. *Parks & Recreation,* 1979, 14:12, 43-46.

Hillman, H., & Abarbanel, K. *The art of winning foundation grants.* New York: Vanguard Press, 1975.

Howard, D. Tapping community power. *Parks & Recreation,* 1976, 11:3, 31-32, 47-48.

Human Resources Network. *How to get money for: Youth, the elderly, the handicapped, women, and civil liberties.* Radnor, Pa.: Chilton, 1975.

Joyce, D.V. Foundation funding. *Parks & Recreation,* 1974, 9:2, 24-25, 47-48.

Kando, T.M. *Leisure and popular culture in transition* (2nd ed.). St. Louis: C.V. Mosby, 1980.

Rankin, J. Legal risks and bold programming. *Parks & Recreation,* 1977, 12:7, 47-48, 67-69.

Ray, P. Programming on a shoestring. *Parks & Recreation,* 1974, 9:6, 57-58, 97-99.

Suchman, E.A. Evaluating education programs: A symposium. *Urban Review,* 1969, 3:4, 16.

Theobald, W.F. *Evaluation of recreation and park programs.* New York: John Wiley, 1979.

Van der Smissen, B. *Overview of liability in parks and recreation.* Paper presented at the National Recreation and Park Association Congress, Phoenix, Arizona, 1980.

Weiss, C.H. *Evaluation research: methods of assessing program effectiveness.* Englewood Cliffs, N.J.: Prentice-Hall, 1972.

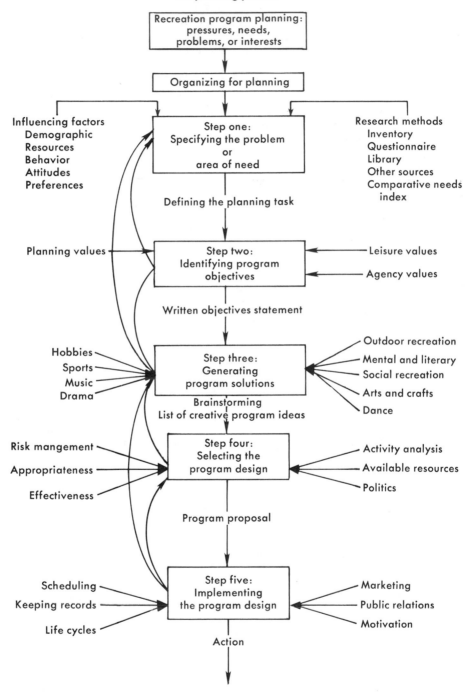

The planning process

Recreation program planning:
pressures, needs,
problems, or interests

Organizing for planning

Influencing factors
Demographic
Resources
Behavior
Attitudes
Preferences

Step one:
Specifying the problem
or
area of need

Research methods
Inventory
Questionnaire
Library
Other sources
Comparative needs
index

Defining the planning task

Planning values

Step two:
Identifying program
objectives

Leisure values

Agency values

Written objectives statement

Hobbies
Sports
Music
Drama

Step three:
Generating
program solutions

Outdoor recreation
Mental and literary
Social recreation
Arts and crafts
Dance

Brainstorming
List of creative program ideas

Risk mangement

Appropriateness

Effectiveness

Step four:
Selecting the
program design

Activity analysis
Available resources
Politics

Program proposal

Scheduling
Keeping records
Life cycles

Step five:
Implementing
the program design

Marketing
Public relations
Motivation

Action

Chapter 7

STEP 5

Implementing the program design

Planning has worth if it leads to implementation. The program ideas conceived and developed in previous planning steps are now ready to be put into action. With one or more program options adopted, the planner has only final preparations to make for the planned implementation. Thus the next step in the program planning process focuses on the transformation of planning into programs.

According to Joseph Bannon (1980), most professionals in the recreation field are idea people. He views them as quick and able to suggest program solutions to constituency needs and interests but not so well prepared to develop and implement them. Bannon complains that program planners typically ignore implementation, assuming that it is an automatic procedure. This criticism may be harsher than necessary, but its warning is important. "Even a 'fair' idea, if it is put to use intelligently and aggressively, may do more good than the most brilliant suggestion that is never followed up" (Mason, 1960, p. 200). Thus the implementation step in planning cannot be ignored; if it were, planning would be merely an intellectual exercise. True creativity means putting creative program ideas into practice.

At this planning stage the following questions must be considered:
- Who will be the best staff to run the program?
- Where is the best place to buy the needed equipment?
- On what date and at what time will the program begin?
- What should be the exact program content?
- How will participants be attracted?

By spelling out such details the planner can bring the intended program to life. This chapter discusses a number of factors to consider and tasks to perform for successful implementation of a program.

The process chart at the beginning of this chapter shows that planning step 5 begins with the approval or adoption of a particular program alternative. The "detailing" then required for implementation of this program will include marketing, motivation, public relations, scheduling, keeping records, and program duration. In order to handle all these details efficiently, many planners have found it helpful to use an implementation strategy. Through such a strategy all the subparts of a program, its details, are brought together to produce program action. This is the task of step 5 in rational program planning.

Implementation strategies

Before the planner can implement a program, he or she must delineate an operational strategy. No matter how simple or complex the program, it is crucial to plan and think about its implementation. The planner also needs to set objectives for implementation: What must be accomplished, and how much time is allotted for it? Thus an implementation strategy not only specifies the various ways of implementing a program but also states who will be responsible for what, and when and how all tasks will be accomplished. Therefore the most basic talent required at this point is the ability to be organized.

Getting organized

Implementing anything requires organization. Recreation program implementation, as well as all the planning that leads to it, is no exception. Therefore I would like to pause and discuss the organizing principle so that the planner will approach this step in planning with a relaxed sense of how diverse details can be brought together.

All concepts of accomplishment, from the simplest system of closet arrangement to the most complex scientific endeavor, share one essential characteristic: an organizing principle. The thesis behind the organizing principle is that "any intellectual or practical system [of organization] always contains a central pole, an essential priority, around which all other components group themselves" (Winston, 1980, p. 25). In fact, the organizing principle defines behavior in all of life. If an individual's first priority is defiance, then that person's behavior will reflect this. If a person's top priority is ease and convenience, then that person will order his or her life to ensure ease and convenience. The key to organization is to find the organizing principle (defiance? convenience?) that is most appropriate for you and allow it to serve as your basic point of reference.

Surrounding this basic principle are three supporting ideas that can help in organizing one's work or personal life. These hints to better organization are:

Hint 1: Use a single notebook for everything.

Hint 2: Divide complex tasks into smaller, manageable segments.

Hint 3: After dividing a complex project into smaller ones, rank them numerically according to how important or necessary they are.

To begin, provide yourself with a notebook. (I prefer loose-leaf so that pages can be added, taken away, or rearranged; but spiral also will work.) The notebook must be small enough to carry around in purse or briefcase. It should become your "master list"—a single, never-ending dialogue that replaces all the small slips of paper tucked into your pocket or wallet. Use the notebook to keep track of errands, things to do or buy, as well as general thoughts or notes to yourself that require future action.

This is the way my notebook works for me. At the beginning of each week (usually Sunday evenings) I review both the jottings I made in my notebook during the previous week and my appointment calendar. From these I compose a detailed to-do list in my notebook. As the week progresses, I mark off each task accomplished and throw away the notation that led to it. Because my appointments are integrated with my to-do list on a weekly basis, the ideal notebook for me does not exist. It would be loose-leaf with room for 20 blank pages at a time, followed by an appointment calendar by the week, followed by an address and phone directory.

Hint 2 is critical to accomplishing anything. All efforts can be divided into significant parts. Because smaller projects are always more manageable than larger complex ones, they are more likely to be carried out. When enough lead-up projects are accomplished, the larger project automatically falls into place. For example, if you want to reorganize the garage, break the effort into smaller parts and accomplish one part a week. Sort the workbench this week, reorganize the laundry area next, take a week off, and then finish by working out the storage for the sports equipment the following week. This way instead of devoting an entire Saturday to the project, you will have spent perhaps only 2 hours a week for 3 weeks.

For particularly difficult or unpleasant projects, Hint 3 offers an additional means of organizing for action. After a major effort has been subdivided into manageable parts, rank each of the items according to how much it irritates you or how important you feel it is. A subtask that creates serious tension has a rank of 1; a more pleasurable task, or one that is not critical, receives a rank of 10. Write the assigned rank next to each item on your list. Do not worry about arranging the projects in complete numerical order (or you may become so involved in figuring out which item should be fourth that you will lose sight of what you are trying to accomplish). Ranking subactions that lead to the accomplishment of a project or the solution of a problem is a vital impetus to action. The lists made in both Hint 2 and Hint 3 should be worked through in the notebook advocated in Hint 1.

With this step of ranking completed, the process of establishing order has begun. The issues have been outlined, priorities have been determined, and a foundation for action has been laid. All that remains is to set aside a specific and regular time for laying the groundwork requested in the three organizing hints. I advise that you make a fixed appointment with yourself (my Sunday evenings) and that you note it in your appointment calendar as if it were a dental appointment. Your "appointments" could be every day for 15 minutes, or twice a week for 1 hour each, or 1 hour a week—whatever is practical for your own life-style.

All organized persons understand time—how it works and does not work. Using time for productive purposes and for enjoyable ones is ultimately a personal decision. Before you even begin to organize yourself or your work, you must learn how to use time to your best advantage.

The secret of time efficiency is to use the notebook advocated in Hint 1 along with an appointment calendar for scheduling all tasks. I suggest the use of a daily to-do list, which serves as an axis around which your day revolves. In composing the to-do list, first decide which items from your notebook and appointment calendar might be better delegated to other people, such as colleagues or subordinates (if at work) or children and domestic services (if at home). Then schedule the remaining tasks in terms of the priority established in Hint 3. Cross each item off the list as you complete it, or transfer unfinished items to the next day or week.

Scheduling for maximization is critical. For example, a task such as report writing, which requires concentration, should be scheduled for quiet, uninterrupted hours. Early morning may be the only comfortable time for yard work. Certain tasks may require special equipment available only between certain hours. Be aware of deadlines, your own biorhythms, and your fatigue level in order to establish a to-do list that is practical and therefore accomplishable.

Because overwork leads to diminishing returns, it must be avoided. A to-do list that helps you foresee projects and space their subparts throughout the week or month helps eliminate overwork. Some people like to schedule their days tightly, on an hourly basis. The important thing is that the to-do list allow for flexibility. For example, if you have difficulty defining schedules that are flexible, reserve at least 1 hour a day for unexpected events or changes and make sure to keep some time for yourself. Do not worry if an item must be transferred to the next day's list, but do not set yourself up for procrastination either. I have made a rule that if an item is transferred to more than three daily to-do lists, I raise its priority ranking to 1, which makes it the first task for the next list.

Stephanie Winston (1980) has listed eight time-savers for better use of your daily to-do list:

1. Barter: Trade or exchange distasteful jobs with others.
2. Make use of services: Rely on professionals as much as you can afford.
3. Double up on time: Do several small tasks at the same time (for example, sign letters while on telephone hold).
4. Make use of bits of time: Plan small projects during waiting periods or bus riding.
5. Plan ahead: Make sure everything is at hand before starting a project.
6. Pool resources: Experiment with cooperative arrangements.
7. Consolidate: Combine errands, telephone return calls, and as much movement as possible.
8. Labor-saving devices: Use modern technology as much as possible.

The advice offered in this section is applicable to everyone in every type of endeavor. The next section focuses on the application these "getting organized" principles have for the implementation step in recreation program planning.

Suggestions for implementation strategy

The need for recreation and park planners and administrators to apply management techniques from other fields is becoming more important in view of increasing demands for accountability and efficiency. Service offerings in recreation agencies can no longer be based solely on "doing what comes naturally." Instead there is a need to draw upon business and economic theories and to acquire workable techniques for realizing more and better program and facility services.

In order to give proper attention to the various details of implementation, it is helpful to divide the task into chronological stages. Program implementation can be visualized as a series of substeps in which certain functions take sequence priority because they must be completed before others can begin. From the fields of business and management come suggestions for implementation strategies.

The Critical Path Method (CPM) and the Flow Chart Method (FCM) are management systems for graphically designated implementation tasks. Both methods have been extracted from a larger systems theory evaluation tool known as PERT. Program Evaluation and Review Technique (PERT) was developed in 1958 jointly by the U.S. Navy, Lockheed Aircraft Corporation, and a private management consulting firm for weaponry development (Evarts, 1964). The primary analytical device in PERT is a flow chart that outlines the steps toward achieving a finished product. This flow chart capacity in PERT has recently been adapted for recreation program implementation, for facility construction completion, and for personnel management, and it has been dubbed with the CPM and FCM titles.

Versatility and adaptability are significant advantages of the CPM and FCM systems. For simple programs, manual development of the time network required to accomplish the tasks is feasible. The system can also be easily converted to computer operations for large-scale or complex projects. Because an application of CPM or FCM to computer programming is beyond the scope of this text, attention here will be limited to manual use.

These strategies for implementation are event-oriented techniques that focus on the planning, scheduling, and controlling of events in a quantitative manner. With this focus they attempt to eliminate oversight, the uncertainty of chance, and last-minute scrambling. Essentially FCM and CPM are systematic forecasting processes that attempt to account for and set a precedent for each task requirement in the organization of a program. The CPM and FCM systems separate the entire program into implementation parts and evaluate each according to what is to be done, when it is to be done, who is to do it, and how long it will take. For example, Tables 15 and 16 present, respectively, the components of a fictional summer playground program and a dramatic presentation. CPM and FCM then combine and fit these various parts onto a "time line" according to a precedence theme to provide the planner with a logical view of the path leading to the accomplishment of the program. The applica-

Table 15   *Checklist for implementation of a summer playground program*

Component	Task	Time required to complete (weeks)	Deadline
Personnel	Prepare job announcements	2	2/15
	Interview applicants	3	4/1
	Prepare leader's manual	6	5/2
	Leaders in-service training begins	1	6/25
Materials	Inventory existing supplies	1	1/19
	Prepare specs for bids	1	3/2
	Order equipment	6	4/25
	Arrange storage	2	5/29
	Distribute materials to sites	1	6/23
Facilities	Inspect sites	2	2/4
	Select tentative sites	2	2/24
	Reconfirm use agreement with school district	1	3/9
	Request maintenance	4	4/23
	Meet with school principals	1	5/18
	Complete maintenance	4	6/21
Program	Review previous years' evaluations	2	1/17
	Meet with playground advisory council	6	3/6
	Establish tentative master calendar	4	3/24
	Complete special events schedule	4	4/18
	Complete program activities manual	8	5/24
Publicity	Visit with local media representatives	1	4/16
	Flyers to printer	3	5/12
	Prepare posters and radio spots	2	6/15
	Newspaper articles	1	6/24

Table 16   *Checklist for implementation of a dramatic presentation*

Component	Task	Time required to complete (weeks)	Deadline
Personnel	A. Select staff	4	2/25
Materials	B. Prepare scenery and props	1	4/22
	C. Install scenery and props	2	5/6
	D. Prepare costuming and effects	4	5/6
Facilities	E. Reserve auditorium	1	5/6
Program	F. Choose and obtain play	3	1/28
	G. Cast actors	2	2/25
	H. Rehearse actors	6	4/8
	I. Dress rehearsal	5	6/10
Publicity	J. Advertise play	7	5/6
	K. Print tickets and programs	3	4/8

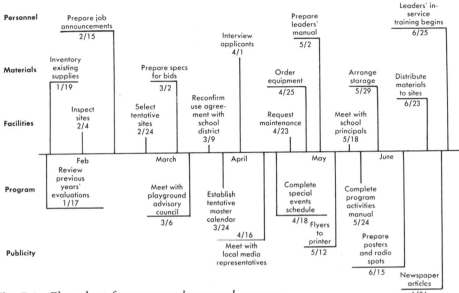

Fig. 7-1 *Flow chart for summer playground program.*

From Murphy, J.F., & Howard, D.R. *Delivery of community leisure services: An holistic approach.* Philadelphia: Lea & Febiger, 1977, p. 200.

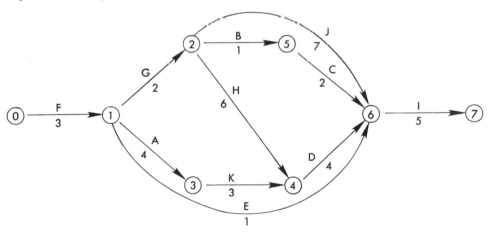

Fig. 7-2 *Critical path for dramatic presentation.*

Adapted from Mittelstaedt, A.H., & Berger, H.A. The Critical Path Method: A management tool for recreation. *Parks & Recreation*, 1972, 7:7, p. 15.

tion of the checklist shown in Table 15 to a time line is presented in Fig. 7-1 for the Flow Chart Method, and the application of the checklist shown in Table 16 to a time line is illustrated in Fig. 7-2 for the Critical Path Method.

Let us review this more specifically. Certain requirements are basic and universal to the effective organization of program activities. Recreation program planners have to bring together money, staff, equipment, facility, schedule, motivation, and publicity resources. Therefore FCM and CPM begin by dividing the entire program into these essential components. The planner is then able to identify the major requirements or tasks necessary for the completion of the program. In the examples in Tables 15 and 16, five major areas are identified: staff, equipment, facility, program content, and publicity. Each of these components is analyzed independently, and a list of relevant tasks is derived. For example, a list of the tasks involved in meeting the staff component would include hiring staff, conducting interviews, writing a leader's manual, and training. To accompany the list, the planner then sets a priority for the completion of each task and an estimated time for completion. Some planners may choose to stop at this point and use the checklist itself as a strategy for implementation.

The next step is to project a time line for FCM or a time path for CPM. This is a graphic ordering of all the tasks that lead to the program experience. The planner must place tasks on the diagram according to priority or urgency for completion and estimated length of time necessary for completion. Some tasks need to be completed before others can be started, so these take precedence in the diagram. Experience, circumstances, and personal preference help the planner determine this ordering.

In the example in Fig. 7-1 approximately 6 months have been allocated to prepare for the playground session. Therefore the flow of tasks begins in January and concludes with the in-service training for leaders in June. Between the initial and final tasks a variety of tasks are arranged in logical order.

In the example in Fig. 7-2 the tail of the arrow on the left, point O, is the start of the implementation procedure. The head of this arrow represents the completion of the first task (Task F). From point 1, other arrows are drawn representing Tasks A, G, and so on, all of which may start only after Task F is completed. From the arrowhead of Task B come three arrows representing subsequent tasks that may not begin until Task B is completed, and so forth. The pathing is continued until the network is completed. Units of time (numbers below task letters) are then applied. Through this method the graph is arranged with the times in which each detail task must be completed if the entire program is to be carried through successfully and on time. The CPM illustrated in Fig. 7-2 derives its name from the "critical path," which is the longest path in the diagram to reach the conclusion of implementation. If any task along this path is lengthened or held up, then the total implementation will require more time.

The only difference between the two systems is that CPM allows for a graphic indication of simultaneous tasks. (As a practicing program planner, I find it more useful to work with the FCM.) Regardless of the appropriate ordering of the tasks, the crucial factor in both strategies is to account for, in some logical manner, all necessary work requirements.

Once a natural flow of tasks is established, the diagram outlines the sequence that should be followed and acts as a road map that helps keep the planner from costly and embarrassing mistakes. The placement of all tasks on a time line or in a path configuration can be difficult and time consuming, depending upon the complexity of the program. However, it is time and effort well spent; particularly for a complicated program such an implementation strategy can be crucial. Although time consuming and subject to imperfection, the CPM and the FCM offer a logical, efficient way to approach program implementation. Some experienced program planners may be able to rely on past experience or memory; but when most planners attempt to organize in their minds the numerous tasks involved in putting into action a major program, the result is usually a more costly use of time and resources.

These implementation strategies also facilitate the delegation of responsibility to other staff members or subordinates. When all tasks for program implementation have been accounted for, the planner can share the CPM or FCM diagram with other members of the program or administrative staff, and together they can specify who will be responsible for each task. The FCM and CPM can also be valuable reference tools for programs provided annually on a seasonal basis. Rather than starting from scratch each season, the program staff can refer to the diagram from the preceding year for a comprehensive picture of the tasks to be completed for the upcoming season.

Additional benefits of CPM and FCM are the following ones noted by Moder and Philips (1970, p. 18):

1. Encourage a logical discipline in the planning, scheduling and control of projects
2. Encourage more long-range and detailed planning of projects
3. Provide a standard method of documenting and communicating project plans, schedules, and time and cost performance
4. Identify the most critical elements in the plan, focusing management attention on the 10 or 20 percent of the project that is most constraining on the schedule
5. Illustrate the effects of technical and procedural changes on the over-all schedule

Occasionally programmers have found it usful to combine the CPM or FCM system with the Gantt Chart. The Gantt Chart (see Fig. 7-3) takes the CPM and FCM logic and converts it into another type of visual management tool. The format of this strategy is basically a bar graph of time. In the Gantt Chart the time periods allocated to perform each implementation task are more visible and allow for a greater sensitivity to difficult tasks. In complex situations the combination of CPM or FCM and the Gantt Chart enables complete implementation tracking for both intra-agency and extra-agency task delegation or assignment.

All three strategies for implementation are designed to stimulate increased program service efficiency, providing an opportunity to increase performance output with decreased dollar investment. For all their advantages, the Critical Path Method, the Flow Chart Method, and the Gantt Chart do not guarantee program success.

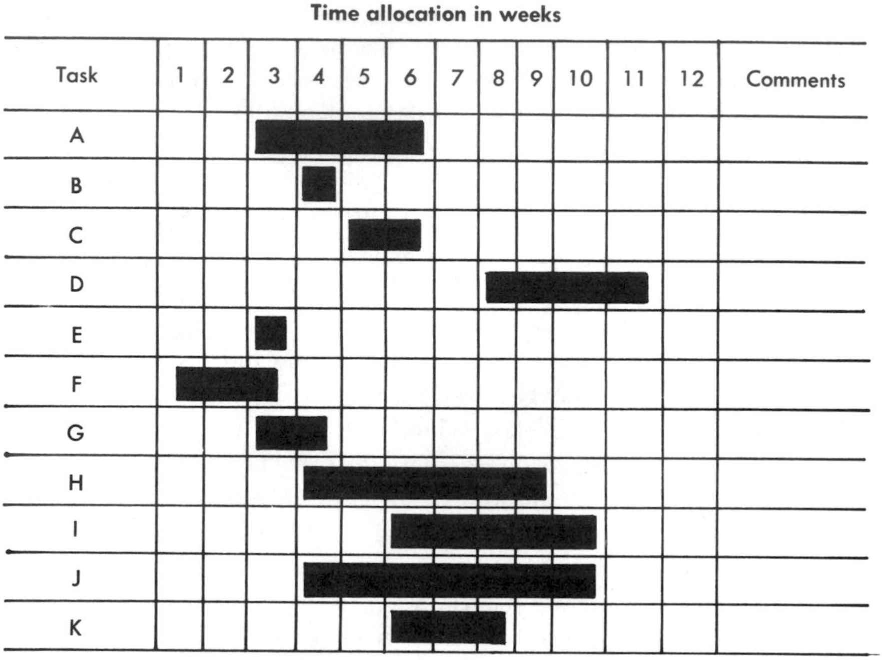

Time allocation in weeks

Task	1	2	3	4	5	6	7	8	9	10	11	12	Comments
A			███	███	███	███							
B				█									
C					███	███							
D								███	███	███			
E			█										
F	███	███	███										
G			███										
H				███	███	███	███						
I					███	███	███	███	███				
J				███	███	███	███	███	███				
K					███	███	███						

Fig. 7-3   *Gantt chart for dramatic presentation.*

Adapted from Mittelstaedt, A.H., & Berger, H.A. The Critical Path Method: A management tool for recreation. *Parks & Recreation*, 1972, 7:7, p. 16.

However they can serve the planner as highly effective coordinating devices for making the details of recreation program implementation come together.

Implementation details

This is the point in the recreation program planning process when the various details must be gathered and coordinated so that the goals of the program have the best chance of being met. There are certain tasks that must be performed for any program to take place. Such detail tasks include marketing, motivation, public relations, scheduling, keeping program records, and determining when to end. Because the previous planning step gave initial attention to budgeting, selection of appropriate leadership, and facility and equipment designation, the planner needs only to finalize these decisions in this planning step. The remainder of this chapter therefore focuses on these other implementation details.

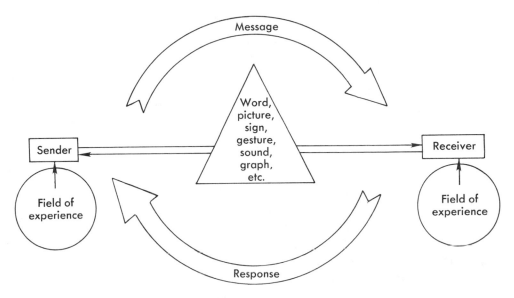

Fig. 7-4 *The communication process.*

Marketing: user recruitment

Futurists and forecasters of recreation behavior generally agree that the next few years will hold some changes in the leisure habits of Americans (Beck, 1980). Energy shortages and inflation are expected to come together, forcing a reduction in expensive vacations and a renewed focus on local facilities and programs. This development will be accompanied by a general increase in free time for the average person. The sum impact of these changes will mean an expanded constituency market for the average recreation and park agency. In order to reap benefits from this potentially expanded constituency, however, program planners will need to develop and perfect recruitment techniques that translate potential users into actual ones. Today's potential recreation program constituent is sophisticated. No longer is it enough to have a good product or program. Therefore recreation program planners must deliberately set up mechanisms for attracting participants. Program marketing, which is the key element in converting potential program users into actual ones, entails communication, persuasion, and timing.

Communication is an exchange of messages between two or more entities. The communication process is a vital link that enables both an individual to express needs to an agency and an agency to identify its program services. The communicative exchange can be packaged in either visual or verbal terms. Typically the communication process is identified as having four elements: the sender, the message, the channel of information distribution, and the receiver (see Fig. 7-4). In recreation program marketing the sender is the recreation agency, made up of its staff and current participants. The general message is the improvement of the quality of life through recreation. The specific message depends on the program being offered and its potential values. Channels of information distribution include such means as advertising, promotion, and printed program schedules. Finally, the communication process requires that the sender direct the message through appropriate channels to receivers. The receivers are the target population for the program services. Through this process of communication, information is focused toward the prospective participant in an attempt to stimulate involvement in the program services.

Marketing not only seeks to inform potential participants; it also attempts to persuade them to use the program services. Therefore marketing must include attention to who the communication receiver should be. For example, persons who are overweight will be especially receptive to a jazzercise program. However, members of a bird watcher's club probably will not be interested in a hunter's safety course. A key factor in persuading potential participants is to show them how the program will benefit their lives. Thus an understanding of the area of need derived in step 1 of program planning is useful again at this stage.

Timing is also an important consideration in marketing. Getting a persuasive message to the potential participant either too late (and thus conflicting with prior commitments) or too early (and thus being forgotten) should be avoided. Determining the ideal timing takes experimentation with local media deadlines, the scope of the program, and the life-style of the constituency.

Given the program marketer's goal of timely, persuasive communication, there are five methods of information distribution available: promotion, advertising, publicity, selling, and the published program schedule. Even though these methods should be used simultaneously, each one serves distinctly different ends. Some detail will now be devoted to each method to emphasize that a successfully marketed program requires a carefully planned strategy that incorporates most, if not all, of these methods.

Promotion The concept of promotion is borrowed from the retail business field. Sales promotion activities go beyond the simple communication of a product's worth and attempt to attract the customer through other means. In order to generate interest in a recreation program, planners often organize special promotional activities such as tasters; contests; exhibits, displays, and demonstrations; novelty items; coupons; and research sampling.

Research sampling, a method of gathering planning data, can also be viewed as an attempt to prepromote a program. While the planner is asking people their opinions about certain programming, naturally their interest is going to be stirred. Following up the research questioning with information about the prospective program, or about the agency as a whole, serves to encourage the interviewee to participate later.

Taster activities are a useful and familiar method of promotion. Commercial health clubs are famous for offering nonmembers a free day or week at the facility to provide a "taste" of the program service in the hope of attracting new members. The class format of programming is particularly well suited to taster activities; an opportunity to sample an experience is offered with the idea of influencing participation in the entire series of lessons.

The use of coupons is a common promotional technique in retailing, but it has yet to be used widely in recreation program promotion. However, the coupon technique has been used successfully in attracting the elderly participant. This application serves two benefits. Not only does the agency attract a group of users normally unavailable to it; it also enhances its community reputation.

Sometimes it is useful to conduct a competitive activity, such as a contest, to stimulate participation in an ongoing related activity. For example, a community-wide flower-growing contest may motivate people to join the garden club. Creating enthusiasm and interest in a regular program can be easy when appealing to the competitive nature of potential participants.

Recreation agencies can use the exhibit, display, or demonstration technique not only to promote their program offerings but to interpret their purposes as well. A display and an exhibit are similar. However, a display is usually only two dimensional, but an exhibit may be more complex and include three-dimensional items. A demonstration involves the use of program participants or agency members to perform or to demonstrate various aspects of the program. This technique allows the potential participant to witness the skills, attitudes, and other benefits that the program offers. Some common examples of the demonstration technique include a gymnastics demonstration at halftime at a basketball game, a pottery wheel demonstration at a shopping mall, and a dramatic troupe performance in a busy park.

Program promotion can also be accomplished through the use of novelty items such as buttons, bumper stickers, and window decals. For instance, the use of T-shirts with slogans or logos is often an effective way of promoting programs. If the novelty items are sold to current participants or if they are donated by commercial companies, they are an inexpensive technique. Key chains, calendars, hats, postcards, pens and pencils, buttons and pins, and toys are effective program promoters that also encourage program unity and loyalty.

The promotion techniques discussed above aim far beyond informing the public of available program services. Promotions are not designed to announce program schedules to current users; instead they are intended to draw out new sources of participants, people who are not in the habit of using these services. The various techniques of promotion can be put into action in either a grand or small fashion, depending upon the scope of the program and the number of participants desired. The planner's only limitation is his or her imagination.

Advertising   Advertising is communication that is paid for. In recreation program marketing, advertising usually is directed at potential program users through the mass media, such as newspapers, radio, television, and signs. Advertising can be an effective marketing method because it enables the agency to reach large numbers of people rapidly. Yet it has been used only sparingly by recreation agencies because it is often expensive and requires some expertise.

According to Edginton, Compton, and Hanson (1980), there are two forms of advertising that are useful for recreation program marketing: direct and indirect. Direct advertising informs the audience of specific events or services, such as the registration deadline for the YMCA youth summer camp. Indirect advertising, on the other hand, tries to create a general, long-term interest in the program services or the agency. For instance, an indirect appeal might merely discuss the agency and its service breadth.

The most widely used agency vehicle for both direct and indirect advertising is the newspaper. It is vital, therefore, that the program planner befriend the newspapers that serve his or her constituency. In purchasing advertising and especially in seeking coverage of news items within the agency, it is important for the planner to be aware of the deadlines and procedures necessary. This involves knowing who to contact at the newspaper and the requirements for submission of materials. The initial decision for newspaper advertising is choosing the format that is most appropriate for the planner's message. Most communities support national, daily, weekly, special interest, and shopper's guide formats. Professional experience and knowledge of the constituency's characteristics will help the planner choose the best option.

Newspapers calculate advertising costs in varying ways. One way is to charge a basic rate per size of the ad, measured in column inches. Often a newspaper offers a "contract rate," or a basic rate that decreases as the size of the ad increases or as the number of runs per year increases. The composition of a well-done, attention-getting newspaper advertisement requires specialized skill. Because advertising layout is a profession, the help of a graphic artist or advertising consultant is often well worth the advertising dollar invested. Many newspapers have "in house" people available for ad layout work at no charge to the advertising customer. Fig. 7-5 offers a sample of an ad that was run twice in a daily newspaper and cost the agency a total of $212.

Radio advertising is somewhat more expensive than newspaper advertising, but it has the benefit of reaching a broader geographic audience. In addition, radio audiences can be defined in terms of age, economic, and educational levels so that the advertising dollar can be targeted to the most likely potential participants. There are two forms of radio (and television) advertising that can be purchased. One is the sponsorship of an entire program, and the other is independent or "spot" ads.

Television yields the best return for the money, but a substantial monetary investment is required for worthwhile results. Because television reaches a large percentage of people, both locally and nationwide, the program service the agency offers must be similarly broad in appeal for this advertising technique to be justified.

Fig. 7-5 *Program advertising sample.*

Finally, television advertising should be professionally prepared. A television ad that is unattractive and lifeless can produce a strong negative impact.

Signs, posters, bulletin boards, and roadside billboards differ from other advertising forms in that they are not directed at a specific audience. Whoever happens by becomes the recipient of the message. For this reason extra care should be taken to ensure that such advertising is strategically placed and dynamically presented. Most of these advertising options are relatively inexpensive to implement. Although billboards can be expensive for commercial agencies, occasionally advertising firms will donate space for use by voluntary or public agencies. When signs are well designed, suitably placed, and well maintained, they can do a great deal of program advertising at a comparatively small cost. Therefore, the planner should never take this advertising option for granted.

Publicity   Publicity is news. For the planner it is communication of the agency's successes and highlights that present a favorable image to the community. For instance, a newspaper feature article on the new dance instructor, an announcement on radio's "community bulletin board" about a citizen's advisory committee meeting, a complimentary letter to the editor, and an interview on a television talk show with the agency's fitness expert all present the agency and its programs in a favorable light—at no charge.

If an agency creates news, publicity is what communicates it to the potential constituency. The goal, of course, is to maintain a productive and favorable publicity posture. Although there are publicity tools available for this, more important is the creation and maintenance of positive, human interest news. Nothing markets a program better than favorable publicity. Because unfavorable publicity can be just as effective, if not more so, a good public relations program should be instituted to avoid this problem.

Releasing news about an agency's future programming is commonly done with a formal news release. News releases are usually issued to newspapers, but they may also be designed for television and radio. A news release is a brief statement of the news facts written by the agency in as concise, factual, and direct a manner as possible. There are specific rules for the composition of a news release: it should always identify what the news is; who it pertains to; and when, where, and how it will take place. Many agencies have found it effective to write the news release on a special form so that after submission it can be readily identified as a news release.

In contrast to a news release, a news article or feature is initiated and written by the newspaper or radio station staff. Usually it pertains to a human interest theme or an issue of broad constituency interest. Because a news article often appears during or after the event or program, its prime value is not in attracting participation for a specific program but in casting a favorable light for future programs. News articles can be encouraged by keeping the media informed of agency news and assisting in fact gathering and photo taking.

Although often overlooked as a publicity technique, favorable "letters to the editor" or editorials in newspaper, radio, or television can be very helpful. (I have known some program planners to write such letters or editorials themselves in order to tap the potential for certain programming.) The planner also needs to respond to unfavorable letters or editorials with as much factual information and cooperation as possible.

Public service announcements are opportunities for communicating agency programming on radio or television at no charge. An agency can usually take advantage of such a publicity format if the nature of the announcement is charitable, educational, informational, or entails the selling of nonprofit agency services. Such announcements typically are short, ranging from 10 to 30 seconds.

Radio and television talk shows, as well as regular columns in newspapers, provide an increasingly beneficial and popular format for agency publicity. This informal approach offers a chance for lengthy exposure to the agency's program services.

Gaining exposure through the news media is a highly regarded method of marketing. However, "making the news" does not suggest staging the news. News is made by offering exciting and innovative programs, by keeping media representatives aware of them, and by encouraging and helping with the coverage of these programs.

Selling   There are times and circumstances when an agency will want to take a more aggressive approach to program marketing by adopting some of the strategies of personal selling. Usually, personal selling involves making a face-to-face appeal to an individual or group. This personal direct contact is perhaps the most effective and persuasive method available for marketing a recreation program.

Instead of talking about knocking on doors and soliciting by phone, let us discuss some of the more widely used techniques of selling employed in the recreation field. First, go where potential users can be found in high concentrations—service clubs, social groups, and businesses that attract the people likely to be interested in the kind of program being marketed. Informal sales pitches, formal public speaking engagements, and slide and film presentations can be effective with such audiences. For example, if the agency needs participants for a 15-kilometer road race, contact the local roadrunners club and make a presentation at one of its meetings; or contact the community garden club when the agency is involved in the planning of a high-yield backyard gardening class.

When speaking to an individual or a group, the planner must keep in mind the purpose and interests of the listeners and tailor the presentation to reflect the program's value to them. Value to the potential user is crucial to any presentation or selling contact, for without this emphasis little interest can be generated. While speaking to an outings club, for example, emphasize the practical value its members can gain from participating in the agency's "Wilderness Gear You Can Make Yourself" seminar. It is also vital that the speaker be in tune with the audience, not only in terms of topic relevancy but also in method of presentation. A joke style or a manuscript reading style is not appropriate in every setting.

When "selling" to a group or club, it may be advantageous to use a slide or film presentation in conjunction with the verbal appeal. By enabling the target audience to visualize program offerings and benefits, this approach makes marketing a bit easier. Some agencies have found it useful to produce their own slides or films, but others prefer to use the audiovisual services of libraries, catalog ordering, and those services available through the National Recreation and Park Association.

The published program schedule   Although the schedule brochure could be grouped with the other publicity techniques, it is treated separately here. Without a doubt, the schedule is one of the most widely used and effective methods of channeling the program message to the constituency. For many years the published schedule has been the main method used in recreation program marketing. In some agencies it is still used exclusively (although this is not recommended as a substitute for a complete marketing plan).

The schedule brochure comes in all shapes and sizes, with varying degrees of professional, artistic, and printing standards applied. It is basically a printed piece that highlights program and facility schedules and is issued on a monthly, quarterly, or seasonal basis. The final cost and the method selected for distribution both relate to the particular circumstances of the agency.

Recreation and park agencies have used three basic types of announcement brochures. Brochures typically are used to:

1. Identify and define programs
2. Provide information on area and facility layout
3. Promote other recreation resources or opportunities

Often two or more of the above purposes are combined in the same brochure. For example, a brochure might include the schedule of recreation events for the summer, a discussion of the location and use of the facilities in which these events will take place, as well as the names and telephone numbers of related resources such as senior citizen centers, referral centers, and special populations services. Therefore brochure content varies according to its purpose. Brochures that highlight scheduled programs will usually include a time-and-date schedule of events, a description of events, their cost, their location, and may include the program leader's name.

The layout and design of the program brochure can be very important to the overall appeal of the program services themselves. The use of photographs, color, graphic designs, print size and style, and catchy wording have all been employed for persuasive purposes. Some programmers publish their brochures through typesetters and printers; others do their own lettering and typing and then run the brochures off on the office mimeograph machine. The adoption of either approach depends upon the scope of the programming, the intended audience, and the available budget. When working with graphic artists, typesetters, and printers, be sure to give all specifications, including such details as paper color and typeface. Always request to see a proof before authorizing the actual printing. Always agree on the price before authorizing the work.

Determining how the potential user will gain access to the finished brochure depends upon available money and the planner's own abilities. Should brochures be mailed out to community residents, delivered to other agencies or service organizations, handed out at schools, advertised in the paper, or simply placed at the information counter at the recreation facility? Because brochure distribution is so important, as many methods as possible should be developed. Timing is critical. Planning the release time to ensure maximum visibility and impact takes great care.

Considerations of brochure content, layout and design, cost, and distribution are highly situational. Regardless of the planner's own resources and intent, as the representative of the agency's services, the planner should make certain that the program brochure is as informational and as professionally presented as possible. The brochure's effectiveness is bounded only by the skill and creativity of those who devise it.

For instance, when the residents of Aurora, Colorado, sit down each year to read the new program brochure of the municipal park and recreation department, they know they are in for a treat. In the first place it is going to take them a while. Over 525 programs, classes, and special events are offered yearly, representing one of the most ambitious and diverse programming efforts in the country. In addition, between 60 and 80 new programs are added each season. Because this agency offers its constituency so many activities, Aurora program planners have felt it necessary to come up with a unique title and description for each program to persuade people into participating. Following is a sampling from the Aurora brochure.*

Yule Giving Surprise your friends and relatives with ideas for gift breads, candy houses, specialty sauces, and cheeses. Other unusual kitchen crafted items will be included as well as suggestions for decoration and packaging. Ages 15 to adult.

Up, Up, and Away Learn to construct a simple kite and fly it that afternoon.

Show Biz Kids For that "ham" in every family, come learn the art of dramatics. Class will include stage productions, acting, costumes, makeup, and actual performance of a one-act play.

Pool Sharks Interested in sharpening up your pool game? Now's your chance to learn the proper shooting techniques.

Pennypinchers Potpourri Help balance your budget with economical family and friend pleasing meals. Tips on how to cut costs in food buying will be included. Class will prepare several thrifty but interesting meals.

Greasy Chick and the Dip Stick An activity for ladies only. Includes general auto-anatomy information, minor maintenance tips, recognition of various warning symptoms, etc.

Mountain Treasures There's still gold in them thar hills. Class discussion will cover gold panning and metal detection techniques, how to build a sluice box, and the legal aspects of staking out a claim.

Public relations

A good relationship between a recreation agency and the community is best achieved by creatively developed program services that match the true needs of the constituency. An important implementation detail that helps develop such a relation-

---

*From Johnson, L. Brainstorming and name forming. Reprinted from the *12:6* (1977, p. 36) issue of *Parks & Recreation* by special permission of the National Recreation and Park Association.

ship is public relations. (It is important to remember that the development of positive public attitudes toward the agency should be an ongoing consideration, not simply a matter for attention at the implementation stage in planning.) Public relations deals with concerns such as the caliber of services, adequacy of information distribution, the manner the public is dealt with on the phone, and the attitude of leaders to participants. To some professionals these concerns may seem automatic. However, public relations should never be left to chance.

A recreation and park agency exists to serve; thus its achievements and its aspirations are of interest to the people it serves. Although the best and most natural public relations effort consists of doing a good job, it is conceivable that the agency may be doing a good job, and the public may not be aware of it. As a result, a public relations program becomes necessary to do more than develop good rapport; it needs to inform the public about the agency—its achievements, programs, plans for the future, and how these relate to the constituency.

Therefore public relations efforts take two main directions: engendering goodwill toward the agency and establishing an understanding of its operations. Both are accomplished through management practices and policies that foster the well-being and interests of the constituency. The "good name" of an agency is its best asset, but it must be cultivated and worked for. There is really no better way to attract participation and support for programs and services than having a good reputation.

Let us now review some commonly used public relations tools. Awards and citations are used primarily as public relations tools. They are ways of recognizing individuals or groups for their contributions to the recreation efforts of an agency. Such recognition is useful not only in a public relations sense; because the presentation of awards or citations is frequently newsworthy, it helps to market the agency's services. An article and photograph in the newspaper about the award recipient also serves as publicity for the agency.

Awards and citations become meaningless if they are handed out indiscriminately or too freely. Yet they certainly should be a part of public relations when there is genuine cause for such presentations. There are several types of contributions individuals and groups make to recreation agencies that deserve recognition. Foremost is the contribution of time and effort toward the operations of an agency. This could include a program activity volunteer, a member of a citizen's advisory council, a local service club that annually sponsors a program, or a member of the agency staff whose efforts are particularly meritorious. The recognition of monetary or material contributions, such as cash, land, buildings, trees, and playground equipment, is also an important public relations opportunity. Wall plaques, site markers, framed certificates, trophies, watches, and silver objects are traditional types of awards, but exactly what to give the recipient is a matter of appropriateness.

The agency's annual report can also be viewed as a public relations tool. As a year-end summary of financial, facility, and program developments and accomplish-

ments, the report is designed to inform the public about the good works of the agency. The annual report is a means of showing the constituency the agency's current (hopefully positive) state of affairs. For this reason the report should be professionally prepared and should emphasize the year's strengths.

Annual reports should be directed toward building both community and board-of-director confidence. The better the information presented, the stronger the confidence. The report should be carefully laid out, graphically designed, and include high-quality photographs, charts, and graphs. Fig. 7-6 shows one page extracted from the 1980 annual report of the Monongalia County Consolidated Recreation Commission in West Virginia.

Although the preparation of the annual report is normally the responsibility of the agency director or administrator, program planners should be familiar with its purpose and construction to ensure that the agency's program services are adequately represented. Kraus and Curtis (1982) have suggested that recreation agencies include the following components in their annual reports:

1. Departmental address and board and staff roster, with or without photographs of key individuals
2. Opening messages, which may be from the mayor, the chairman of the recreation and park board, or administrator of the department
3. Table of contents and acknowledgments of appreciation to those individuals or organizations that served the department during the year
4. Organization chart
5. Financial report, consisting of a simple statement of the authorized budget and sums actually spent. This may include summaries of past and future or predicted budgets
6. A report of physical resource development—the major facilities operated by the department, as well as acquisition, maintenance, or refurbishment projects carried out during the course of the year
7. Report of attendance and participation in programs, usually done by major department divisions or types of activities

Information kits should also be made available as a public relations tool. Material that offers background information about the agency, its program and facility services, and its staff should be prepared in a convenient "kit" format to provide the constituency with easy access to these details. Such an information package is useful not only for communicating with the public but also in meeting and working with other recreation or service agencies, the press, and other professional contacts.

A carefully organized and well-presented information kit can make a positive, lasting impression and provide an interested individual with good insight into the agency. Edginton, Compton, and Hanson (1980, pp. 323-324) suggest the following inclusions in such a kit:

1. A history of the organization: such information could provide insight as to why a given agency provides certain services and not others

Morgantown Municipal Ice Rink

The year-round facility was used for ice skating in winter and roller skating, basketball, soccer and football practice in milder seasons.

The year 1980 was the first complete year of operation for the $1.3 million skating facility. During the winter months, 50,096 daily admissions were recorded during public sessions, an average of 300 per day. Additionally, hockey clinics and leagues were also held, as was figure skating instruction. Summary for 1980:

Season Pass Sales		Public Skating Sessions Total Daily Admissions	
Children	40	Children	12,388
Teens	54	Teens	11,781
Adults	26	Adults	17,101
Family	36	Pass Admission	8,826
Total	**156**	**Total**	**50,096**

Santa and his Elves take a break from a busy schedule to host a skating party prior to Christmas Day.

The Rink provides a comfortable warming area with a four-sided fireplace, and lockers for storage of street shoes.

Rental stakes are available for roller skating and ice skating. Rental inventory totals 350 ice skates and 200 roller skates.

Roller skating sessions were held on 75 days in 1980. A total of 5,819 daily admissions were recorded.

Skaters enjoyed over 46 hours of public sessions per week during ice skating season. The ice skating season lasted 166 days in 1980.

Fig. 7-6 *Annual report sample page.*

From Anderson, V. *1980 Annual report.* Morgantown, W.Va.: Monongalia County Consolidated Recreation Commission, 1981.

2. An organizational chart: this could assist in making contact with the specific staff person that relates to the constituent's own interests
3. Biographical sketches of staff members: this information allows the agency to seem more human and inspires confidence and respect
4. Agency services: this could entail the seasonal program brochure, facility maps, or specific program flyers
5. The annual report
6. Reprints of newspaper articles or other media materials: articles that are especially valuable emphasize the end result of services
7. Photographs of activities or services: these should be carefully selected to provide a well-rounded view of the agency

A newsletter is another useful means for public relations. It is used primarily for communicating with an agency's own membership or already identified constituency. Like other tools of public relations, the newsletter's major objective is both to inform and to create a positive image. Newsletters either may originate from the membership, thus representing the broad viewpoint of the agency's constituency, or may originate from the administrator, thus communicating the viewpoint of the agency's chief executive. Agency newsletters come in a variety of sizes and formats and have varying degrees of printing sophistication. These considerations are not as important as directing the newsletter to the audience it is designed to reach (for example, through technical or personal approaches) and developing and maintaining a mechanism for news gathering. Depending on the size of the agency, news gathering can involve an entire staff or only a single contact person.

Motivation

Motivation, the inner drive that excites participation and causes behavior, is an area of program implementation that is hard to grasp. This text has already discussed participant needs and interests, leadership and facility provision, and program marketing; but all these merely lead people to the brink of involvement. What stimulates the participant's complex motivational machinery is often considered the mystique of programming. It is conceivable that a planner can carry out each step in the program planning process with care and accuracy, but then face a participation motivation problem during implementation.

In psychological terms, *motivation* can be defined as an inner drive that causes behavior that is directed toward a goal. People are involved in a recreation program or a pursuit because their needs for fulfillment are pushing them to a point of interest and readiness. Thus the basic motivation cycle can be thought of as:

Need → Drive → Goal

Need may be defined as deficiency; *drive* may be thought of as deficiency with direction. Attainment of goals reduces or alleviates needs and drives, thus completing the motivation cycle. The cycle can be complex or simple, depending upon the needs, drives, and goals involved. The temper of the motivation cycle offers the program planner and leader a most challenging function. The recreation program professional can use this cycle concept to determine the deficiencies that individuals are experiencing and to help them discover the ability to reduce or eliminate these deficiencies. If the planner can capture interest and readiness for recreation activity, he or she can manipulate certain motivational devices to initiate vigorous, joyful, and dedicated program participation.

Some of the motivational devices useful for recreation programs are environment, status, planned progression, success recognition, and social facilitation. Let us consider each device and how it can be manipulated to achieve more successful program implementation.

Sometimes humorous consequences occur through the inappropriate use of the environment motivational device. One such example in planned recreation concerns the lighting of social dances. As Tillman (1973) relates, because of moral prudery, or just plain fear, programmers have been known to light the gymnasium or recreation room like a holiday living room, expecting joyous social interaction to happen; instead they have ended up with wax museums. The visual and atmospheric properties of the program environment can be manipulated to produce almost automatic responses. By using balloons, costumes, sports equipment, music, sunshine, crepe paper, or clean water, the program implementer can set the stage for recreation. In such a prepared recreation environment participants are likely to have a good time.

Participants in recreation programs, as in all areas of life, tend to be motivated by status. Status involves the need to belong and to be recognized; it culminates in the striving for a unique identity. In recreation programs status is related to both the type of activity engaged in (yachting vs. rowboating) and the distinctive equipment that accompanies some activities. The most common "equipment" example is the uniform; it allows the wearer to visibly associate himself or herself with an activity that he or she thinks impresses people. Other examples are ski and surfboard racks on the car roof, a Casio runner's watch on the arm, and toe clamps on bicycle peddles—all of which help to create status. Because each recreation activity has a status position in American society, programmers should not overlook the motivating force of membership cards, uniforms, and equipment as status indicators.

If a recreation participant's effort is directed toward some far-off goal, disinterest will occur rapidly. It is human nature to lose interest in doing anything if one. does not experience a sense of improvement or progress in the activity. Therefore the program implementer must use systems that offer growth opportunities. Planned progression systems provide one of the best motivational devices for structured growth. The classic example is the merit badge system used by youth organizations such as the Girl Scouts and the Boy Scouts. The YMCA's swim program classifications, in which polliwogs strive to become sharks through a progressions of tests, is another successful example. In sports programming, planners have found it useful to form first-, second-, and third-string team rankings. The competition program format often includes all-neighborhood, all-city, all-county, all-state, and all-American progression devices.

Planned progression can be tricky to operate if care is not taken. It requires an astute recreation professional to devise and conduct a system that motivates participation without producing a stressful, tense environment. Instead of determining a winner and then moving on, a well-thought-out progression system makes the participant feel comfortable in continuing to strive for the award. Errors are made, but the participant never really loses. Planned progression lets the recreation participant know exactly what growth is required, but it leaves the timing and level of growth up to the individual.

Distinct from the motivation for growth and achievement is the motivation for success. The participant is also driven to recreation program involvement by a need to be recognized for coming out on top. Winners in competitive recreation expect a tangible award that demonstrates to themselves and others that they were "the best." The blue ribbon, the medal, the trophy, the certificate are all motivators of the psychological need for success. The major danger of material awards, however, is the substitution of award interest for activity interest. Despite the argument that awards often make the recreation experience inappropriately competitive, awards do work to hold interest and lend an element of excitement. Still there is need for professionally researched analyses and systematic studies to keep programmers in control of what happens as a result of awards for success.

Closely related to the other motivational forces just discussed is the need to interact with others. Most individuals are influenced to some degree by others, and ultimately they seek peer approval. The recreation program implementer must be able to recognize, encourage, and use group and peer dynamics as motivational means. Often the enthusiastic, positive force found in socially relaxed recreation situations makes it difficult for participants to stand idly by or to resist involvement. Congenial, happy, socially attentive groups give life to an activity. Several devices help the program implementer create all this. Some planners work through a bridging concept; extroverts from the group are encouraged to initiate participation and a chain reaction begins. Others have found that there is nothing like the "limited seating" device or the waiting list to enhance an activity's desirability. Because most recreation program involvement is facilitated by group pressures, understanding the basics of the group process is an important recreation leadership skill.

Should program implementers manipulate motivation through the devices discussed above, or should the participant be left to seek out whatever is of interest? Remember, the energizing force that is motivation is operative only because there are within each person basic needs, drives, and goals. There can be no motivation, no matter how skillful the leader, without these intrinsic forces. Although the participant in the recreation program experience may be intrinsically motivated toward

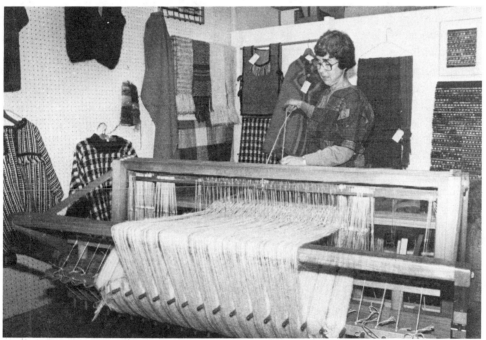

participation, at some point he or she will also seek external sanction and encourage-ment. Therefore knowledge of the motivation process is important in developing, initiating, and maintaining program interest during the implementation state of planning.

Scheduling

Another implementation detail that must be handled aptly by the planner is the scheduling of the chosen program. Scheduling entails designating the length, dura-tion, day(s) of the week, and time of day that the program will be offered. The appropriate scheduling of a program is a strong determinant of its success. It is obvious that scheduling a tiny tots program in the evening or a fitness program for industry employees in midafternoon is probably inappropriate and will lead to weak participation.

Scheduling can be innovative and still be workable, however. Many length, duration, and time combinations can be adopted to the advantage of the program itself. Two critical rules must be adhered to, no matter how creative the schedule, in order to ensure appropriateness:

1. The scheduling of a program must be aligned with the availability and life-style of the participant.
2. The scheduling should complement the format of the recreation experience. Realistically, these important rules must often be accommodated in terms of prior facility commitments and busy activity specialists and program leaders.

Recreation programs can be scheduled according to three different patterns. The first pattern involves calendar seasons; that is, it may be most appropriate to schedule fall, winter, spring, and summer programs. Fig. 7-7 illustrates a winter program for a facility of the San Diego Park and Recreation Department in California. The seasonal concept is most useful for programs of the class format; classes and other programs that convene regularly can be easily designated a single season duration. All programs with the same seasonal distinction then can be grouped and coordinated as a single package for marketing purposes; promotion, publicity, and advertising efforts can be unified to economic advantage.

The second scheduling pattern involves a shorter duration focus, such as a month or week. This pattern is usually most appropriate for facility-centered pro-grams where the constituency traffic flow is constant and regular. Fig. 7-8 illustrates a monthly schedule for a commercial agency facility, a bookstore. This type of sched-uling pattern would also be useful for an ice rink or a swimming pool, where program activities occur the same day each week indefinitely. Communicating the program schedule by the week or the month would help to keep regular users informed and reminded.

The third pattern is the daily time-frame schedule. This is a highly regimented scheduling pattern that serves to organize the life-style of program participants. It is

Text continued on p. 276.

Fig. 7-7, A *Seasonal program scheduling.*

From *Winter 1980 program brochure.* Standley Community Park, La Jolla, Calif., 1980.

Continued.

```
                    STANDLEY COMMUNITY PARK
                       3585 Governor Drive
                          452-8556


                       WINTER PROGRAM 1981
                   Jan. 19 - March 27, 1981
                   (Make-up Week March 30th)

                       REGISTRATION WEEK
                   Jan. 12 - Jan. 16, 1981
               Additions may be made as late as the second
               class meeting if minimum enrollment is met.


        *           *           *           *           *


   Parents! Please remind your children that for reasons of safety,
   bicycles and skateboards are not to be ridden on sidewalks at
   the Park.  Bikes must be locked in the bikeracks provided, and
   skateboards carried while on Park grounds.  Skateboards may be
   checked in at the Office.  Skates are not allowed in the building.
   Children under the age of five must be accompanied by an adult.
   Please be aware that we have been experiencing numerous break-ins
   to autos parked in the parking lots (Pool & Center).  We advise
   that you not leave valuables (purses, wallets, etc.) in your car!
   Thank-you!


        *           *           *           *           *


   CENTER STAFF:
   Steve Lyons...................................U.C. Area Manager
   Rose Vieira.....................................Center Director
   Earl Jaeggi................................Grounds Maintenance
   Denise Knobloch............................Grounds Maintenance
   Ralph Fink.................................Grounds Maintenance
   Tom Medigovich.............................Recreation Leader
   Terry Smith................................Recreation Leader
   Carol Cracolice............................Recreation Leader
   Kevin Haupt................................Recreation Leader
   Patti Jungers..............................Recreation Leader
   Linwood Mackey.............................Recreation Leader
   Laura Boas.................................Recreation Leader


        *           *           *           *           *


   HOURS OF OPERATION (Center)          SWANSON MEMORIAL POOL:
   Monday - Friday   9:00am-10:00pm            453-9770
   Saturday          9:00am- 5:00pm        Opens in April
   Sunday            1:00pm- 5:00pm
```

Fig. 7-7, cont'd B *Seasonal program scheduling.*

PROGRAM REGISTRATION INFORMATION

REGISTRATION for the WINTER 1981 program will be held Jan. 12-16, 1981. Most of the programs at Standley Park will operate on a ten-week basis, with an additional week at the end of the session for class make-ups (Classes cancelled by the instructor only). Make-up week will be March 30 - April 4. A few classes will be conducted on a five-week basis; please check the duration column in the activities schedule to be sure of the class length. See below for additional Special Registration Information.

ALL CLASS FEES ARE DUE AT THE TIME OF REGISTRATION. CHECKS OR MONEY ORDERS ARE PREFERRED. IF PAYING CASH, PLEASE HAVE THE EXACT AMOUNT! NO REFUNDS AFTER THE SECOND CLASS.

SPECIAL REGISTRATIONS: See Schedule of Activities for more details.

YOUTH GYMNASTICS   REGISTER
Returning Fall '80 Students   Jan. 12, 3:15 - 5:00pm
New Students and Jr. High Students   Jan. 14, 3:15 - 5:00pm

TENNIS INSTRUCTION

Session I - Register Sat. Jan. 3 for classes held Jan. 20 - Feb. 21
Session II - Register Sat. Feb. 21 for classes held March 9 - April 10

CREATIVE COOKING   MONTHLY!!!
PRESCHOOL - Thurs. 1:30 - 2:30 pm
          Class held Jan. 29   (Register Starting Jan. 19)
          Class held Feb. 19   (Register Starting Feb. 9)
          Class held March 19   (Register Starting March 9)
PEE WEE - Fri. 3:30 - 4:30pm & ELEMENTARY Fri. 4:45 - 6:00pm
          Class held Jan. 30   (Register Starting Jan. 19)
          Class held Feb. 20   (Register Starting Feb. 9)
          Class held March 20   (Register Starting March 9)

TAP DANCE, JAZZ DANCE, and RHYTHMIC AEROBICS
TAP DANCE
      Register Jan. 6, 1981
      Classes will start on Jan. 13, 1981
      2:45pm - Preschool 4 & 5 years (age must be verified)
      3:30pm - 1st grade to 18 years (levels Beginning to Advanced)
JAZZ DANCE - Tues. Jan. 6, 1981
      5:45 & 6:30pm - 7th grade to 18 years (Beginners Welcome!)
RHYTHMIC AEROBICS - Thurs. Jan. 22
      9:30am - Adults 18 years and older

Fig. 7-7, cont'd C *Seasonal program scheduling.*   *Continued.*

ADULT ACTIVITIES

TIME	DAY	CLASS	FEE	DURATION
9 – 11	M-Sat.	Adult Tennis Lessons-Day	15.00	5 wks.
9 – 4:30	W	Adult Educ. - Gourmet Cooking	*	16 wks.
9:30-10:30	Th	Rhythmic Aerobic Dance	6.00	10 wks.
9:30- 1:00	T	Adult Educ. - Landscape Painting	*	16 wks.
10:00-11:30	M,W,F	Womens Rhythmic Slimnastics	15.00	10 wks.
10:00- 3:00	F	Senior Citizens Club	---	Continuous
5:30-6:30	M,W,Th	CO-ED Aerobic Slimnastics	$10.00	10 wks.
To resume in April		Jazzerobics	10.00	8 wks.
6:00-10:00	M-Sat.	Adult Tennis Lessons-Eve.	15.00	5 wks.
7:00-9:45	Th	Free Play Volleyball	---	Continuous
7:30-9:00	Th	University City Recreation Council		Monthly
		Meeting (Public Welcome!)	---	4th Thurs.
7:00-8:00	T,F	Pre&Post Natal Excerise Class	25.00	8 wks.

*See North Region Adult Education Class Schedule For Fee (273-3221).

TEEN ACTIVITIES

		(With exp.)		
4:15-6:15	Th	Jr. Theater Wkshp. (10-15 yrs.)	32.00	16 mtgs.
4:15-5:15	W	Jr. High Gymnastics	14.00	10 wks.
5:30-6:30	M,W,Th	CO-ED Aerobic Slimnastics	10.00	10 wks.
To resume in April		Jazzerobics	10.00	8 wks.
5:45-6:45	T,Th	Aikido-Ki Development	25.00	10 wks.
		(10-15 years---Beg. & Int.)		
5:45-7:30	T	Jazz Dance	6.00	10 wks.

ELEMENTARY AGE ACTIVITIES

3:00-6:00	M-F	Child Tennis Lessons	15.00	5 wks.
3:00-4:00	M,W,F	Game Room Open	---	Continuous
3:15-5:15	M or W	Elem. Gymnastics & Tumbling	14.00	10 wks.
		(5 yrs. and older)		
3:30-4:30	M　Beg.	Jr. Theater Wkshp. (5-9 yrs.)	Reg.	March 2, 1981
3:15-4:15	W	Kindercrafts (Kindergarten Only)	2.00	10 wks.
3:15-4:15	T,Th	Aikido-Ki Development	25.00	10 wks.
		(6-9 yrs. Intermediate)		

Fig. 7-7, cont'd　**D**　*Seasonal program scheduling.*

ELEMENTARY AGE ACTIVITIES (CONT.)

TIME	DAY	CLASS	FEE	DURATION
4:30-5:30	T,Th	Aikido-Ki Development	25.00	10 wks.
		(6-9 yrs. Beginning)		
3:30-4:30	M	Creative Crafts (Grades 1-4)	3.00	10 wks.
3:30-4:30	T	Snoopy Sports (Grades K-2)	---	10 wks.
3:30-5:45	T	Tap Dance(All Levels, 1 hr. each)	6.00	10 wks.
3:30-5:00	F	Lots 'o Pots (Grades 3-6)	20.00	10 wks.
3:30-4:30	F	Creative Cooking (Grades K-2)	2.00	Monthly
4:30-6:30	Th	Jr. Theater Wkshp. (10-15 yrs.)	32.00	16 mtgs.
4:45-6:00	F	Creative Cooking (Grades 3-6)	2.00	Monthly
3:15-4:15	Th	Stage Dance & Musical Dance	15.00	10 wks.
		Theater (7-12 yrs.)		
10:00-11:30	S	Adv. Beg. Lots of Pots (Grades	20.00	10 wks.
		3rd and over) must have some exp.		

PRESCHOOL ACTIVITIES

TIME	DAY	CLASS	FEE	DURATION
9:30-10:15	T	Kindergym (2-3½ yrs.)	12.00	10 wks.
10:30-11:15	T	Kindergym (3½-5 yrs.)	12.00	10 wks.
10:00-11:30	M,W	Tiny Tots (See Act. Descrip.)	20.00	10 wks.
1:30-2:30	Th	Creative Cooking (Preschool)	2.00	Monthly
2:45-3:30	T	Tap Dance (4-5 yrs.)	6.00	10 wks.

FOR DETAILED INFORMATION CONCERNING CLASSES, PROGRAM FLYERS FOR MANY
OF THE CLASSES ARE AVAILABLE IN THE LOBBY OF THE MAIN PARK BUILDING.
CLASSES CAN BE HELD ONLY IF A MINIMUM NUMBER OF STUDENTS ARE ENROLLED,
VARIES ACCORDING TO THE CLASS.

UNIVERSITY CITY RECREATION COUNCIL - Meets the fourth Thursday of each
month. The public is welcome to attend the meetings. We encourage
community input regarding programs and activities at the park.
Volunteers are always welcome.

  *   *   *   *   *   *

 SWANSON POOL - 453-9770 Open swim and lessons will resume
in April.

Fig. 7-7, cont'd E *Seasonal program scheduling.*   *Continued.*

ACTIVITY DESCRIPTIONS

ADULT

1. <u>Physical Fitness</u> - Several fitness programs are offered at the Park. <u>Women's Rhythmic Slimnastics</u> and the CO-ED Slimnastics are programs primarily using calisthenics, stretching and jogging, with individual supervision using the Universal Gym Equipment. <u>Jazzerobics</u> is a vigorous exercise program using Jazz Dance steps and movements in addition to aerobic dance techniques. <u>Rhythmic Aerobics</u> combines dance, music, and aerobic exercise all in one class.

TEEN

1. <u>Aikido-Ki</u> - Non-competitive form of self defense. Coordination of mind and body. Smoothness and softness are stressed rather than aggressive and fierceness. Instructor: Martin Katz

PRESCHOOL & ELEMENTARY AGE

1. <u>Lots 'o Pots</u> - A clay class for elementary age children, grades 3 - 6. Learn different techniques of forming clay into a variety of projects. Instructor: Mona Alpert

2. <u>Jr. Theater Workshop</u> - A very popular class that introduces children to the inner workings of the theater: directing, script, set design, and staging as well as dramatic experience. Instructor: Susan Jackson-Beehler

3. <u>Stage Dance and the Musical Dance Theater-</u>
Auditing, Poise, Performance, Coordination.
For children interested in dancing on the stage and in musicals. Includes a performance at the end of the series. Instructor: Susan Jackson-Beehler

4. <u>Tiny Tots</u> - for children $3\frac{1}{2}$ to 5 yrs. Children 2 to $3\frac{1}{2}$ yrs. may enroll if their mother is enrolled and participates in the Women's Rhythmic Slimnastics class at the park. (arts, crafts, stories, games, and social activities.)

Fig. 7-7, cont'd F *Seasonal program scheduling.*

THANKS

The staff at Standley Park Recreation Center depend heavily on volunteers to maintain a quality program. These are just a few of the many people we would like to thank for donating their time to the park in 1980:

GENE McELROY   BOBBIE BENSHOOF and RACQUET

DEBBIE MALLOY-CHAPIN   CHUCK OSBORNE

U.C. KIWANIS   NELLIE FENNER

U.C. OPTIMISTS   STEPHANIE WELLS

BETH ENSCH   JOE VECA

CHRISTINE WHITMAN   BECKY RIOS

                                  KATHY SHELY

Fig. 7-7, cont'd   G   *Seasonal program scheduling.*   *Continued.*

Special Events

St. Patricks Day

Washington's Birthday

PIE EATING CONTEST

Family Night

FUN!

Monday - February 16, Roller
Skating trip (additional information
see flyer at desk).

Friday - February 13, Cherry Pie
eating contest,   pre-school 10a.m.
                 K-2nd 10:30 a.m.
                 3rd-4th 11 a.m.
                 5th-6th 11:30 a.m.

Sunday - March 15, Family Ice
Skating (free at the U.C. Town
Center) For more information see
flyer at desk).

Monday - February 16 Movie
Darby O'Gill and the Little
People.
        2 shows Noon - 1:45 p.m.
and 2:45 - 4:00 p.m.
        50 cents for Children
and a dollar for 16 yrs. and over.

Fig. 7-7, cont'd   H *Seasonal program scheduling.*

Fig. 7-8 *Short-term program scheduling.*

EXPLORING WINTER WONDERS WEEKEND

NORTH BEND STATE PARK

JANUARY 30 - FEBRUARY 1, 1981

We are pleased to announce new this year our plans for a special event-
"EXPLORING WINTER WONDERS WEEKEND" at North Bend State Park, January 30 -
February 1, 1981.

This weekend will prove enlightening and provide fun and experiences
you won't want to miss....so plan now to be with us for this occassion.
You will have an opportunity to join in the entertainment. See note on the
talent show on next page.

RESERVATIONS for both rooms and meals will be made by using the
attached form. Be certain to forward no later than January 29, 1981,
to be assured of a reservation.

The cost will be $44.00 per person. This includes two nights lodging
in either the lodge or a cabin, five delicious meals and registration
fee which includes a sleigh ride and two social hours.

Our program is as follows:

FRIDAY, JANUARY 30, 1981

2:00 p.m.   Registration - Lodge Lobby

4:00 p.m.   Techniques of Outdoor Photography   (For early arrivals)

6:15 p.m.   Dinner - Lodge Dining Room

8:00 p.m.   Program Convenes - Lodge Conference Room

9:00 p.m.   SKY SPLENDORS - Bob Gardner, SUNRISE, Charleston

10.00 p.m.   Refreshments - Lodge Lobby

Fig. 7-9A *Daily program scheduling.*

From *Exploring winter wonders weekend.* Charleston, W. Va.: West Virginia Department of Natural
Resources, 1980.

SATURDAY, JANUARY 31, 1981

7:15 a.m.   Breakfast - Lodge Dining Room

9:00 a.m.   Animal Tracking and Wildlife Observation
to   OR
11:00 a.m.   Three Mile Winter Walk

12:00 noon   LUNCH - Lodge Dining Room

1:30 p.m.   Tree and Plant Identification in Winter
to   OR
3:30 p.m.   Who's Who in the Bird Kingdom

4:00 p.m.   Outdoor Winter Games

                    Sleigh Riding
                    Snowball Battle
                    Fox and Goose
                    Cross Country Skiing   (Bring your skis)

6:00 p.m.   Dinner - Lodge Dining Room

7:00 p.m.
to   Winter Sleighride or Hayride
8:30 p.m.

9:00 p.m.   Program - Lodge Conference Room

             Talent Show - Get your act together. Register it at the
                            Registration Desk when you check in. Participants
                            will provide entertainment. (Sing, dance, play
                            musical instrument, recite, etc.)

SUNDAY, FEBRUARY 1, 1981

7:15 a.m.   Breakfast - Lodge Dining Room

9:00 a.m.   Exploring the Wonder of Winter (Hike)
                            OR
             Winter Survival - Conference Room

11:00 a.m.   Weekend program concludes. However, you are invited to
             stay for lunch on your own and enjoy the facilities of
             the North Bend State Park.

     Use the attached form to make your reservations. The lodge rooms
have two double beds. The cabins are two-bedrooms and three-bedrooms.
The three-bedrooms have two baths.

     If you need additional information, call Charleston (304) 348-3370.

Fig. 7-9, cont'd   B   *Daily program scheduling.*

employed most appropriately with the conference and seminar program format and other programs (such as camp) where participants remain on the program site overnight or longer. Fig. 7-9 illustrates a weekend time schedule for a program sponsored by the West Virginia Department of Natural Resources.

Usually the daily pattern of scheduling focuses on five distinct time periods. The morning program session rarely begins before 9 AM and may include the noon meal. This session is commonly reserved for athletic programming. The early afternoon session follows lunch and often incorporates activity at a lower level or even rest and meditation. Next is the highly participatory time of the late afternoon session. The early evening session follows dinner and is a popular time for class format programming or social recreation. Depending upon the age and life-style of the participants, one of two (usually not both) additional daily blocks can be used. The prebreakfast session is common in athletic camps and health resorts and features the predawn hike or workout; the late evening session is normally found in socially oriented programs such as cruise ships (this time block can extend well into the early morning hours).

No matter which organizing pattern is used, schedules must constantly relate to the participant's life-style and to the format and content of the program in order to serve their function properly. Scheduling should complement the participant and the program by facilitating their coming together.

Keeping program records

It is common practice for implementing planners to be required by their agency to maintain accurate records of programs. These are necessary to facilitate progress reporting, health and safety of the participant, and the program evaluation stage; therefore this responsibility should never be taken lightly. Such records are maintained on a weekly or monthly basis. In addition to regular records and reports are those special reports required under certain circumstances, such as accidents, theft, or vandalism. Records usually kept by the program planner fall into the following categories.

Program records Not always required by an agency, program records normally follow a prescribed format. They consist of a description of the general activities that were conducted, including special events. Program records should sum up the major details of the program, how it was planned and carried out, those who participated, what facilities and equipment were involved, and other relevant information (time schedules are usually kept on file). If the records appear in order, they will be maintained for a certain period of time (usually a year). If they reveal an inadequacy or a departure from agency policy, they may become the basis of staff meetings, training sessions, or other supervisory efforts.

Personnel records Individual staff members usually are requested to report their work record. This record includes such detailed information as time cards, overtime, lateness, illness, special leaves, and vacations. When personnel records are kept in a meaningful way, better allocation and assignment of staff to programs is frequently possible.

Attendance records   Elaborate attendance or activity participation records are the most popular records required. In fact, program planners have a tendency to rely heavily on attendance records to define everything from the program's popularity to its ultimate value. Attendance information does play an important role in program evaluation and therefore should be as efficient as possible. In some cases these records are not accurate; often program leaders boost the attendance figures to make themselves appear more successful. Many times it can be difficult to keep precise participation statistics because of the size of the event or the program format. For example, in programs where preregistration is required, it is possible to keep complete and accurate records of attendance; on the other hand, playground or open facility attendance is much more difficult to determine and thus the results are less accurate.

Other records   Most recreation and park agencies request that the following circumstances also be recorded and reported: (1) accidents or injuries both to program participants and staff; (2) permissions for children to leave the program site; (3) vandalism, damage, or theft; (4) disciplinary problems and their solutions; (5) inventory of equipment and supplies; (6) maintenance and equipment conditions; and (7) the use of petty cash funds. Record keeping within each of these areas is normally detailed by the agency; procedural guidelines and particular formats are predetermined for the program planner.

Although it is vital to program worth that accurate records be kept, there is also the danger of creating unnecessary paperwork. Only those records that are truly necessary and make a contribution to the program should be implemented. Record-keeping chores should be carried out swiftly and efficiently; records should be filed promptly or forwarded to the appropriate supervisor.

Program life cycles

The concept that recreation programs have life cycles is based upon an analogy with human biological development. The periods of growth, maturity, and decline are useful in describing the recreation program life cycle. Although this evolutionary process can be modified by careful leadership, the decline of a program's appeal is inevitable.

According to Crompton (1979), the life cycle of a recreation program consists of five stages. As shown in Fig. 7-10, the vertical scale represents the number of program participants, and the horizontal scale represents time. The first life-cycle stage is the introduction, in which user acceptance is light and slow; the second is the take-off stage, a period of rapid growth. Third is the maturity stage, when the growth rate slows down; fourth is saturation, when no further growth takes place and con-

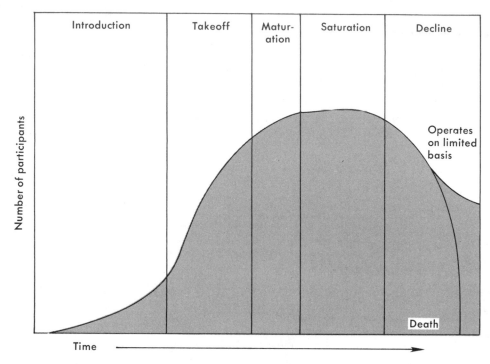

Fig. 7-10 *Program life cycle.*

Adapted from Crompton, J. L. Recreation programs have life cycles, too. *Parks & Recreation*, 1979, *14:10*, p. 53.

stituency interest begins to wane. Fifth is the decline stage, in which the program ceases altogether or shows a substantially reduced level of involvement over an indefinite period of time.

At the implementation step in planning the program the life cycle concept can be vital in determining program duration and resource allocations (later it will be important in interpreting evaluation results). Let us therefore explore the characteristics of each life cycle stage more carefully.

In the introduction stage the program planner applies marketing devices to generate support and acceptance for the new program. Publicity, advertising, and promotions costs are high at this point. Compared to the number of participants involved so far, a disproportionate leadership effort and facility commitment is being made. As attendance in the program slowly grows, satisfied participants begin to spread the word. Therefore it is most important that program quality and standards be fully operable at this early stage. The newer the program idea, the more important that the early participant has a good first impression.

At the second, or take-off, stage in the program life cycle participation grows rapidly. Less marketing effort is now required because all the details of initiating the program have been accomplished and program participants take care of the remaining publicity needs. This stage is concluded when the rate of participation increase begins to slow down. According to Crompton (1979, p. 54), the actual length of these first two stages depends upon (1) the program's familiarity, (2) the degree of skill complexity required by the activity, (3) the cost of the necessary equipment, (4) the presence of competitors for this particular program, (5) the ease of participation, (6) the visibility the program has attained in the community, and (7) its compatibility with other agency programs.

During the third stage, maturity, the number of participants continues to increase, yet the rate of this increase declines significantly. It is unrealistic to expect any program to experience rapid growth indefinitely; a leveling off is inevitable. At this stage imitators will begin to emerge. When a program is obviously very successful, other agencies (particularly commercial) will want to include it in their service offerings. When this happens, the original programming agency is no longer concerned with how to persuade people to try the program, but rather with the more difficult challenge of making them prefer their program over competing ones.

The fourth, or saturation, stage finds the program relying on repeat business. By this time there are no newcomers to the program. Hence if the existing participants drop out, there are fewer others to take their place. It is at this stage that program planners have the greatest opportunity to alter the program to extend its duration. Occasionally regeneration strategies, such as assigning new leaders, using a different facility, undertaking a second marketing campaign, or developing an alternative program format, can revitalize a program in the saturation stage. However, not all programs can be revitalized, so it is important for the planner to recognize these cases and to cut back on time and money invested.

In the final, or decline, stage the program's end is usually imminent. Planners may decide to mount a primary advertising and promotion effort aimed at potential participants, but it is more likely that this stage in the life cycle will involve the decision to terminate the program. At this point competitive programs have become more attractive to participants, and the number of participants remaining is too small to justify continuance at the same level. An alternative to program termination may be to offer the program intermittently or less frequently. If this is done, the participation decline may level off, resulting in a small number of true enthusiasts capable of maintaining the program themselves. It is during the decline stage that careful program evaluation is important. Each year agency programs that are in the decline stage should be identified for evaluation; a comparison should be made between the resource commitment to number of participants and their satisfaction with the program. Any decision to terminate a program should be carefully planned, with consideration given to the well-being of those remaining in the program. Termination is an important decision; for if a program is truly in its final life-cycle stage, the resources used to support that program can soon be liberated for new program ideas.

The illustration used in Fig. 7-10 is meant only as a generalization of the life-cycle concept. The actual time span of each stage in the cycle is subject to the complex variations of reality. When the concept is applied to particular programs, some stages may be very brief and others quite long. Some programs may have a minimal introduction stage; others may have none, going directly into the take-off stage. If a new program were introduced and failed to gain much support, this would be shown by an irreversible descending curve.

Determining a program's life cycle requires strict attention to the individuality of the locale, agency, and constituency. It is particularly important to distinguish between the life cycle of the generic group of programs and that of the particular program in an individual community. The life cycle curve for tennis in the United States, for instance, is likely to be very different from that of a children's tennis instruction program in one particular city. On the whole, the life-cycle time frame will be longer for the broader generic program group. The life cycle of a particular tennis program in a particular agency may be only one year, whereas tennis programs in America have already enjoyed more than a 25-year life span.

As Crompton (1979) has said, "Many recreation managers may be intuitively aware of the life cycle concept which has been described, but unfortunately, few have recognized its usefulness as a management tool" (p. 56). Knowledge of program life cycles allows for preplanning; that is, for the planner to take the initiative in program implementation details instead of being forced to react to what has already happened. Program development can be planned more systematically because the life-cycle concept identifies the pattern a new program is likely to follow.

When a new program is being implemented, it is vital to arrange for a series of appropriate actions to be used at each stage in the program's existence. For example, each stage requires a different marketing strategy as well as differing allocations of leader, facility, and budget resources. Considerable publicity and promotional effort is necessary at the introduction stage, but little value is likely to result from such effort in the saturation stage. In addition, once a program reaches the saturation stage, the sponsoring agency will want to reallocate some resources to the development of new programs. The likelihood of sound implementation decisions will increase if there is knowledge of where programs stand, both individually and collectively, in their respective life cycles. With this information programs are more likely to receive an appropriate mix of resources.

Because of the inevitability of the program life cycle and its implementation planning implications, there is a constant demand for new program ideas to replace those in the decline stage. The recreation and park agency's status is usually dependent upon that of its program and facility services. The life-cycle concept provides a guide for assessing both the current status and the potential of particular programs. This powerful implementation tool provides a framework for program expectations.

CONCLUSION

If any program is to be successful, the planner must approach implementation strategically and with great attention to details. After the selection of appropriate leadership, the determination of facility availability and adequacy, and the acquisition of sufficient funds (discussed in Chapter 6), at this step the planner must make a diverse collection of implementation details come together in a timely and effective manner. This chapter has recommended the use of a specifically designed implementation strategy for this task. When implementation is approached in an organized, logical manner, the planner can rest assured that his or her professional responsibility has been performed as conscientiously as possible. All that remains is to wait and see how it all goes.

References

Anderson, V. *1980 Annual Report*. Morgantown, W.Va.: Monongalia County Consolidated Recreation Commission, 1981.

Bannon, J.J. *Problem solving in recreation and parks* (2nd ed.). Englewood Cliffs, N.J.: Prentice-Hall, 1980.

Beck, D. Make the most out of changing leisure habits. Recruit! *Parks & Recreation*, 1980, *15:1*, 93-94.

Crompton, J.L. Recreation programs have life cycles, too. *Parks & Recreation*, 1979, *14:10*, 52-57, 69.

Edginton, C.R., Compton, D.M., & Hanson, C.J. *Recreation and leisure programming: A guide for the professional*. Philadelphia: Saunders College, 1980.

Evarts, H.F. *Introduction to PERT*. Boston: Allyn & Bacon, 1964.

Johnson, L. Brainstorming and name forming. *Parks & Recreation*, 1977, *12:6*, 36, 78.

Kraus, R., & Curtis, J. *Creative management in recreation and parks* (3rd ed.). St. Louis: C.V. Mosby, 1982.

Mason, J.G. *How to be a more creative executive*. New York: McGraw-Hill, 1960.

Mittelstaedt, A.H., & Berger, H.A. The Critical Path Method: A management tool for recreation. *Parks & Recreation*, 1972, *7:7*, 14-16.

Moder, JJ, & Phillips, C.R. *Project management with CPM and PERT* (2nd ed.). New York: Van Nostrand Reinhold, 1970.

Murphy, J.F., & Howard, D.R. *Delivery of community leisure services: An holistic approach*. Philadelphia: Lea & Febiger, 1977.

Tillman, A. *The program book for recreation professionals*. Palo Alto, Calif.: Mayfield, 1973.

Winston, S. *Getting organized*. New York: Warner Books, 1980.

Winter 1981 program brochure. Standley Community Park, La Jolla, Calif., 1981.

The planning process

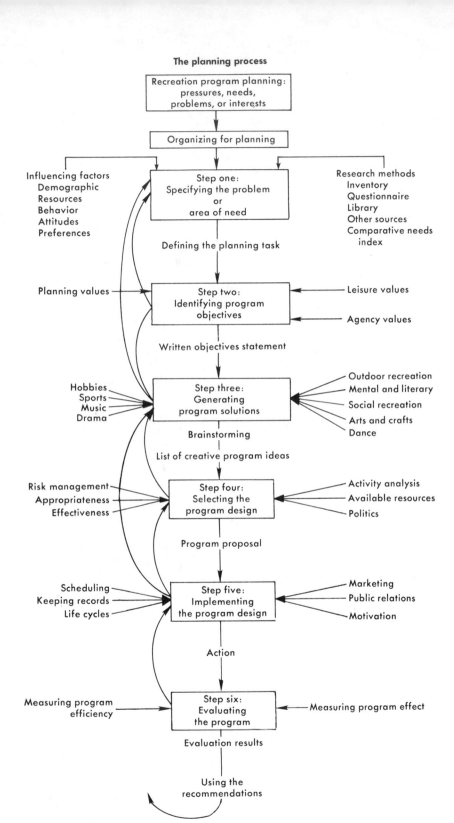

Chapter 8

STEP 6

Evaluating the program

A phrase that is frequently quoted from the poet Robert Burns is that our best-laid plans "gang aft a-gley." Our world has grown much more complex since Burns made his wry comment about planning, but one thing has not changed: the need to determine the success of our plans. We have come to that point in the planning process where the actions that were planned and programmed in the previous stages are now taking place. In step 6 of the process this action is observed and evaluated; this step calls for program evaluation.

Program evaluation begins when the planner takes action to implement a given program, and it continues until evaluation results show that the program should be changed or terminated. As shown by the graphic representation of the planning process at the beginning of this chapter, decisions may be made from evaluation until the resulting program bears little resemblance to the original plan. Decisions derived from evaluation often concern improving the quality of program services for the constituency as well as determining the value of continued spending for these services. Because most major program decisions are subsequently based on such an assessment, the outcome of evaluation is crucial.

Although evaluation is one of the most important aspects of recreation program planning, it is one of the least understood, most confused aspects of program services. It is an often discussed but infrequently used planning step. This may result from an unclear view of exactly what evaluation is and ought to be. For example, citing several definitions of evaluation in the recreation literature, Bannon (1976, p. 267) shows the following diversity and resulting lack of clarity:
- Evaluation is measurement; evaluation involves the development of an instrument to collect data that can then be compared with some normative criteria.
- Evaluation is a statement of congruence between performance and objectives.
- Evaluation is a professional judgment of the merits of the program.
- Evaluation is the determination of worth in order to intentionally produce a change in the participant or the agency; it is the measurement of desirable or undesirable consequences of an action intended to advance some ulterior motive.

- Evaluation is the final step in the decision-making process; its sole purpose is to report summary data useful to decision makers in selecting among alternatives.

Each of the above definitions implies the notions of judgment and appraisal; in other words, evaluation attempts to assess something's worth. That much seems to be agreed upon. The confusion and disagreement both in the literature and among practicing planners come with the attempt to define evaluation in terms of purpose, use, and means. This problem may result from the fact that in the not-so-distant past recreation planners evaluated their programs simply by counting the program attendance. Yet the current cry for accountability and professionalism has forced planners to develop accurate qualitative and quantitative measures of evaluation. Planners are now expected to be able to assess what actually happened to the participant as a result of experiencing a particular program, in addition to assessing the program conduct and content worth.

With this in mind, I propose that the definition of evaluation in program planning be the following:

> Evaluation is a continuing, ongoing function whereby pertinent information is gathered in order to assess the efficiency of program conduct and content and the effect of the program on the participant; this information is then used to determine the adequacy of the program in reaching its stated objectives so that future program decisions may be made wisely.

Thus the foundation for this discussion is that evaluation is a continuous, ongoing enterprise; that it is concerned with assessing both program efficiency and effectiveness in order to compare them with program and performance objectives; that it is intended to assist in future decision making; and that it uses both qualitative and quantitative appraisals. This chapter presents material on the purpose and use of evaluation so that the main discussion of measuring program efficiency and effectiveness can be appreciated better. For the sake of providing practical assistance to the planner at the evaluation stage, the chapter also discusses specific evaluation tools, as well as how to deal with evaluation results.

Purposes of evaluation

There are a host of reasons to evaluate a recreation program, ranging from the sincere and logical to the cosmetic and appeasing. Theoretically the purpose of evaluation is to systematically judge, assess, and appraise the entire workings of a program to gain information that indicates whether or not the planner is getting results and the program is going where it was intended to go. The ultimate reason for engaging in evaluation is for the planner to become more proficient and more effective in meeting participants' and society's recreational needs.

One of the most fundamental purposes of evaluating the program is to determine whether or not it is doing what it is intended to do. Is the program achieving its objectives? Now is the time to determine the program's ability to meet the clearly defined and specific program and performance objectives that were established in step 2 of the planning process. In evaluation it is the objectives that form a basis for both the appraisal of the program and the details of measurement and data collection. This places a great deal of emphasis on the need for accurately determined and precisely defined objectives. In fact, there are evaluation theorists who consider the bedrock of an evaluation to be the clear and precise definition of objectives. Objectives must be stated specifically so that the planner, as well as the constituency, can tell whether they have been achieved. The statements that were written in planning step 2 to represent the program and performance objectives need to be clear enough to now provide a yardstick for measuring program success.

Related to the measurement of objectives is a second and equally valid purpose of evaluation. Evaluation can determine whether the stated objectives are the actual ones upon which the program is operating, and, if so, whether the objectives are appropriate. According to Theobald (1979), determining whether a program's objectives are or are not met (and the reasons for their success or failure) offers another chance for the planner to study the objectives themselves. It is conceivable that some program or performance objectives are not being achieved because the planner or the participants do not identify them as the objectives. Therefore occasionally the evaluation step will result in a redefinition of objectives (as shown by the upward arrows in the diagram at the beginning of this chapter).

The bottom line in evaluation is determining whether or not the objectives of the program have been or are currently being realized. A third purpose of evaluation focuses on the approach taken to make this determination. Historically most recreation programs have been evaluated from a subjective vantage point. Leaders or participants simply have been asked how satisfied they are with a particular program; or, worse yet, the leaders have measured program success by "feeling" that the participants were or were not (usually it ended up that they were) having a good time. This subjective method of determining program worth is based on the assumption that expressed satisfaction measures the quality of service provided. Such subjective evaluation can be misleading because expressed satisfaction may not be affected by any characteristics of that program. Thus the third purpose of evaluation is to combine a systematic method with subjective indications to gain a useful understanding of a program's worth.

The fourth purpose of evaluation is to provide a systematic procedure or method by which accurate and reliable knowledge is produced. The goal in evaluation is, therefore, to provide systematic and comprehensive evidence of the program's ability to achieve its intended objectives. This makes evaluation one of a number of scientific research techniques—"all of which share certain basic tenets such as the logic and design of research and the verifiability of findings" (Theobald, 1979, p. 21). Research is that field of inquiry characterized by the employment of scientific methodologies in order to be as objective, as unbiased, as systematic, and as comprehensive as possible.

The fifth purpose of evaluation is to aid in decision making. As discussed earlier, the development and implementation of a recreation program requires the selection of a specific action from an assortment of alternatives. To choose among the alternatives, the planner needs to apply the process of decision making, which relies upon evaluative behavior. Likewise when operating budgets are cut or expanded, when new facilities or leaders are acquired, or when constituencies change or increase, evaluation assists the planner in making decisions about the usefulness of existing programs and the probability of their achieving the desired result. In this way evaluation helps the planner in making decisions about future programming efforts.

A sixth reason that evaluation is included in the program planning process is to make the agency a better, more worthwhile organization. Evaluation stimulates the quality of all the services the agency provides. How is this accomplished? When used wisely, evaluation can promote staff growth and education; ascertain the flexibility of policies and internal systems; appraise personnel quality and worth in relation to the agency's entire service scheme; develop firmer foundations for the agency's philosophy; appraise the adequacy of existing physical properties; and avoid unnecessary or wasteful financial expenditures. A systematic evaluation of programs can assist the agency in not only bettering program services but in these other related operations as well.

A final purpose for evaluation is the pure and simple contribution the results can make to the body of professional recreation knowledge. Outmoded concepts, invalid ideas, and inadequate understandings are replaced through meaningful evaluation. Thus the seventh evaluation goal is to increase the knowledge gained through practice and to test current practice so that the professional knowledge base becomes increasingly broader and stronger.

Successful planners constantly question the effectiveness and the efficiency of their programs. Are the programs accomplishing what they were intended to do? Should they be expanded, cut back, eliminated? In summary, the purposes of evaluation are:

1. To determine the achievement of program and performance objectives
2. To determine the appropriateness of the objectives themselves
3. To be sensitive by considering subjective indications of a program's worth
4. To be trusted by providing systematic, unbiased evidence of a program's worth
5. To aid in decision making
6. To improve the agency itself
7. To increase the professional knowledge base in order to improve current practice

In addition to all the right reasons just discussed, Weiss (1972) proposes a number of wrong reasons for using evaluation: postponement or avoidance of taking action, avoidance of responsibility or criticism, public relations, grant requirements, and increased agency prestige. The procrastination strategy of "sending the matter up for evaluation" has no relation to the established purposes of evaluation. Using evaluation as an excuse to avoid making a decision or taking action is not a professional mode of behavior. Evaluation can also be used to avoid responsibility or criticism; the planner can blame an unpopular decision on the evaluation instead of assuming responsibility himself or herself. As stressed in Chapter 7, good public relations are essential to recreation programs. However, calling for an evaluation that the planner thinks will be positive merely to draw attention to the agency's good relationship with its constituency is an improper expenditure of evaluation time and money. In addition, conducting an evaluation study simply as a means of acquiring grant money is not justified. Finally, an agency with poor programming, unprepared staff, or inadequate facilities sometimes conducts a "selective" evaluation to enhance its prestige. This action attempts to justify a weak program by evaluating only its strong aspects.

Uses of evaluation

Overall, evaluation's usefulness is in determining the relationships between planned programming and desired outcomes. Its main concern is to assist program personnel in planning and then modifying their activities in order to increase the potential of achieving delineated objectives. In addition, evaluation has a number of specific uses.

Knutson (1961, p. 109) has suggested 10 utilitarian examples for program evaluation:

1. To demonstrate to others that the program is worthwhile
2. To determine whether or not a program is moving in the right direction
3. To determine whether the needs for which the program is designed are being satisfied
4. To justify past or projected expenditures
5. To determine the costs of a program in terms of money or human effort
6. To obtain evidence that may be helpful in demonstrating to others what is already believed to be true regarding the effectiveness of the program
7. To support program expansion
8. To compare different types of programs in terms of their relative effectiveness
9. To compare different program methods or approaches in terms of effect
10. To satisfy someone who has demanded evidence of effect

These 10 circumstances can be viewed as the basis or the rationale for evaluation of recreation programs. Evaluation must be able to furnish planners with information

RAY BELLAROSA

to answer such questions as these: Should a poorly attended program be continued as is, altered, or dropped? Should more or fewer program resources be allocated to it? Should it be reworked completely or just given more growth time? Even the determination of when these questions should be asked can be answered by well-conducted evaluation studies.

There are two distinct approaches to evaluation: process and outcome. Process evaluation is undertaken during program development and implementation to allow for improvement of the program before it is terminated. Process evaluation provides information that may permit the planner to make small specific decisions about the program's conduct or potential for obtaining the objectives. As such, this approach requires study of more than a simple comparison between objectives and results.

Such a comparison is the task of outcome evaluation. An approach used only after the program has been completed, outcome evaluation is useful in providing information about the overall effectiveness and efficiency of the program as measured against the stated objectives. This method is particularly useful for comparing two or more programs because it is designed to measure which programs work and which do not.

Ideally, the two approaches should operate simultaneously during the evaluation. Evaluation efforts cannot take place in a vacuum. Better program services are possible when the planner is apprised of the program's efficiency and effectiveness both during and after its occurrence.

Subject of evaluation

The question must always be asked: Evaluation of what? Each program or planned activity in recreation has value for some purpose. But it makes little sense to ask whether a specific program has value without specifying value for what. Even though evaluation mainly concerns to what extent the program has achieved its objectives, it also can be seen as the study of change. In this light the program itself is the causal factor of the change, and the stated objective is the effect of the change. Viewing evaluation in this manner requires the planner to consider the end result (objectives) as well as the means toward that end (that is, the specification of what it is about the program that is expected to produce these results).

Therefore in addition to asking whether or not the program achieved the end result or objectives is the equally important question of why the program succeeded or failed. The answer to the latter question is sometimes more important than the answer to how well the program worked. If evaluation is viewed as a process "to improve rather than prove or disprove" (Theobald, 1979, p. 61), an answer to the question of why or how a program failed can be of immeasurable value to future planning and allocation of resources.

Consequently this text maintains that the subject of evaluation is twofold. First is the measurement of program means; that is, the value of the program conduct and content that makes it possible for the program to succeed or fail. I have labeled this the *measurement of program efficiency*. Second is the measurement of program ends; that is, the results or the degree to which the program achieved its performance objectives. I term this the *measurement of program effectiveness*.

Measuring program content and conduct: efficiency

Program efficiency, the assessment of program content and conduct, compares the effectiveness-effort ratio in terms of money, time, staff, facilities, and equipment. Program efficiency assessments should determine the extent to which the *program objectives* are achieved when measured against the number and cost of the resources required. How economically does the program achieve its desired effectiveness results? Could another program achieve the same results at a lower cost?

Areas to be evaluated   There are four basic aspects of the programming undertaking that are necessary to its success. These program objectives include the administration under whose auspices the program is conducted; the face-to-face leadership that brings the program to the participant; the physical properties (such as facilities and equipment) that assist and support the program; and the program content itself. All these areas must be fully efficient if the total program is to have the desired effect upon the participant.

For example, the administrative facet concerns evaluating the competency of program planning, organizing staffing, training, directing work, exerting control, and inspiring creativity. Is the agency being administered so that it is doing its required program work efficiently? Is financing being handled wisely and being dispersed creatively? Because the functions of an administrator usually include planning, organizing, directing, and controlling the work of others, an evaluation of administrative efficiency should be carried out within this framework. The level of efficiency is the extent to which the agency administration is able to (1) work with subordinates, (2) work as a joint member of a complete system, (3) be innovative, (4) complete projects, (5) meet the job requirements of the position, and (6) work with other parallel administrators (Reddin, 1971, p. 3).

It is important to recognize that the program administration should be evaluated not only in terms of the above broad objectives but also in terms of how well the objectives of the leadership were met. Whether or not the leadership objectives were met is probably relevant to how well the leaders were administered or managed.

Leadership or personnel is a key area because poor or inadequate leadership can destroy the most well-conceived and well-planned program. Is the leadership qualified for the program it is responsible for? What is its performance in that role? How effective is the leadership? Most of the evaluation concerned with staff is directed to the following purposes: (1) selecting qualified staff members for various levels of responsibility; (2) reviewing the effectiveness of individual staff members as a guide to advancement, in-service training needs, and future assignments; (3) evaluating specific leadership techniques and methods; and (4) providing a basis for recommendations designed to improve overall staff performance within a department (Kraus, 1966, p. 421).

An evaluation of the performance of all program staff members should be undertaken at least once a year. Some recreation professionals advocate that this process should include self-evaluation, participant evaluation, and supervisor evaluation. Although the specifics of personnel evaluation are the domain of the planner's favorite recreation leadership text, such an evaluation should focus on (1) both general and specific traits of the leaders, (2) the effectiveness of leadership style, and (3) a comparison with other parallel employees. The planner must also consider the impact of the unique circumstances of the situation on leader performance.

Usually the evaluation of recreation leaders is conducted by a supervisor who observes them on the job and holds periodic joint evaluation conferences. This procedure is made more objective and thorough when a standard rating form is used. Such a form is usually kept in the individual's personnel file. It provides a basis for the evaluation conferences and a means of judging improvement over time.

Evaluation of physical properties includes the level of efficient management of areas and facilities; the adequacy of their design, construction, and maintenance; and their appropriateness to the program itself. Are equipment and facilities safe? Do they contribute to or hinder the conduct of the program?

It has been suggested by Shivers (1967) that what needs to be evaluated in terms of the physical support systems of programs is their adequacy, safety, availability, accessibility, appropriateness, and multiple use. However, the important consideration is whether or not the facilities and equipment complement and contribute to the program, facilitating the meeting of program and performance objectives.

In addition to the administrative, leadership, and physical property facets of program conduct, program content should also be evaluated. What is the adequacy of the schedule? Is the content appropriate for the desired participant? Were program marketing techniques effective in attracting participation? Is the program subject matter really related to participant needs? Were the refreshments tasty? Did the program or event move smoothly from one activity to another? Evaluation of program content mainly concerns appropriateness to the participant and the circumstances; it is considerably important to the evaluation step in planning.

Thus in the evaluation of recreation program efficiency, the attributes of the program that make it successful or unsuccessful must be identified. Specification of a program's attributes requires an analysis of the program's parts (such as leaders and facilities) and an identification of those aspects that detract from or contribute to program efficiency. For example, an inadequate provision for safety might negate an otherwise successful boating program, or a new potter's wheel might make a pottery program more successful.

Standards   The evaluation of these four facets of program efficiency is frequently conducted by comparison to standards. Standards are statements of desirable practice or minimum levels of performance for a given situation. They enable evaluation by comparison; that is, if prestated desirable practices are followed, the program should be efficient (van der Smissen, 1972). Today the use of standards in recreation program evaluation is a very common approach. It allows a program's efficiency to be evaluated in terms of preset standard criteria, such as so many campers per counselor, so many ball diamonds per team, so many playgrounds per capita of children, so many sit-ups per participant, or so many years of education or experience per leader. As distinguished from norms, which tell us what *is*, standards tell us what *should be*. The set of standards is usually a measurement tool that consists of a checklist with occasional interview questions that serve a supportive role.

This type of evaluation is prevalent in the recreation and park field because it is relatively inexpensive, requires little research training or skills to perform, and allows for regional and even national comparisons (if the same standards are used). The difficulty in using standards for evaluation arises when such comparisons are interpreted. The interpretation of the results of a standards-oriented evaluation is often couched in inexplicit, personal terms. Sometimes it is too global in nature, yielding data that are too general to be useful or making it impossible to weight the more important components. Standards usually do not allow for "equally good, but different" interpretations (Bannon, 1976); what may be an appropriate standard for one agency may be obsolete, outdated, or plainly inappropriate for another. For these reasons great care is advocated in the use and interpretation of standards.

Where do these administrative, leadership, facility, and program content standards come from? In most cases standards are developed in response to a need felt by those professionals responsible for the agency or service. In addition, national organizations such as the American Camping Association and the National Recreation and Park Association have developed standards for use by recreation and park agencies. Examples include *Standards of the American Camping Association*, National Recreation and Park Association's *Evaluation and Self-Study of Public Recreation and Park Agencies*, Berryman's *Standards and Criteria Checklist*, and Wolfsenberger's *Program Analysis of Service Systems*.

The planner's agency may choose to adopt, in whole or in part, one of these pretested and researched published standards, or the planner may choose to devise his or her own. In order to develop standards, the first step is to delineate the major areas of criteria. Common to most standard sets are the general areas of philosophy and long-range goals, administration, program content, personnel, physical properties, and evaluation itself. Following this general determination, specific criteria for measuring each of these areas are developed. Usually this is done in work groups or committees. After much debate and reworking, the specific criteria finally adopted represent a consensus of the entire agency. There is also the need to develop a scoring system for use in assessing the degree of attainment of each standard criteri-

RAY BELLAROSA

on. Usually the research tests for reliability, validity, and objectivity of measurement instruments are applied to ensure the adequacy of standards for the agency's situation.

When choosing standards to evaluate program efficiency, whether they are adopted from an outside source or developed within the planner's own agency, several points of adequacy should be ensured. Farrell and Lundegren (1978, p. 217) specify them as follows:

1. Do the standards cover all the areas adequately that need to be evaluated for efficiency?
2. Are there specific criteria listed for each standard? Are they clear and scorable?
3. If you use this set of standards, what will you know when you finish? Will this information help you evaluate the program's efficiency in the best way possible?
4. Is the scoring system clear and meaningful?
5. Are there implications within the scoring system for remediation?

Cost-benefit analysis Concern for program efficiency has recently led to the utilization of cost-benefit ratios. First summarized, fixed program costs (including staff, facilities, and maintenance) are determined. Then the benefits (objectives) are likewise determined, and a resulting ratio is established between the two. If the cost-to-benefit ratio is too high, an attempt is made to reduce it (hopefully without disturbing program quality). If this cannot be done, the program is usually discontinued.

Proponents of this form of program efficiency evaluation see cost-benefit systems as the wave of the future in terms of accountability. Several cost-benefit approaches have been enthusiastically proposed in recent years. One example is the Economic Equivalency Index (EEI) developed by Robert Wilder (1977). The EEI is based upon the concept that time is money, and therefore every working hour has value. It assumes that a program's social value to the community can be expressed in economic terms and is equivalent to what a constituency would be willing to pay or give up for that program.

The mathematical formula proposed for the Economic Equivalency Index is as follows:

$$PH \times NP \times MW \div AF = EEI$$

PH represents the number of hours of participant activity involvement; *NP* represents the number of participants in the activity; *MW* is the current federal minimum wage; and *AF* stands for an age-group factor. Wilder distinguishes the age factor with a point system whereby:

> Adults (19 years of age and older) = 1
> Youth (13-18 years of age) = 2
> Children (12 years of age and younger) = 3

A hypothetical example of the formula is as follows:

PH		*NP*		*MW*		*AF*		*EEI*
100	×	100	×	\$3.10	÷	1	=	\$31,000
participation hours		participants		hourly min. wage		adult		

For instance, if there were 100 hours of participation in a ceramics class program by 100 adults, and the minimum wage were \$3.10 per hour, the Economic Equivalency Index would be \$31,000.

Wilder maintains that the EEI can be adjusted to allow for differences in the type of participant. Based on the principle that greater resources are required to provide program services to special groups of participants, a multiplier can be applied to the equation. For example, Wilder proposes that senior citizens and the disabled be given a multiplier of 5, the economically deprived 4, and children and youth 3. Applying the multiplier to the previous example is done in the following way:

PH	*NP*	*MW*	*AF*	*EEI*	*Multiplier*	
100 ×	100 ×	\$3.10 ÷	1	= \$31,000 ×	4	= \$124,000

Here \$124,000 would be the Economic Equivalency Index for a ceramics program for economically disadvantaged adults.

To apply the EEI to program cost-benefit analysis, the figure of \$124,000 must be compared to the actual costs of the program. Let us suppose that both the direct and indirect costs for the program are \$62,000 a year; then the ratio is 1:2 or .50. Wilder further suggests that criteria be established to eliminate a program or that fees be charged to any program that exceeds a .50 ratio. This ratio provides the planner with an answer to how economical the program is.

Application of the cost-benefit analysis and other similar formulas all have been subject to one major criticism. It is very difficult to provide a logical and consistent rationale for placing a dollar figure on the value of satisfying recreation experiences to the participant. For example, nothing in the EEI equation allows for individual participant differences or for small or new programs that require high initial costs. As a result, the more innovative programs might be eliminated in favor of larger traditional ones with high attendance, such as boy's baseball programs.

Because of this difficulty I recommend the use of cost-benefit analysis in conjunction with both standards-oriented evaluation and the evaluation approaches to be discussed in the next section of this chapter. However, commercial or private recreation agencies may find the cost-benefit analysis approach to program efficiency much more beneficial in regard to their net profit concerns.

Attainment of program objectives As discussed in Chapter 4 of this text, program objectives are the guideposts for the program itself. These objectives pertain to the program support systems (such as facilities, equipment, administration, and leadership) and to the content of the program itself. They specify the standard of care the program participant can expect, such as the quality of leadership, the adequacy of the facility, and the safety of the equipment.

In order to evaluate a program meaningfully, the planner must determine the degree of success in meeting these program objectives. A good appraisal of such success leads to a revision of program objectives; more equitable and relevant agency policies; and ultimately a better, stronger operational program base. If the program objectives are as specific as possible (as advocated in Chapter 4), assessing the degree of attainment can be relatively simple. Take the following example: One of the program objectives for a preschool swim program concerns leadership qualification; the objectives specify that there be one leader per five children and that each leader have at least an American Red Cross water-safety instructor certificate. In this case evaluating the program's success in meeting the objectives involves a simple count and a check of credentials.

Two currently used approaches to assist the planner in determining the program's success in meeting program objectives are standards and cost-benefit analysis. In addition, a great deal can be learned about the success of some facets of program objectives when other ones are evaluated. For example, suppose a program objective concerned with program content calls for the participants to be able to perform a certain skill a certain number of times. Suppose also that all the participants meet this objective 50% of the time. This reveals a great deal about the adequacy of the program instructional format and also about how successful the leadership is.

Evaluation is a process that must deal with varying degrees of tangibility. Measurement of the attainment of program objectives is the most tangible evaluation available to the planner. For example, to measure the attainment of a program objective of having 75% of the campsites in a park occupied during the weekend is certainly a more tangible evaluation task than measuring whether or not attitudes toward preservation of the wilderness have improved for 75% of the campers. Both measures should be undertaken to obtain a complete evaluation picture. There are some recreation professionals who further specify that the tangible evaluation indicators should be given more weight than the nontangible ones, on the theory that ultimately criteria such as attitudes and opinions will correlate positively with the more tangible indicators (Rossi and Williams, 1972).

Measuring the program participant: effectiveness

In evaluating recreation programs, the planner must analyze the program not only in terms of its characteristics but also in terms of the characteristics of the participants and the effects that the program has produced upon them. In large measure, the techniques that assess program effectiveness depend upon the performance objectives delineated earlier in the planning process. Because recreation and park professionals are currently very concerned with specifying the effectiveness of their programs, they are devoting a great deal of professional literature space to discussing the best way of approaching this aspect of evaluation.

As a complement to financial accountability, program effect accountability represents a new and sometimes difficult challenge. The provision of a program service that merely contributes to the recreational pleasure of people is no longer an acceptable justification. The judgment of worth extends beyond head counts and checklists to the documentation of the program's effect upon the participant. There are three basic areas of program effect that will be discussed here. They are measures of behavioral change, attitude, and opinion.

Behavioral change   In recreation programs for particular populations, most evaluation efforts attempt to measure physical or psychological changes in the program participant. These evaluations usually include the use of techniques for assessing each participant's behavioral characteristics and studying the change in these characteristics over the course of the program. For example, a crafts program may expect to impact basic knowledge about the craft as well as specific skills (such as eye-hand coordination). Naturally the program planner hopes that the program will change the participant's behavior in a positive direction.

These behavioral changes can be categorized into four types. According to Farrell and Lundegren (1978, p. 218), a planner may be looking for one or a combination of the following types when evaluating program effect:

1. *Psychomotor*. These behavioral change effects include skill development; development of positive body image; improvement in strength, endurance, fitness, stress recovery; and rehabilitative or therapeutic impact.
2. *Psychological*. These behavioral change effects include development of a positive self-concept; ability to deal constructively with stress; and self-actualization.
3. *Sociological*. These behavioral change effects concern the development of positive collective behavior, for example, belongingness, sharing, and integration; and the development of positive social organization as in a reduction of delinquency.
4. *Educational*. These behavioral change effects refer to the enhancement of knowledge, as in learning the rules of the game.

Information for assessing participant behavior is usually collected by means other than checklists, questionnaires, or tests. It can be gathered from individual self-reports or from reports by people who have contact with the participant. For example, in many therapeutic institutions, behavior data about each client are obtained from a group meeting of institution staff members who assess the participant's progress. This progress is charted primarily by observing the participant. Behavioral-change evaluation data can be difficult and time consuming to gather and interpret, but it is the most meaningful route to understanding program effectiveness.

Attitude   In most recreation programs, a large part of the evaluation of a program's effect on the participant relies on attitudinal measures. An attitude is a learned predisposition to think, feel, and perceive, which in turn influences the nature of behavior toward an object, person, or situation (Kerlinger, 1973, p. 495). Although it is true that attitudes greatly influence behavior, because attitudinal evaluation is simpler to conduct, most planners prefer it and then make inferences from attitude to behavior. For example, questions regarding attitude will often be interpreted to include behavioral changes; therefore a positive attitude toward society might be interpreted as leading to a less asocial life. Behavioral change is difficult to measure, particularly in a noninstitutional setting. Therefore many evaluators rely upon indexes of attitude to indicate accompanying behavioral change. Attitudes are generally measured by means of a paper and pencil test or a questionnaire.

Opinion   One of the most traditional and widely used measures of recreation program effectiveness is the opinions of participants toward the program. Participants are frequently asked these questions: Did you enjoy the program? What did you like most (and least) about it? Would you participate in another program? Would you recommend this program to a friend? How would you improve the program?

Knowing whether or not the program had participant appeal and popularity produces some vital data, but there is a danger in relying too heavily on measures of opinion. Measures of opinion can be misleading. People frequently participate in recreation programs for differing reasons, and these reasons can be totally unrelated to the stated performance objectives. For example, some people may participate in a square dance club for the exercise; others because they want to improve their dance skill, still others desire the social atmosphere and companionship. Participant opinions are solely an indication of individual participant needs and interests. Therefore the responses to an evaluation opinion questionnaire can be irrelevant to the objectives of the program. Does this mean the program was a failure? No, it merely means that the program was popular for reasons different from the ones the planner assumed it would be. Even though indicators of program appeal can be interesting and helpful, recreation programs that are based solely on the popular opinion approach to evaluation are woefully inadequate in instructing the planner in program effectiveness (Theobald, 1979).

Attainment of performance objectives   If performance objectives have not yet been adopted, the process of evaluating the program's effects is made more difficult and ultimately meaningless because there are no standards against which to measure effectiveness. One person can look at the program from the perspective of his or her own personal values and assumptions about the program's purpose and pronounce it a dismal failure. Another person can look at the same program, but with a different personal bias, and acclaim it a resounding success. This returns us to the subject of clearly stated performance objectives (as advocated in Chapter 4). De Boer (1970, p. 108) relates a clever analogy to the importance of establishing clear performance objectives:

> In the sport of archery there is one sure way even for beginners to hit the bull's-eye on the side of the barn every time—paint the bull's eye on the barn after the arrow has

landed. A program that is launched without a clear statement of goals is like such an arrow; though wide of the mark intended by its launchers long ago, it may be dubbed "on target" by anyone who can paint a convincing bull's-eye.

Thus in recreation programs the sequence of the attainment of participant effects begins with the establishment of specific performance objectives. A causal sequence then sets in motion a series of actions or events (such as assigning the leaders, publicity, and equipment purchases) that may bring about the desired outcome. Without any intervening variables (the leader quits mid-program, vandalism destroys the ceramics projects, or publicity is inaccurate), the planner can assume a direct causal relationship between the program and attaining the desired objective. Intervening variables may, however, directly affect performance objective attainment. This is why evaluation considerations should include two approaches: the more tangible measures of efficiency and the less tangible measures of effectiveness. The degree to which recreation agencies modify program characteristics or reallocate resources (program objectives) may be in direct proportion to the degree to which the performance objectives of effectiveness are achieved.

The task of identifying criteria of effectiveness success (often elusive to the planner) is influenced by a number of factors. First, some of the desired participant outcomes (behavior, attitudes, opinions) are easier to measure in some areas than in others. Psychomotor skill development in basketball and ballroom dancing, for instance, is readily observable. Other outcomes, such as the sociological development of a sense of sharing in a tiny tots play program, may require intermediate or proxy measures. Still other effects are highly subjective; because they depend upon interpretation by an observer or the participants themselves, they reflect special biases. Examples of such subjective outcomes are the improvement of parent-child relationships in a father-son weekend camping trip or the improvement of self-esteem in a modeling and etiquette class. Even when behaviorally specific effects are identified, the meaning of the behavior can be misinterpreted. Hence the planner's strategy must be to do the best he or she can by being at least aware of the difficulties of measurement accuracy and subjectivity. Those planners who work with programs that lend themselves to precise measurement of participant effect should vigorously document their results so that some interpretive assistance is available for programs that are more difficult to measure.

A second factor affecting the criteria of effectiveness success is the timing of the evaluation. Some changes in behavior, attitude, or opinion can be recorded immediately upon completion of the program. Other changes are not desired or expected until a later time. Collecting data on the attainment of behavioral performance immediately following the program may be much simpler than obtaining this data 6 months or a year after the participants have left the program. This factor is of particular concern in long-term, residential types of programs, such as summer camps and hospital recreation services.

RAY BELLAROSA

The degree of behavior, attitude, or opinion change desired is the third factor affecting the criteria for success. Clearly, the greater the change that is desired, the less likely the chance of success. Suppose that instead of selecting as a tennis program performance objective the development of the backhand, the objective chosen is for 85% of the participants to win a city-wide tennis tournament. Success is less likely than if the former objective had been chosen. This does not mean that large or difficult objectives are inappropriate; they simply make success more difficult to achieve.

Because some program effects on participants are more measurable than others, because the point at which evaluation measurements are undertaken can affect outcomes, and because success can be influenced by the degree of change expected, it is essential that recreation program planners and administrators not fall into the trap of unduly favoring those programs that can readily demonstrate success. Professional care and judgment in appraising a program's effectiveness are also required.

Evaluation design

One of the most troublesome problems faced by recreation program planners is the need to adequately evaluate recreation programs even though procedures for conducting a scientifically tight assessment are not readily available or not always understood. Frequently programmers are so involved with program operation on a day-to-day basis that they think they cannot conduct more than a cursory evaluation. This common failure to determine whether or not program and peformance objectives are being achieved can also stem from an inadequate recognition of the basic elements of an evaluation design.

A design for evaluation is a plan stating what will be measured (observed, tested) and when (which groups and at what times). A design also prescribes the measurement instruments and who the evaluator will be. Because the evaluator's report can affect important future planning decisions, the evaluation findings must be substantiated soundly. Backing up findings is easier when the evaluation's design has been given professional consideration. In summary, evaluation design dictates the kind of information, from whom it will come, when it will be gathered, by whom, and with what instrumentation.

Who is the evaluator?

The evaluation step in planning often involves participation by many people—from the on-site activity leader to the district supervisor to the board of directors. System-wide program evaluation can even be conducted by outside consultants (as discussed in Chapter 2). The issue of who is best qualified to conduct an evaluation (trained vs. untrained or internal vs. external personnel) is determined by the degree of complexity of the evaluation circumstances. I want to emphasize that all program evaluations must be conducted by qualified personnel in order to be meaningful. This means that the evaluator must possess qualifications appropriate to the level of evaluation desired. Some may be relatively simple self-appraisal types of evaluations that require minimal research skills and knowledge. Other evaluation efforts may be highly sophisticated, detailing a great deal of behavioral change data, and therefore require advanced knowledge of statistics and research techniques.

There is a debate currently underway in the recreation and park field about which is more desirable: outside consulting evaluators or in-house evaluators. Some professionals favor using outside evaluators to provide a bias-free judgment, to offer a fresh "outside" view, and to study the program objectively. Others argue that inside evaluators, who may not have the same precise training and expertise, have more first-hand knowledge of the overall program, will be accepted by the staff, and can function in a less obtrusive manner in conducting the evaluation (Edginton, Compton, and Hanson, 1980). Of course, agency finances are also a determinant.

Regardless of the agency's position on this debate, it is important that whoever is designated as the program evaluator be adequately prepared and qualified to meet the task. Remember, the goal of evaluation is better programming. The degree of research sophistication required to produce evaluation results that truly contribute to the improvement of future programs is what is important.

Are there some guidelines for the minimal degree of evaluation competencies? Farrell and Lundegren (1978) and Edginton, Compton, and Hanson (1980) have discussed some suggested evaluator competencies that are presented here in check-list form. Are those persons who are to conduct program evaluation in the planner's agency able to:

☐ Know the place of evaluation in recreation programs and its relationship to the planning process?

☐ Understand the subject of the evaluation, or the specific efficiency and effectiveness areas that need to be evaluated?

☐ Select the appropriate evaluation design and put it into effect?

☐ Identify appropriate instrumentation for collecting data?

☐ Analyze and interpret the results?

☐ Effectively communicate the evaluation results to others, and convert them into practice?

At least some mastery of these six competencies is essential for acquiring useful program evaluation results. In addition, whether the evaluator is from inside or outside the agency, there are certain ethical considerations that should be reviewed at this point. Each individual evaluator will approach the evaluation step in planning from a different background, with unique values and perceptions, and with a different repertory of skills and favorite techniques. As such, the evaluator's responsibility transcends basic competence in evaluation. It includes being honest about what evaluation can do and cannot do, being as open about the evaluation design as possible, obtaining and presenting the findings as objectively and honestly as possible, maintaining accuracy in data collection and reporting, and checking all personal or professional predispositions as much as possible.

Above all, professionals who are involved in the evaluation step must constantly consider the ramifications of their work. Deviations, miscalculations, errors, or unethical maneuverings in any aspect of evaluation can have considerable implications for the future of the program, the agency, the participant, or the staff member. "The evaluator should respect evaluation but never fear either the process or the outcome" (Edginton, Compton, and Hanson, 1980, p. 357).

Procedure

It would appear from the presentation in this text so far that all the program planner has to do to conduct an evaluation is this: determine the program's objectives, translate these objectives into measurable indicators of objective achievement, gather information on these measurable indicators from the program participants, and then compare these findings with the original objectives. Although this is conceptually, if not ideally, the procedure that occurs, recreation and park programs are customarily not as accommodating and neatly ordered as the evaluator would like. Often intervening circumstances and unique situations make the procedure more complex.

With this qualification in mind, the discussion now turns to an overview of the basic evaluation procedure. There is no single "best" design available to the recreation program evaluator. The selection of design and measurement techniques depends upon the intended use of the results, the decisions necessary to make, and the research capabilities and interests of the agency. In reality the designation of a particular evaluation procedure often is a compromise between the ideal and the feasible. In spite of the lack of a single model for recreation program evaluation, Theobald (1979) has offered a conceptual model of the procedure that practitioners may find adaptable to their own situation.

As Fig. 8-1 indicates, the program evaluation model is composed of two phases: the research phase and the information dissemination phase. The research evaluation phase first identifies the purpose of evaluation study. Then basic assumptions and hypotheses may be proposed, although they are not crucial to every evaluation effort. Unique or potentially misunderstood terms are defined. Any previous evaluation reports relating to the agency, or to similar agencies or programs, are reviewed so the evaluator will understand this background. A sample of specific activities and/or specific participants is then selected. Data-gathering techniques and measurement instruments are also selected. Then the evaluation itself is conducted: information is gathered, questions are asked, and participants are observed or tested. Finally, the results of the evaluation are assembled, analyzed, and interpreted; conclusions and recommendations for future programming are drawn up.

The second phase in the evaluation model is information dissemination. This begins when the evaluator presents the findings and proposes recomendations to the agency administrator or supervisor, the program staff, and (if appropriate) the program participants themselves. Based upon these presentations and discussions, the evaluator then has the option of making revisions or modifications to the final evaluation report. This final report is usually written and presented to the agency; in some cases it is also released to the general public.

Theobald (1979, pp. 156-158) illustrates the evaluation procedure model presented in Fig. 8-1 with the following example:

> The manager of a large state park may have received complaints about the quality of exhibits in the park historical museum. In addition, the number of visitors during the past year has decreased at the rate of approximately 4 percent per month. None of the staff can propose a viable cause for this situation, so the manager seeks to have the museum exhibits evaluated in order to determine the cause(s).
>
> An evaluator is selected and together with the manager and staff, he begins to review the goals and objectives of the museum program. One of the most significant

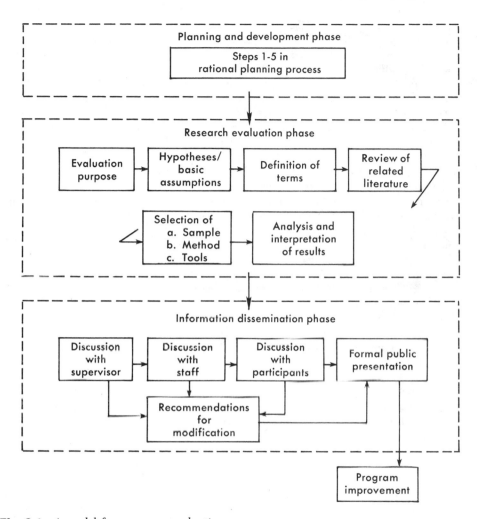

Fig. 8-1 *A model for program evaluation.*

Adapted from Theobald, W.F. *Evaluation of recreation and park programs.* New York: John Wiley, 1979, p. 155.

findings of this process is the realization that although the museum objectives are appropriate, there are no written measures for suggesting the task to be accomplished. The evaluator and the staff agree on a set of objectives that are clear, specific, and measurable. Next, they identify guidelines or criteria to help determine how the objectives will be measured. The final task of this initial phase is to select and agree upon the objectives of the evaluation itself, or more simply, what the evaluation hopes to accomplish.

From the previous information gained during the process of the planning-development phase, the evaluator succinctly states the problem as underutilization of the museum exhibit program. The purposes of the study are (1) to determine the cause of this problem and (2) to make specific recommendations that will enhance public participation in the program. For the purposes of this study, no assumptions or hypotheses were made. After defining the terminology in the study, the evaluator decides to limit the investigation to potential users of the museum and to limit the duration of the study to a twelve-month period. All printed information about the museum, its collection, and exhibits is reviewed. In addition, any similar literature and studies that deal with the problem of underutilization of museum exhibits is also reviewed.

The sample consists of a randomly selected group of visitors, both entering and exiting from the exhibits, as well as a number of individuals who have signed the guestbook and provided addresses during the past calendar year. The methodology selected consists of (1) a mail questionnaire to individuals selected from names in the guestbook, (2) a short, sequence-structured interview of those individuals who have or will see the exhibits, and (3) a duration-interval measurement to determine the amount of time visitors spend viewing individual exhibits. The analysis technique will consist of frequency distributions, percentages, and cross-tabulations with regard to age, sex, occupation, income, education, and number of previous visits to other museums (of all types). After the study has been completed, and the data both tabulated and analyzed, the evaluator proposed a series of recommendations:

1. Changing individual exhibits with greater frequency.
2. Hiring two additional curatorial staff and a Director of Education.
3. Soliciting nationally for additional exhibition material pertinent to the museum locale and the genre of the permanent collection.
4. Adding 30 new parking spaces adjacent to the museum entrance.
5. Purchasing and installing professional exhibition panels and a rear screen projector.
6. Enlarging the scope of the museum permanent collection in order to appeal to greater visitor diversity.
7. Embarking on a major fund-raising drive or capital campaign in order to enlarge the size of the museum.
8. Installing an air-conditioning system.
9. Establishing a volunteer docent program in order to provide group visitor tours.
10. Providing in-service training program on the museum and its collection for the entire park staff.

The evaluator discusses the findings and recommendations with the administrator and the staff. Additional recommendations might arise, or recommendations might be modified or deleted depending upon practicality and the limitations of potential for use. After any revisions are made, the evaluator submits the final report to the sponsoring organization, then to the public with a suggested method and timetable for implementation.*

As indicated earlier, the selection of evaluation samples, information-gathering methodology, specific measurement tools, and techniques for analysis of data depends upon the purpose of the evaluation. This purpose includes the intended use of the information and the expected decisions to be made. Actual practice has shown that much about the evaluation procedure also depends upon the limitations of the agency, including the restrictions of time, location, and expertise. An additional, and all too real, limitation is funding. Frequently there are no funds specifically allocated for a large evaluation study. When funding is low, this limits how much of the program can be evaluated and for how long.

Data-gathering techniques

As indicated in the preceding discussion, the planner must take some action to measure specific qualities, traits, or actions that are the focus of the evaluation. The evaluator must be able to determine the specific measures that are available and appropriate to assess the extent of objective attainment. This requires the selection and use of specific data-gathering tools that are appropriate to the purpose of the evaluation and the nature of the program. This phase of the evaluation procedure can often be demanding and difficult.

The discussion below presents certain minimal requirements for measurement instruments and then presents commonly employed methods of data collection for both program efficiency and participant effectiveness.

Measurement instrument requirements Perhaps the most important attribute of any evaluation technique of information collection is that the instrument possess reliability, validity, and objectivity. These basic research terms are critical minimal requirements for ensuring that the information derived from the measurement instrument is dependable, useful, and unbiased. If the measurement tool used in a program evaluation does not possess these three qualities, the planner can put little faith in the data resulting from its use.

Reliability refers to the measurement's consistency of dependability. For instance, a data collection tool is said to have reliability if similar information is obtained from repeated use in similar conditions. That is, a test is reliable if the same person takes it twice and receives the same score. Reliability is expressed by location on a scale from 0 to + or − 1.00, with +1.00 indicating a perfect, positive correlation between the two scores. If the agency is reviewing published evaluation tools for adoption, the instrument's location on the reliability scale should be indicated. The more reliable the instrument, the more it can be counted on to yield the information desired.

An evaluation measuring tool is considered valid if it measures what it claims to measure. For example, counting the audience at a modern dance performance is a valid measure of how many people attended the program but not of how many people enjoyed it. A measurement instrument is said to have validity if it measures the factors about which conclusions are to be made.

Objectivity refers to an unbiased quality in the measurement instrument. This implies that two evaluators viewing the same quality or action will judge it the same way. Objectivity represents an attribute of agreement among various users of the instrument; that is, there is a lack of personal influence or opinion from the evaluator on the resulting information.

In addition to being reliable, valid, and objective, measurement tools should be appropriate. Appropriateness in a selected instrument refers to whether or not it measures the important factors or those factors reflected by the program and performance objectives. The instrument should also be appropriate to the participants being evaluated by matching their reading level, skill level, and cultural characteristics.

The measuring techniques selected should also be operational within a reasonable time period and relatively simple to prepare and administer. The resulting information should be readily tabulated and interpreted. Ultimately the measurement device should obtain unique information; that is, data that have not already been obtained from other instruments or in other ways.

Measurement instruments for use in recreation program evaluation can be obtained in numerous ways. The planner can choose to develop his or her own; published library materials can provide suggestions; commercial research firms offer them for sale; graduate students in college recreation and park programs are constantly developing them to satisfy degree requirements; tried and true tools can be shared among similar agencies; and national professional organizations can suggest the use of their standards. For example, previous evaluations may have been done on similar program and performance objectives or on similar activities in related agencies. If this is the case, the planner can save time and effort by adopting or modifying these measures. Some professionals advocate seeking existing valid and reliable measures rather than attempting to develop new ones.

The evaluator's principle task is selecting and using a data-gathering technique or combining techniques to produce the necessary information at a minimal cost. Following are some typical measurement instruments in recreation program evaluation.

Instruments that measure program efficiency A number of evaluation techniques have been successfully used to measure the efficient attainment of program objectives. These program-monitoring techniques include procedures for reviewing the general operations of the program, auditing for administrative accountability, and charting staff behavior.

Perhaps the most useful, and certainly the most economical, is the instrumentation that already exists in the form of conscientiously kept *program records*. For example, program records on registrations and registration fees can be used to indicate total attendance and participation hours (total time spent using the service), the number and percent of different participants or nonparticipants for each program, and the ratio of recreation staff to participants. A systematic sampling of an agency's total programming at various times can indicate comparative attendance and participant use as well as an index of variety (number of different programs available at various times).

The *user rating instruments,* on the other hand, are brief questionnaires or checklists in which the planner asks the participant to respond to several criteria of efficiency. For instance, program participants could be asked to rate the physical attractiveness of the recreation sites and facilities, the convenience or suitability of the hours of operation of programs, the helpfulness of the staff, the appropriateness of program fees, and indexes of crowdedness (such as waiting lines, waiting lists, and the ratio of capacity of service to usage). The box on p. 308 supplies a hypothetical illustration of a user rating instrument.

Standards checklists, which were already discussed in this chapter, can also be useful measurement instruments of program efficiency because they offer a comparison against some professionally designated standard. For example, such checklists can help indicate to the planner the desired number and percent of persons living within so many minutes or miles of a recreation program service, the minimal degree of safety (usually expressed in number of accidents per number of user days as recorded on program accident reports), and the minimal number of programs per number of constituency.

Self-appraisals are other program-monitoring techniques that are potentially useful in evaluating program efficiency. Self-appraisals may be in either checklist, rating, questionnaire, or interview formats; they require the agency as a whole, an individual staff member, citizen advisory boards, or recreation and park governing commissions to apply self-judgment or self-evaluation to certain criteria. These self-appraisal criteria are usually concerned with certain organizational characteristics that predict program efficiency, such as (1) need for such recreation program services, (2) task orientation by recreation commissions or boards, (3) supervisory and personnel competency, (4) managerial style, (5) agency size, and (6) organizational configuration.

A large assortment of program-efficiency monitoring indexes may also be found within the financial records of the agency. For example, program or agency *financial auditing* techniques for accountability purposes are often useful for reviewing existing records on program expenditures; for studying resource allocations including staff, budget, equipment, facilities; and for reviewing other operating functions. Audits are essentially reviews of existing financial records that are kept on an individual program or department basis. Unless the agency retains its own accountants, most financial audits are conducted by specialist consultants from outside the agency.

A final means of determining program efficiency to be discussed here is the *time-and-motion study*. This measurement refers to those techniques that attempt to quantify the time spent by program staff on program services both under development and in operation (Theobald, 1979). Time-and-motion studies measure the amount of staff effort against the time devoted to a particular program. This is done to

Name of program ————————————————————————————

Days and times of participation ————————————————————

Please rate the following criteria on a numerical scale of one to five (1 to 5) with:
    1 = unsatisfactory
    3 = satisfactory
    5 = outstanding

	1	*2*	*3*	*4*	*5*
1. Is the scheduling of this program convenient to your own life-style?	☐	☐	☐	☐	☐

COMMENTS:

2. Is the facility provided for this program conducive to its enjoyment?	☐	☐	☐	☐	☐

COMMENTS:

3. How would you rate the leadership of this program?	☐	☐	☐	☐	☐

COMMENTS:

4. Was this program adequately marketed so that all those who were interested were notified of its existence?	☐	☐	☐	☐	☐

COMMENTS:

5. Is the fee charged a reflection of the program's use of resources?	☐	☐	☐	☐	☐

COMMENTS:

6. Is the program atmosphere safe?	☐	☐	☐	☐	☐

COMMENTS:

Table 17 *Summary of evaluation data-gathering tools*

Instrumentation	What is measured	Assumptions	Comments
Measures of program efficiency			
Program records	Attendance, participant hours, same or different participants, program variety, etc.	Assumed to indicate meeting of constituency interest	Low attendance or lack of variety may indicate lack of need rather than poor program
User rating	Physical attractiveness of program sites, schedule suitability, staff attitudes, crowdedness, etc.	Assumed that attractive sites, convenient schedules, perky staff, etc. attract participants	May wish to look at the number of potential users who stay away because of these
Standards checklists	Desired safety levels, desired participant-to-staff ratios, desired number of programs, etc.	Assumed that maintaining a certain level of standards will attract more participants	Important to look not only at preset standards but also participants' perceptions of these standards; criteria can often be vague
Self-appraisals	Need for programs, supervisory and leadership competency, managerial style, organizational size and configuration	Assumed that certain types of agency characteristics are directly associated with more efficient programs	Must be conducted with objectivity and unbiased care to be worthwhile
Financial auditing	Program expenditures and income	Assumed that high expenditures and low income are inefficient	Depends on the financial resources of the agency
Time-and-motion study	Staff time and energy expenditures	Assumed that low staff time commitments and much program productivity are efficient	Depends on newness and creativity of the programs
Measures of program effectiveness			
Attitude scales	Learned ways of thinking and feeling	Assumed that a participant's attitude will indicate program behavior and thus enjoyment	Before the scale can be trusted, it must be sure of reliability, validity, and objectivity
Case and field study	A specific program or participant, in-depth and all-inclusive	Assumed that complete understanding of an entity will reveal why or why not it is effective	Very time consuming, requires some research skills
Sociogram	Internal nature of groups, attainment of sociological performance objectives	Assumed to indicate how participants are affected by their involvement in a program group	Can also be useful in dividing participants into compatible groups
Behavior observation	Recreational skills, actions, behavior of program participants	Assumed that a change in behavior at end of program reflects program effect	Requires extreme objectivity
Opinion questionnaire	Program appeal and popularity	Assumed that a popular program is an effective program	Such measures do not always truly indicate program effect

review the efficiency and adequacy of staff resources. The measurement is frequently determined by the use of staff diaries or self-reports. For instance, by determining the amount of working hours necessary for each activity in the recreation program, unanticipated time spent can be measured, and staff resources can be reallocated according to the relative priority of each program. This means that if the staff time spent on developing and operating a special event, such as a Christmas tree lighting ceremony, is out of proportion with other ongoing, regularly scheduled activities, a decision to change the magnitude of this event may be made.

Instruments that measure program efficiency can be as simple as reviewing program registrations or as complex as conducting financial audits or time-and-motion studies. Yet a great deal of efficiency evaluation depends upon thoroughly kept program records; all programs should at least have records maintained on staff and money expenditures, safety, facility maintenance, and program content. Table 17 summarizes the instrumentation commonly used for measuring program efficiency.

Instruments that measure program effectiveness   From another perspective there is a group of commonly used data gathering techniques for measuring the attainment of performance objectives. These techniques entail a more systematic investigation of participant attitudes, opinions, and behavior. Therefore the interpretation of the results requires some knowledge and expertise in the methodology of scientific investigation. The data-gathering techniques for determining the program's effect on the participant that will be briefly discussed here are: attitude scales, case and field studies, sociograms, behavioral observations, and opinion questionnaires. Additional study and practice are recommended for the student planner who is unfamiliar with these measurement instruments. Citations provided throughout this discussion will aid such study.

The measurement and subsequent interpretation of an individual participant's attitude are normally difficult. Its desirability is based on the premise that a participant's attitude toward a program will reveal his or her satisfaction and enjoyment in the program. Several data-collection instruments can be used. The five major types of *attitude scales* currently in use are: the Likert (a summation scale), the Thurstone (an equal-appearing intervals scale), the Guttman (a cumulative scale), the semantic differential scale, and the Q-sort.

The most widely used of these is the Likert attitude scale. In this technique a series of statements are listed and the respondent is asked to provide his or her degree of agreement or disagreement with each statement according to a five-point scale. For example, the statement "Recreation programs should be provided free of charge" would yield a strongly agree, agree, undecided, disagree, or strongly disagree response from each participant queried. Usually the more positive the attitude, the more extreme is the agreement (or disagreement, depending upon how the statement is worded). The box on the opposite page offers an illustration of the Likert

Below are listed a number of free time activities. Using the scale values given, indicate what, in your opinion, society's position regarding these activities should be.

This activity should be:	*Scale values*
Very strongly encouraged	7
Strongly encouraged	6
Encouraged	5
Neither encouraged nor discouraged	4
Discouraged	3
Strongly discouraged	2
Very strongly discouraged	1

Free time activities   *Your position*

a. Activities emphasizing mental endeavors such as studying,   _____
taking adult education courses, etc.

b. Activities involving the taking of habit-forming drugs   _____

c. Activities that consist basically of doing nothing, being idle,   _____
"hanging around," etc.

d. Activities involving active participation in social affairs, such as   _____
volunteer work, club activities, etc.

e. Activities that consist basically of artistic and creative efforts,   _____
such as writing, painting, or playing an instrument

f. Activities involving the consumption of alcohol   _____

g. Activities involving productive efforts, such as hobbies like   _____
woodworking, leather tooling, sewing, etc.

h. Activities involving physical exercise, such as sports and calis-   _____
thenics, hunting and fishing, or just walking

From Neulinger, J. *The psychology of leisure: Research approaches to the study of leisure*, 1978, p. 170. Courtesy of Charles C Thomas, Publisher, Springfield, Illinois.

attitude scale as developed by John Neulinger (1978). Although there are many Likert scales on the market, it is occasionally desirable to tailor a scale that is specific to the planner's program situation. Consult Shaw and Wright (1967), Kerlinger (1973), Kohr (1974), and Farrell and Lundegren (1978) for the procedure to be followed in developing such an attitude scale.

The Thurstone scale of attitude measurement is one in which the totality of items is considered as an ordered set, with each item differing in value and the intervals between items being equal. The respondent is asked to check those items with which he or she agrees. That person's score is the median value of the items checked. The box below provides an illustration of the Thurstone-type scale as applied to a recreation program leader. The program participants are asked to mark with a check those statement items that they think apply to the leader, and mark with an X those statement items that they think do not apply to the leader. The leader's score would be the median of the scale values of the items with which the participants agree. This type of attitude scale is difficult to construct, and so I recommend Oppenheim (1966) for a complete discussion.

The Guttman scale consists of a small set of items that are homogeneous and unidimensional. All the items measure only one attitude, and the scale is considered to be cumulative so that if a person responds positively to any given attitude item, he or she will likewise usually respond positively to all attitude items of milder rank. Kerlinger (1973) should be consulted for additional information on the development and use of this scale.

The essence of the semantic differential attitude technique is the establishment of bipolar adjective pairs (such as pleasant-unpleasant, beautiful-ugly) and a rating scale in between where the participant can select a position. The rating scale usually consists of seven points between the two adjectives, and by asking the program participant to declare a position between each adjective pair, a numerical measure of attitude toward a specific concept can be derived. The box on the opposite page, excerpted from Neulinger's 1974 study of leisure, provides an illustration. For further assistance, consult Osgood and others (1967).

DIRECTIONS: Please mark with an X those statements that you disagree apply to this leader and mark with a ✔ those statements that you agree apply to this leader.

_____ 1. Is perfect in very way

_____ 2. Makes the subject matter interesting

_____ 3. Treats all participants fairly

_____ 4. Is an aid in developing high ideals

_____ 5. Is always polite

_____ 41. Exerts an influence for wrong

_____ 42. Has more bad points than any leader I know

_____ 43. Has an ungovernable temper

_____ 44. Does not know the subject matter

_____ 45. Is a failure as a recreation leader

Adapted from Shaw, M.E., & Wright, J.M. *Scales for the measurement of attitudes.* New York: McGraw-Hill, 1967, p. 497. NOTE: There are 45 items on the scale, and the top and bottom five are shown here.

The Q-sort technique is a complex means of having a participant rank order a large number of concepts or subjects. The participant is asked to sort a number of cards containing verbal or pictorial statements regarding a particular attitude orientation into a certain number of piles. The piles range from most meaningful on the extreme left to least meaningful on the extreme right. The participant is permitted to put only a certain number of statements in each pile, with the two extreme piles

---

Below are 16 seven-point scales, each referring to a word pair. Use these scales to describe what *leisure* means to you. The scale points indicate the following:

1 = Extremely
2 = Quite
3 = Slightly
4 = Neutral or unrelated
5 = Slightly
6 = Quite
7 = Extremely

Put a check mark at that point on the scale that best describes what leisure means to you. For example, if the word pair is

beautiful 1 2 3 4 5 6 7 ugly

and you feel that leisure is quite beautiful, you would check 2 on the scale; on the other hand, if you feel that leisure is extremely ugly, you would check 7 on the scale.

Word pairs

Leisure is:

Boring	1	2	3	4	5	6	7	Interesting	(51)
Solitary	1	2	3	4	5	6	7	Sociable	(52)
Honest	1	2	3	4	5	6	7	Dishonest	(53)
Empty	1	2	3	4	5	6	7	Full	(54)
Desirable	1	2	3	4	5	6	7	Undesirable	(55)
Necessary	1	2	3	4	5	6	7	Unnecessary	(56)
Powerful	1	2	3	4	5	6	7	Powerless	(57)
Mature	1	2	3	4	5	6	7	Developing	(58)
Valuable	1	2	3	4	5	6	7	Worthless	(59)
Meaningful	1	2	3	4	5	6	7	Meaningless	(60)
Passive	1	2	3	4	5	6	7	Active	(61)

From Neulinger, J. *The psychology of leisure: Research approaches to the study of leisure.* 1978, pp. 175-176. Courtesy of Charles C Thomas, Publisher, Springfield, Illinois.

receiving the fewest number of cards and the center, undecided pile receiving the most. Refer to Farrell and Lundegren (1978) for additional information.

All the attitude scales introduced here may be subjected to statistical analysis both by hand and with the help of a computer. If the planner is unable to apply formal statistical procedures, he or she can simply look at the most salient and least salient responses in the attitude scale to determine general attitudinal orientations.

The *case or field study* approach is an in-depth observation and investigation of an individual participant, a specific program, an individual agency or unit within that agency, or a particular situation. Depending upon the purpose of the study, the evaluator may observe only a portion or the entirety of the targeted situation. Because of its intensive approach, the field study will often reveal a great deal about the person or program, aspects of which can later be singled out for further evaluation by other means.

In the case study data-gathering technique, a wide variety of information is gathered by means of anecdotal records, action observations, rating forms, direct interviewing, and skill testing. The results of a case study are usually written in a narrative format. The goal is to gather as much relevant information as is available to explain a given situation as it stands at the time of the study. For instance, a case study could be undertaken to investigate a uniquely successful program in order to identify all possible elements that contribute to its success. After these elements are identified and studied, they can be adopted for use in similar programs that are less successful. Case studies, as a data-gathering technique, are time consuming and often limited in usefulness or application. They are most beneficial when there is a particular problem in a program, or with a leader or facility, that has been elusive to the program planner. The case study often brings to the surface the specific area of difficulty, making further evaluation or solution clearer.

The *sociogram* is a measurement instrument that evaluates the nature of the internal structure of a group. It also helps to identify which group members are accepted and which ones are not. In determining the attainment of performance objectives of a sociological nature, the sociogram can help to evaluate the degree of unity of a particular program group. It can also help to evaluate communication patterns within a group, compatible subunits, and emergent leaders or prestigious members. Interpretation of the results are assumed to indicate how program participants are affected by their membership in the group.

Sociograms are a method of studying the interactions or the relationships among group members. The participant is asked a question reflecting a social choice, such as "Name three people in your Girl Scout troop with whom you would like to be in the same tent at camp." The situation must be meaningful to the program group, and group members must already be familiar with each other. All group members' responses are then plotted on a graph to show either all three choices or simply the mutual choices. Plotting a sociogram gets increasingly complex as the number of group members becomes larger. Therefore to ease difficulty in interpretation, the sociogram probably should not be used on groups of more than 25 persons.

In order to plot these social choices in diagram format for analysis, the following steps, as adapted from Farrell and Lundegren (1978, p. 230), should be taken:

1. Draw four concentric circles. Each circle can then be considered to represent four occasions of choice from highly chosen to isolated. The circles may be labeled according to the number of times chosen.

2. If it is necessary to subdivide the group, such as according to sex, experience level, or place of residence, a vertical line can be drawn to divide the circles accordingly. Different symbols can be used to further distinguish this subdivision.

3. Enter each group participant onto the concentric circles according to the number of times he or she was chosen by someone else. That is, the nearer the center of the circles, the more chosen that person is.

4. Draw arrows from and to each person to indicate who chooses who and who is chosen. Double-headed arrows refer to mutual, reciprocal choices. First choices only may be plotted if a less complex sociogram is desired.

Fig. 8-2 presents a sample sociogram.

Behavior observation is another data-gathering tool for measuring program effectiveness. It is a preplanned and systematic single observation, or series of observations, designed to note and record specific, selected actions or behaviors. The purpose is to determine a positive relationship between the behavior specified in the performance objectives and the behavior observed in the evaluation. Unlike other measurement instruments, behavior observation does not necessarily require the direct involvement of the program participant. In fact, provided that the observer is discreet and maintains confidentiality, behavior observation may take place without the person(s) being observed even aware.

Several minimal requirements are advised if the data obtained from behavior observations are to be useful and trusted. In all observations, for example, it is essential that the observers be objective, be trained in how to observe, and know how to record correctly what is observed. As much as is possible, observer inference and interpretation should be kept under control. At the outset the specific behavior to be observed must be clearly delineated; the observer must know exactly what actions to record.

Behavior observations are usually conducted on a time-sampling or event-sampling basis. In time sampling the target behavior is watched for at specific time intervals during a program, such as the final 10 minutes each week in the crafts program at the hospital. In event sampling an entire program event is selected for behavior observation, such as the backgammon game at the senior citizens center. The tools used to guide the evaluator during behavior observations range from simple checklists to anecdotal narrative records and rating scales.

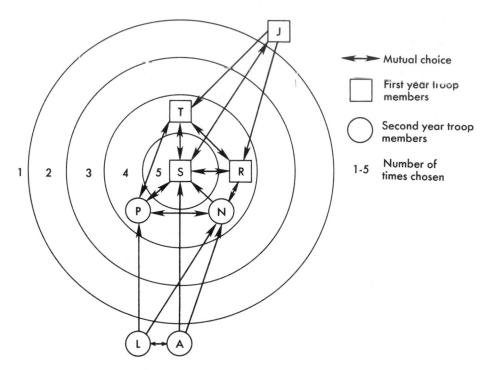

Fig. 8-2   *Sample sociogram for a Girl Scout troop. Scouts were asked to answer the question, "Name three people in your Girl Scout troop with whom you would like to be in the same tent at camp."*

The most frequently adopted measurement of program effect is the *opinion questionnaire*. The opinion questionnaire asks participants to express their opinion on certain issues by responding to a written or orally administered series of questions. The questionnaire tool has already been discussed in Chapter 3 in its other role of offering descriptive information about the program constituency. That discussion should be referred to again in reference to questionnaire design and construction. The opinion questionnaire is useful both in steps 1 and 6 of the planning process. In step 6 its purpose is to ask participants questions about their opinion on specific concerns regarding the program being evaluated. Sample questions follow:

- Did you enjoy the dance class program this session?
- Would you like to see it continued next season?
- Were you encouraged to attend each class session more because of the fee charged?
- Do you consider that you learned quite a bit about the techniques of modern dance from this program?

• What is your overall opinion of this program?

These examples show the nature of opinions sought. The responses are then tallied and summarized to reveal the major and minor opinions. In general, the evaluator uses the opinion questionnaire to indicate what the participants thought about the program and what improvements they would like.

Instruments that measure program effectiveness can be useless unless adequate forethought is given to exactly what effect is intended to be measured. All such instruments discussed here—attitude scales, case and field studies, sociograms, behavior observations, and opinion questionnaires—can be meaningful evaluation data-gathering techniques if used conscientiously and interpreted cautiously. Table 17 should be reviewed as a summary of the instrumentation commonly used for measuring program effectiveness.

Evaluation results

Once the planner has collected and analyzed the evaluation data, the next step is to disseminate and use the results. Whether or not evaluation results are ultimately useful often depends on how these findings are written and communicated to agency decision makers. Therefore the final portion of this chapter is devoted to the written evaluation report—how it is constructed, communicated, and used.

Writing the evaluation report

An outline for a written evaluation report is presented below. It is intended to be used by the planner in one of several ways. If the planner is required to write a technical report, which is likely in a large, all-inclusive outcome approach to evaluation, then the report will need to follow this outline exactly. In this case the planner would simply follow the entire outline in as much detail as is appropriate. On the other hand, if the form of the report can be less formal, the planner can use this outline as a checklist of contents. The planner can then organize the material according to his or her own needs, with the assurance that no important information is being omitted. Some recreation and park agencies and departments use a specific form or questionnaire that the program planner merely fills out with the evaluation procedures and results. Whether or not a form is used, the outline presented below indicates the typical report content.

Outline of typical evaluation report

    I. Cover page
   II. Summary
  III. Program background information
  IV. Description of evaluation design
   V. Results

VI. Analysis of results
VII. Costs and benefits (optional)
VIII. Conclusion and recommendations

The front cover should provide the basic information about the program: the name of the program, date(s), time(s), and recreation site. It should also include the name of the evaluator and the date the report was written.

The summary section contains an overview of the report. It explains why the evaluation was conducted and lists its major conclusions and recommendations. Because the summary is designed for those agency staff members who are either too busy or not directly involved enough to read the full report, it should be brief. Although the summary is placed first in the report, it is usually written last.

The next section of the report concerns the program background information; it sets the program in context. It describes how the program was initiated and what its objectives were. A brief description of the program constituency, as well as the program materials, activities, and administrative arrangements, should be included in this section. A discussion of the program's leadership is also appropriate. If the report will be the sole lasting record of the program, then this section should contain considerable detail. For example, such items as a program flyer, several photographs, and copies of news releases may also be desirable inclusions.

The description of the evaluation design section should next explain why the evaluation was conducted, what it was intended to accomplish, and what it was not intended to accomplish. The remainder of this section describes the procedure, telling how the program was evaluated. Samples of all data-gathering techniques should also be included. If other decision makers are to have faith in the recommendations of the evaluation, they need to know how the information that led to these recommendations was obtained. It is therefore important that this description be as detailed as possible.

The next section presents the results of the various measurements described in the previous section. If the measurement tools were relevant, reliable, and valid, these results constitute hard data about the program. Soft data, such as anecdotal descriptions or participant testimonies, may also be included. The data presented in this section have already been tabulated and are often presented in table or graph format. Results from questionnaires can be summarized on a copy of the questionnaire itself.

Interpretation and analysis of each result make up the next section of the report. These results should be discussed with particular reference to the previous section on the purposes of the evaluation. There are two major issues to be addressed in this section:

1. How certain is it that the program caused the results? Are there alternative explanations for the program results? At this point the planner should attempt to anticipate and deal with arguments against his or her explanation of

RAY BELLAROSA

program efficiency and effectiveness that might be raised by the skeptic.

2. How good were the results of the program? How well did the results compare with what would have been expected had there been no program at all? How do the results compare with what was expected?

The next section is an optional one. Its inclusion depends on the planner's opinion of its worth for the particular planning situation. If the planner has elected to calculate a cost-benefit ratio, this section lists the dollar costs associated with the program and then expands to include a summary of other nondollar or qualitative costs. The benefits of the program are then described and weighed against these costs. It may be helpful to review the previous discussion in this chapter on making a cost-benefit analysis.

The final section in the evaluation report contains the conclusions and recommendations. Often presented in list form, the recommendations can be the most influential aspect of the report. Therefore the planner must be sure to make clear which conclusions are being tentatively, rather than firmly, drawn.

Communicating the results

All that has taken place in the entire evaluation step is irrelevant if the results are shelved and forgotten. The communication of evaluation recommendations must be extended not only to the sponsoring agency but to others involved with the agency and the program as well. If the program and its evaluation methodology or results are unique or significant, this communication should be directed to professional journals and meetings.

Even if the evaluation results indicate poor programming, or the evaluation design was poorly conceived and carried out, the lesson will never be learned if it is not communicated. Worse yet, if the results are not communicated, the program errors could easily be repeated. Those persons who are in a position to use the evaluation should certainly be informed of its recommendations. It is the planner's responsibility to see that the results are at least adequately communicated.

Utilizing the recommendations

After the evaluation has been completed, the planner must decide what to do with it. The results of evaluation studies do not always show how improvements in recreation programs can be accomplished. One reference (Tripodi and others, 1971, p. 135) suggests four questions that may assist the planner in deciding where to begin:

1. What do the findings mean in terms of the program objectives?
2. How can the findings be utilized to bring about changes in a particular program?
3. What implications would the implementation of findings have for the overall program?
4. What next steps are necessary, such as new evaluation efforts, implementation of change, or movement to new stages of program development?

The adoption and subsequent implementation of evaluation recommendations can be aided by discussions and involvement with all related program staff and agency administrators. The planner would make a devastating error by suggesting program changes or cancellations without first discussing them with those program leaders who would be most affected. The greater the involvement of program staff in the interpretation of evaluation results and the formulation of recommendations, the more likely that the recommendations will be accepted and implemented.

Evaluations that suggest program changes can be difficult to implement in the face of reluctance or hostility from the participants. For example, if a movie has been shown at a convalescent facility every Friday night for 2 years, and the planner suggests that based on an evaluation the movie showing be changed to Sunday nights (or replaced completely with a fitness program), there might be such an outcry by the patients that the values of the change would be drowned out. Even though evaluative research has suggested that recreation activities like basketball, baseball, and football have little lifetime, carry-over value, they continue to exist in large quantities in recreation programs because of constituency demand (Theobald, 1979, p. 169). In order to deal with potential participant resistance to change, the planner must involve the participants in deciding how to use the evaluation results. Gradual changes are often easier to introduce than sudden ones.

Evaluation studies provide information on the strengths and weaknesses of programs. They cannot, however, provide all the answers. Yet evaluation recommendations that are useful and practical, and reflect compatability with other agency programming and agency policies, almost always are implemented.

CONCLUSION

The recreation field needs more and better program evaluation. Except in therapeutic recreation, where there is a strong emphasis on assessing the effects of programming, evaluation in recreation program planning seems to rely on impressionistic and instinctive rationale. The neglect is complicated by problems of design and measurement. For example, this chapter has shown that one of the major obstacles to adequate evaluation is the desperate need for better performance measures. The effective delivery of recreation program services depends upon knowing if objectives are being achieved. Yet, despite their importance, very few adequate measures of effectiveness have been devised

However, faced with increasing demands for more responsive, efficient, and effective recreation and park programs to meet the complex needs of society, evaluation has become increasingly important as an indicator of direction. Specifically, evaluation has the following functions:

1. It suggests those programs that work, and so it can recommend alternatives for better program operation.
2. It helps to identify ways of conducting program activities that assist in achieving specific objectives.
3. It provides information that can help clarify the gains and losses of different planning decisions.

Program evaluation is, therefore, an integral and vital part of the rational planning process. Evaluation is the back-up step in the process that validates the usefulness of the preceding steps. It creates objectives for the program in light of the agency's program planning purpose; it judges the continuing validity of these objectives; and, finally, it measures the performance of the program against these objectives. Failure to recognize the relationship of the evaluation step to the entire planning process is why many agencies do not take action to avoid ill-conceived programs that continue long after their original need or purpose has been forgotten.

Whenever the evaluation step shows that a given program is missing its intended target, the planning process returns to planning step 1 for a redefinition of the planning task. The cycles of evaluating a program, revising it, reevaluating the results, and again revising the program can be compared to progressing up a spiral staircase, with each revolution representing the six planning steps.

References

Bannon, J.J. *Leisure resources: Its comprehensive planning*. Englewood Cliffs, N.J.: Prentice-Hall, 1976.

De Boer, J.C. *Let's plan: A guide to the planning process for voluntary organizations*. Philadelphia: Pilgrim Press, 1970.

Edginton, C.R., Compton, D.M., & Hanson, C.J. *Recreation and leisure programming: A guide for the professional*. Philadelphia: Saunders College, 1980.

Farrell, P., & Lundegren, H.M. *The process of recreation programming: Theory and technique*. New York: John Wiley, 1978.

Kerlinger, F.N. *Foundations of behavioral research* (2nd ed.). New York: Holt, Rinehart & Winston, 1973.

Knutson, A.L. Evaluation for what? *Proceedings of the Regional Institute on Neurologically Handicapping Conditions in Children*, 1961, University of California-Berkeley, p. 109.

Kohr, R.L. *Likert-Likert attitude scale analysis*. University Park: Pennsylvania State University, Computer Center, 1974.

Kraus, R. *Recreation today: Program planning and leadership*. New York: Appleton-Century-Crofts, 1966.

Neulinger, J. *The psychology of leisure: Research approaches to the study of leisure*. Springfield, Ill.: Charles C Thomas, 1978.

Oppenheim, A.N. *Questionnaire design and attitude measurement*. New York: Basic Books, 1966.

Osgood, C.E., Suci, G.J., & Tannenbaum, P.H. *The measurement of meaning*. Urbana: University of Illinois Press, 1967.

Reddin, W.J. *Effective management by objectives*. New York: McGraw-Hill, 1971.

Rossi, P.H., & Williams, W. *Evaluating social programs: Theory, practice, and politics*. New York: Academic Press, 1972.

Shaw, M.E., & Wright, J.M. *Scales for the measurement of attitudes*. New York: McGraw-Hill, 1967.

Shivers, J.S. *Principles and practices of recreational service*. New York: Macmillan, 1967.

Theobald, W.F. *Evaluation of recreation and park programs*. New York: John Wiley, 1979.

Tripodi, T., Fellin, P., & Epstein, I. *Social program evaluation: Guidelines for health, education, and welfare administrators*. Itasca, Ill.: F.E. Peacock, 1971.

Van der Smissen, B. *Evaluation and self-study of public recreation and park agencies: A guide with standards and evaluative criteria*. Arlington, Va.: National Recreation and Park Association, 1972.

Weiss, C.H. *Evaluation research: Methods of assessing program effectiveness*. Englewood Cliffs, N.J.: Prentice-Hall, 1972.

Wilder, R.L. EEI: A survival tool. *Parks & Recreation*, 1977, *12*:8, 22-24, 50-51.

Part Three

Conclusion

Chapter 9

Toward the future

Sid Sackson is one of the legends of the game industry. More than 30 of his board games have been published by major companies like Milton Bradley, Parker Brothers, and Ideal. These include *Acquire, Sleuth, Executive Decision,* and his newest, *Can't Stop,* which is expected to sell at least a million copies in 1982. Sackson, whose first job was as a structural engineer, has a library of game books dating back to 1580, and three rooms of his home in the Bronx, New York, are piled from floor to ceiling with the largest and most extensive private collection of games in the world.

As Sackson relates, "The 'Golden Age of Games' was the 1960s. Then the war games began—even one called *Vietnam* (seventh shelf, west wall, first room)—and then there were the ecology games, sports games, and the enormous growth in the adult market. In the 1980s you'll see great growth in electronic games" (Mariani, 1980, p. 22).

Like Sid Sackson, Julius Cooper was an avid game player as a child. Having turned from an engineering career to toy inventing in 1949, Cooper is currently vice-president of product development for the Ideal Toy Corporation. Cooper has a particular interest in dolls. "The mechanical dolls of the 60s have faded," he claims. "The cycle today is swinging back to cuddly dolls like the vinyl ones Ideal first made in the 30s—snuggle dolls that serve as a security blanket." Mechanical dolls are still around, however. Cooper has applied the technology of pneumatics to create Karen and Her Magic Carriage: the child puts the doll in the carriage and activates the doll's movements by manipulating the carriage handlebars (Mariani, 1980, p. 23).

In every civilization in the world, toys and games bring life down to a manageable level. What does the future hold? For those of us who make a profession out of designing "fun and games" for both today's and tomorrow's players, where do we go from here? Is the era of simplicity coming to a close (as Sid Sackson suggests), or is there still a craving for old-fashioned, simple play (as Julius Cooper maintains)? Offering parting thoughts for this book on planning programs for recreation, this chapter takes one last look at the status of the endeavor today and then poses challenges, mandates, and goals for the future.

Status of recreation program planning today

Recreation planners and practitioners have built a legitimate and growing profession on the provision of pleasurable, enriching, and regenerative experiences for free time. We have made some significant changes in programming methods and techniques since our beginnings as a profession around the turn of the century, but this goal has always served us well. Commercial, public, voluntary, and private agencies have been in the past, and are today, concerned about providing program services that offer a worthwhile use of free time. With this as our goal, we have enjoyed astounding success and growth.

Even though the social problems and issues of the 1960s and the 1970s continue to disturb our society, as long as the economy has flourished, so have recreation and park agencies. The recent growth in commercial theme parks, outdoor recreation facilities and programs, and resort opportunities has been phenomenal. Programming in these areas focuses on free-time services for those who can afford to purchase them. Up to the present, recreation has been a lucrative and expansive profession. Programs in recreation have been complemented by an increasing pace of life, affluence, and materialism.

The beginnings of a break with traditional activities and program formats are now evident in program services. There is a quest for new markets, new participants, and new ways of doing things. At the same time, participants are still responding most enthusiastically to sport and competitive programming, spectator opportunities, and fitness programs.

Although things have never been better, the astute student of change can detect that the recreation profession is on the crest of an era. In light of the rapid changes and the complexity in our nation's social, economic, and political institutions, it is becoming increasingly difficult to determine the true status of recreation program planning today. Is the pattern of growth and affluence continuing as an ever-changing constituency requires more sophisticated program services; or are the problems and uncertainties of today forcing us back into traditional, "security blanket" program services? No one seems to know for sure.

However, many professionals in recreation are aware of certain disturbing issues, ones that—if not dealt with adequately now—could become trends for the future. These current trouble spots are the following:

1. *Lack of systematic planning.* With or without the complexity and uncertainty of today, planners have always tended to choose programs spontaneously and from a hit-or-miss orientation. This lack of systematic planning has frequently resulted in program services that have little relevance to the needs of the target constituency.

2. *Lack of long-range planning.* Program planning seems to be concerned with only today's needs, having almost no regard for 2, 5, or 10 years from now. As a result, programs not only go out of date rapidly but are frequently behind

the times. Very little attempt is made to predict the future and to design long-range programming goals accordingly.

3. *Traditional service provisions.* In spite of some stirrings to the contrary, most agency program schedules continue to contain a rehash of the same old activities and formats year after year. Very little varies in either the program content or the method of presenting it. Baseball leagues and crafts classes still constitute the majority of the programs. Although there is no harm in having traditional programs, there is cause for concern when the reason is lack of creativity, fear of being sued, or inability to change.

4. *Lack of programming professionalism.* People who are trained, educated, and experienced in the recreation profession usually do not remain in program services. All too frequently recreation professionals move into facility management, district supervision, or agency administration. This is only natural; these are the higher paying positions. Yet that leaves the face-to-face planning and running of the programs to temporary, seasonal, or part-time personnel who are less committed than the professional to achieving a high degree of quality. There seems to be very little emphasis on the provision of, or adequate recognition of, professional program planning and leadership.

5. *Concern for revenue.* With the current threat of restrictive public funding and decreased consumer spending, an almost paranoid concern for financial security has erupted in most recreation agencies. The reality that is fast upon us is that those programs that do not at least pay for themselves will be eliminated. The social welfare approach to recreation that prevailed in the first half of the century is rapidly giving way to a more commercial approach. Will some worthwhile programs and deserving constituency be lost in the process?

6. *Single-use resources.* At professional meetings there are frequent references to the multiple use of recreation areas and facilities. But most of the speakers are not really committed to this idea. In reality, recreation resources are designed and thus programmed for single use only. Program planners have yet to truly appreciate the potential of the alternative scheduling and the alternative purposes of our vast recreation resources.

Even though the status of recreation program services today is backed by an almost glamorous history of growth, expansion, and increasing sophistication, some current issues and concerns are beginning to be bothersome. What will all this mean for the future?

Predictions for tomorrow

Predicting the future (unless it involves the results of a closely monitored scientific experiment) is difficult, and some would say impossible. Predictions of the future behavior of people, professions, and society include such a wide array of unmanageable variables that they have only limited usefulness. At the First Global Conference of the Future, held in Toronto in late 1980, 5000 professional futurists could not come to a consensus on a clear picture of the next decade.

Perhaps a better approach for addressing the future is a discussion of preferred changes in public, professional, and institutional actions and the goals that must precede such changes. This justification for "predicting" the future is based on the premise that we will be and do what we intend to be and do. Therefore I suggest that we take a look at the future of recreation programming by discussing future goals. What we decide to be our professional future will determine our professional future because our future is dependent on what we decide about ourselves today.

Future challenges in program planning

There are several challenges that should be delineated and optimistically met by professionals in program development beginning right now. Some are the gift of the society and time in which we live; others are inherent in the increasing growth and sophistication of our profession and our constituency. Our success in providing meaningful program services to Americans depends upon our belief in and resolve toward these challenges. The four challenges of the future, as I see them, are innovation, relevancy, accessibility, and accountability.

Innovation   Perhaps the greatest challenge for the program planner is staying on top of, and even creating, change. The provision of dynamic and creative opportunities for individual and community recreational fulfillment will require that the program planner be bold and innovative. This means that the planner must be willing to take programming risks if the recreation profession is to continue to make a meaningful and legitimate contribution to the leisure needs of Americans. Participants in our programs must be encouraged to experience thrilling, creative, exploring, independent, spontaneous, vertigo-like moments of genuine play. To afford this we will need to reappraise those current program offerings that are historically prescribed, static, and unimaginative.

Relevancy   Being able to relate to the matter at hand is a professional challenge that is increasing in importance. Relevant programming means paying attention to changing life-styles, tastes, values, and needs. It also means leading the way in setting new trends, establishing new customs, and changing behaviors. This entails expanding our professional knowledge by drawing upon other disciplines and professions. We must be willing to go beyond our own limitations and biases and meet head-on those recreational values and norms that are different from those that are familiar to us. The program planner not only must know why he or she assumes a particular approach to programming; the planner also must have insight and command of the accompanying effects that given programs have upon the group of participants and the individuals in that group.

Accessibility   This future challenge suggests that program planners must pay particular attention to the elimination of physical, social, and psychological barriers to program experiences. As society becomes more complex and cash flows get tighter, the temptation will be to consider only those who can keep up with the pace or afford to pay. Instead, we must never forget that recreation meets some basic and critical needs of both the individual and society. The elimination of physical barriers could include actions such as widening doors on program facilities, locating programs in geographically convenient places, and modifying recreational equipment or rules. Social and psychological barriers are more difficult to see and thus more difficult to remove. They might include poor communication, prejudice, discrimination, and status seeking. The consideration of program accessibility as a professional challenge will become major throughout the recreation profession.

Accountability   At long last, recreation professionals are being held accountable for their decisions and actions. This is a result of both diminished resources and a more sophisticated and better educated constituency. Professionalism is no longer taken for granted; in particular, those who use public funds to plan and produce programs must do so in an increasingly efficient and effective manner. Even commercial and private agencies have had to become more conscious of the value of their services and the scrutiny of their constituency. We literally cannot afford to continue to organize programs in a sloppy, unaccountable way. If we are going to survive and grow, we must be able to manage our human, fiscal, and physical resources efficiently.

Long-range planning: a mandate

Most of the attention in this book has been devoted to short-term planning— making informed decisions about programs that are to take place in the next year or two. However, there is a type of planning that is not intended to be an immediate, programmatic response to a particular concern. Indeed, things may be going quite well when such long-term planning is undertaken. This planning is a response to long-range concerns or goals. It attempts to determine where the agency wants to be in the future. It seeks to answer the trouble spots and challenges already presented in this chapter. Given current trends in the environment, life-style changes, population movements, changes in constituency socioeconomic characteristics, and changes in needs, long-term planning attempts to project the agency's future response and role. Long-range planning also aims to influence change in the direction the planner thinks it should go.

What this planning process amounts to is making informed estimates about the agency's "world" 5 to 10 years in the future and projecting various programming options for measuring up to the expected circumstances. This is important for three reasons. First, certain program changes or ideas require lead time to plan and implement. Particularly large or creative programming formats may require several years to be adequately developed; with long-term planning there is plenty of time to accomplish it all. The second reason is inertia. Quite naturally all persons tend to resist efforts to change; and it takes time to overcome inertia. Therefore planning needs to take account of this by projecting far enough into the future so that if recommended objectives are adopted, there will be enough time to motivate and activate the agency to the projected point by the projected time. The third, and most obvious, reason is organizational survival. In order to stay alive, useful, and effective today, an agency must prepare to be alive and effective in the future.

The general sequence of the planning process as discussed in this book can be applied to long-term program planning; however, there are certain differences in the time spans required for the six steps. For example, the step of adopting objectives is still most important. Yet instead of specific situation objectives, long-term planning works with broader, more philosophical goals. As the long-range plans progress and the implementation phase nears, these long-range goals are converted into specific, definitive program and performance objectives. In addition, the process of long-term planning will turn up some facets that need to be developed and implemented right away, within the year ahead. Other facets will not be developed for 3, 5, or even 10 years in the future.

The long-range plan itself will list the changing factors that need to be accounted for as time goes by. Noting the difficulties seen as blocks to the achievement of the long-range goals, it will call for periodic assessment of the success or failure of the plan in overcoming these difficulties. The plan will also estimate the times in the future when certain programs will need to be implemented, and it will include a calendar of specific dates when the various decisions about these programs will need to be made.

Long-term program planning aids short-term program planning. This is because the agency has a long-range strategy that can serve as the framework within which the smaller yearly, or even daily, decisions can be made. Yet few of the recreation and park agencies that I have worked with or consulted with have planned programs for even 1 year ahead. This means that whenever a major or minor crisis develops and a programming decision must be made, it is done with a haunting uncertainty about its effect upon the long-term health and goals of the agency. The agency staff muddles along and, if they are lucky, they muddle through. Long-range planning can offer some assistance to luck.

A new professional goal

Free time has traditionally been the major time frame during which a person can experience the personal pleasures and fulfillments of recreation. Historically, the recreation and park profession has maintained as its goal the provision of recreation services during this free time. By most measurements, we are well on the way to meeting our professional goal. Today just about anyone can find planned recreational outlets for his or her free time in the comprehensive service network that the recreation profession has established. Then what is our future goal?

The professional goal that I (and others like me in the recreation field) propose is that we go beyond a concern for free time and aim to improve the overall quality of life. Underlying this new direction is the premise that recreation experiences are not, and cannot be, restricted to an individual's free time. It must now be recognized that it is possible for pleasure, enrichment, and regeneration to be experienced at other times as well. With this expanded concept of recreation, we free ourselves to look upon nonrecreation hours, nonrecreation places, and nonrecreation participants as legitimate times and places and participants for planned program services.

If the recreation program planner accepts the challenge of this new goal, he or she will be innovative and experimental in providing programs that enlarge on opportunities for recreation that the constituency is yet unaware of. The program planner will also be determined to make the planning process a continuous one and to base it on increasingly scientific techniques. This enlightened programming will help people cast off familiar, stereotypical, and thus limiting recreation patterns by breaking down traditional time frames, spaces, and target clientele. The keystone of programming will no longer be what is convenient or easiest for programmers. It will be what meets the quality-of-life needs of the public.

Reference

Mariani, J. Designing fun and games for tomorrow's players, *Next*, 1980, *1*:5, 22-28.

Appendix

FURTHER READINGS
A comprehensive bibliography for recreation and park program planning

Art

Canaday, J. *What is art? An introduction to painting, sculpture, and architecture.* New York: Alfred A. Knopf, 1980.

Huyck & Reber. *Art survival guide for the elementary teacher.* Belmont, Calif.: Pitman Learning, 1976.

Preble, D. *We create art creates us.* New York: Harper & Row, 1976.

Art—children

Brittain, W.L. *Creativity, art and the young child.* New York: Macmillan, 1979.

Hardiman, G., & Zernich, T. *Art activities for children.* Englewood Cliffs, N.J.: Prentice-Hall, 1981.

Herberholz, B. *Early childhood art.* Dubuque, Iowa: William C. Brown, 1979.

Jenkins, P.D. *Art for the fun of it: A guide for teaching young children.* Englewood Cliffs, N.J.: Prentice-Hall, 1980.

Lasky, L., & Mukerji, R. *Art: Basic for young children.* Washington, D.C.: National Association for Childhood Education, 1980.

Oole, E.M. *Art is for children.* Minneapolis: Augsburg, 1980.

Schuman, J. *Art from many hands.* Englewood Cliffs, N.J.: Prentice-Hall, 1980.

Art—technique

Chaet, B. *An artists' notebook: Techniques and materials.* New York: Holt, Rinehart, & Winston, 1979.

Elspass, M.L. *Tips and notes for the artist, Book 1.* West End, N.C.: RaMar Press, 1980.

Street, J.C. *Artist's aids.* New York: Vantage, 1978.

Camp counseling

Blackstock, B., & Latimer, J. *Camp counsellor's handbook.* New York: Vanguard, 1976.

Mangan, D., & Fehr, T. *How to be a super camp counselor.* New York: Franklin Watts, 1979.

Mitchell, V.A., and others. *Camp counseling.* New York: Holt, Rinehart, & Winston, 1977.

Camping

Bauer, E. *The digest book of camping.* Chicago: Follett, 1979.

Bauer, P., & Bauer, E. *Camper's digest.* Chicago: Follett, 1980.

Bearse, R. *The canoe camper's handbook.* Tulsa, Okla.: Winchester Press, 1979.

Boy Scouts of America. *Camping skill book.* Dallas/Fort Worth: Boy Scouts of America, 1978.

Brown, T., & Hunter, R. *The concise book of winter camping.* New York: Vanguard, 1978.

Cary, B. *Winter camping.* Brattleboro, Vt.: Stephen Greene, 1979.

Curtis, S. *Harsh weather camping.* New York: David McKay, 1980.

Graves, R. *Bushcraft: A serious guide to survival and camping.* New York: Warner Books, 1978.

Johnstone, B.D. *Guide to canoe camping.* Martinsville, Ind.: American Camping Association, 1980.

Riley, M.J. *Mountain camping.* Chicago: Contemporary Books, 1979.

Roscoe, D.T. *Your book of camping.* Lawrence, Mass.: Merrimack Book Service, 1980.

Sherwood, M. *How to build a comfortable campsite: A beginner's guide.* Northbrook, Ill.: Quality Books, 1979.

Thomas, L.J., & Sanderson, J.L. *First aid for backpackers and campers.* New York: Holt, Rinehart, & Winston, 1979.

Waterman, L., & Waterman, G. *Backwoods ethics: Environment concerns for hikers and campers.* Washington, D.C.: Stone Wall Press, 1979.

Camps

Hartwig, M.D., & Meyer, B.B. *Camping leadership: Counseling and programming.* St. Louis: C.V. Mosby, 1976.

Musselman, V. *The day camp program book.* Chicago: Follett, 1980.

Wilkinson, R.E. *Camps: Their planning and management.* St. Louis: C.V. Mosby, 1981.

Citizen participation

Delbecq, A.L., Van de Ven, A.H., & Gustafson, D.H. *Group techniques for program planning: A guide to Nominal Group and Delphi processes.* Glenview, Ill.: Scott, Foresman, 1975.

Webb, K., & Hatry, H.P. *Obtaining citizen feedback: The application of citizen surveys to local governments.* Washington, D.C.: The Urban Institute, 1973.

Crafts

Allison, L., & Allison, S. *Rags: Making a little something out of almost nothing.* New York: Crown, 1979.

Baldwin, E., & Baldwin, S. *Makin' things for kids.* San Diego, Calif.: A.S. Barnes, 1980.

Better Homes and Gardens Books Editors. *Better Homes and Gardens treasury of Christmas crafts and foods.* Des Moines, Iowa: Meredith, 1980.

Billar, C.F. *The art of nutcraft.* New York: Carlton, 1979.

Bodger, L., & Ephron, D. *Crafts for all seasons.* New York: Universe, 1980.

Boyd, M.A. *Catalogue sources for creative people: Where to buy craft, needlework and hobby supplies by mail.* Barrington, Ill.: Countryside Books, 1980.

Brabec, B. *Creative cash: How to sell your crafts, needlework, designs, and know-how.* Barrington, Ill. Countryside Books, 1979.

Brunner, M.A. *Pass it on: How to make your own family keepsakes.* New York: Sovereign Books, 1979.

Chatterton, P. *Coordinated crafts for the home.* New York: Marek, 1980.

Cotton, A., & Haddon, F. *Learning and teaching through art and crafts.* North Pomfret, Vt.: David & Charles, 1979.

Donald, E.B. (Ed.). *The book of creative crafts.* New York: Mayflower Books, 1978.

Droge, D., & Glander-Bandyk, J. *Woman's Day book of calligraphy.* New York: Simon & Schuster, 1980.

Dubana, J., & Friend, D. *Kid crafts.* New York: Simplicity, 1980.

Ethe, J. *Easy-to-make felt bean bag toys.* New York: Dover, 1980.

Fiberarts Magazine (Ed.). *The Fiberarts design book: The best of contemporary weaving, needlework, wearables, quilting, surface design, papermaking, basketry and felting.* Asheville, N.C.: Fiberarts, 1980.

Hill, J. *The complete practical book of country crafts.* North Pomfret, Vt.: David & Charles, 1979.

Jeffery, V. *The flower workshop.* New York: Hearst Books, 1980.

Johnson, M.E., & Pearson, K. *Naturecrafts: Seasonal projects from natural materials.* Birmingham, Ala.: Oxmoor House, 1980.

Lindbeck, J.R. and others. *Basic crafts.* Peoria, Ill.: Bennett, 1979.

Mills, S. (Ed.). *The book of presents: Easy-to-make gifts for every occasion.* New York: Pantheon, 1979.

Reader's Digest. *Reader's Digest crafts and hobbies.* New York: Norton, 1980.

Shoemaker, K. *Creative Christmas: Simple crafts from many lands.* Minneapolis: Winston Press, 1978.

Stuart, M., & Soper, G. *The bazaar stall.* Lawrence, Mass.: Merrimack Book Service, 1979.

Torbet, L. *Encyclopedia of crafts* (3 vols.). New York: Charles Scribner's, 1980.

Dance

Arnheim, D.D. *Dance injuries: Their prevention and care.* St. Louis: C.V. Mosby, 1980.

Gioseffi, D. *Earth dancing: Mother Nature's oldest rite.* Harrisburg, Pa.: Stackpole, 1980.

Hall, T.J. *Dance! A complete guide to social, folk, and square dancing.* New York: Arno, 1980.

Kitching, J., & Braun, S. (Eds.). *Dance and mime film and videotape catalog.* New York: Dance Films, 1980.

Kuntzleman, B.A., & Consumer Guide Editors. *The complete guide to aerobic dancing.* New York: Fawcett, 1979.

Lavelle, D. *Latin and American dances.* New Rochelle, N.Y.: Sportshelf & Soccer, 1979.

Mettler, B., & Warner, J. (Eds.). *Materials of dance as a creative art activity.* Tucson, Ariz.: Mettler Studios, 1979.

Murray, J. *Dance now.* New York: Penguin, 1979.

Reynolds, N. (Ed.). *The dance catalogue.* New York: Crown, 1979.

Rogers, F.R. *Dance: A basic educational technique.* Brooklyn, N.Y.: Dance Horizons, 1980.

Schlaich, J., & Dupont, B., (Eds.). *Dance: The art of production.* St. Louis: C.V. Mosby, 1977.

Shreeves, R. *Movement and educational dance for children.* Boston, Mass.: Plays, 1980.

Steinberg, C. (Ed.). *Dance anthology.* New York: New American Library, 1980.

Vincent, L. *The dancer's book of health.* Fairway, Kan.: Andrews & McMeel, 1978.

Wayburn, N. *The art of stage dancing.* New York: Chelsea House, 1980.

Dance—children

Barlin, A. *Teaching your wings to fly: The nonspecialists guide to movement activities for young children.* Santa Monica, Calif.: Goodyear, 1979.

Joyce, M. *First steps in teaching creative dancing.* Palo Alto, Calif.: Mayfield, 1973.

Nelson, E.L. *Singing and dancing games for the very young,* New York: Sterling, 1977.

Decision making

Adelman, C. *Smarter not harder.* Hillside, N.J.: IBMS Corporation, 1979.

Anderson, D., and others. *Essentials of management science: Applications to decision making.* St. Paul, Minn.: West Publishing, 1978.

Arnold, J.D. *The art of decision making: Seven steps to achieving more effective results.* New York: American Management, 1980.

Blinn, L. *Making decisions.* Albany, N.Y.: Delmar, 1980.

Brandstatter, H., and others. (Eds.). *Dynamics of group decisions.* Beverly Hills, Calif.: Sage, 1979.

Dalkey, N.C. *Group decision theory.* Reading, Mass.: Addison-Wesley, 1981.

Dombrocki, T. *Creative problem solving: The door to progress and change.* Hicksville, N.Y.: Exposition, 1979.

Fisher, B.A. *Small group decision making: Communication and the group process.* New York: McGraw-Hill, 1980.

Goslin, L.N., & Rethans, A.J. *Basic systems for decision making.* Dubuque, Iowa: Kendall/Hunt, 1980.

Hill, P.H., and others. *Making decisions: A multi-*

disciplinary introduction. Reading, Mass.: Addison-Wesley, 1979.

Hogarth, R.M. *Judgment and choice: Strategies for decisions.* New York: John Wiley, 1980.

Sperry, L. *The decision book.* San Diego, Calif.: Beta Books, 1980.

Wheeler, D.D., & Janis, I.L. *A practical guide for making decisions.* New York: Free Press, 1980.

Drama

Chilver, P. *Teaching improvised drama.* North Pomfret, Vt.: David & Charles, 1978.

George, K. *Rhythm in drama.* Pittsburgh, Pa.: University of Pittsburgh Press, 1980.

Klock, M.E. (Ed.). *Bibliography of creative dramatics.* Washington, D.C.: American Theater Association, 1975.

McCaslin, N. *Creative drama in the classroom.* New York: Longman, 1980.

Mersand, J. (Ed.). *Guide to play selection: A selective bibliography for production and study of modern plays.* Urbana, Ill.: National Council of Teachers of English, 1975.

Polsky. M.E. *Let's improvise: Becoming creative, expressive and spontaneous through drama.* Englewood Cliffs, N.J.: Prentice-Hall, 1980.

Roland, L.B. *The technique of the one-act play: Study in dramatic construction.* Darby, Pa.: Arden Library, 1978.

Salem, J.M. *Drury's guide to best plays.* Metuchen, N.J.: Scarecrow, 1978.

Samples, G. *The drama scholar's index to plays and filmscripts: A guide to plays and filmscripts in selected anthologies, series and periodicals.* Metuchen, N.J.: Scarecrow, 1980.

Siks, G.B. *Drama with children.* New York: Harper & Row, 1977.

Spotlight on drama. Martinsville, Ind.: American Camping Association, 1979.

Upton, G. (Ed.). *Physical and creative activities for the mentally handicapped.* New York: Cambridge University Press, 1979.

Vaughn, J.A. *Drama A to Z: A handbook.* New York: Frederick Ungar, 1978.

Evaluation

Council on Accreditaton. *Standards and evaluative criteria for recreation, leisure services and resources: Curricula baccalaureate and master's degree programs.* Arlington, Va.: National Recreation and Park Association, 1975.

Dolbeare, K.M. (Ed.). *Public policy evaluation.* Beverly Hills, Calif.: Sage, 1975.

Epstein, I., & Tripodi, T. *Research techniques for program planning, monitoring and evaluation.* New York: Columbia University Press, 1977.

Franklin, J.L., & Thrasher, J.H. *An introduction to program evaluation.* New York: John Wiley, 1976.

Hatry, H., Blair, L., Fisk, D., & Kimmell, W. *Program analysis for state and local governments.* Washington, D.C.: The Urban Institute, 1976.

Stake, R.E. *Evaluating educational programs: The need and the response.* Washington, D.C.: Organization for Economic Cooperation and Development, 1976.

Struening, E.L., & Guttentag, M. (Eds.). *Handbook of evaluation research.* Beverly Hills, Calif.: Sage, 1975.

Van der Smissen, B. *Evaluation and self-study of public recreation and park agencies: A guide with standards and evaluative criteria.* Arlington, Va.: National Recreation and Park Association, 1972.

Evaluation—instruments

AAHPER youth fitness test manual. Available from: AAHPER (American Alliance for Health, Physical Education & Recreation) Publication-Sales, 1201 16th Street, N.W., Washington, D.C., 1976.

Bruininks-Oseretsky test of motor proficiency. Available from: American Guidance Service, Inc., Circle Pines, Minn., 1976.

California psychological inventory. Available from: Consulting Psychologists Press, Inc., 577 College Avenue, Palo Alto, Calif., 1975.

Coopersmith behavior rating form. Available from: The Self-Esteem Institute, San Francisco, Calif., 1975.

Coopersmith self-esteem inventory. Available from: The Self-Esteem Institute, San Francisco, Calif., 1975.

Kohr, R.L. *Likert attitude scale analysis.* Available from: The Computation Center, Pennsylvania State University, College Park, Pa., 1974.

Leisure activities blank. Available from: Consulting Psychologists Press, Inc., 577 College Avenue, Palo Alto, Calif., 1975.

Managerial philosophies scale. Available from: Teleometrics International, P.O. Drawer 1850, Conroe, Tex., 1975.

Motor fitness testing manual for the moderately mentally retarded. Available from: AAHPER Publication-Sales, 1201 16th Street, N.W., Washington, D.C., 1976.

Robinson, J.P., & Shaver, P.R. *Measures of social psychological attitudes.* Ann Arbor, Mich.: Survey Research Center, Institute for Social Research, 1973.

State-trait anxiety inventory for adults. Available from: Consulting Psychologists Press, Inc., 577 College Avenue, Palo Alto, Calif., 1973.

State-trait anxiety inventory for children. Available from: Consulting Psychologists Press, Inc., 577 College Avenue, Palo Alto, Calif., 1973.

Testing for impaired, disabled and handicapped individuals. Available from: AAHPER Publication-Sales, 1201 16th Street, N.W., Washington, D.C., 1975.

Grant writing

Alkin, M.C., and others. *Conducting evaluations: Three perspectives.* New York: Foundation Center, 1980.

Annual register of grant support: 1980-1981. Chicago: Marquis, 1980.

Conrad, D.L. *How to get federal grants.* San Francisco, Calif.: Public Management, 1979.

Foundation Center. *The foundation grants index, 1979.* New York: Foundation Center, 1980.

Hillman, H. *Art of winning corporate grants.* New York: Vanguard, 1980.

Kurzig, C.M. *Foundation fundamentals: A guide for grantseekers.* New York: Foundation Center, 1980.

National directory of grants and aid to individuals in the arts, international. Washington, D.C.: Washington International Arts, 1980.

Public Management Institute Staff. *The grant writer's handbook, nineteen seventy-nine to nineteen eighty.* San Francisco, Calif.: Public Management, 1980.

Smith, C., & Skjei, E. *Getting grants.* New York: Harper & Row, 1980.

White, V.P. *Grants for the arts.* New York: Plenum, 1980.

Hobbies

Doering, H. (Ed.). *The World Almanac book of buffs, masters, mavens and uncommon experts.* New York: World Almanac, 1980.

Lewis, S. *Things kids collect.* New York: Holt, Rinehart, & Winston, 1980.

MacDonald, C. *At your leisure.* San Diego, Calif.: Beta Books, 1980.

Smaridge, N. *Choosing your retirement hobby.* New York: Dodd, Mead, 1976.

Legal liability

Bodenheimer, E. *Philosophy of responsibility.* Littleton, Colo.: Fred B. Rothman, 1980.

Van Biervliet, A., & Sheldon-Wildgen, J. *Liability issues in community-based programs.* Baltimore, Md.: Paul H. Brookes, 1980.

Marketing

Amarchand, D., & Varadharajan, B. *An introduction to marketing.* New York: Advent Books, 1980.

Bell, M.L. *Marketing: Concepts and strategy.* Boston: Houghton Mifflin, 1979.

Cundiff, E.W., and others. *Fundamentals of modern marketing.* Englewood Cliffs, N.J.: Prentice-Hall, 1980.

Diamond, J., & Pintel, G. *Principles of marketing.* Englewood Cliffs, N.J.: Prentice-Hall, 1980.

Garfunkle, S. *Developing the marketing plan: A practical guide.* New York: Random House, 1980.

Gelb, B., & Gelb, G. *Marketing is everybody's business.* Santa Monica, Calif.: Goodyear, 1980.

Nickels, W.G. *Marketing communications and promotion.* Columbus, Ohio: Grid, 1980.

Seltz, D.D. *Handbook of innovative marketing techniques.* Reading, Mass.: Addison-Wesley, 1980.

Mental and literary activities

Ahl, D.H. (Ed.). *Basic computer games: TRS, Vol. 2.* Morristown, N.J.: Creative Computing, 1980.

Barry, S.A. *Super-colossal book of puzzles, tricks, and games.* New York: Sterling, 1978.

Carlsen, G.R. *Books and the teenage reader: A guide for teachers, librarians, and parents.* New York: Harper & Row, 1980.

De Vito, J. *Elements of public speaking.* New York: Harper & Row, 1980.

Makay, J.J. *Speaking with an audience: Communicating ideas and attitudes.* Dubuque, Iowa: Kendall/Hunt, 1980.

Moy, V. *Easy clues make reading fun.* New York: Vantage, 1979.

Peterson, B.D., and others. *Speak easy: Introduction to public speaking.* St. Paul, Minn.: West Publishing, 1980.

Shortz, W. *Brain games.* New York: Simon & Schuster, 1979.

Music

Glennon, J. *Understanding music.* New York: St. Martin's, 1980.

Hopkins, A. *Understanding music.* Totowa, N.J.: Biblio Distribution, 1980.

Leyerle, A., & Leyerle, W.D. *Song anthology: One.* Mt. Morris, N.Y.: William D. Leyerle, 1980.

Music—children

Andress, B. *Music experiences in early childhood.* New York: Holt, Rinehart, & Winston, 1980.

Bramscher, C.S. *Treasury of musical motivators for the elementary classroom,* Englewood Cliffs, N.J.: Prentice-Hall, 1979.

Burton, L., & Hughes, W. *Music activities for young children.* Reading, Mass.: Addison-Wesley, 1980.

Nye, V.T. *Music for young children.* Dubuque, Iowa: William C. Brown, 1979.

Outdoor recreation

Alton, D. *Valuing outdoor recreation benefits: An annotated bibliography* (Public Administration Series: P 258). Monticello, Ill.: Vance Bibliographies, 1979.

Brockman, C.F., & Merriam, L.C., Jr. *Recreational use of wildlands.* New York: McGraw-Hill, 1979.

Cooper, D., and others. *The outdoor handbook.* Central Islip, N.Y.: Transatlantic, 1978.

Doan, M. *Starting small in the wilderness: The Sierra Club outdoors guide for families.* San Francisco, Calif.: Sierra Club, 1979.

Fleming, J. (Ed.). *The outdoor idea book.* Portland, Ore.: Victoria House, 1978.

Knudson, D.M. *Outdoor recreation.* New York: Macmillan, 1980.

Leonard, W. *One thousand one tips for the great outdoors.* Contemporary Books, 1978.

LeRoy, D. *The outdoorsman's guide to government surplus.* Chicago: Contemporary Books, 1978.

Sparano, V. *Complete outdoors encyclopedia.* New York: Harper & Row, 1980.

Thomas, D. *Backyard roughing it easy.* New York: Fawcett, 1980.

Van Doren, C., and others. (Eds.). *Land and leisure: Concepts and methods in outdoor recreation.* Chicago: Maaroufa Press, 1979.

Outdoor recreation—high risk

Bernstein, J. *Ascent: Of the invention of mountain climbing and its practice.* Lincoln: University of Nebraska Press, 1979.

Clarke, A. *Starting rock climbing.* New York: Barrie & Jenkins, 1979.

Cleare, J. *Mountaineering.* New York: Sterling, 1980.

Darvill, F.T. *Mountaineering medicine: A wilderness medical guide.* Mt. Vernon, Wash.: Darvill Outdoor, 1980.

Franks, D.E. *The canoe and white water: From essential to sport.* Buffalo, N.Y.: University of Toronto Press, 1977.

Hadley, D. *Hang gliding.* Central Islip, N.Y.: Transatlantic, 1979.

Moravetz, B. *The big book of mountaineering.* Woodbury, N.Y.: Barron's, 1980.

Neate, W.R. *Mountaineering and its literature.* Seattle, Wash.: Mountaineers, 1980.

Poynter, D. *Hang gliding: The basic handbook of skysurfing.* Santa Barbara, Calif.: Parachuting Publications, 1979.

Radlauer, E. *Some basics about hang gliding.* Chicago: Childrens, 1979.

Riley, M.J. *Mountain camping.* Chicago: Contemporary Books, 1979.

Rock climbing. New York: David McKay, 1980.

Schneider, S. *High technology: A guide to modern mountaineering equipment.* Chicago: Contemporary Books, 1980.

Setnicka, T.J. *Wilderness search and rescue: A complete handbook.* Boston: Appalachian Mountain, 1980.

Questionnaires

Berdie, D.R., & Anderson, J.F. *Questionnaires: Design and use.* Metuchen, N.J.: Scarecrow, 1974.

Orlish, D.C. *Designing sensible surveys.* New York: Two Continents, 1979.

Risk management

Crockford, N. *An introduction to risk management.* Boston: Herman, 1980.

Green, M.R., & Serbein, O.N. *Risk management: text and cases.* Reston, Va.: Reston, 1978.

Leuz, M., Jr. *Risk management manual.* Santa Monica, Calif.: Merritt, 1978.

Williams, C.A., Jr., & Heins, R.M. *Risk management and insurance.* New York: McGraw-Hill, 1980.

Social recreation

Adair, I. *The complete party planner.* San Diego, Calif.: A.S. Barnes, 1978.

Barrett, S.L. *Parties with a purpose.* Springfield, Ill.: Charles C Thomas, 1980.

Patten, M. *The hostess book of entertaining.* North Pomfret, Vt.: David & Charles, 1980.

Post, E., & Staffieri, A. *The complete book of entertaining from the Emily Post Institute.* New York: Lippincott & Crowell, 1981.

Ross, D., & Schaffer, E. *The birthday party book.* Maplewood, N.J.: Hammond, Inc., 1979.

Von Welanetz, D., & Von Welanetz, P. *The art of buffet entertaining.* Los Angeles, Calif.: J.P. Tarcher, 1978.

Social recreation—children

Bioff, D.A. *Birthday parties for children.* Grand Rapids, Mich.: Baker Books, 1978.

Fiarotta, P., & Fiarotta, N. *Confetti: The kids' make it yourself, do it yourself party book.* New York: Workman, 1978.

Wolfsohn, R.B. *Successful children's parties.* New York: Arco, 1979.

Sports

Anderson, D. *Sports of our times.* New York: Random House, 1979.

Buxbaum, R.C., & Michieli, L. J. *Sports for life: Fitness training, injury prevention and nutrition.* Boston: Beacon Press, 1979.

Consumer Guide Magazine (Ed.). *Spectators' guide to sports: Rules, scoring, strategy and competing.* New York: New American Library, 1976.

Cuddon, J.A. *The international dictionary of sports and games.* New York: Schocken, 1980.

Doherty, J.K. *Track and field omnibook.* Los Altos, Calif.: Tafnews, 1980.

Eitzen, D.S., & Sage, G.J. *The sociology of American sport.* Dubuque, Iowa: William C. Brown, 1978.

Fitzgibbon, H., & Bairstow, J. *The complete racquet sports player.* New York: Simon & Schuster, 1980.

Gipe, G. *The great American sports book.* Garden City, N.Y.: Doubleday, 1978.

Hindman, D.A. *Kick-the-can and over 800 other active games and sports.* Englewood Cliffs, N.J.: Prentice-Hall, 1978.

Home video tape-disc guide: Sports and recreation. New York: New American Library, 1980.

Johnson, S.E. *Frisbee.* New York: Workman, 1975.

Johnson, W. (Ed.). *Sport and physical education around the world.* Champaign, Ill.: Stipes, 1980.

Keith, H. *Sports and games.* New York: T.Y. Crowell, 1976.

Lipsey, R. (Ed.). *Sportsguide for individual sports, Vol. 1,* Detroit: Gale, 1980.

Michener, J.A. *Sports in America.* New York: Fawcett, 1977.

Morbock, C., & Morbock, P. *New American guide to athletics, sports and recreation.* New York: New American Library, 1979.

Official rules of sports and games. New Rochelle N.Y.: Sportshelf & Soccer, 1979.

Roberts, G.C., and others. *Social science of play, games and sport: Learning experiences.* Champaign, Ill.: Human Kinetics, 1979.

Shrader, R.D., & Everden, S. *Team sports: A competency based approach.* Dubuque, Iowa: Kendall/Hunt, 1977.

Sports trader annual buyers guide 1980. New York: Nichols, 1980.

Sysler, B., & Fox, E.R. *Life-time sports for the college student: A behavioral objective approach.* Dubuque, Iowa: Kendall/Hunt, 1980.

Sports—accidents and injuries

Asinof, E. *Bleeding between the lines.* New York: Holt, Rinehart, & Winston, 1979.

Benjamin, B.E. *Sports without pain.* New York: Summit Books, 1979.

Colson, J.H., & Armour, W.J. *Sports injuries and their treatment.* New Rochelle, N.Y.: Sportshelf & Soccer, 1979.

Dornan, P. *Sporting injuries: A trainer's guide.* New York: University of Queensland Press, 1980.

Fahey, T.D. *What to do about athletic injuries.* New York: Butterick, 1979.

Gambordella, T.L. *End of injury.* Chicago: Contemporary Books, 1980.

Golanty, E. *No strain, no pain: A guide to understanding and preventing sports injuries.* San Diego, Calif.: A.S. Barnes, 1979.

McMaster, J. *ABC's of sports injuries.* Huntington, N.Y.: Krieger, 1981.

Schiari, M. *Athletic trainers guide to injuries of young athletes.* New York: Lion, 1980.

Verney, P. *Sports fitness: A practical guide to conditioning and injury prevention in more than fifty-five major sports.* New York: Paddington, 1980.

Sports—children

Galton, L. *Your child in sports: À complete guide.* New York: Watts, 1980.

Guidelines for children's sports. Washington, D.C.: AAPHER, 1979.

Humphrey, J.H., & Humphrey, J.N. *Sports skills for boys and girls.* Springfield, Ill.: Charles C Thomas, 1980.

Vandeweghe, E.M., & Flynn, G.L. *Growing with sports: A parent's guide to the young athlete.* Englewood Cliffs, N.J.: Prentice-Hall, 1978.

Sports—dictionaries

Cuddon, J.A. *The international dictionary of sports and games.* New York: Schocken, 1980.

Diagram Group. *The official world encyclopedia of sports and games: The rules, techniques of play and equipment for over 400 sports and 1000 games.* New York: Paddington, 1979.

Menke, F.G. *The encyclopedia of sports.* San Diego, Calif.: A.S. Barnes, 1978.

Neft, D.S., and others. *The sports encyclopedia: Baseball.* New York: Grosset & Dunlap, 1979.

Wright, G. *Illustrated dictionary of sports.* Chicago: Rand McNally, 1979.

Sports—officiating

Clegg, R., & Thompson, W.A. *Modern sports officiating: A practical guide.* Dubuque, Iowa: William C. Brown, 1979.

Richards, J., & Hill, D. *Complete handbook of sports scoring and record keeping.* Englewood Cliffs, N.J.: Prentice-Hall, 1974.

Sports—organization and administration

De Vrye-Park, C. *Sports promotion and fund raising.* New York: Vantage, 1980.

Hendy, D.M., & McGregor, I. *Intramurals: A teacher's guide.* West Point, N.Y.: Leisure Press, 1979.

La Point, J.D. *Organization and management of sport.* Dubuque, Iowa: Kendall/Hunt, 1980.

Index